Bridging Worlds – Building Feminist Geographies

This book marks the 30th anniversary of the IGU Commission on Gender and Geography, honouring the contributions of Janice Monk in establishing the field of feminist geography. The collection is published as part of the series International Studies of Women and Place that Janice Monk co-edited with Janet Momsen for over 30 years. The chapters, from over 45 leading international scholars, encompass key areas Monk has contributed to within feminist geography.

The collaborative nature of this project reflects the networks and themes Monk nurtured throughout her long and impactful career. The book provides critical insights to wide-ranging topics that include the development of feminist geography in different global contexts, gendered geographies of work and everyday life, and gender and environmental concerns.

Diverse voices and perspectives in this book will serve as invaluable resources for scholars interested in gender and feminist geographies, the history of the IGU Commission on Gender and Geography, career trajectories of women geographers in different parts of the world, gendered geographies of the life course, as well as feminist analyses of environmental issues. The book will be useful to students, educators, and activists in gender studies, development studies, and human geography.

Anindita Datta is Professor at the Department of Geography, University of Delhi and the current Chair of the IGU Commission on Gender and Geography. Her work focuses on gendered and epistemic violence, indigenous feminisms, spaces of resistance and geographies of care. A member of several international editorial boards and collaborations such as the NORAD, Linnaeus Palme and Erasmus Mundus programmes, Anindita is committed to feminist mentoring and building transformative networks of care across differences. Her recent books include *Gender, Space and Agency in India: Exploring Regional Genderscapes* and the *Routledge Handbook of Gender and Feminist Geography* (co-editor).

Janet Momsen was a founding member of the Gender Commission in 1988 and was Chair from then until 1996, continuing as Treasurer until 2006. She is Emerita Professor of Geography, University of California, Davis. Her research is mainly on gender and agricultural development. She has also taught in England, Canada, Brazil, Costa Rica, the Netherlands and South Africa. She has published 17 books, founded and is current editor of the Routledge series on *International Studies of Women and Place*.

Ann M. Oberhauser is Professor of Sociology at Iowa State University and holds a PhD in Geography from Clark University. Her research focuses on feminist economic geography, gender and globalization, feminist pedagogy, and critical development studies with an emphasis on rural economic strategies in Appalachia and sub-Saharan Africa. Her publications include *Feminist Spaces: Gender and Geography in a Global Context* and *Global Perspectives on Gender and Space*. Oberhauser is a long-time member of the International Geographical Union Commission on Gender, the Society of Woman Geographers, and the Feminis the American Association of Geographers.

Routledge International Studies of Women and Place
Series Editors: Janet Henshall Momsen
University of California, Davis

Feminist Political Ecology
Global Issues and Local Experience
Edited by Dianne Rocheleau, Barbara Thomas-Slayter, and Esther Wangari

Women Divided
Gender, Religion and Politics in Northern Ireland
Rosemary Sales

Women's Lifeworlds
Women's Narratives on Shaping their Realities
Edited by Edith Sizoo

Gender, Planning and Human Rights
Edited by Tovi Fenster

Gender, Ethnicity and Place
Women and Identity in Guyana
Linda Peake and D. Alissa Trotz

Brokering Circular Labour Migration
A Mobile Ethnography of Migrant Care Workers' Journey to Switzerland
Huey Shy Chau

Climate Change, Gender Roles and Hierarchies
Socioeconomic Transformation in an Ethnic Minority Community in Vietnam
Phuong Ha Pham and Donna L. Doane

Intersectional Lives
Chinese Australian Women in White Australia
Alanna Kamp

Bridging Worlds – Building Feminist Geographies
Essays in Honour of Janice Monk
Anindita Datta, Janet Momsen and Ann M. Oberhauser

Bridging Worlds – Building Feminist Geographies
Essays in Honour of Janice Monk

Edited by Anindita Datta, Janet Momsen and Ann M. Oberhauser

LONDON AND NEW YORK

First published 2023
by Routledge
4 Park Square, Milton Park, Abingdon, Oxon OX14 4RN

and by Routledge
605 Third Avenue, New York, NY 10158

Routledge is an imprint of the Taylor & Francis Group, an informa business

© 2023 selection and editorial matter, Anindita Datta, Janet Momsen and Ann M. Oberhauser; individual chapters, the contributors

The right of Anindita Datta, Janet Momsen and Ann M. Oberhauser to be identified as the authors of the editorial material, and of the authors for their individual chapters, has been asserted in accordance with sections 77 and 78 of the Copyright, Designs and Patents Act 1988.

All rights reserved. No part of this book may be reprinted or reproduced or utilised in any form or by any electronic, mechanical, or other means, now known or hereafter invented, including photocopying and recording, or in any information storage or retrieval system, without permission in writing from the publishers.

Trademark notice: Product or corporate names may be trademarks or registered trademarks, and are used only for identification and explanation without intent to infringe.

British Library Cataloguing-in-Publication Data
A catalogue record for this book is available from the British Library

ISBN: 978-1-032-27562-8 (hbk)
ISBN: 978-1-032-27563-5 (pbk)
ISBN: 978-1-032-27561-1 (ebk)

DOI: 10.4324/9781032275611

Typeset in Times New Roman
by SPi Technologies India Pvt Ltd (Straive)

Contents

List of Figures viii
List of Tables ix
List of Contributors x

1 Bridging Worlds – Building Feminist Geographies: Essays in Honour of Janice Monk 1
ANINDITA DATTA, JANET MOMSEN AND ANN M. OBERHAUSER

PART I
Gender and Feminist Geographies: Perspectives from around the World 7

2 Connecting Distant Academic Landscapes, Inspiring Researchers: Jan Monk's Role in Developing Gender Geography and Geohumanities in Spain 9
MARIA DOLORS GARCIA RAMON AND ANTONI LUNA

3 Crossing Borders, Exotic Women and the Challenge of Teaching Gender in World Regional Geography and Area Studies Courses 19
HOLLY M. HAPKE

4 Centering Fireside Knowledge and Utu Feminisms: On Writing Feminist Margins from the Margins 29
MARY NJERI KINYANJUI

5 The Value of Feminist Scholarship: Renegotiating Spaces for Gender and Geography in Post-Communist Romania 37
SORINA VOICULESCU AND MARGARETA AMY LELEA

6 Women in Geography: The Case of the International
  Geographical Union   48
  JOOS DROOGLEEVER FORTUIJN

PART II
**Career Trajectories of Women Geographers – Strategies to
Survive and Thrive**   61

7 "Making Zonia Known": Discussing Baber's
  "Peace Symbols" (1948)   63
  MARCELLA SCHMIDT DI FRIEDBERG

8 Janice Monk and Evelyn Stokes: Two Women Geographers
  from Down Under Break New Ground   73
  ROBYN LONGHURST AND LYNDA JOHNSTON

9 The 'Excluded Half of the Human' in Brazilian Geography:
  The Life Course of Women in a Scientific Field   84
  JOSELI MARIA SILVA, MARCIO JOSE ORNAT AND TAMIRES REGINA AGUIAR
  DE OLIVEIRA CESAR

10 Being (From) There: Antipodean Reflections on
   Feminist Geography   97
   RUTH FINCHER, KATHERINE GIBSON AND LOUISE C. JOHNSON

11 Valuing Mentoring: Jan Monk's Role in Creating a Community
   of Support for Early Career Researchers   111
   MICHAEL SOLEM AND KEN FOOTE

12 Students' Evaluation of Instruction: A Neoliberal Managerial
   Tool Against Faculty Diversity   121
   MARTINA ANGELA CARETTA AND FEDERICA BONO

PART III
**Gendered Geographies of the Life Course: Work and
Everyday Life**   133

13 Migrant Women's Everyday Lives and Work Burdens: Insights from
   Kusumpur Pahari, Delhi   135
   SWAGATA BASU

14 Challenging Instability: Women's Multigenerational Narratives
of Work in the Margins of Central and Eastern Europe   145
DORIS WASTL-WALTER, ÁGNES ERŐSS AND MONIKA MÁRIA VÁRADI

15 Life Course in the New Processes of Re-Ruralization in Spain   157
MIREIA BAYLINA, MARIA DOLORS GARCIA RAMON, MONTSERRAT
VILLARINO, Mª JOSEFA MOSTEIRO GARCÍA, ANA Mª PORTO CASTRO AND
ISABEL SALAMAÑA

16 Independence and Entrepreneurship Among Arab Muslim
Rural and Bedouin Women in Israel   169
RUTH KARK, EMIR GALILEE AND TAMAR FEUERSTEIN

PART IV
Gender and Environmental Concerns: Change, Crisis and Recovery   179

17 Social Change in Griffith, NSW, Australia: Discourses of
Indigeneity, Identity, Justice and Well-Being over Fifty Years   181
JANICE MONK, RICHARD HOWITT, CLAIRE COLYER, CANDY KILBY,
LYNETTE KILBY, STEPHEN COLLINS, BEV JOHNSON, DAVID CREW AND
ROGER PENRITH

18 Gender and the Food History of the Caribbean: The Case of
Cassava in Barbados   204
JANET MOMSEN

19 COVID-19 and Tourism in the Island Pacific:
Gender Tribulations and Transformations in Different Seas   212
JOHN CONNELL

20 Women and Waste Recycling in the State of São Paulo, Brazil   221
MARGARIDA QUEIRÓS

21 Women's Stories of Loss and Recovery from Climatic Events in the
Pacific Islands   233
RACHEL CLISSOLD AND KAREN E. MCNAMARA

Index   247

Figures

6.1	Percentage of women in the IGU Commissions and Task Forces steering committees, 2020–2022	55
7.1	Distribution of Peace Monuments	67
9.1	Structure of a general network of female discourse on their scientific trajectories	89
10.1	Janice Monk (USA), Saraswati Raju (India), Maria Dolors Garcia Ramon (Spain), IGU Gender and Geography Conference, Jerusalem, 2010	106
10.2	Janice Monk, Vincent Del Casino, Paul Robbins, Sarah Moore, Katherine Gibson, Sallie Marston, Julie Graham and Daoquin Tong at dinner after presenting the Jan Monk Lecture, Tucson, 2010	108
17.1	New South Wales showing the birthplaces of adult Aboriginal people living in the communities in Monk's PhD study in 1965 and indicating the movement of people to Griffith from across Wiradjuri Country	183
17.2	New South Wales, showing the six towns included in Monk's PhD	185
17.3	An information table about the Monk Archive at the Griffith Family History Day	188
20.1	Mural with the beginnings of Cooperlix	226
20.2	At Cooperlix site: plastic objects separated by composition and market value, ready to be transported to destination	227
20.3	A shelter for working women: the shed from inside, the conveyor belts and the separation process	228
20.4	The Cooperlix shed from outside	228
20.5	The Cooperlix: a detail of a showcase of collected and reused materials for room decoration	229
21.1	Map of Vanuatu and the approximate locations of the marketplaces that participants' livelihoods are tied to	236
21.2	Location of the Cook Islands in relation to Australia and New Zealand	237

Tables

6.1	Percentage of women and men in the IGU Commissions and Task Forces steering committees, 2004–2022	53
6.2	Percentage of women and men in the IGU Commissions and Task Forces steering committees by continent, 2020–2022	54
6.3	Countries with an equal number or majority of women steering committee members of the IGU Commissions and Task Forces, 2020–2022	54
6.4	IGU Commissions and Task Forces with a woman as (co-)chair, 2020–2022	55
14.1	Background of the research participants	148
15.1	Young women and men entrepreneurs. Basic information	159
17.1	Key community statistics 1965, 2011 and 2016	187

Contributors

Swagata Basu is Associate Professor and Head of the Department of Geography at SSV College, Hapur, India. Swagata's research interests are in the area of Violence against Women (VAW) and Intimate Partner Violence (IPV) as well as issues related to women's right to the city. Swagata works closely with women's organisations associated with livelihood issues of women in low-income urban neighbourhoods.

Mireia Baylina is Senior Lecturer in Geography at the Universitat Autònoma de Barcelona (UAB). Her interests of research and publications are related to women's work and daily life in rural areas, representation of gender and rurality, and geographies of children and youth from a gender and intersectional perspective. She has been editor of the journals *Documents d'Anàlisi Geogràfica* and *European Urban and Regional Studies*, board member of the Commission of Gender and Geography of the International Geographical Union and coordinator of the Interuniversity and Interdisciplinary Doctorate Program on *Gender Studies: Cultures, Societies and Policies* for the UAB.

Federica Bono is Assistant Professor of Human Geography in the Department of Sociology, Social Work and Anthropology at Christopher Newport University. She teaches undergraduate-level Geography and GIS courses and researches informality and solidarity relations through the lens of food production and food access and, most recently, cross-border networks. She has conducted fieldwork in Belgium, the UK, Cuba, Gibraltar, and Spain. Additionally, she is interested in research ethics in sensitive settings.

Martina Angela Caretta is a Senior Lecturer at the Department of Human Geography at Lund University, Sweden. She holds a PhD in Geography from Stockholm University. She is a feminist geographer with expertise in water, climate change adaptation, gender and participatory methodologies. She is the Coordinating Lead Author of the 'Water' Chapter WGII IPCC 6th Assessment Report. She has carried out extensive fieldwork in East Africa, Latin America and Appalachia, USA. She is a member of the IGU Gender and Geography Commission steering committee. Her work has been published in *Gender, Place & Culture*; *Annals of the AAG*, *Climate & Development*, *Frontiers Water*, *Qualitative Research* among others.

Contributors xi

Rachel Clissold is a Senior Research Assistant in the School of Earth and Environmental Sciences at The University of Queensland (UQ) and her research interests include the gender, socio-political and livelihoods dimensions of climate change, natural hazards and sustainable development. Rachel has been involved in policy-relevant and applied research on climate change adaptation, disaster risk reduction, social vulnerability, gender, resilient livelihoods and non-economic loss and damage in the Asia-Pacific region for five years.

Stephen Collins is from the Yamandhu Marang Social Research Reference Group, Griffith, Australia.

Claire Colyer completed her PhD in Human Geography at Macquarie University in 2014. Her PhD research explored the role of mainstream not-for-profit organisations in community development and service delivery in Aboriginal communities in Australia. She has also worked in a collaborative research project on the social and economic well-being of Aboriginal people in rural towns in New South Wales through Macquarie University, and on a qualitative evaluation of a pilot project on amelioration of the health impacts of overcrowding in Aboriginal housing for the New South Wales Government.

John Connell is a Professor of Human Geography in the School of Geosciences, University of Sydney. He works mainly on development issues in small island states and especially in Melanesia. His most recent book, edited with Yonique Campbell, is *COVID in the Islands: A Comparative Perspective on the Caribbean and the Pacific* (2021).

David Crew is from the Yarkuwa Indigenous Knowledge Centre, Deniliquin, Australia.

Anindita Datta is Professor at the Department of Geography, University of Delhi and the current Chair of the IGU Commission on Gender and Geography. Her work focuses on gendered and epistemic violence, indigenous feminisms, spaces of resistance and geographies of care. A member of several international editorial boards and collaborations such as the NORAD, Linnaeus Palme and Erasmus Mundus programmes, Anindita is committed to feminist mentoring and building transformative networks of care across differences. Her recent books include *Gender, Space and Agency in India: Exploring Regional Genderscapes* and the *Routledge Handbook of Gender and Feminist Geography* (co-editor).

Joos Droogleever Fortuijn was Associate Professor in Human Geography at the University of Amsterdam and served from 2008 to 2015 as Chair of the Department of Geography, Planning and International Development Studies. She published on urban geography, rural geography, gender, ageing and teaching geography in higher education. She was Vice-President of the International Geographical Union (2012–2020) and steering committee member (1992–2000) and chair (2000–2004) of the IGU Commission on Gender and Geography and. From 1990 to 1998 she coordinated the ERASMUS/SOCRATES network on Geography and Gender, a teaching network of six European universities funded by the European Commission in the ERASMUS/ SOCRATES programme.

Ágnes Erőss is a geographer and research fellow at the Geographical Institute Research Centre for Astronomy and Earth Sciences (GI RCEAS) and a post-doctoral researcher at the Institute of Political Science and Public Administration, University of Opole. Her research tackles symbolic space appropriation strategies in ethnically–culturally diverse urban settings in Central and Eastern Europe (CEE). Besides, she has been exploring how family and individual livelihood strategies develop in the context of transnational migration and kin-state politics in CEE. Recently, she has been interested in the gender aspect of transnational migration and the immobile local communities in Transcarpathia, Western Ukraine.

Tamar Feuerstein is a geographer, who directs the National Gardens Section at the Society for the Protection of Nature in Israel.

Ruth Fincher is Professor Emeritus at the University of Melbourne, where she worked for 30 years following earlier positions in Canada. Her research in feminist urban geography examines the inequality and locational disadvantage associated with multiculturalism and difference in cities. She has held positions of leadership in and for geography with the International Geographical Union, the International Social Science Council, the International Science Council and the Institute of Australian Geographers. Her books include *Cities of Difference* (1998, co-edited with J Jacobs), *Planning and Diversity in the City* (2008, with K Iveson) and *Everyday Equalities* (2019, with K Iveson, H Leitner and V Preston).

Ken Foote is Professor of Geography and Director of the Urban and Community Studies Program at the University of Connecticut. He is a past president and fellow of the American Association of Geographers and a past president of the National Council for Geographic Education. Along with his interests in landscape history and GIScience, Ken has worked with Jan and Michael Solem for over 20 years on projects and programs to improve support for graduate students and early career geographers.

Emir Galilee is a scholar at Ben Gurion University, and Kaye collage. He has authored, both individually and collaboratively, a book and a number of papers, focused on the geography and history of nomadic and Muslim societies in Israel and the Middle East. His areas of interest include historical, social and cultural geography; focused on ethnic, religious, nomadic and indigenous groups; tourism and minorities; immigration of minorities from the Middle East.

Maria Dolors Garcia Ramon is Emerita Professor of Geography at the Autonomous University of Barcelona and has been Professor/research fellow at several universities in the USA, UK and Argentina, and is a member of the Academia Europea. She has published several books and many articles on rural geography, urban public spaces and the history of geography. She has been the coordinator of many international and national research projects. She has been a pioneering figure in Spain on gender studies as well as member of the editing board of several international journals. She was a founding member and secretary of the Gender and Geography Commission and was awarded the *Laureat d'Honneur* (IGU) and the Vautrin Lud Award.

Katherine Gibson is a Professorial Fellow in the Institute for Culture and Society at the Western Sydney University. She is an economic geographer with an international reputation for innovative research on economic transformation and over 30 years' experience of working with communities to build resilient economies. As J.K. Gibson-Graham, the collective authorial presence she shares with the late Julie Graham, her books include *The End of Capitalism (As We Knew It)* (1996), *A Postcapitalist Politics* (2006), *Take Back the Economy* (2013) co-authored with Cameron and Healy and *Manifesto For Living in the Anthropocene* (2015) co-edited with Rose and Fincher.

Holly M. Hapke, PhD is a feminist geographer and interdisciplinary social scientist whose research explores the intersection of culture, environment and political economy in the Global South. Her principal research projects focus on globalisation and development in small-scale fisheries in southern India. She is particularly interested in the social and cultural economy of fish markets and the role gender and other social identities play in shaping economic organisation and change. Dr. Hapke earned her PhD at Syracuse University. She is currently a research Professor and Director of Research Development in the School of Social Sciences at the University of California, Irvine.

Richard Howitt is Emeritus Professor at the Department of Geography and Planning at Macquarie University. His research focuses on Indigenous rights and the interface between Indigenous communities, natural resource development, governments and corporations at the scales of the project, the community, the landscape and the nation. His teaching covers areas of cultural, social and environmental geography at undergraduate, honours, master's and PhD levels.

Bev Johnson is from the Yamandhu Marang Social Research Reference Group, Griffith, Australia.

Louise C. Johnson is an Honorary Professor at Deakin University and Honorary (Professorial Fellow) at the University of Melbourne. She taught for over 40 years in Australian and New Zealand universities and has a solid record of research, policy development, leadership and community activism. A human geographer, she has long put a feminist perspective on researching

Geelong's textile industry, displaced car industry workers, women in the service sector, the growth of the creative industries and most recently analysed the city's economic resilience and socio-spatial disadvantage. In 2011, she received the Institute of Australian Geographers *Australia and International Medal* for her contribution to urban, social and cultural geography.

Lynda Johnston is a Professor of Geography at the University of Waikato with research interests in the challenges and spatial complexities of inequalities. Specifically, Lynda draws attention to the exclusionary ways in which various forms of marginalisation and discrimination – such as sexism, homophobia, transphobia and racism – shape people's places and spaces. Lynda would not have pursued a PhD, and subsequent academic career, without the financial support of an Evelyn Stokes scholarship. Lynda is currently the Assistant Vice-Chancellor Sustainability.

Marcio Jose Ornat is a Professor of Geography in the graduate programme at the State University of Ponta Grossa and vice-coordinator of the Group of Territorial Studies at the same university. His research is focused on the relationships between space, gender, sexualities and religion.

Ruth Kark is Professor at the Hebrew University of Jerusalem and has written and edited 27 books and 200 articles on the history and historical geography of Palestine/Israel. Her research interests include, among other topics, land and settlement activity, policy and law, Western civilisations and the Holy Land, Women and gender, as well as Bedouin in the Middle East and dissent and conflict surrounding landownership in Israel.

Candy Kilby is from the Yamandhu Marang Social Research Reference Group, Griffith, Australia

Lynette Kilby is from the Yamandhu Marang Social Research Reference Group, Griffith, Australia.

Mary Njeri Kinyanjui is a feminist geographer and activist. She is a Steering Committee member of the IGU Commission on Gender and Geography. Her research interests include women and the informal economy in African cities, international trade justice, education, women and pain, gender-based violence and femicide, women and the survival of indigenous economic activities in the global economy. Apart from these themes she has also published on 'utu feminism'. Her current research examines the logics, norms, values and institutional arrangements of 'Wanjiku'. Wanjiku represents the subaltern or the ordinary woman engaged in small-scale production and distribution in Africa.

Margareta Amy Lelea is a Senior Scientist at the German Institute for Tropical and Subtropical Agriculture (DITSL) and also works for the University of Kassel. Her PhD dissertation is a feminist geography of changing livelihoods along Romania's western border. Recent publications include the topic of gendering post-harvest loss research.

Robyn Longhurst has a long-standing interest in gender, equity and social justice. She researches in the broad area of social and cultural geography, with a particular interest in gender and embodiment. Robyn was Chair of the Commission on Gender and Geography, International Geographical Union from 2008 to 2012 providing her with rich opportunities to work with Janice Monk. She was from 1992 a member of the Department of Geography at the University of Waikato with Evelyn Stokes until Evelyn died in 2005. Robyn is currently the Deputy Vice-Chancellor Academic at the University of Waikato.

Antoni Luna is Professor of geography at the Universitat Pompeu Fabra of Barcelona since 1996. He holds a BA from the Universitat Autònoma de Barcelona and a master's and a doctorate from the University of Arizona. His main areas of research are geography education, working in several international projects; in social urban geography (with a strong focus on gender perspectives and public space) and history of geographic thought, particularly on the history of urban planning and urban design and on travel writing. He is a member of the Geohumanities Research Group at the UPF.

Karen E. McNamara is an Associate Professor in the School of Earth and Environmental Sciences at The University of Queensland (UQ). She is a development geographer who is ultimately interested in how livelihoods (in the broadest sense) can be enhanced to respond to the triple crises of poverty, disaster risk and climate change. Karen has been undertaking applied and policy-relevant research in resilient livelihoods, climate change adaptation, non-economic loss and recovery, human mobility and gender for over 15 years, partnering with governments and inter-governmental and non-governmental organisations throughout the Asia-Pacific region.

Janet Momsen was a founding member of the Gender Commission in 1988 and was Chair from then until 1996, continuing as Treasurer until 2006. She is Emerita Professor of Geography, University of California, Davis. Her research is mainly on gender and agricultural development. She has also taught in England, Canada, Brazil, Costa Rica, the Netherlands and South Africa. She has published 17 books and founded and is current Editor of the Routledge series on International Studies of Women and Place.

Janice Monk is a feminist geographer and Emeritus Professor at the University of Arizona. As a former president and senior fellow of the AAG, and director of the Southwest Institute for Research on Women, she has been instrumental in foregrounding how gender has shaped the development of geographic institutions and women's experiences within them. She has also worked on projects which addressed women's employment, education, health and culture.

Mª Josefa Mosteiro García is Senior Lecturer in Research Methods and Diagnosis in Education of the Department of Pedagogy and Didactics of the University of Santiago de Compostela. She is area coordinator, Secretary of the Institute of Education Sciences and member of the Interdisciplinary Center for Feminist Research and Gender Studies (CIFEX). She has participated in national and regional research projects on gender, education and geography and has publications in this field. Her teaching is linked to the research methodology in education and in the studies of women and gender.

Ann M. Oberhauser is Professor of sociology in the Department of Sociology at Iowa State University and holds a PhD in geography from Clark University. Her research focuses on feminist economic geography, gender and globalisation, feminist pedagogy and critical development studies with an emphasis on rural economic strategies in Appalachia and sub-Saharan Africa. Her publications include *Feminist Spaces: Gender and Geography in a Global Context* and *Global Perspectives on Gender and Space*. Oberhauser is a long-time member of the International Geographical Union Commission on Gender, the Society of Woman Geographers and the Feminist Geographies Specialty Group of the American Association of Geographers.

Tamires Regina Aguiar de Oliveira Cesar is a PhD in geography researcher of the Group of Territorial Studies at the State University of Ponta Grossa. Her post-doctoral research is on 'Actor's networks and emerging themes in the Brazilian Geographical Scientific Production between 1987-2019'.

Roger Penrith was a highly respected community member and Director of the Griffith Clontarf Academy. Roger took great pride in his role and made a significant impact on the lives of the young people with whom he worked. He encouraged Aboriginal students to take pride in themselves and their culture.

Ana Mª Porto Castro is a senior lecturer in Research Methods and Diagnosis in Education of the Department of Pedagogy and Didactics of the University of Santiago de Compostela (USC). Director of the Institute of Education Sciences of the USC since 2012 and coordinator of the IDEA Research Group (Investigation, Educational Diagnosis and Evaluation) in which she has directed and participated in national and regional projects on gender and education. She is the founder of the Interdisciplinary Center for Feminist Research and Gender Studies (CIFEX) and her publications are related to gender, education and geography.

Margarida Queirós has a PhD in Human Geography from the University of Lisbon. She is currently Associate Professor at the Institute of Geography and Spatial Planning (IGOT-UL) and a researcher at the Centre for Geographical Studies of the University of Lisbon. Her research interests include gender, environment, and spatial planning. She is the national coordinator of RIDOT network (Ibero-American Network for Territorial Observation) and a founding member of the REGGSILA network

(Studies of Ibero-Latin American Geography, Gender and Sexuality) and a recognised expert by the Portuguese Commission for Citizenship and Gender Equality as a reference on gender studies.

Isabel Salamaña is geographer, Senior Lecturer at the Department of Geography, Universitat de Girona (UdG). She is specialised in rural studies, gender, territorial planning and public spaces, issues on which she has done research. She is a member of the Permanent Commission of the Interuniversity Institute for Women and Gender Studies (iiEDG), of the Institute of the Environment (UdG), of the Chair of Geography and Territorial Thought (UdG) and of the Geography and Gender Research Group of the UAB. Moreover, she is nowadays head of Gender and Diversity of the Faculty of Arts of the UdG and editor of the journal *Documents d'Anàlisi Geogràfica* (UAB-UdG).

Marcella Schmidt di Friedberg is full Professor of Geography, at the 'Riccardo Massa' Department of Human Sciences for Education (University of Milano-Bicocca, Italy). She is Chair of the Commission on the History of Geography of the International Geographical Union (IGU) from 2016 and vice-director of the Marine Research and High Education Center (MaRHE) in Faaf-Magoodhoo (Rep of Maldives). Her research interests concern Cultural Geography, Gender Geography, Hazard and Resilience, and History of the Geographical Thought. She has been working and publishing extensively on the relations between nature, culture, memory and landscape in different contexts, from the Mediterranean to Japan.

Joseli Maria Silva is a Professor of Geography in the postgraduate programme at the State University of Ponta Grossa. She is coordinator of the Group of Territorial Studies at the same university. Her research is focused on the relationship between space, gender and sexualities, with special attention on trans-sexualities.

Michael Solem is a Professor of Geography at Texas State University. After 14 years directing educational programs at the American Association of Geographers, he continues to serve the AAG as Senior Advisor for Geography Education and Co-Director of the National Center for Research in Geography Education. Since 2002 Michael has contributed to the AAG's annual Geography Faculty Development Alliance workshops for early career faculty. He is co-chair of the International Geographical Union's Commission on Geographical Education and is a member of the editorial board for the *Journal of Geography in Higher Education*. In 2015, Michael received AAG Gilbert Grosvenor Honors in Geographic Education.

Monika Mária Váradi is a sociologist and Senior Research Fellow at the Institute for Regional Studies (CERS ELKH). Her research focuses on transnational migration, the socioeconomic transformation of local communities and rural poverty. Recently, Váradi was the leader of a research project on how international (circular) labour migration from Hungary transforms the life of communities in lagging rural regions, and how it impacts livelihood and mobility strategies of individuals and families. Her research interest includes the changing patterns of gender roles in families in the context of (transnational) geographical and social mobility.

Montserrat Villarino is Senior Lecturer of geography at the University of Santiago de Compostela. Montserrat teaches human and economic geography and specialisation courses: Master's Degree in Education, Gender and Equality (University of Santiago). She has done research in geography and gender and rural development, alone and with the Geography and Gender Research Group of the UAB since its beginnings. She has participated in Development cooperation projects in Latin America with several universities in Ecuador and in Argentina. She is co-founder of the Interdisciplinary Center for Feminist Research and Gender Studies (University of Santiago) and Deputy Director of the Interdisciplinary Center for American Studies 'Gumersindo Busto' (University of Santiago).

Sorina Voiculescu is an Associate Professor in the Department of Geography, West University Timisoara (WUT). She was a member of the steering committee of the Gender and Geography Commission of the International Geographical Union (2004–2012). She is a leading figure in the Romanian academic system for research in the field of gender and geography.

Doris Wastl-Walter is Professor emerita of Human Geography at the University of Berne, Switzerland. Her research interest is Social and Political Geography and Gender Studies. She has been Chair of the IGU Commission for Geography of Governance and President of the interdisciplinary Centre of Gender Studies at the University of Berne. There she has also served as Vice-rectrice for Quality including Equal Opportunities and Sustainability. She has also been the President of the Federal Swiss program for equal opportunities at universities. Among her numerous publications are the Research Companion for Border Studies and Gender Geographien. Jan Monk has always been a role model for her regarding Mentoring, feminist Geographies and institutional development.

1 Bridging Worlds – Building Feminist Geographies
Essays in Honour of Janice Monk

Anindita Datta, Janet Momsen and Ann M. Oberhauser

The metaphor of a bridge connecting feminist scholarship across different worlds best describes the supportive figure Jan Monk has been to feminist geographers of different generations and social locations. Her seminal essay with Susan Hanson 'On Not Excluding Half of the Human in Human Geography' (Monk and Hanson 1982) questioned the androcentricity of geography and the invisibility of women and its subjects and practitioners. This book, published in the Tricenary year of the IGU Commission on Gender and Geography, is our heartfelt tribute to Jan Monk. Borrowing her words from the title of one of her papers, this collection emphasizes how she has been instrumental in "connecting people, places, and ideas" (Monk 2008) besides laying the foundations of feminist geography and working tirelessly to extend the field.

Together with Janet Momsen and Maria Dolors Garcia Ramon, Jan lobbied for a place for geographies of gender at the International Geographical Union (IGU) meeting in Sydney in 1988. In 1989, the working group held its first conference at Newcastle University in the UK, chaired by Janet Momsen. The conference focused on Gender and Development and attracted nearly 100 academic geographers and other social scientists from over 40 countries. Papers from this conference were published in *Different Places, Different Voices* edited by Janet Momsen and Vivian Kinnaird in 1993 (Momsen and Kinnaird 1993), as the first volume in the Routledge series on *International Studies of Women and Place*, co-edited by Janet Momsen and Jan Monk. The series now has 35 volumes published and others in press. As a result of these and many other efforts, the working group was finally granted the status of a full-fledged Commission on Gender and Geography in 1992.

Born in Sydney, Australia, Jan studied at the University of Sydney for her bachelor's and master's degrees. She then moved to the USA and obtained her doctorate at the University of Illinois, Champagne, conducting research on indigenous communities in Australia under Charles Alexander's mentorship. In her long and impactful career, she has held several important positions, including Research Social Scientist Emerita – Women's Studies, Professor of the School of Geography and Development, University of Arizona and Senior Fellow, and President of the American Association of Geographers. Throughout, Jan worked to highlight women's experiences and

DOI: 10.4324/9781032275611-1

to foreground the lens of gender within geographical research and knowledge production. She was committed to supporting feminist geographers, introducing them to relevant networks, promoting their research, and advocating for their inclusion and recognition within international groups, universities, and other academic bodies. Jan's key research has focused on historical studies of women geographers, women's roles in the southeastern USA, women in the Caribbean, women and work, women's education, and mentorship of young women academics.

Women were present in the IGU meetings since 1871, but it was only towards the latter half of the 1950s that their presence in the IGU was acknowledged through social events organized by a few women geographers. This came after Marguerite Lefevre was appointed First Vice President from 1949 to 1952. In her essay 'Many Roads: The Personal and Professional Lives of Women Geographers,' Jan observed how academic trajectories were influenced by social and political cultures and that geographic knowledge needs to be contextualized both spatially and temporally (Monk 2001). In a later essay, she described ways in which the history of education in the USA had placed women and men differently within the discipline (Monk 2004) accounting for the androcentricity of geography (Ibid). Today we recognize that these forms of marginalization are evident in many other countries and contexts as well. Jan's work with Cindi Katz (Katz and Monk 1993) extended the field of gender geography, demonstrating the importance of place and time in women's lives through autobiographical methods, an intergenerational approach, and contextualizing women's lives within their geographical settings and life courses. Writing with Vera Norwood, *The Desert is No Lady* (Norwood and Monk 1997) examined the way in which the desert landscape of the southwest had been interpreted by Hispanic, Mexican, and American Indian women, influencing their creativity and art. The book highlighted the importance of a gendered perspective, stemming from women's readings of their native landscapes. Jan's most recent research involved updating her doctoral study in Australia.

As part of her geographical engagement, Jan attended conferences and established institutional and personal connections with scholars, activists, and practitioners across the globe. Building connections with feminist geographers outside the Anglo-American world in Brazil, India, Taiwan, China, Japan, Ghana, Nigeria, and Kenya among others, Jan noted that "place matters, it is perhaps inevitable that where we are shapes our ways of looking at the world" (Monk 1994; Silva 2010, 156). Her body of work has been very influential in shaping the initial contours of feminist geography and in nurturing the community of feminist geographers worldwide.

As editors, our connections to each other have also involved Jan's efforts to bridge feminist scholarship and activities. Our professional and personal associations with her have helped us "survive and thrive" – a theme for a panel Jan organized at the IGU Annual Meeting in Kraków in 2014. As outlined here, our associations with Jan and with each other reflect the different facets of her work in building feminist geographies.

Janet Momsen first met Jan Monk in 1978 at the 74th Annual Meeting of the Association of American Geographers held in New Orleans (Monk 1981) where they both gave papers. After that first meeting, they went on to work and travel together, organizing conferences to encourage other women geographers, and negotiating for a Working Group and finally a full-fledged Commission within the IGU. Janet Momsen served two terms as the first Chair of the Working Group besides being Treasurer of the Commission until 2004. Jan edited the Commission's biannual newsletter until 2014, keeping many of us connected and updated with news of publications, conferences, and feminist geography events from around the world. They also co-edited publications in the Routledge series *International Studies of Women and Place*. Janet recalls the challenge of finding an appropriate title for their series at a time when "gender" was not a widely used term and notes that the series was initially focused on gender and development but has widened its scope and has been among the most successful and the longest running of such series.

For Anindita, Jan has been an invaluable mentor, inspiring her to persist in her work despite several structural barriers and introducing her to other feminist geographers. She encouraged Anindita to participate in international events, often paying for her membership and generously hosting her at international events. These efforts included advising her to build connections across institutions, get involved in editorial boards, and participate in the IGU Commission on Gender and Geography. In 2013, Jan introduced Anindita to Janet Momsen at an RGS-IBG meeting at London. In their first meeting Anindita remarked how influential the Routledge series had been and that Janet's *Gender and Development* (now in its third edition) was the first feminist geography book she had bought! Noting her interest and emerging work, Janet subsequently invited Anindita to contribute to the new edition, forging a collaboration almost a decade ago. Similarly, Ann and Anindita met in 2012 at the Commission's pre-conference at Nara, Japan. Both recounted with warmth their association with Jan and her impact on their academic life as they worked together in the Steering Committee of Commission, forging a strong bond and camaraderie.

Ann Oberhauser is pleased to contribute to this collection which recognizes the influence and significance of Jan Monk's career and legacy for her and many other feminist geographers. Her strongest ties to Jan have been in the academic spaces of conferences and through feminist geography scholarship. This book underscores the impact of Jan's work on the professional arena and scholarship of the discipline of geography. As noted above, much of this impact was organically formed and grown in local, national, and global gatherings of feminist geographers. Ann recalls how her first experiences at AAG conferences entailed a certain degree of trepidation and uncertainty. Over the years, however, she met and learned from a strong and supportive community in the Geographical Perspectives on Women (GPOW), now Feminist Geographies Specialty Group (FGSG) of the AAG, and the IGU Commission on Gender and Geography. In addition to the scholarship and academic exchanges at these meetings, she developed networks, allies, and friendships in some otherwise sterile and unwelcoming environments. As these networks grew, Jan Monk became a constant, a confidante, and a role model for younger scholars and activists. She gave critical feedback and was extremely generous in writing recommendation letters and providing resources that are still on Ann's bookshelf and hard drive. Fittingly, in 2021 Ann was awarded the Jan Monk Service Award of the Feminist Geographies Specialty Group.

Given the way that Jan connected so many of us to each other, it is no coincidence that the editors of this festschrift are the first and current Chairs as well as the Treasurer and Steering Committee member of the Gender Commission. The seeds for this book were sown in one of the many friendly conversations we have shared with each other over the years.

Jan Monk's ground-breaking writings and visual materials on women and work, cultural landscapes, the life course, indigenous peoples, and more have left an indelible mark on feminist and critical geography as a whole. This festschrift acknowledges and honours the legacy of her friendship, mentoring, tireless leadership, and contributions to this field. These efforts also reflect her commitment to improving our local communities and broader, diverse landscapes of geography. Jan's amazing ability to build community and develop collaborations ensure the continuity of this legacy.

Out of the numerous abstracts submitted for this book, we selected those that build on Jan's own research interests. The geographical distribution of chapters included in this book is three from the USA, eight from Europe (Spain, Portugal, France, UK, Romania, Germany, the Netherlands and Italy, Switzerland, Sweden, and Hungary), five from Australia and New Zealand, plus one each from Brazil, India, Israel, and Kenya. Several chapters examine Jan's specific contributions to gender and geography in various parts of the world as at the University of Arizona, in Spain, Australia, and New Zealand. The contributions are organized around the themes of placing gender and feminist geographies within the discipline, career trajectories, and survival strategies among women geographers, the theme of everyday lives, women's work and life courses, and the intersections of gender and environmental concerns. A major chapter in this collection is a tribute to Jan's final research project which revisited her doctoral work on Australian indigenous people.

This book encompasses the themes close to Jan's heart and is also a product of the networks she has so passionately nurtured. Altogether the book's contents provide a broad overview of the development of feminist geography worldwide. Although focused on Jan Monk's career, it will offer a valuable reference for students highlighting the impact of Jan's work. As one feminist geographer reminds us, this field entails "greater concerns with the complexities of difference, diversity, subjectivity, and the body, as well as to thinking of knowledge as socially, culturally and politically constructed, and as intertwined with power relations" (Silva 2010, 155). Of note to this growing emphasis on difference and diversity in feminist and gender geography is the emergence of scholarship about and representation of the LGBTQ community, experiences and topics. These themes recognize and celebrate non-binary dimensions of gender identity and sexual orientation.

Finally, in revisiting the metaphor of the bridge, we find our feminist networks appear more like complex webs as our journeys intersect and overlap. Yet the bridge is key for its role in connecting and enabling multidirectional flows to connect these webs. Without the crucial bridge, many of these multiple webs would remain unconnected. For many of us, Jan Monk has been that bridge.

References

Katz, Cindi, and Janice Monk. 1993. *Full Circles: Geographies of Women over the Life Course*. London: Routledge.

Momsen, Janet H., and Vivian Kinnaird ed. 1993. *Different Places, Different Voices: Gender and Development in Africa, Asia and Latin America*. London: Routledge.

Monk, Janice. 1981. "Social Change and Sexual Differences in Puerto Rican Rural Migration." *Papers in Latin American Geography in Honor of Lucia C. Harrison*, edited by Oscar H. Horst, 28–43. Indiana. (Special Publications of the Conference of Latin Americanist Geographers, Volume 1).

Monk, Janice. 1994. "Place Matters: Comparative International Perspectives on Feminist Geography." *Professional Geographer*, 46 (3): 277–288.

Monk, Janice. 2001. "Many Roads: The Personal and Professional Lives of Women Geographers." In *Placing Autobiography in Geography*, edited by Pamela Moss, 167–187. Syracuse: Syracuse University Press.

Monk, Janice. 2004. "Women, Gender, and the Histories of American Geography." *Annals of the Association of American Geographers*, 94 (1): 1–22.

Monk, Janice. 2008. "Connecting People, Places, and Ideas: Reflections on the History of the International Geographical Union Commission on Gender and Geography." *Report to the International Geographical Union Gender and Geography Commission*.

Monk, Janice, and Susan Hanson. 1982. "On Not Excluding Half of the Human in Human Geography." *The Professional Geographer*, 34 (1): 11–23.

Norwood, Vera, and Janice J. Monk. ed. 1997. *The Desert Is No Lady: Southwestern Landscapes in Women's Writing and Art*. Arizona: University of Arizona Press.

Silva, Joseli Maria. 2010. "On Not Excluding Half of the Human in Human Geography: Interview with Janice Monk." *Revista Latino-Americana de Geografia E Genero*, 1 (1): 153–556.

Part I
Gender and Feminist Geographies

Perspectives from around the World

2 Connecting Distant Academic Landscapes, Inspiring Researchers

Jan Monk's Role in Developing Gender Geography and Geohumanities in Spain

Maria Dolors Garcia Ramon and Antoni Luna

Introduction

Jan Monk has been a very active geographer for almost 50 years, and during that time she has created a network of researchers across the world on gender issues in geography as well as other areas such as geography of education and cultural geography. In this chapter we analyze her role in the development of the field of geography of gender and the development of geohumanities approaches internationally and more specifically in Spain.

Monk made profound contributions to advance international collaborations on gender and geography, geography of education, and cultural geography. She has been well recognized as a leader in supporting the advancement of women within her discipline around the world; nevertheless, she has also supported and advised some male researchers around the world. As Executive Director for 25 years of a regional research institute on gender at the University of Arizona, she fostered interdisciplinary research, educational and outreach programs that addressed ethnic and cultural diversity, bringing together scholars from many American universities and Northern Mexico.

In addition to her work in the United States, Jan Monk has been a sustained supporter of international collaboration. Her contacts and interactions eventually spread across the world, including to Latin America and Southern and Eastern Europe. Jan has acted as a human bridge across a variety of academic communities in different countries and contexts using solely geography and gender as a lingua franca. While it is true that Anglophone work has been a key inspiration for diverse perspectives on gender and sexuality in many other places and has become very powerful in local academic communities (Garcia Ramon and Monk 1987; Hancock 2002; Garcia Ramon 2003; Garcia Ramon, Simonsen and Vaiou 2006; Kitchin 2005; Browne 2015), Jan Monk used her privileged position – being an "insider" and an "outsider" within the Anglo-American world – to support all kinds of international collaboration and somehow counterbalance this hegemony. Her work on gender approaches in geography and her early work in arts and landscape have been an inspiration to scholars on the other side of the Atlantic.

DOI: 10.4324/9781032275611-3

Jan's role in the development of international gender geography

Jan Monk hails from the Southern Hemisphere from her beloved Australia; although, she has lived during most of her academic life in the United States, very close to the Mexican border, within a very enriching cultural landscape that inspired her personally and professionally. It is important to point out that in her early education in Australia, she was educated on a "colonial" view of the world dominated by the British and by European history (Garcia Ramon and Luna 2007). Her own choice of topics of research for her PhD in the 1970s – cultural aspects of aboriginals in some towns of eastern Australia – also situated her outside the dominant arenas of research in geography of her time, identifying her as a "deviant geographer" by choice (Monk and Allen 2021). Nevertheless, she has a long engagement with Anglo-American geography, even becoming the President of the Association of American Geographers (renamed the American Association of Geographers) in 2001. Working as an "insider" and as an "outsider" has allowed her to develop a special sensibility for varied approaches and an increasing interest in fostering new types of academic relationships away from the hegemonic Anglo-American discourse. Jan has been extremely active in the promotion of "real" international scholarship (Monk and Garcia Ramon 1997). It is clear that this "positionality" has shaped and enhanced her contribution to the development of geography of gender in a large number of countries (Monk and Garcia Ramon 2013).

One of Monk's key projects in developing this field has been the Geography and Gender Commission of the International Geographical Union (IGU). In effect, this Commission has been the most important agent for internationalizing gender within geography and making the discipline more inclusive. In the IGU congress of Paris in 1984, Jan Monk sent a written request (never answered) to the local organizers for a meeting time and space to discuss the possibility of creating a group. Nevertheless, a "spontaneous" meeting took place, organized by Jan, and created an informal list of people who showed some interest in the gender approach. In the following IGU Regional Conference in Barcelona in 1986, a well-attended Round Table was organized within the program of the conference hosted by the Autonomous University of Barcelona (UAB) due to Jan's contacts with the Spanish local colleagues. About one year later, important steps towards initiating the Commission were taken in informal conversations between Jan Monk, Janet Momsen, and Maria Dolors Garcia Ramon in December 1987 at a conference hosted by Maria Dolors in Barcelona on agriculture and gender. These were soon followed by discussions at British meetings, after which Janet Momsen took the lead in preparing an application and shepherding it through the IGU Executive Committee, drawing on her long-standing networks. At the Sydney IGU Conference in 1988, Jan Monk was invited to give one of the plenary lectures on "Encompassing Gender: Progress and Challenges in Gender Research". The Gender and Geography Study Group was approved with Janet Momsen as the founding Chair, Jan Monk as Vice-President and Maria Dolors Garcia

Ramon as Secretary. The Study Group was "upgraded" to Commission status at the conference in Washington in 1992 with the same team.

An early example of the Commission's potential to disseminate research by scholars from multiple regions of the world and making international geography really inclusive was the book series International Studies of Women and Place. Janet Momsen and Jan Monk edited it and the series has been published until the present by Routledge in almost 40 volumes. This Festschrift in honor of Jan is published in this series.

In terms of inclusivity, we would like to point out the publication of the Newsletter of the Commission. It began in 1988, and in May 2021 reached issue number 65 (since 2006 it has also been circulated to all members in Spanish and French to widen the audience in those regions of the world where English is not so common in academia). Jan Monk was the editor for more than 30 years (up to 2018 and for 60 issues), playing a vital role in showcasing emerging research and connecting feminist geographers worldwide through the Newsletter (Huang et al. 2017). Joos Droogleven Fortuijn from Amsterdam is the current editor. The Newsletter reports Commission activities and publishes academic and scientific news of feminist geographers, publications as well as gender-related activities around the world. Jan has long practiced an international and inclusive geography and argued for the rights of those who must struggle to have their voices heard and who lived outside the Anglophone realm. Therefore, when she was compiling the Newsletter, she made an effort to include the work of researchers who have published in languages other than English. The Newsletter contains a great deal of information about gender and geography around the world and, in particular, about publications (in English as well as in many other languages). It has been an excellent means of circulating work and information from the non-hegemonic margins as well as the hegemonic mainstream.

She personally wrote and distributed the Commission's newsletter, all the while providing invaluable personal encouragement to many women in geography in countries where professional paths for women are difficult to negotiate. It is worthwhile remembering that she has held visiting appointments in Australia, New Zealand, Taiwan, the Netherlands, Israel, Canada, and Switzerland and has sustained ties with geographers at the UAB (as we will explain in the section that follows in detail). Her work has been published as original or translated pieces in Catalan, German, Italian, Japanese, Portuguese (the latter in Brazil), and Spanish. And of course, she has hosted numerous international scholars at the University of Arizona, including those from Australia, Azerbaijan, Canada, Spain, France, Iceland, India, New Zealand, Norway, and Sri Lanka. After these visits she has kept in touch with most of these individuals, strengthening the relationship with them and their home institutions as well as sharing professional and personal interests. All these international contacts have offered Jan the chance to learn how geography and also gender studies are conceptualized in different contexts and to reinforce her interest in seeing how we can share and how we can deal with the differences.

Jan's involvement in the development of gender geography in Spain

As we have seen, Jan has provided intellectual stimulus to the community of feminist geographers worldwide for more than four decades. One of the countries that she has had a more intensive relationship with is Spain, and in particular with the Universitat Autònoma de Barcelona (UAB). One of the co-authors of the chapter (Maria Dolors) met her at the congress of Paris in 1984 and together with her they organized a half-day session on gender at the IGU regional congress in Barcelona in 1986. It was the first time that a session on the topic of gender was organized at the IGU and also it was the first time that Jan visited Barcelona. Since then, she has visited Barcelona many times and also a number of Catalan geographers (in particular Mireia Baylina, Antoni Luna, and Maria Dolors Garcia Ramon) have spent periods of various length at the University of Arizona and contacts between Arizona and Spain (in particular Catalonia) have multiplied. Jan has visited Barcelona more than 15 times, the last being in July 2017 for a late celebration of her 80th birthday in the UAB Department.

Seven of her visits were lengthy (sabbaticals in 1992 and 2006) and others were shorter (at least one week), and in this case Maria Dolors hosted her. Some of the visits were to give lectures or workshops, to help organize international congress, to discuss the development of research projects, or work with Maria Dolors in editing books or journals issues. All her visits were very fruitful exchanges between academics not only from UAB but also from other Catalan universities such as the University of Barcelona or University of Pompeu Fabra at Barcelona, as well as the University of Girona.

She also participated in three of the workshops of the Erasmus Intensive Course that the UAB organized together with seven European universities 1990–1998 (a total of eight workshops, almost one per year). Two of the workshops took place in Barcelona (1993 and 1998) and the third one took place in Athens in 1994 which she attended as a member of the Barcelona team. The Erasmus Intensive Course was an EU teaching initiative that she highly valued and allowed her many contacts among European colleagues working on gender (Monk and Garcia Ramon 1997). The workshops of the course were built on the very different traditions in geography and gender studies that both staff and students had previously experienced in their own universities. This experience forced students and staff to deal with and learn about differences of approach (methodological as well as theoretical). Jan was very enthusiastic in particular about the one we organized in 1993 in Barcelona. She gave the opening lecture entitled "Place Matters", published in Spanish (Monk 1995) and in English (Monk 1994), where she discussed very interesting strategies to engender geography and at the same time challenged certain practices of Anglo-American geography. The topic of this Erasmus intensive course was Women's Work and Daily Life with an emphasis on Southern Europe. The importance of place and the differences between the North and South of Europe was extremely enriching, and this was reflected afterwards in the book that Jan and Maria Dolors co-edited during one of Jan's lengthy stays in Barcelona (Garcia Ramon & Monk 1996).

Thus, co-authoring and editing with non-Anglo colleagues has been a good instrument for Jan towards fostering and pushing international publications and the circulation of non-hegemonic traditions. The book co-edited with Maria Dolors *Women of the European Union: The Politics of Work and Daily Life* (Garcia Ramon and Monk 1996) is a good example. The original materials came from the seminar held in Barcelona where they were presented by Spanish, French, German, Danish, Dutch, British, Italian, and Greek colleagues. The editors decided to give more space in the book to women of Southern Europe, a fact that was quite uncommon in the international geography of Europe. They were also very aware that Northern or hegemonic models of interpreting the world, for example the family unit, could not be taken for granted for Southern Europe. Moreover, a majority of the authors who were included were not native speakers of English and worked outside English-speaking countries. These choices on the emphasis and authors reflect the editors' own awareness that place is important in the construction of knowledge.

Another example of Jan's interest in giving voice to peripheral/marginal voices is her enthusiasm in an international seminar she co-organized with us in Barcelona in 2006. The title was 'Gender and Geography Worldwide: Contesting Anglo-American Hegemony'. Our aim was not only to give an inclusive view of gender geography but also to discuss strategies to break this hegemony. We invited speakers from a wide variety of countries and geographical traditions and nationalities (Hungary, Singapore, Brazil, Argentina, Ghana, UK, Switzerland, Turkey, United States, and Spain) and we were also able to enlarge the pool of countries with the discussants (Netherlands, Israel, India, Greece, and the United States).

A selection of the papers was published in English and in French in a special monographic issue of the Belgian journal (BELGEO 2007) with Maria Dolors and Jan Monk as invited editors. We thought that in this way the results of the seminar would have a wider diffusion as compared to only through the main "international" Anglophone journals. In order to foster a truly international gender geography, this monographic issue gave the opportunity to speak to other voices (and not only the hegemonic ones) and also draw a "real" picture of the work being done internationally in gender geography (Garcia Ramon and Monk 2007a; Garcia Ramon and Monk 2007b).

Jan has also contributed towards giving visibility within the international arena to some Catalan and Spanish geographical journals (*Treballs de la Societat Catalana de Geografia* and *Documents 'd'Anàlisi Geogràfica*) where a good number of her articles on gender have been published (Monk 2001a., 2001b., 2006). The first journal, mostly written in Catalan, is published by the Societat Catalana de Geografia. It might be thought of as a "marginal" or peripheral journal within Spanish geography; although, its quality and evaluation standards are high. Jan has been an active member of the board, in particular as a referee for articles that are submitted in English and that are evaluated before they are translated. She is also author of one article in a monographic issue on the contribution of foreign geographers to Catalan geography (2007). In this way her contribution to make the journal more international is quite remarkable. Jan has also published several articles in Spanish in *Documents 'd'Anàlisi Geografica*, a journal published in Barcelona in Spanish and Catalan since 1982 (see references). It has a wide influence in Spain and in Latin America, and it has been a pioneer in introducing gender geography in the Latin American world.

Jan's involvement in non-hegemonic traditions of geography has helped not only us but also her. She has been able to connect not only to gender geographers in other continental European countries but also in Mexico and other Latin American countries.

Jan's impact among Catalan geographers has been steady, strong, and very fruitful since 1986 until today, in particular with geographers of the Autonomous University of Barcelona. This is why the Rector of the Autonomous University of Barcelona gave Jan Monk the highest honor of the university, the honorary degree of Doctor Honoris Causa in a very solemn act in the fall of 2013. Her brilliant speech on "Braided Streams: Spaces and Flows in a Career" was published in *Documents 'd'Analisi Geografica* (Monk 2015).

In this way Jan Monk has made Spanish and Catalan cultural gender geography more visible at the national and international levels. At the same time, we have helped Jan in enlarging her professional horizons and connecting her to new people, new places, and new ideas.

Jan's role in the development of geohumanities approaches in Spain

The impact of Jan's work in Spain goes beyond geographies of gender as she also helped geographers from Spain in other areas such as geography education, cultural and social geography, and more recently on geohumanities. The connection between the University of Arizona and the Autonomous University of Barcelona in particular was fruitful and extended over different generations of geographers. In this section we want to add on the contributions of Jan Monk in new approaches in geography in Spain.

Jan Monk arrived at the University of Arizona in the early 1980s to work at the Southwestern Institute of Research on Women (SIROW), where she became Executive director between 1983 and 2004. She was also affiliated scholar at the Geography and Regional Development in the same university. SIROW was a very important platform to link with scholars and activities across the Southwestern States and also to parts of Northern Mexico. She maintained effective activities with different educational institutions in the area and brought together feminist scholars in the area to work not only in geography but also in the social sciences and also, and most remarkably, in the arts and humanities. We believe geography for Jan has neither disciplinary boundaries nor geographic limitations. Language and cultural differences were always overcome with mutual trust and enthusiasm.

One example of these activities is the project funded by the Rockefeller Foundation, titled "Vision of Landscape: Women Writers and Artists in the

Southwest 1880-1980" in which she worked as co-PI with University of New Mexico Scholar, Dr. Vera Norwood. In this project Monk and Norwood focused on the concept of a landscape from a very different perspective of the traditional studies on Landscape of the American Cultural Geography. This was groundbreaking work that resulted in an edited volume (Norwood & Monk 1987). The book unfolded the richness of the different cultures that form the Southwest. Anglos, Mexican, and Native women speak about their perception of the landscape that surrounds them, and also the way their creative work is shaped by the different places. She focused on women artists, writers, poets, painters, and photographers in different sections of the American Southwest.

This project could not easily be labeled by any of the 1980s paradigms in geography; it is an interesting mix of traditional cultural geography and humanistic approaches (Monk 1984). It draws from the work of both Yi Fu Tuan and Glacken Jackson but from a distinctive gender perspective. Their conceptualization of landscape is closer to that of Cosgrove and to some of the new cultural geography that was developed more or less at the same time that explains culture more as a process than as material artifacts. Finally, it also has some influence on the behavioral geography of Thomas Sarinen, one of her fellow geographers at the University of Arizona.

This work was rapidly introduced to Spain, a review of the book appeared in 1990 *Documents d'Analisi Geografica*, the journal of the department of Geography of the Autonomous University of Barcelona. The author of the review was Joan Nogué (1990) who just a few years before defended the first dissertation in Humanistic Geography in Spain under the supervision of Maria Dolors Garcia Ramon. Nogué's analysis of the landscape of the rural region of la Garrotxa was highly influenced by his contact with the University of Wisconsin–Madison and Yi Fu Tuan. In the early 1980s, the perspective of his work was still not gender sensitive, but his later work became more "genderized" in part thanks to the impact and evolution of the Geography Department of Barcelona and the productive relationship, as we explained before, between Jan Monk and Maria Dolors Garcia Ramon.

In 1995, Jan's book became a movie, a documentary, directed by Shelley Williams in collaboration with Susan Palmer with the supervision of Jan Monk and Vera Norwood. The documentary was shown in different festivals and received several awards such as the Best Documentary of San Antonio Cine Festival in 1996 and was screened and broadcasted in different TV stations in North America and Western Europe.

The film was widely used as a teaching material in human and cultural geography classes. In Spain, both Maria Dolors and Toni Luna, authors of this chapter, have been using it in some of their courses for geography students or for humanities students at Pompeu Fabra University. Toni Luna, who studied extensively the US–Mexico border for his PhD at the University of Arizona, also used to show the cultural diversity of the American Southwest to his humanities students. The theme of the relation between landscapes and gender issues also began to develop in some publications (Luna & Cerarols 2015).

Eventually, Toni Luna and Rosa Cerarols, both geographers at Pompeu Fabra started to work in the area of geohumanities organizing in 2016 an International Conference on Geohumanities, the first of this kind in Spain (Cerarols & Luna 2017; Cerarols, Nogué & Luna 2017). The work developed by mostly British geographers such as Oli Mould, Tim Cresswell, or Harriett Hawkins became the inspiration for their work. In 2021, they also organized a new colloquium on Creative Landscapes together with the Landscape Observatory of Catalonia (http://paisatgescreatius.catpaisatge.net/en/presentation/). Their work on Catalan and Spanish Artists is clearly inspired by the groundbreaking work of Jan Monk almost 30 years earlier. Landscape and creativity as well as gender are again the source of this seminar and future publication, very much like the way Jan explained it in her 1980s work on women artists.

Final remarks

In this chapter we have analyzed three different aspects of Jan's work. First, we mention her unstoppable activities towards the development of an international network of women geographers and the creation of the IGU's Gender and Geography Study Group. Second, and in part connected with the first, we explain her prolific influence of the development of gender approaches in geography in Spain, and more particularly in Barcelona, and the long relationship with Maria Dolors Garcia Ramon. Finally, we analyze the impact of her work also in the development of geohumanities approaches in Catalonia.

Monk's work on gender perspectives in geography is well known and has been widely recognized around the world and by different geographic institutions. In this chapter we wanted to point out other significant contributions of Jan Work's prolific career, her tireless efforts to connect scholars across borders and also her pioneering work in the relations between arts, creativity, and landscape. With a work that she considered to be on the margins of the discipline, and with a "deviant" professional career as she defines it, Jan Monk's work has been able to enlighten and inspire geographers of different nationalities, gender, and trajectories.

References

Browne, Kath. 2015. "Contesting Anglo-American Privilege in the Production of Knowledge in Geographies of Sexualities and Genders." *Revista Latino-Americana de Geografia e Genero* 6 (2): 250–270.

Cerarols, Rosa, and Toni Luna. 2017 "Geohumanidades. El papel de la cultura creativa en la intersección entre la geografía y las humanidades." *Treballs de la Societat Catalana de Geografia* 84: 19–34.

Cerarols, Rosa, Joan Nogué, and Toni Luna. 2017. "Tancant Cercles, obrint horitzons. Les contribucions del Col·loqui internacional en Geohumanitats." *Treballs de la Societat Catalana de Geografia* 84: 9–18.

Garcia Ramon, Maria Dolors. 2003. "Globalization and International Geography: The Questions of Languages and Scholarly Traditions." *Progress in Human Geography* 27 (1): 1–5.
Garcia Ramon, Maria Dolors, and Antoni Luna. 2007. "Challenging Hegemonies through Connecting Places, People and Ideas." *Gender, Place and Culture* 14 (1): 35–41.
Garcia Ramon, Maria Dolors, and Jan Monk. 1987. "Geografia Feminista: Una Perspectiva Internacional." *Documents D'Anàlisi Geogràfica* 10: 147–157.
Garcia Ramon, Maria Dolors, and Jan Monk, ed. 1996. *Women of the European Union: The Politics of Work and Daily Life*. London and New York: Routledge.
Garcia Ramon, Maria Dolors, and Jan Monk. 2007a. "Feminist Geographies around the World" (guest edited special issue of Belgeo).
Garcia Ramon, Maria Dolors, and Jan Monk. 2007b. "Gender and Geography: World Views and Practices." *Belgeo* 3: 247–260.
Garcia Ramon, Maria Dolors, K. Simonsen, and D. Vaiou. 2006. "Does Anglophone Hegemony Permeate Gender, Place and Culture." *Gender, Place and Culture* 13 (1): 1–5.
Hancock, Claire. 2002. "Genre et géographie: les apports de géographies de langue anglaise." *Espaces, Populations, Societés*, 3: 53–69.
Huang, Shirlena, Janice Monk, Joos Droogleever Fortuijn, Maria Dolors Garcia Ramon, and Janet Momsen. 2017. "A Continuing Agenda for Gender: The Role of the IGU Commission on Gender and Geography." *Gender, Place and Culture* 24 (7): 919–938.
Kitchin, Rob. 2005. "Disrupting and Destabilizing Anglo-American and English-Language Hegemony in Geography." *Social and Cultural Geography* 6 (1): 1–15.
Luna, Antoni, and Rosa Cerarols. 2015. "Paisaje, cine y género." In Toni Luna and Isabel Valverde, eds. *Paisaje y emoción el resurgir de las geografías emocionales*. Barcelona: Observatori del Paisatge de Catalunya, Universitat Pompeu Fabra.
Monk, Jan. 1984. "Approaches to the Study of Women and Landscape." *Environmental History* 8 (1): 23–33.
Monk, Jan. 1994. "Place Matters: Comparative Perspectives on Feminist Geography." *The Professional Geographer* 46 (3): 277–288 (Translation into English of Monk 1995 in Catalan).
Monk, Jan. 1995. "El Lloc Compta: Perspectives Internacionals Comparades Sobre la Geografia Feminista." *Documents D'Anàlisi Geogràfica* 26: 241–255 (Translation of Monk 1994).
Monk, Jan. 2001a. "Teaching the 'Other'?: Linking Knowledge, Emotions and Action." *Treballs de la Societat Catalana de Geografia* 52: 383–392.
Monk, Jan. 2001b. "Continuidades, cambios y retos de la geografía contemporánea en los Estados Unidos." *Documents d'Anàlisi Geogràfica* 39: 75–95.
Monk, Jan. 2006. "Teixint una teranyina (Weaving a Spider's Web)." *Treballs de la Societat Catalan de Geografia* 61–62: 117–182/183–187.
Monk, Jan. 2007. "Generizando la geografia: personas, lugares e ideas." *Documents d'Anàlisi Geogràfica* 49: 21–42.
Monk, Jan. 2015. "Braided Streams: Spaces and Flows in a Career." *Documents d'Anàlisi Geogràfica* 61(1): 5–20.
Monk, Jan, and Casey D. Allen. 2021. "The Deviant Geographer." *The Geographical Bulletin* 62 (1): 45–47.

Monk, Jan, and Maria Dolors Garcia Ramon. 1997. "Infrequent Flying: International Dialogue in Geography in Higher Education." *Journal of Geography in Higher Education* 21 (2): 141–145.

Monk, Jan, and Maria Dolors Garcia Ramon. 2013. "Bridges and Barriers: Some Cartographies of 'International' Practice in Gender Studies." *Querelles, Jahrbuch für Frauen und Geschleterforschung* 16.

Nogué, Joan. 1990. "Review of *The Desert Is No Lady*." *Documents d'Anàlisi Geogràfica* 16: 140–143.

Norwood, Vera, and Janice Monk. 1987. *The Desert Is No Lady*. Yale: Yale University Press.

3 Crossing Borders, Exotic Women and the Challenge of Teaching Gender in World Regional Geography and Area Studies Courses

Holly M. Hapke

One of the great contributions Janice Monk has made to the discipline of geography is in geographic education and the integration of women, gender and feminist scholarship in the geography curriculum. As early as 1983, Monk argued the need to "include in basic geography courses material that examines how gender shapes response to place, how the visible features of regions reflect values about male and female roles, and how the geographical organization of society affects women and men differently" (Monk 1983, 271). By the early 2000s Monk's interest broadened to consideration of the "Other" in geographic education and internationalizing the study of women and gender. In a 2000 issue of *Journal of Geography in Higher Education* (JGHE) she tackled the issue of the "Other" as it appears in the journal, exploring "ways in which teaching addresses aspects of students' values and attitudes, and the importance of linking knowledge, emotion, experiential learning and action"(2000, 163). A focal point of this interest necessarily centers on gender in non-Western contexts, how we teach about the "Other" and how the ways we teach have bearing on students' responses to "Others". In *Encompassing Gender: Integrating International Studies and Women's Studies*, Monk and her co-authors asked,

> How do we think and teach comparatively and relationally about women's lives and gender arrangements in locations around the world? How do we bring international perspectives to bear on women's lives and gender arrangements in any given location, including the United States?
> (Lay, Monk and Rosenfelt 2001, 2)

These perennial questions resonate with those of us who are inspired by Jan's quest to understand and teach gender in broad geographic contexts in a manner that can cultivate student empathy. They frame the broad context in which the following essay is situated.

Instruction about gender systems, women and women's issues in non-Western contexts presents pedagogical challenges for feminist geographers and area studies scholars teaching students in the West who have had little exposure to cultures and societies outside their own. One challenge we face is the question of how to teach about patriarchy and what, if anything, to teach

DOI: 10.4324/9781032275611-4

about patriarchal violence (see Nagar 2002; Staeheli and Nagar 2002). The critical question for me has been how to teach American students about patriarchy and patriarchal violence in non-Western societies, specifically in South Asia, without victimizing non-Western women in the eyes of students. How do we talk and teach about the realities of life for women living in different types of patriarchal societies in non-Western countries without falling into a Western discourse that constructs non-Western women singularly as victims of masculine control and traditional culture (Mohanty 1988; see also Abu-Lughod 1998; Hapke 2013; Datta 2021)? How do we communicate to students the full experience of women's lives, including the ways women are empowered and exercise agency as well as the ways they are oppressed? This question is part of a larger problem of exoticism when teaching about "other" regions of the world. How can we teach courses (or write textbooks) about non-Western cultures and societies in a way that inculcates nuanced understanding and empathy and at the same time retain critical analysis?

My contemplation of these questions has been prompted by a couple of experiences in which students have blurted out statements in class that reveal simplistic and completely misconstrued understandings of issues such as female infanticide and arranged marriage. Secondly, in reviewing pedagogical materials on Asia, I have felt discomfort over how issues such as dowry murder and infanticide have been presented and discussed as examples, indeed icons, of gender issues in Asia – but in isolation from broader social, economic, political and cultural processes and as phenomena that occur "there" but not "here".

The challenge for feminist geographers as well as world regional geography and area studies education more generally is to teach complexity, historical context and cultural difference in a manner that de-exoticizes other peoples and places. The question is how might this be accomplished? In this chapter I discuss my attempts to do just this. What I report on is an iteration of a 20-year experiment in pedagogical practice in a course I teach on South Asia in which I used the film, *Water*, in combination with supplementary readings and lecture material to teach about gender and patriarchy.

My argument is twofold. First, we need to find ways to de-exoticize non-Western people and societies by drawing parallels to our own society – but neither in a manner in which Western culture and feminism function as the norm against which the "Other" is evaluated (see Mohanty 1988) nor in a manner that falls prey to the paralysis of cultural relativism. Rather, as instructors we need to assess our own understandings and biases to help students develop a critical, interrogative understanding of their own society as they learn about others. This requires that we teach students to reflect on their own society in a more nuanced way than what they might be accustomed to doing. Second, we cannot present particular gender issues in isolation from larger cultural processes. For example, the issue of dowry murder in India should not be presented as a phenomenon by itself but as part of a more general problem – one of social hierarchies and violence. This requires that as instructors we do what we can to deepen our own understanding of social issues and that we understand particular social issues as embedded in broader scale economic, political and cultural processes. We need to make sure that we are reading and assessing material in a nuanced, critical way.

The inspiration and theoretical context I draw on in making this argument derives from Uma Narayan's essay, 'Cross-Cultural Connections, Border Crossings, and "Death" by Culture: Thinking About Dowry-Murders in India and Domestic Violence-Murders in the United States' (Narayan 1997). This essay is a meditation on Western (mis)understanding of dowry murder in India in which Narayan identifies two problems underlying the project of learning and teaching about other cultures that are pertinent to feminist world regional geography and area studies education. First is the effect national contexts have on the construction of feminist issues and the ways these are then (mis)understood when they cross national borders (e.g., through media). Second is the way "culture" is invoked in the absence of contextualized information to explain forms of violence and oppression of Third World women, but not Western women: the "death by culture" phenomenon or culturalist explanations of problems that are in fact rooted in social political economy.

With respect to the first problem, Narayan argues that feminist issues in different countries are constructed in particular ways according to the national political context, and the ways "issues emerge in particular contexts ... affect the information that is readily available for connection-making and hence our abilities to make connections across these contexts" (Narayan 1997, 86). For example, she observes that in the United States, domestic violence activism has focused on providing shelters and other resources to victims to assist them to leave abusive partners; but in India, social, economic and institutional circumstances make this approach unfeasible, so domestic violence activism initially focused on the more extreme outcome of murder because it was an issue around which Indian women's groups could easily organize. However, important contextual knowledge and understanding underlying the construction of particular issues gets lost when news about a given issue crosses the border into another country. So, although roughly equivalent numbers of women (in terms of proportion of population) in the United States and India are killed by domestic partners each year, such murders in the United States are obfuscated by the particular ways we have come to understand the problem of domestic violence, which focus on beating and shelters. These types of failures ultimately impede cross-cultural understanding because they impact the "sense of 'similarities and differences' one develops" (Narayan 1997, 96), constructing as different a phenomenon that may in fact be quite similar viewed from a different angle.

With respect to the second problem – selective culturalism, Narayan argues that the decontextualization that occurs when information about issues such as dowry murder crosses national borders not only facilitates misunderstanding, it encourages problematic cultural explanations of phenomena that seem culturally alien, mysterious or exotic. Dowry murder (or female infanticide in China or clitoridectomy in parts of Africa), though observed only since the late 1970s and only within particular communities, is explained as rooted in Indian culture writ large rather than as a contemporary problem related to particular socio-economic developments in the late 20th century. "Culture" is deployed to explain violence against women in India but not in the United States. Such explanations are problematic because, devoid of the detail of material and historical context, they fail to provide any real explanation. Rather than facilitate cross-cultural understanding, such explanations obfuscate meaning and perpetuate Orientalist constructions of "Us" and "Other" (see Said 1979).

These issues are compounded by another set of problems within the discipline of geography related to the use of the region as a methodological tool in teaching geography courses (Silverman 1977 by Brooker-Gross 1991). One is the problem of scale in which detail is sacrificed to extensive coverage. It is these details that provide necessary contextual information to fully understand a phenomenon. Second is the tendency to search for or focus on "regional markers", that is, cultural features or characteristics that "define" a given region, which results from a persistent onto-epistemological approach that essentializes places and people and relies on forms of classification that construct knowledge in hierarchical and binary ways (see Said 1979; Panelli 2008; Ash 2020; Datta 2020). Most world regional geography textbooks devote some space to descriptions of the *culture* of each region covered in the text. But, as Narayan (1997) observes, the phenomena that cross borders most frequently are those that seem different or alien, and these then become *the* issues that are taught about and studied – becoming "iconic" and "representative" of the region. Decontextualized and reduced to culturalist explanation, such issues lead to cultural *mis*understanding.

A third, related problem is the issue of scholarly inclusion, canonization and citation and the way biases in these practices shape the production of knowledge. Janice Monk addressed this issue in her 2012 article, 'Canons, Classics, and Inclusion in the Histories of Geography' (Monk 2012), in which she noted the preponderance of white, British men in geographic research that is considered classic and thus canonized. Scholars across diverse disciplines have noted citation practices that exclude scholarly work by women, people of color and scholars from the Global South (e.g., Mott and Cockayne 2017; Kim 2020) as others have noted the exclusion of writings by women, people of color and Global South scholars from course syllabi (e.g., Smith et al. 2020). The effect of these exclusions, of course, is to privilege and reproduce colonial and masculinist ways of knowing (Datta 2020). Students are schooled in a narrow range of perspectives that reify hegemonic onto-epistemologies and circumscribe their understanding of the world.

Some scholars have argued that one of the ways we can avoid these pitfalls is to adopt a type of border pedagogy that strives "to unsettle the accepted knowledges promoted through conventional education, and … to break down the borders that divide here from there, self from other" (Ansell 2002, 355). Border pedagogy is rooted in a body of radical education theory that has been critical of traditional, "banking" approaches to education in which "correct" ways of understanding the world are deposited in students' minds, which students then represent in examinations and coursework (Cook 2000). The idea of border pedagogy comes from Giroux's (1991, 1992) contemplations on a critical pedagogy that strives to unsettle accepted knowledges promoted through conventional education and break down the borders that divide here from there, self from other. It "aims to replace such education with an alternative that empowers its recipients to construct oppositional knowledges" (Ansell 2002, 357). Ansell argues that for teaching students in the West about "Other" places; however, a different kind of border pedagogy is required – one that helps students interrogate their own images of those places to explore their origins, the ways they reflect historical and contemporary power relations and their relationships to the material circumstances of "Other" people's lives.

Such a border pedagogy rests on students' capacity to transgress "borders" between themselves and others – to recognize the "powerfully co-implicated histories of different places and peoples" (Cook 2000, 16). Incorporating literary materials such as novels, films and documentaries, accompanied by pedagogical practices that "address texts as social and historical constructions and allow students to analyze texts in terms of their presences and absences and dialogically through a configuration of many voices" (Giroux 1991, 358) is one way of accomplishing this. For example, Ansell (2002) uses films from/about Africa to teach students the geography of a region about which they have little prior knowledge. Brooker-Gross (1991) found novels effective for "motivating students, providing information, fostering cross-cultural comparisons and contrasts and creating empathy with different peoples" (p. 36). Rajgopal (2010) has used documentary films demonstrating how Hollywood images have been used to "Other" specific immigrant populations to raise student consciousness about the way race and gender oppression influence them on a daily basis. She argues that

> through an examination of such films students can learn to develop what hooks calls "an oppositional gaze", a critical gaze, ... which realizes that looking at is not a mere acceptance of the images and stereotypes represented but can also be a process of contestation and confrontation (hooks 1996).
>
> (Rajgopal 2010, 159)

Orientalism and the problem of border crossing

My approach to teaching about South Asia begins in my introduction of the course to students in which I recite the adage, "whatever one can say is true of India, the opposite is also true" and present South Asia as a "landscape of contestations" between competing ideologies and socio-economic and ecological interests. So, from the first day of class I emphasize to students that there is no such thing as *an* India or *a* South Asia, that is, a single, homogenous cultural entity. Rather, within a set of general observations we might make about a region, there lies considerable room for diverging views about what it means to be Indian or Pakistani or Nepali and so on, and that a big part of studying a region of the world is about contemplating the range and interplay of ideas, interests and power relations that exist within any society. This, of course, requires us to understand culture as a dynamic, iterative process, rather than a static state of existence. I then begin the course with a unit that problematizes the study of other peoples and places by introducing students to the concept of Orientalism and post-colonial critiques of West-generated knowledge about the non-Western "Other". We start with an exercise in which students brainstorm their images of India and South Asia and then discuss where these images come from and why they exist. Next, we read and discuss excerpts from Edward Said's (1979) book, *Orientalism*, and then we turn to Narayan's essay.

Narayan's essay provides the starting point for a comparative discussion about violence against women in India and the United States, the manner in which social problems are constructed in political action and differences in how data are categorized and reported across countries, all of which influence how we understand the same social issue in different ways for different places. Knowledge about places is constructed in specific contexts, of which we need to be aware if we are to make critical sense of the information we receive. In contrast to when I taught this course in the late 1990s when dowry murder garnered a fair amount of attention in the Western press, in recent years most students have not been familiar with the issue and find reading about it disturbing, often with counterproductive effects. I have thus found it necessary to preface assignment of the essay with a "warning" about its content and an instruction to focus not on the phenomenon described but on Narayan's arguments about the problems that surround studying "the Other", i.e., loss of context when information crosses borders and culturalist explanations.

In class discussion of the essay, to underscore her reckoning that roughly comparable numbers of women in India and the United States are killed by domestic partners, I share anecdotal observations I have made about assaults reported in our local daily newspaper in which a high proportion of those committed against women are by boyfriends, husbands, or former male partners or spouses. Although I have observed this to be an effective way to create connections between social experience in the United States and India – the information about assault perpetrators makes a visible impression on students, I think the point about comparability of experience could be made even more strongly if students are assigned the task to gather and tabulate assault-perpetrator data from local crime reports and then compare them to data from India.

Structures and ideologies of hierarchy and difference

The next unit of the course focuses on social structures and ideologies of hierarchy and difference. The unit covers caste, class, religion, patriarchy and gender and their intersections. In my presentation of lecture material on patriarchy and the geography of gender in South Asia, I draw on diverse sources of scholarship, especially research conducted by scholars based in South Asia. I emphasize geographic variation and diversity within South Asian patriarchal systems, how different intersecting factors shape women's experiences (e.g., caste, class, region, community, family structure, family ideology, age, life course stage), the women's movement and how women exert agency within their particular social situations. Students are assigned supplemental reading that includes a set of personal narratives of women from different social backgrounds (Mukhopadhyay 2007) and asked to answer a series of questions based on the material. Discussion of the assigned reading reiterates and reinforces lecture points about geographic variation, social location and agency. With this background in hand, we then view the film *Water* by Deepa Mehta (2005), which explores the lives of widows in the city of Varanasi in the 1930s, and simultaneously read and discuss several reviews of the film (e.g., Onesto 2006; Kaul 2007) and two academic articles, one from a film/literary criticism perspective (Chaudhuri 2009), the other by an anthropologist who was studying widows and society's treatment of them in Varanasi the same year Mehta first attempted filming (Courtney 2007). We view the film in segments so that particular content can be immediately debriefed, historical and cultural references can be explained and students may seek clarification on any points of misunderstanding.

Set in British-occupied India in 1938 when child marriage was a common practice, *Water* tells the story of several widows living in an ashram through the eyes of its most recent arrival, eight-year-old Chuyia who is left at the ashram by her parents, head shaven and dressed in white, to live out her life in renunciation and penance. Through its depiction of the widows' extreme poverty and deprivation, some forced into prostitution by the priests who run the ashrams, the film critiques Hindu society's treatment of widows and challenges the religious subjugation of women in India more generally. At the time of its initial filming in Varanasi in 2000, Hindu nationalists destroyed the set and threatened the crew, and Mehta was forced to close production. Ultimately, Mehta resumed filming in Sri Lanka four years later, but when the film was finally released, another wave of violent backlash and protest ensued.

Students read reviews of the film from a variety of voices: Indian and non-Indian, based in India and the West, and those that are "positive" and "negative". The two academic articles help situate the reviews and the controversy surrounding the making of the film in larger social-cultural processes as both offer interesting insights into the film and public response to it. Chaudhuri places the film in the larger context of contemporary world cinema and the cultural heterogeneity and multicultural allegiances of global audiences, noting that "Mehta's status as a migrant woman filmmaker, her export success, and competing visions of a globalized 'India' have been the key factors in the antagonism towards her" (2009, 8). Courtney locates the backlash toward the film and Mehta herself in the necessity to defend-through denial-the self-idealisation Benarasi men hold and assert about themselves, which is embodied in the ideality of the purity and restraint of Hindu widows. Criticism of how widows are treated unearths guilt and the threat of humiliation and dishonour.

(2007, 116–117)

Students are assigned a set of questions to consider as they view the film and relate their reading of the film to the commentaries and reviews. Including a diverse array of reviews and discussion of the controversy surrounding the film reveals to students the ways culture can be contentious, underscoring the idea of India as a landscape of contestation. Interrogation of the Director Mehta's positionality and authority further underscores the way contentions often constitute cultural process.

I am not suggesting that *Water* is necessarily the best film to use for teaching about gender in South Asia – its focus on the treatment of widows and the controversy and objection from conservative Hindus it provoked have the potential to perpetuate negative stereotypes (Mehta's perspective is uncompromising and critics charge her with pandering to Western audiences by peddling negative stereotypes). On the other hand, the controversy surrounding the film, the various reviews and the commentaries provided ample material to illustrate the complexity surrounding gender as well as the challenges facing individuals who want to tackle social issues. By reading opposing viewpoints of the film and about the controversy the film provoked, students gained insight into the way social and cultural issues are contested even within Indian "culture" and society itself.

Conclusions

I found in this pedagogical experiment of using the film *Water* as described above that students really enjoyed the film. Indeed, as I and others have observed in general, students gravitate toward fiction or fiction-like material, in part because its narrative form is very accessible. But film (and fiction) cannot be left to speak for itself, and issues addressed in films such as *Water* require contextualization and full discussion from various perspectives. It is especially important to include voices and scholarship from the non-Western (or Global South) places we are teaching about. Incorporating supplemental material about the controversy and reviews of film that were both positive and negative (which we probed and interrogated) provided entry points for discussion that helped illustrate the complexity of gender and, based on students' exam answers, appears to have been an effective way of talking about "exotic" issues in a nuanced, de-exoticized way.

Afterward

Janice Monk pioneered the inclusion of women and gender and feminist perspectives in geographic research and education and has served as a role model and mentor to scores of women geographers. She not only concerned herself with expanding geographic curricula, she explored ways of teaching that could cultivate students' empathy for the "Other". Further, Jan assiduously encouraged the inclusion of scholars from the Global South in international networks, editorial boards and collaborations. Her work has been truly inspirational and stands as an example of how we might advance a more humane way of understanding the world.

Acknowledgements

I would like to express my heartfelt appreciation to Jan Monk for encouraging this work as well as my research more generally over the past 25 years. The mentorship and support she has provided to me, and no doubt to generations of women and feminist geographers, has been invaluable and critical to our success as scholars. I also thank the anonymous reviewers who provided helpful comments on this chapter.

References

Abu-Lughod, Lila. 1998. "Contentious Theoretical Issues: Third World Feminisms and Identity Politics." *Women's Studies Quarterly* 26: 25–29.
Ansell, Nicola. 2002. "Using Films in Teaching about Africa." *Journal of Geography in Higher Education* 26: 355–368. doi: 10.1080/0309826022000019927.
Ash, James. 2020. "Flat Ontology and Geography." *Dialogues in Human Geography* 10: 345–361. doi: 10.1177/2043820620940052.
Brooker-Gross, Susan R. 1991. "Teaching about Race, Gender, Class and Geography through Fiction." *Journal of Geography in Higher Education* 15: 35–47.
Chaudhuri, Shohini. 2009. "Snake Charmers and Child Brides: Deepa Mehta's Water, 'Exotic' Representation, and the Cross-Cultural Spectatorship of South Asian Migrant Cinema." *South Asian Popular Culture* 7: 7–20.
Cook, Ian. 2000. "'Nothing Can Ever Be the Case of "Us" and "Them" Again': Exploring the Politics of Difference through Border Pedagogy and Student Journal Writing." *Journal of Geography in Higher Education* 24: 13–27.
Courtney, Sheleyah A. 2007. "The Storm of Deepa's *Water*: From Violent Tempest in Varanasi to Glacial Account of Hindu Widowhood." *The Australian Journal of Anthropology* 18: 115–120.
Datta, Anindita. 2020. "Patriarchal Bargains and a Triple Bind: On Writing Geographies of Gender in India." In *Handbook on Gender in Asia*, edited by Shirlena Huang and Kanchana N. Ruwanpura, 13–27. Cheltenham UK and Northampton, MA: Edward Elgar. doi: 10.4337/9781788112918.00008.
Datta, Anindita. 2021. *Gender, Space and Agency in India: Exploring Regional Genderscapes*. Oxon, New York: Routledge.
Giroux, Henry A. 1991. "Democracy and the Discourse of Cultural Difference: Towards a Politics of Border Pedagogy." *British Journal of Sociology Education* 12: 501–519.
Giroux, Henry A. 1992. *Border Crossings: Cultural Workers and the Politics of Education*. New York: Routledge.
Hapke, Holly M. 2013. "Theorizing Patriarchy: Development Paradoxes and the Geography of Gender in South Asia." *Gender, Technology & Development* 17: 1–29.

Kaul, Kaveeta. 2007. "'Water' by Deepa Mehta – A Review." *Sachinita*. Last modified March 13, 2007. https://sachiniti.com/2007/03/13/water-by-deepa-mehta-a-review/

Kim, Annabel L. 2020. "The Politics of Citation." *Diacritics* 48: 4–9. doi: 10.1353/dia.2020.0016.

Lay, Mary M., Janice Monk, and Deborah S. Rosenfelt 2001. *Encompassing Gender: Integrating International Studies and Women's Studies*. New York: The Feminist Press at the City University of New York.

Mohanty, Chandra Talpade. 1988. "Under Western Eyes: Feminist Scholarship and Colonial Discourses." *Feminist Review* 30: 61–88. doi: 10.1080/00221348308980417.

Monk, Janice. 1983. "Integrating Women into the Geography Curriculum." *Journal of Geography* 8: 271–273.

Monk, Janice 2000. "Looking out, Looking in: The 'Other' in the Journal of Geography in Higher Education." *Journal of Geography in Higher Education* 24: 163–177.

Monk, Janice. 2012. "Canons, Classics, and Inclusion in the Histories of Geography." *Dialogues in Human Geography* 2: 328–331. doi: 10.1177/2043820612468550.

Mott, Carrie, and Daniel Cockayne. 2017. "Citation Matters: Mobilizing the Politics of Citation toward a Practice of 'Conscientious Engagement'." *Gender, Place and Culture* 24: 954–973. doi:10.1080/0966369X.2017.1339022.

Mukhopadhyay, Swapna. 2007. *The Enigma of Kerala Women: The Failed Promise of Literacy*. New Delhi: Social Science Press.

Nagar, Richa. 2002. "Footloose Researchers, 'Traveling' Theories, and the Politics of Transnational Feminist Praxis." *Gender, Place and Culture: A Journal of Feminist Geography* 9: 179–186. doi: 10.1080/09663960220139699.

Narayan, Uma. 1997. "Cross-Cultural Connections, Border Crossings, and 'Death' by Culture: Thinking about Dowry – Murders in India and Domestic-Violence Murders in the United States." In *Dislocating Cultures: Identities, Traditions, and Third World Feminisms*, edited by Uma Narayan, 81–117. London and New York: Routledge.

Onesto, Li. 2006. "Reflections on *Water*." *Revolution #049*. Last modified June 4, 2006. http://www.lionesto.net/articles/onesto/water-review.html

Panelli, Ruth. 2008. "Social Geographies: Encounters with Indigenous and More-than-White/Anglo Geographies." *Progress in Human Geography* 32: 801–811.

Rajgopal, Shoba Sharad. 2010. "'The Daughter of Fu Manchu': The Pedagogy of Deconstructing the Representation of Asian Women in Film and Fiction." *Meridians: Feminism, Race, Transnationalism* 10: 141–162.

Said, Edward. 1979. *Orientalism*. New York: Vintage Books.

Silverman, Sherman E. 1977. "The Use of Novels in Teaching Cultural Geography of the United States." *Journal of Geography* 76: 140–146.

Smith, Amy Erica, Heidi Hardt, Philippe Meister, and Hannah June Kim. 2020. "Gender, Race, Age, and National Origin Predict Whether Faculty Assign Female-Authored Readings in Graduate Syllabi." *PS: Political Science and Politics*. doi: 10.1017/S1049096519001239.

Staeheli, Lynn A., and Richa Nagar. 2002. "Feminists Talking Across Worlds." *Gender, Place and Culture: A Journal of Feminist Geography* 9: 167–172. doi: 10.1080/09663960220139671.

4 Centering Fireside Knowledge and Utu Feminisms
On Writing Feminist Margins from the Margins

Mary Njeri Kinyanjui

I was inspired to write about women at the margins through my interactions with Janice Monk. I first met her during the International Geographical Union (IGU) meeting in Durban, South Africa. Professor Agnes Musyoki, my friend and teacher who has extensive interest in gender, development and rural market systems, facilitated my participation in the IGU meeting. Between Agnes and Janice Monk, my costs of participation in the conference were kept to a minimum as my university had no vote head for such conferences. Being one of the founders of the IGU Commission on Gender and Geograph, Jan was determined to visibilize and advance the course on Women in Geography. Monk's significant contributions to social and cultural geography (Monk 1982, 1984, 1993, 2004, 2010, 2011), with a particular focus on the livelihoods and health of women and minority groups in the United States and Mexico, have been documented in more than 100 articles authored by her in various scholarly journals on the development and history of feminist geography. Her diligence, commitment to the gender course and organization skills were quite exemplary and impressive. From her, I learned the importance of pursuing research on women to foreground the contribution of women within development, especially in my country, Kenya.

Accordingly, this chapter addresses the production of fireside knowledge and the practice of utu feminism by women located at the margins of the academy. Fireside knowledge refers to knowledge produced at the margins and rendered irrelevant in epistemological maps within the development academy; while 'utu feminism' is a humanistic approach to feminism addressing the lack of an African feminist epistemology informed by the lived reality of women situated in these contexts. I coin the term 'fireside knowledge' from my Agikuyu tradition. It is a term which refers to knowledge passed on in the woman's fireside in the kitchen and is seen as separate and in contrast to that which is handed down in the men's hut. The phrase '*cia riiko ti cio cia thingira*' (What is spoken at the fireside-woman's kitchen is different from what is spoken in the man's house) conveys the distinction between these two forms of knowledge (Kinyanjui 2019b). Fireside knowledge is thus a feminist form of knowledge generation consisting of identifying women's perspectives of knowing, logic, norms, values, methods and strategies of doing and engaging the world (ibid. 2019b). Fireside knowledge and utu feminism are grassroots

DOI: 10.4324/9781032275611-5

features that are expressed by ordinary women in their everyday lives in Kenya. Using these concepts as analytical frames, I bring to the fore aspects of the everyday lived experiences of ordinary women located at the margins of the academy.

My positionality in this writing is dual. I am not only a researcher and writer of development but also a subject of development at the same time. I had the privilege of studying in major universities in the world. I obtained a PhD in geography from Fitzwilliam College, University of Cambridge, United Kingdom, a Master's degree in Geography from Kenyatta University and a Bachelor's degree in Education from the University of Nairobi. I have been actively involved in the development process by working with peasant farming activities in my rural Ng'ethu village in Gatundu North, Kiambu County, Kenya. I have participated in the process of urbanization by building my own home in Nairobi. I am affected by the development processes and have full experience of the devastating effects of neoliberal policies in Kenya. As a woman of color, my lived experiences in a Third World country which are a mixture of positive and negative encounters influence my development research.

My positioning in development as a subject and a consumer of development defines the epistemology methods I deploy in gathering data and interpreting my findings. This shapes my outlook and methods of understanding development as a feminist scholar. I also borrow from decolonial feminists who use their personal experiences as a canvas for analysis (Asher et al. 2019), and as a woman of color, I am drawn to their idea of how racism shapes their analytical frameworks. This coupled with my experience in the development academy in turn shapes my analytical frameworks, values, norms, beliefs and logic. It allows me to challenge the modernist assumptions of absolute truths, grand narratives and objectivities. The story of my lived experiences is a valid and logical explanation of my worldview of experiences. Therefore, I deploy autobiography and autoethnography as a method of analysis in my work on the women's lived experiences (Moss 2001; Ellis 2004; Ellis et al. 2011).

In my early life, I studied geography with a lot of enthusiasm. Geographical knowledge answered most of the questions I encountered on a daily basis at home, on the farm and on my way to school. It explained my family's livelihood – why my parents grew cash crops. It also explained the landform patterns in my village as well as phenomena such as soil erosion. It helped me understand vegetation types, their distribution and the impact and life cycle of rivers. Later, I became critical about the things I read. I began questioning the half-truths of universal social theories and grand narratives that tended to explain most social and economic phenomenon. Looking at the positioning of Africa in the global development discourse, I began questioning dependency theories between developed and developing countries. My curiosity led me to inquire into trade relations between, Africa and Europe – Between the coffee producers in Africa or the coffee consumers in Europe and North America, who is more dependent on the other? These reflections led to the realization that Africa carried the burden of the world as a supplier of raw materials that are found in abundance on the continent. Despite this, in dominant Western portrayals, Africa and its contributions therein remained inconspicuous and unacknowledged within larger global trade flows.

The United Nations Environment Programme (UNEP) notes that the African continent is home to some 30 per cent of the world's mineral reserves, 8 per cent of the world's natural gas and 12 per cent of the world's oil reserves (UNEP n.d.) The continent has 40 per cent of the world's gold and up to 90 per cent of its chromium and platinum. The largest reserves of cobalt, diamonds, platinum and uranium in the world are in Africa. Africa holds 65 per cent of the world's arable land and 10 per cent of internal renewable fresh water source. Hence, there is a scramble for dominion over this continent that serves as the mine of the world. Alliances of African rulers are connected to the global resource economy and multinational companies from the West and the East in extractive and plundering deals that are most often cloaked in corporate secrecy. According to Davey (2020), Africa loses an estimated $195 billion annually of its natural capital through illicit financial flows, illegal mining, illegal logging, illegal trade in wildlife, unregulated fishing, environmental degradation and loss among others. Thus, without African resources, the industrialization in the developed world would not have taken place. Yet, African economic geography is portrayed negatively in scholarly and literary work. The developed world is filled with narratives on African poverty, disease, corruption, underdevelopment and conflict, instead of the skewed global market system that does not act in the continent's favor.

Monk and I communicated extensively by email between 2004 and 2014. She would recommend me to participate in forums which considered my expertise as crucial and presented opportunities for growth and networking. Consequently, I got to know many geographers who updated me on emerging research issues and current trends in the world of geography. Through these interactions, my focus on researching at the margins, albeit being located in the margins of knowledge hegemonies myself, was sharpened. Each time, I met Monk or received a letter from her, it was either a reminder of the work I had on writing and researching feminist geography at the margins or an encouragement to hang in there because other women feminists were doing the same thing in different parts of the world. Scholars like Mohanty (1984), Sarkar (2004) and Chowdhury (2016) have documented the way in which knowledge from the third word is treated as secondary and marginal to knowledge from the West. Knowledge generation and production are thus hierarchically ordered; and its significance is determined by social location.

In Africa, as in most of the formerly colonized world, knowledge generated from the West is valued significantly more than local African knowledge. Further, the conceptual and theoretical analysis generated by Western scholars is valued more than the homegrown or native insights. As a result of this recognition, many African scholars opt to study in foreign universities rather than those located in their native place. In such situations, our scholars are largely involved only in confirming the absence or presence of proposed

Western theoretical concepts in the African environment. Most often, they conclude that the knowledge attributes under investigation are missing. For example, in questions regarding whether, African businessmen and women can be called entrepreneurs or not. Using frameworks based on Western male entrepreneurs, there is a tendency for scholars to conclude that African women are not entrepreneurs. This surmise then fuels the need for entrepreneurial sensitization programs and to recast entrepreneurial attributes in reference to local cultural context.

I started my long journey of decolonizing existing pedagogy and epistemology, through critiquing the effect of structural adjustments imposed upon Africa by the Bretton Woods institutions, on indigenous institutions. I also question the methods of gathering data and sharing information in the research process. For example, in what language should surveys and interviews related to African economic geography be conducted and can these really be translated? Inconsistencies arise when trying to convert the thought process from a native language to English. How does one translate the terms 'very agreeable,' 'agreeable,' 'not agreeable' and 'not very agreeable' into Gikuyu while interviewing? These situations are bound to arise when the questionnaires are written in English and researchers translate the questions into any other language. A respondent usually answers in a vernacular language and the researcher then translates the answer into English; in such a situation, whose response does the answer become? Further, I question why the area in Kikuyu surrounding the Church of the Torch, built between 1928 and 1933 following an initiative by Dr John Arthur, has not prospered or undergone transformation like his homeland in Scotland. I compare the ability of the priest at Kiriko Catholic Church in Kenya to mobilize peasants to construct a church while a school head teacher in the same region is not able to do the same.

Through my research work I also inferred that people, mostly women, located at the margins, are often overlooked. Their contributions towards livelihood have not been documented in literature within geography and development studies related to African contexts; yet their everyday lived experiences and practices significantly contribute to the livelihood economy within these contexts. Their ways of living are not rehearsed but informed through inter-generational practices they receive from the 'fireside' (Kinyanjui 2019b). These women have their own unique ways of navigating life and making ends meet at the margins of the capitalist economy as traders, peasants and artisans, and these feminist ways of living in the margins are disregarded and glossed over. I endeavor to bridge this gap with an agenda to make their experiences and contributions visible to the world. Through my work I draw attention to the logic, norms, values and institutional arrangements they engage with in their everyday lived experiences as co-contributors to the informal economy and peasant agriculture. Their effort is aimed at bequeathing their offspring a good future. The margins are spaces of self-reliance, mutual engagement and resistance. The margins are vibrant with agency, celebration of life, resilience, production and exchange, solidarity, learning and innovation as opposed to doom and gloom.

My writing is informed by stories of feminists who are situated in the margins of the economy and are also from a marginal position in an African university. Some African universities are situated at the bottom of the global knowledge hegemonies. They do not perform well on global rankings of reputable world class universities. They are relatively younger than universities in Europe and North America which are centuries old. My former university, the University of Nairobi, is about 50 years old. It is underfunded and does not have a profound academic tradition that can be built upon and its alumni are few. It is an uphill task to engage in reasonable academic endeavor when resources are restricted and the academic tradition is shaky. I have navigated this environment to come up with my feminist research on women situated at the margins of the economic ladder (Kinyanjui 2019a, 2019b, 2019c). I describe my work in the margins as 'fireside knowledge.' I have envisioned and positioned my scholarship as situating fireside knowledge in development discourse of the feminist development academy. Fireside knowledge involves giving visibility and recognition to those who operate in the margins of society. Fireside knowledge represents an African feminist form of knowledge that consists of women's perspectives of knowing, norms, values, methods and strategies of doing and engaging the world.

Most knowledge systems that have evolved from the works of Western philosophers and scholars create an impression that knowledge is constructed and organized through a masculine frame. In contrast to this, norms and values shared by African women are regarded as irrational and non-scientific. Perspectives from the cited works suggest that women to approach their household economies as businesses; based on monetary exchanges that reinforce patriarchal global commodity production, labor and financial circuits at the margins. Advocating for the use of fireside knowledge espouses survival, self-reliance, resilience, solidarity, self-determination, justice, sharing and reciprocity. This knowledge is gained from women's lived experiences and participation in the daily household and community activities. Fireside knowledge is therefore experiential, affective, practical and is tested in the lived environment. Fireside knowledge is free and not commercialized in the knowledge market system of textbooks, journals, schools or college. It is passed on from one generation to the next in households and African market places. It is the knowledge that sustains activities of women peasants, artisans and traders in Kenya. While the emphasis on care and caring is fairly recent in geography (Lawson 2007), fireside knowledge is an inherent practice of care among women of Kenya for many centuries.

Feminist economic margins are populated by ordinary subaltern women working in activities that are considered to be at the bottom of the economic ladder. They are ordinary traders, artisans, fisher folk and peasants. They are treated as outlaws from whom nothing can be learned, consequently in need of rescue from subalternity. The women operating at the margins have a kind of feminism that is different from that espoused by elite communities. Their feminism exhibits what I refer to as utu feminism (Kinyanjui 2018). 'Utu' in the vernacular means humanness. It refers to a type of feminism that upholds values that extend the norms and values of being human. It includes the creation of thriving communities by transferring life from one generation to the next. Utu feminism comprises the following tenets, namely, continuity of life to the next generation; peace and harmony; pain management; food security; making work easier and tolerable; socialization and education for the next generation; connecting human beings in family, community and nation; creating thriving and flourishing communities; and creating solidarity and community (Kinyanjui 2018, 265). That is why a woman here will engage in the informal economy despite the conditions therein. She is required to sustain life by engaging in livelihood negotiation. In the absence of state and corporations to create, she has to create jobs for herself and her offspring. Where there are no realtors or municipal authorities to provide housing, she has to provide housing for herself. She relies on an indigenous logic of self-reliance, mutual aid and resistance. This utu feminism thus predates the theories of mutual aid and feminist solidarity that are now being revisited (Kropotkin 1902).

Through these principles of utu feminism, Kenyan women have been able to contribute to the survival of their mode of production and exchange into the 21st century. Hence, I argue that, they serve as a model of an 'economic woman' who synthesizes life and livelihood together. The economic woman is motivated to engage in business by her logic of caring and nurturing. She builds her business to meet the everyday needs of her family and community (Kinyanjui 2021). She works in solidarity with other workers and practices cooperative competition. She engages in solidarity entrepreneurialism (Kinyanjui 2014) to reduce transaction costs in transport, room hire and security.

As my work on feminism is from a marginal position in an African university constrained by resources and overwhelmed by knowledge hegemonies, I have used a variety of cost-saving methodologies that include archival research, case studies, popular music, everyday journaling and linkages with international feminist organizations such as the IGU Commission of Gender and Geography and the Janice Monk lectures at the AAG. My networking with feminist organizations and participation in these settings have challenged me to delve into understanding of feminist lives at the margins in my community. I have an understanding of women who have no experience of the corporation and government boardrooms. The fireside in their houses is their boardroom. That is where they organize care and production. My efforts to situate fireside knowledge in the development feminist academy include Kinyanjui (2012, 2014, 2019b, 2021). In these works, I have made efforts to present knowledge, philosophies, norms and values of subaltern women. I have also made efforts to come up with different vocabulary to describe the activities they are involved in.

In conclusion, I argue that women at the margins are engaged in different forms of alternative economies whose distinct features should be acknowledged in mainstream literature on livelihood, gender and development. This chapter points to these alternative economies and feminisms arguing that such women are not helpless individuals but are imbued with resilience and commitment to hard work. Their feminism is one that connects generations and regions in order to preserve and transfer life to the next generation. Feminists at the margins take risks and stand up in solidarity to defend their position as women and their offspring. They resiliently survive at the margins and care for others so that they can create institutional arrangements that have made the informal economy survive even in the 21st century. To bring them out of the margins requires addressing the structural barriers of colonialism and neoliberalism which relegate some at the margins, making them fodder for exploitation and extraction by others at the top of the ladder.

References

Asher, Molly, Cristina Leston-Bandeira, and Viktoria Spaiser. 2019. "Do Parliamentary Debates of e-Petitions Enhance Public Engagement with Parliament? An Analysis of Twitter Conversations." *Policy & Internet* 11: 149–71.

Chowdhury, Elora Halim. 2016. "Development Paradoxes: Feminist Solidarity, Alternative Imaginaries and New Spaces." *Journal of International Women's Studies* 17 (1): 117–132.

Davey, Charlotte. 2020. *The Economic Growth of Africa Depends on the Successful Management of its Natural Capital*. URL: https://earth.org/africa-natural-capital/

Ellis, Carolyn. 2004. *The Ethnographic I: A Methodological Novel About Autoethnography*. Walnut Creek, CA: Alta Mira Press.

Ellis, Carolyn, Tony E. Adams, and Arthur P. Bochner. 2011. "Autoethnography: An Overview." *Forum: Qualitative Social Research* 12 (1), Art. 10.

Kinyanjui, Mary Njeri. 2012. *Vyama Institutions of Hope: Ordinary People's Market Coordination and Society Organization Alternatives*. Nairobi: Nsemia Publishers.

Kinyanjui, Mary Njeri. 2014. *Women and the Informal Economy in Urban Africa: From the Margins to the Centre*. London: Zed Publishers.

Kinyanjui, Mary Njeri. 2018. "Feminine Utu: Rethinking African Feminism in Kabira Wanjiku and Nkatha Kabira." In *Changing the Mainstream: Celebrating Women's Resilience (1800-2018)* (pp. 255–268). Nairobi: African Women Studies Center.

Kinyanjui, Mary Njeri. 2019a. "A Lone Ranger: My Journey Towards Becoming a Feminist Geographer in Nairobi, Kenya." *Gender, Place & Culture* 26 (7-9): 1159–1169. doi: 10.1080/0966369X.2018.1556616.

Kinyanjui, Mary Njeri. 2019b. "Situating Fireside Knowledge in Development Feminist Academy." *Journal of Language, Technology and Entrepreneurship in Africa* 10 (2): 1–15.

Kinyanjui, Mary Njeri. 2019c. *The Sweet Sobs of Women in Response to Anthropain*. Newcastle Upon Tyne: Cambridge Scholars Press.

Kinyanjui, Mary Neri. 2021. *Wanjiku in Global Development: Everyday Ordinary Women Livelihood Economy in Kenya*. Nairobi: Nsemia Publishers.

Kropotkin, Peter. 1902. *Mutual Aid: A Factor of Evolution*. New York: McClure, Philips & Co.

Lawson, Victoria. 2007. "Presidential Address: Geographies of Care and Responsibility." *Annals of the Association of American Geographers* 97 (1): 1–11. doi: 10.1111/j.1467-8306.2007.00520.x.

Mohanty, Chandra Talpade 1984. Under Western Eyes: Feminist Scholarship and Colonial Discourses. *Boundary* 2 (12): 333–358.

Monk, Janice. 1984. "Approaches to the Study of Women and Landscape." *Environmental Review* 8 (1): 23–33. doi: 10.2307/3984519.

Monk, Janice. 2004. "Women, Gender, and the Histories of American Geography." *Annals of the Association of American Geographers* 94 (1): 1–22. doi: 10.1111/j.1467-8306.2004.09401001.x.

Monk, Janice. 2010. "Time, Place, and the Lifeworlds of Feminist Geographers: The US in the 1970s." *Gender, Place & Culture: A Journal of Feminist Geography* 17 (1): 35–42.

Monk, Janice. 2011. "Politics and Priorities: Placing Gender in Geographic Education." *International Research in Geographical and Environmental Education* 20 (3): 169–174.

Monk, Janice, and Susan Hanson. 1982. "On Not Excluding Half of the Human in Human Geography." *The Professional Geographer* 34 (1): 11–23.

Monk, Janice, and Cindi Katz. 1993. *When in the World Are Women? In Full Circles. Geographies of Women over the Life Course*. London: Routledge.

Moss, Pamela. 2001. *Placing Autobiography in Geography*. Syracuse: Syracuse University Press.

Sarkar, Mahua. 2004. "Looking for Feminism." *Gender & History* 16 (2): 318–333.

UNEP. n.d. Our Work in Africa. URL: https://www.unep.org/regions/africa/our-work-africa

5 The Value of Feminist Scholarship

Renegotiating Spaces for Gender and Geography in Post-Communist Romania

Sorina Voiculescu and Margareta Amy Lelea

Introduction: place-ing gender studies in Romanian geography

Internationalization of gender and geography does not just happen in a vacuum or in uniform trajectories worldwide. Although geographic scholarship emphasizing the need to bring the perspectives of women into geographic research was pioneered in the 1970s in Euro-American literature (Burnett 1973; Hayford 1974; Tivers 1978), it took time for it to disseminate and spread further. Introducing gender and geography into international geography institutions (Huang et al. 2017), and having gender taught as part of geography curricula (Monk and Hanson 1982; Monk 1997) requires the sustained commitment of individuals over the span of their careers (Monk 2015). However, what constitutes research and teaching in gender and geography, and the degree to which feminist scholarship can be integrated, varies in different countries and regions (Blidon and Zaragocin 2019).

Gendered geographies are missing in most countries of CEE like Poland (Narkowicz and Korolczuk 2019) and Russia (Blidon and Zaragocin 2019). A focus on gender is not considered geographical but is rather associated with disciplines such as Sociology or concentrated within interdisciplinary Gender Studies, like in Albania (Danaj et al. 2019). In Romania, gender and geography is not a distinct subfield of geography, but rather research and teaching are promoted as an individual endeavor within existing institutional structures. This is also similar to Hungary (Timár 2019). Exceptions in which feminist and gendered geography have been more accepted into the larger body of Human Geography are the Czech Republic and Slovakia (Pitoňák and Kamila 2019). The tensions surrounding the integration of feminist scholarship in geographic study play out at multiple levels including what is considered a legitimate topic of study and also at the epistemological level regarding critical approaches to knowledge production in Human Geography (Pitoňák and Kamila 2019).

In Romania, as in the rest of countries on the eastern side of the former Iron Curtain, gender and geography could only be introduced after the fall of communism because officially there could be no sexism, classism, or racism in communist "utopias" (Voiculescu and Lelea 2005) as the question of gender equality had been addressed through quotas mandating women's

DOI: 10.4324/9781032275611-6

participation in politics and government-funded childcare centers. However, unspoken horrors during this period included the ban on abortion due to the regime's pro-natalist policies that, for example, entailed surveillance of women's bodies in the workplace to check for pregnancy (Kligman 1998). Indeed, even the way that women could express feminine gender identities with their bodies was suppressed during the communist period (Voiculescu 2004).

Romania's independence came after 45 years of communism and a bloody revolution in 1989, but the context underlying this is even more challenging than most can imagine. The democratization of everyday life and of institutions was finally solidified through accession to the European Union (EU) in 2007. The educational system was no exception to the process of reform. In fact, of all the reform activities, that of education was among the most difficult due to the generations of politicians who followed only their own self-interest for financial gain and closed their eyes to corruption, under-financing, lack of resources and inefficient reforms. In Romania, education remains centralized and dependent on the Ministry of Education which channels power through agencies such as the Romanian Agency for Quality Assurance in Higher Education (ARACIS).[1] Their control – of faculty performance, course content and study program management, among other things – made university autonomy illusory. More than 30 years after the fall of communism, there remain measures that instill conformity and obedience, creating the obsolescence and failure of a system that should at its best, resonate with the requirements of society and serve student needs. Resistance to the inclusion of gender and geography into the curricula in Eastern Europe initially came from these regulatory structures rather than an overt critique of the theoretical foundations of gender and geography (Timár and Fekete 2010). However, this has changed in recent years with the backlash and resistance to such themes coming from the anti-genderism movement.

Following Jan Monk's arguments to include the lens of gender in geography curriculum and her large body of work on this theme (Monk and Hanson 1982; Monk et al. 2004) in this festschrift contribution, we connect to the question she posed, "How does the context affect the incorporation of gender into geographic education?" (Monk 2011). Our answer to this question interweaves personal reflections with broader themes.

In 2004, we worked together to teach gender and geography at West University in Timisoara (WUT). The course was proposed to the WUT faculty by first author (Sorina Voiculescu) and she was assisted by second author (Margareta Lelea). We wrote an article about the establishment of the course (Voiculescu and Lelea 2005) in which we review how gender and geography is taught around the world and the introduction of the course in Romania. In this chapter, we reflect on what has happened since then as Voiculescu continued to teach the course: namely the process of (re)negotiating spaces to teach gender and geography within a Romanian university for 15+ years, and the grit required to overcome structural, ideological and political barriers to integrating feminist scholarship into geographical studies. Our analysis is based on the ways in which systems develop and change, namely geographical curricula in Romania, and the continuous negotiations and tensions between acceptance and rejection for teaching gender and geography. We conclude our chapter with a discussion about the rising current of anti-genderism in Eastern Europe and the urgency to promote and sustain solidarity through international networks for gender and geography.

Institutional structures to foster cross-border personal and professional networks

Flows and exchanges of ideas across spaces and places are vital for the evolution of knowledge and associated disciplinary changes. Structures in the system that facilitate these movements can take the form of international exchange programs and international professional bodies. Both of these have played a pivotal role for raising the awareness of scholars trained behind the Iron Curtain on emerging research topics that were inaccessible in the former totalitarian regimes. In the case of introducing gender and geography in Romania, the U.S. Fulbright exchange program and the International Geographical Union (IGU) Gender and Geography Commission were significant.

Change needed to be learned. In our case an important role was played by the Institute of International Education which organizes the U.S. Fulbright exchange program. The first author of this chapter (Voiculescu) is a Junior Fulbright scholar from Romania to the USA at Rutgers University with Joanna Regulska (1998–1999). Regulska has written extensively on gender and political space in Eastern Europe and introduced her to gender and geography ideas and networks. From networks established during her time at Rutgers, Voiculescu also met Janet Momsen a gender and geography pioneer whose scholarship includes women farmers in the Caribbean and gendered entrepreneurship in Eastern European border regions. Momsen remembered the connection when her then PhD student, second author (Lelea), applied for a Junior Fulbright scholarship. In 2003, Lelea was granted a scholarship for her PhD research for a feminist geography of Romania's Western borderlands. She was based at the Department of Geography, Chemistry and Biology at WUT, Romania with Voiculescu as her mentor. In this way, the layering of personal and professional networks between different generations of feminist geographers was facilitated by the structure of the U.S. Fulbright international exchange program.

Voiculescu was able to use the visibility of Lelea's exchange to strategically leverage more credibility for her proposal to her department to introduce a course on gender and geography. This course was approved to be taught starting in the Fall of 2004. Together, Voiculescu and Lelea developed the course content. Lelea collected materials online, read through feminist geography books that she had brought from the USA as well as her rapidly growing collection of books on gender published in Romania. She donated all of these books for the continuation of the course when she left so that students would have more access to this literature. Later, she brought a copy of

Momsen's *Gender and Development* (2004) which then became the main text book for the course. Students were impressed that what they considered to be an esoteric topic (gender and geography) was seriously covered by a reputable publisher – Routledge. These books were important since during this period, Romanian universities had scarce access to international publications.

Inclusion in the IGU Gender and Geography Commission was another important step towards validating gender research in Romanian geography. The people who made up this Commission created a space that was inclusive, supportive and collaborative. Janice Monk, Janet Momsen, Janet Townsend, Robyn Longhurst, Joos Drooglever Fortuijn and Tovi Fenster encouraged gender and geography to become more visible in Central and Eastern Europe. Both Judit Timár from Hungary and Voiculescu were part of the Commission's steering committee (1996–2004, 2004–2012). Through this international body, researchers from Eastern Europe, and beyond who otherwise would have had no chance to meet, were able to exchange and develop knowledge linked to their specific scientific interests in the region (Timár and Fekete 2010) – specifically gender and geography.

In 2009, this support translated into the first and until now the only conference in the region organized in the frame of IGU Gender and Geography Commission through a joint effort between the Universities of Szeged in Hungary (Timár) and WUT in Romania (Voiculescu). To our knowledge, this was also the first IGU conference between Hungary and Romania on any subfield of Human geography. The theme was "Post-socialism, neo-liberalism – old and new gendered societies and policies". Timár and Fekete (2010) extensively referred to the importance of this conference in the region.

Jan Monk explained that the IGU Gender and Geography Commission strategically had a conference "… in the border region of Hungary and Romania where gender themes had been largely missing in geography" (2018, 5). To increase the impact of the results of the conference, she organized a Special Issue in the journal *International Research in Geographical and Environmental Education* and wrote the Guest Editorial about 'Perspectives on teaching geography and gender in a post socialist, neoliberal-dominated world' (2011). Another important outcome of the conference was the 2010 volume edited by Voiculescu and Robyn Longhurst in *Annals of West University of Timisoara* that

> … included articles on rural spaces, on institutional politics in diverse areas of public and private employment, and of themes such as the challenges of combining household work and careers. The articles show ways that political regimes can have bearing on interest in gender.
> (Monk 2018, 5)

The IGU offered support after Voiculescu failed to be promoted from Lecturer to Assistant Professor. There was overt and covert critique of Voiculescu for promoting some "crazy stuff" she brought from the USA (i.e. gender in geography). Such topics challenged the traditional character of the geographical knowledge sustained in Romanian universities by the hard-liners and possibly their positions of power that they ruthlessly performed. About this situation, Jan Monk wrote: "On the negative side, however, a Romanian geographer engaging with gender research found that publishing on gender was detrimental to her promotion when she was evaluated nationally by more traditional colleagues" (Monk 2018, 6). A further consequence of having gatekeepers who are not supportive of gender and geography is that the resistance to having feminist scholars advance in their careers within geography also has consequences for not having PhD students who could carry the torch forward. Similar attitudes in which feminist geographers are pushing against the grain, is India where Anindita Datta (2019) reports ontological blindness from the Indian university culture which trivializes and tries to silence specific issues of geographies of gender (sexuality, disability, race, class) that reveal how patriarchy, caste and misogyny shape everyday lives.

Through challenges and successes, these examples show the crucial role of *inclusive* academic international networking with personal and professional relationships interweaving institutional structures that together shape the spaces of possibility for gender and geography in Eastern Europe.

Reflections from teaching gender and geography for the past 15+ years

Establishing a gender and geography course in one university in Romania offers insights about the process of creating space for feminist scholarship in geographic curriculum. However, starting the class was no guarantee that it would continue. Different strategies were required for sustaining the space for more than a decade and a half. In this section, we focus on how teaching gender and geography is influenced by Romania pulling closer to the EU, such as through the adoption of the Bologna system and, more recently, the attempted ban on gender studies following the anti-gender current in Eastern Europe which is culturally and politically a rebuttal of EU influence.

The gender and geography course at WUT was introduced as a required course before Romania's EU accession. As Romania adopted the Bologna teaching system to facilitate the movement of students and recognition of their degrees across the EU, undergraduate study programs were shortened from eight to six semesters. A consequence was that it drastically reduced the mandatory curricula bringing into question whether gender and geography would continue. The number of classes that were offered needed to be drastically restricted and individual universities had their hands tied by the ARACIS, the agency that *formulates* and reviews "national reference standards and performance indicators for quality evaluation and assurance in higher education".[2] With this reduction of teaching hours some courses lost their pre-Bologna status from compulsory to optional. This was the case with gender and geography because it was not placed on the ARACIS list of recognized topics in geography. Who were the representatives of geography in the agency? Mostly those who made the rules before were representatives of physical geography and quantitative human geography. They did recognize cultural geography, so integration of gender into cultural geography courses was a potential entry point. This presented one way that secured studies on gender through teaching social and cultural values and practices (Monk 2011). We were also successful at WUT to split social from cultural geography and open the floor for new qualitative geographies and critical approaches integrating gender, race and class.

The gender and geography class went from mandatory to optional and students were asked to choose between this course and glaciology. Although there are many optional courses in neoliberal universities such as in the USA, this was a new development in the Romanian system which had more mandatory sequences of courses and the same group of students spent more time together as a cohort. With these new course restrictions resulting from adaptation to the Bologna criteria, the choice between the two courses was made through a vote by the students. Those who lost considered themselves punished to take a class they didn't want. There were years when the gender course won and others when glaciology was selected. The reason why we describe this situation in detail is to explain how carefully the themes that have been presented needed to be selected in order to attract and sustain student interest.

Feminist theoretical lenses in geographic research and teaching lead to questions about what drives gender differences and ultimately power relations that shape individual experiences in society. A view on the social construction of gender opens up more nuanced questions about how bodies are gendered, sexualized and racialized as well as specifically how pregnant, ill, disabled and even dead bodies are connected to identities formed in specific spaces and places (Bell and Vallentine 1995; Duncan 1996; Butler and Parr 1999; Teather 1999; Brown 2000; Longhurst 2000). Thus, new lines of inquiry can be drawn in the process of building feminist geographies of difference, relation and construction (Dixon and Jones III 2006).

Tracing the patterns made by patriarchy and misogyny across economic, political and social spaces link gender and sexuality to other axes of difference through intersectional approaches. In line with these emerging topics and considering all these missing themes in Romanian literature on gender, Voiculescu and Lelea have published about feminist and genderqueer spaces (Lelea and Voiculescu 2017) and about the definition of family and acceptance of LGBT families (Voiculescu and Groza 2021). However, the presentation of course concepts needed to take a slower approach to introducing this gender fluidity both due to student resistance and also push-back from other faculty in the university who were keen to protect patriarchal spaces in the university. In order to adapt to this situation, Voiculescu decided to introduce masculinity studies as well as starting by presenting women's struggle for the right to vote within a human rights framework. This enabled resistant students an entry point to connect to the feminist scholarship before going deeper into the material.

Connecting with current events from news headlines that involved gender aspects in Romania also made the course content more immediately relevant for students. For example, in 2019, themes surrounding gender-based violence came to the fore when two girls were kidnapped on their way back from high school and were later found killed and cremated in the backyard of the killer. This tragedy gripped the country and so in the gender and geography course, this was immediately linked to broader themes of violence, human trafficking and sex work. Making these changes was not always easy because optional courses have increased time restraints with only seven lectures and seven seminars per semester.

Within the Master's program on Sustainable Territorial Planning and Development, *Gender and safe cities* has been a successful class since its incipient stages in 2003 when it was offered both at WUT and Alexandru Ioan Cuza University of Iassy, funded first by New Europe College. Ever since then, many Master's theses in both universities analyzed different aspects of gender in urban planning. Popular topics were about safety in public spaces of different municipalities in Romania. Since mapping is mandatory for every graduation paper, Geographic Information Systems (GIS) were always used for mapping safety issues.

Although these advances for continuing to teach gender and geography were won within the institutional context of the universities, the broader political context is now very threatening. As Helen Lewis writes, "It's the job of feminism to make us equal. Each wave gets us a little closer. Each advance prompts a backlash. We march forward" (2020, 320–321). Unfortunately, the backlash in Central and Eastern European (CEE) countries has intensified in recent years. Although there were also anti-gender demonstrations in France, Germany and Italy on the issue of school curricula, these did not gain the same traction politically as in CEE countries. The Istanbul Convention (2014) was ratified by 28 states but not by Bulgaria (Squire 2018) and Romania who were part of the signatories of the opposition letter in March 2018. The letter sent to the Secretary General of the Council of Europe specifically referred to what was described as "gender ideology" and demanded a ban on teaching items such as sexual orientation (Schonard et al. 2018). In the same vein, the Bulgarian Academy of Sciences stopped the application process for a project entitled, *"Forum for gender balanced model at school: the Bulgarian case"* (Monova et al. 2018).

In Hungary the government stopped programs in gender studies at state-run universities by claiming that they are based on ideology rather than science, connecting the Hungarian anti-feminist and radical right movements (Bodil and Axlid 2017; Williams 2018; Timár 2019). In 2013, a Russian federal law was enacted against non-traditional relationships in order to "protect" children from "exposure to homosexuality". In Poland as of January 2021, abortion is only allowed in cases of rape, incest or when there is risk of death of the mother.[3] In June, 2021, Hungary passed a new law banning LGBT education for minors. There are concerns that this law could even extend towards punishing those who display pride flags or even could result in banning content on entertainment media that cover LGBT themes (Verseck 2021).

Two major developments in Romania were connected to these anti-gender movements in the region. The first was in 2018, revolving around sexual citizenship and right to marriage of people identifying on the LGBTQI spectrum. A referendum was set up by NGOs that coalesced under the umbrella of Coalition for Family supporting by the governing political alliance (Social Democratic Party-The Alliance of Liberals and Democrats). Even though the referendum failed due to lack of quorum, marriage in Romania continues to be restricted to a man and a woman (Voiculescu and Groza 2021). The second was the most directly threatening to teaching gender and geography at the university level in Romania. It came unexpectedly in 2020 as Amendment seven to the National Education Law (2011) which clearly prohibited "activities in view of the promotion of theories or opinions about gender identity, understood as theory or opinion that gender is a concept different from biological sex and that the two do not always correspond"[4] (L87/2020, p. 1).[5] These restrictions were applicable to "entitites... [such as] institutions of higher learning and... all of the spaces designated for education or professional development"[6] based on the principle of "the violation of moral norms"[7] because they endanger "the health and physical or psychological integrity of children and youth with respect to the teaching staff, auxiliary teaching and non-teaching staff, just like with activities of a political nature or religious proselytism"[8] (Anexa nr. 1 la Raportul suplimentar nr. Nr. XXVIII/44/05.06.2020, p. 1).

This amendment failed due to "unprecedented national and international solidarity to protect academic freedom and freedom of thought in Romania".[9] A coalition of universities including the National University of Political Studies and Public Administration in Bucharest and WUT, among others came together and was backed by supporters, from all over the world including support from the well-known gender scholar Judith Butler. The coalition elaborated an *Amicus curiae* – friend of the court – advocating for the unconstitutionality of the amendment as contravening the principles of academic freedom, freedom of speech and university autonomy in violation of international treaties and EU law. The Romanian Parliament passed this bill in June of 2020[10] and after that an international campaign was launched targeting the Romanian President, Klaus Iohannis to intervene. In December 2020, it was deemed invalid by Romania's constitutional court.[11] And now in 2022, gender and geography can continue to legally be taught in Romania!

Conclusion

What we would like to emphasize using Jan Monk's words (1994, 279) is that "because the field is relatively small, the role of individuals is quite important" and so is the role of places, networks and exchange programs. We affirm the importance of personal networks in the struggle to shape institutional spaces of higher education to make the teaching of gender and geography more accessible. This work at the institutional level within universities is one part of influencing the broader space in society for feminist dialogue and progress. The work is not finished yet!

Notes

1 https://www.aracis.ro/en/about-aracis/.
2 https://www.aracis.ro/en/history/.
3 https://www.euronews.com/2021/05/12/100-days-since-poland-banned-abortion-polish-women-are-fighting-back.
4 Original text: *(Activitatile in vederea raspandirii teoriei sau opiniei identitatii de gen inteleasa ca teoria sau opinia ca genul este un concept different de sexul biologic si ca cele doua nu sunt intotdeuna aceleasi).*
5 All translations between Romanian and English are done by the authors.
6 *unitatile… institutiile de invatamant si … toate spatiile destinate educatiei si formarii profesionale.*
7 *incalcarea normelor de moralitate.*
8 *sanatatea si integritatea fizica sau psihica a copiilor si a tinerilor, respectiv a personalului didactic, didactic auxiliar si nedidactic, precum si activitatile de natura politica si prozelitismul religios.*
9 http://snspa.ro/en/unprecedented-national-and-international-solidarity-to-protect-the-academic-freedom-and-the-freedom-of-thought-in-romania.
10 https://www.reuters.com/article/us-romania-lgbt-rights-idUSKBN28Q2NF and https://eua.eu/news/536:romanian-president-moves-to-reject-ban-on-gender-studies.html.
11 https://www.reuters.com/article/us-romania-lgbt-rights-idUSKBN28Q2NF.

References

Bell, David, and Gill Vallentine, eds. 1995. *Mapping Desire: Geographies of sexuality.* London: Routledge.
Blidon, Marianne, and Sofia Zaragocin. 2019. "Mapping gender and feminist geographies in the global context." *Gender, Place & Culture* 26 (7-9): 915–925. DOI: 10.1080/0966369X.2019.1636000.
Bodil, E. I., and D. Axlid. 2017. *Ambivalent situation for gender studies in Hungary, Swedish Secretariat for Gender Research.* Retrieved from https://www.genus.se/en/newspost/ambivalent-situation-for-gender-studies-in-hungary/
Brown, Michael. 2000. *Closet Space: Geographies of Metaphor from the Body to the Globe.* New York: Routledge.
Burnett, Pat. 1973. "Social change: the status of women and models of city form and development." *Antipode* 2 (5): 57–61.
Butler, Ruth, and Hester Parr, eds. 1999. *Mind and body spaces: Geographies of illness, impairment and disability.* London: Routledge.
Danaj, Ermira, Edvin Lame, and Daniela Kalaja. 2019. "Gender and feminist studies in Albania – a brief state of the art." *Gender, Place & Culture. A Journal of Feminist Geography* 26 (7–9): 926–934.
Datta, Anindita. 2019. "But this is not geography…! Of ontological circumcisions and writing feminist geographies from India." *Gender, Place & Culture. A Journal of Feminist Geography* 26 (7-9): 1103–1110. DOI: 10.1080/0966369X.2019.1609428.
Dixon, Deborah P. and John P. Jones III. 2006. "Feminist geographies of difference, relation, and construction." In *Approaches to Human Geography*, edited by Stuart Aitken Stuart and Gill Valentine, 42–56. London: Sage
Duncan, Nancy, ed. 1996. *BodySpace: Destabilizing Geographies of Gender and Sexuality*, London: Routledge.
Hayford, Alison. 1974. "The geography of women: an historical introduction." *Antipode* 6 (2): 1–18.

Huang, Shirlena, Janice Monk, Joos Droogleever Fortuijn, Maria Dolors Garcia Ramon, and Janet Henshall Momsen. 2017. "A continuing agenda for gender: the role of the IGU Commission on gender and geography." *Gender, Place & Culture: A journal of Feminist Geography* 24 (7): 919–938. DOI: 10.1080/0966369X.2017.1343283.

Kligman, Gail. 1998. *Politica Duplicitatii: Controlul reproducerii in Romania lui Ceasescu*, Trad. Marilena Dumitrescu, Humanitas, Bucuresti.

Lelea, Margaret A., and Sorina Voiculescu. 2017. "The production of emancipatory feminist spaces in a post-socialist context: organization of ladyfest in Romania." *Gender, Place and Culture: A Journal of Feminist Geography* 24 (6): 794–811. DOI: 10.1080/0966369X.2017.1340872.

Lewis, Helen. 2020. *Difficult Women: A history of feminism in 11 Fights*. London: Jonathan Cape

Longhurst, Robyn. 2000. *Bodies: Exploring Fluid Boundaries*. London: Routledge.

Momsen, Janet. 2004. *Gender and Development, Routledge Perspectives on Development*, London and NY: Routledge, p. 272.

Monk, Janice. 1994. "Place matters: comparative international perspectives on feminist geography." *Professional Geographer* 46 (3): 277–288.

Monk, Janice. 1997. *Women in the Curriculum: Geography: Discipline analysis. National Center for Curriculum Transformation Resources on Women*. Baltimore: Uptown Press.

Monk, Janice. 2011. "Politics and priorities: placing gender in geographic education." *International Research in Geographical and Environmental Education* 20 (3): 169–174. DOI: 10.1080/10382046.2011.588491.

Monk, Janice. 2015. "Braided streams: spaces and flows in a career." *Documents d'Analisi Geografica* 61 (1): 5–20.

Monk, Janice 2018. "Finisterra annual lecture: placing gender in geography directions, challenges, and opportunities." *Rev. Finsterra LIII* 108: 3–14.

Monk, Janice, and Susan Hanson. 1982. "On not excluding half of the human in human geography." *The Professional Geographer* 34 (1): 11–23.

Monk, Janice, Joos Droogleever Fortuijn, and Clionadh Raleigh. 2004. "The representation of women in academic geography: contexts, climate and curricula." *Journal of Geography in Higher Education* 28 (1): 83–90. DOI: 10.1080/0309826042000198657.

Monova, Miladina, Ana Luleva, Albena Nakova, and Shaban Darakchi. 2018. Bulgarian Academy of Sciences Researchers on the Campaign against a Project on Gender Equality. *LEFTEAST*. Retrieved from: http://www.criticatac.ro/lefteast/bulgarian-academy-of-sciences-researchers-on-the-campaign-against-a-project-on-gender-equality/

Narkowicz, Kasia, and Elzbieta Korolczuk. 2019. "Searching for feminist geographies: mappings outside the discipline in Poland." *Gender, Place & Culture: A Journal of Feminist Geography* 26 (7-9): 1215–1222.

Pitoňák, Michal, and Klingorová Kamila. 2019. "Development of Czech feminist and queer geographies: identifying barriers, seeking progress." *Gender, Place & Culture: A journal of Feminist Geography* 26 (7-9): 1001–1012.

Schonard, Martina, Borbála Juhász, Enikő Pap, Christiane Ugbor, Sophie Hansal, Gabriella Ilonszki, Siusi Casaccia, Zuzana Maďarová, Laura Albu, and Małgorzata Tarasiewicz. 2018. *Backlash in gender equality and women's and girls' Rights. Women's rights and gender equality, Study Requested by the FEMM Committee*. Online at: http://www.europarl.europa.eu/RegData/etudes/STUD/2018/604955/IPOL_STU(2018)604955_EN.pdf

Squire, Isobel 2018. *Gender ideology and the Istanbul Convention in Bulgaria*. M.Sc. Development and International Relations (specialization Global Gender Studies). Retrieved from https://projekter.aau.dk/projekter/files/281553551/Istanbul_Convention_in_Bulgaria_300518.pdf

Teather, Elisabeth, ed. 1999. *Embodied Geographies: Spaces, bodies and rites of Passage*. London: Routledge.

Timár, Judith. 2019. "Hungarian feminist geography in a curved space?" *Gender, Place and Culture: A Journal of Feminist Geography* 26 (7-9): 1094–1102.

Timár, Judith, and Fekete, Eva. 2010. "Fighting for recognition: Feminist geography in East-Central Europe. Gender", *Place and Culture*, 17: 775–790.

Tivers, Jacqueline. 1978. "How the other half lives: the geographical study of women." *Area* 10 (4): 302–306.

Verseck, Keno. 2021. "Hungary approves law banning LGBTQ+ content for minors." *Deutsche Welle*. https://www.dw.com/en/hungary-approves-law-banning-lgbtq-content-for-minors/a-57909844

Voiculescu, Sorina. 2004. "Rethinking women's bodies; from uniforms to sexual freedom." In *Gendered Cities: Identities, Activities, Networks. A Life Course Approach*, edited by Gisella Cortesi, Flavia Cristaldi and Joos Droogleever Fortuijn, 57–68. Rome: IGU/SGI.

Voiculescu, Sorina, and Octavian Groza. 2021. "Legislating political space for LGBT families: the 2018 referendum on the definition of family in Romania." *Area* 53 (4): 679–690. DOI: 10.1111/area.12729.

Voiculescu, S., and Margareta A. Lelea. 2005. "A review of gender and geography and its development in Romania." *Analele Universitatii de Vest din Timişoara, GEOGRAFIE* 13: 123–144.

Williams, Thomas D. 2018. Hungary discontinues gender studies programs: 'Ideology, not Science'. Retrieved from https://www.breitbart.com/europe/2018/08/10/hungary-discontinues-gender-studies-programs-ideology-not-science/

6 Women in Geography
The Case of the International Geographical Union

Joos Droogleever Fortuijn

Introduction

Half a century ago, former president of the Association of American Geographers AAG (renamed American Association of Geographers) Wilbur Zelinsky exclaimed in his article 'The strange case of the missing female geographer':

> I bear evil tidings. By every objective measure that can be mustered, the lot of the female geographer is, and has been, a discouraging one; and there is little assurance of substantial improvement during the foreseeable future ... the evidence indicates that, just as in any other scientific discipline, any young woman contemplating a professional career in geography can look forward to substantially less in both the short and long run in terms of material and non-material rewards, such as attainment of higher degrees, rank, appointment to prestigious institutions, salary, power, honors, office in national organizations, or the opportunity for creative scholarships, than is the case for a young man of the same age and native ability.
> (Zelinsky 1973, 101)

Zelinsky's article is the first one in a long series of publications about the under-representation of women in geography. All these articles, express the same 'discouraging' message that, although the situation has improved, women are still under-represented in the discipline of geography, especially in secure positions and higher ranks (see Special Issue of *Gender, Place & Culture*, edited by Marianne Blidon and Sofia Zaragocin 2019). This applies to the situation in the United States (Lee 1990; Domosh 2000; Falconer Al-Hindi 2000; Kaplan and Mapes 2016; Caretta et al. 2018) as well as in other parts of the world: the UK (McDowell 1979; Maddrell et al. 2016), Canada (Momsen 1980; MacKenzie 1989; Hall et al. 2002), Spain (Garcia Ramon et al. 1988; Diaz Cortés et al. 2007), The Netherlands (Droogleever Fortuijn 2004), France (Creton 2007; Blidon 2019), Hungary (Timár 2007), the German speaking countries (Buehler and Baechli 2007; Bauriedl et al. 2019), Brazil and Argentina (Veleda da Silva and Lan 2007), Anglophone

DOI: 10.4324/9781032275611-7

Africa (Awumbila 2007), Romania (Voiculescu 2011), Israel (Fenster 2011), Taiwan and Hong Kong (Chiang and Liu 2011; Chiang and Stephenson 2019), New Zealand (Longhurst 2011; WGGRN et al. 2019), Switzerland (Duplan 2019), Ireland (Gilmartin et al. 2019), India (Datta 2019), Iran (Bagheri 2019), Ghana (Wrigley-Asante and Ardayfio-Schandorf 2019) and Kenya (Kinyanjui 2019).

The situation is not the same in all countries (Garcia Ramon and Monk 2007). While in most countries the share of women geographers in the student and staff population has increased, Diaz Cortés et al. (2007) report a decrease in the share of female students and staff in Spain as a result of a transformation in the discipline of geography into a more technical, GIS related discipline. Other authors report differences between universities within a country (Garcia Ramon et al. 1988; Longhurst 2011; Kaplan and Mapes 2016; Villagrán 2019).

In line with Zelinsky, these articles demonstrate the 'evil tiding'. Janice Monk is one of the very few feminist geographers who is not focusing on the 'missing female geographer', but on the 'present female geographer': women geographers who, often under difficult conditions, succeeded in making a career in geography and contributing to the development of geographical knowledge. In 'Women's worlds at the American Geographical Society', Janice Monk (2003) reports the opportunities for women geographers by the AGS at a time that university positions were almost inaccessible for women. Several women geographers, mainly from middle-class families, were employed as librarians and editors and made important contributions to the field of geography. In her article 'Women, gender, and the histories of American geographers', Janice Monk (2004) tells the story of the role of women in geography in the United States in the first half of the 20th century. She demonstrates that the first decades of the 20th century were 'a period in which feminist efforts and the social and economic contexts opened new educational opportunities for women' (Monk 2004, 9), while the 1920s and 1930s was a period in which opportunities for women geographers declined. Janice Monk organized at the IGU Regional Conference in Krakow 2014 a discussion around 'Surviving and Thriving as a Woman Geographer', encouraging women geographers of different generations and contexts to reflect on this issue.

Furthermore, she explained how careers of women academic geographers were very different from the careers of men. Many women started their careers at normal schools and as teachers before a university education, a doctorate in geography and an academic career.

This reminds me of my grandmother who was a biologist. She was born in 1886. After completion of the normal school, she finished grammar school and went to university where she obtained a master degree in biology. In 1926, married with three children (my father, a younger brother and a younger sister), she followed her husband to Beijing, where my grandfather was appointed as full professor at the Peking Union Medical College, founded by the Rockefeller Foundation to educate Chinese students in Western medicine.

My grandmother became a teacher in biology and sciences at the Peking American High School. In 1942, they left China under Japanese occupation and traveled via Mozambique, the United States and United Kingdom to Surinam, where my grandmother became a researcher at the Department of Agriculture of the Surinamese government. In 1946, after the Second World War, my grandparents went to Indonesia during the independence war. My grandfather was invited to establish a new Medical Faculty in Surabaya and my grandmother was appointed as reader in this new faculty. They were everything: teacher, researcher, student advisor, examination board, dean of the faculty, financial director, building master, purchasing manager, head laboratory and lab practical supervisor where they made the microscopic sections with their own hands. I always thought that my grandmothers' career – normal school-university-high school teacher-researcher-university reader – was exceptional. But after reading Janice Monk's work I realized that this was typical for women scientists in the first half of the 20th century.

In the 1970s the situation and prospects for women geographers changed substantially. 'As increasing numbers developed new aspirations for graduate education and professional work, stereotyping, discrimination, the lack of mentoring, and the challenges of a job market whose peak has passed presented difficulties' (Monk 2006, 259). In this period, women geographers were more often from lower middle class or working-class origin than in earlier decades (Zelinsky et al. 1982).

In this chapter, I will focus on the (under) representation and presence of women in the International Geographical Union IGU during the 100 years of its existence. This chapter is an extension of my article on Women in the IGU (Droogleever Fortuijn 2019) in the *Boletín de la Asociación de Geógrafos Españoles* and a chapter in a book to be published at the centennial of IGU in 2022.

The IGU and its membership

An international community of geographers already existed before the foundation of the International Geographical Union (IGU) in 1922 (Kish 1992; Robic 1996). The first International Geographical Congress (IGC) was organized in 1871 in Antwerp, followed by congresses in Paris (2 times), Venice, Bern, London, Berlin, Washington, Geneva and Rome. The congress in Antwerp was dedicated to geographical, cosmological and commercial sciences, a meeting of about 600 geographers, cartographers, explorers, military, traders and academic scientists. As Mechtild Rössler (1996) reports in an essay about women in the IGC, almost no women participated in the early congresses: 'Women in sciences existed in two forms: outside the scientific institutions and universities or as wives, daughters or secretaries accompanying male scientists' (Rössler 1996, 259, see also Monk 2003, 2004), participating in the 'ladies program' of the congress.

One of the first female IGC participants was Elina González Acha de Correa Morales from Argentina, who participated in the IGC in 1891 in

Bern (Rössler 1996, 260). She was a remarkable teacher, scientist, women's rights and indigenous rights activist and painter. Her career was in line with the careers of American women geographers in the first half of the 20th century as reported by Janice Monk (2004). Elina González Acha de Correa Morales (1861–1942) went to normal school and became a teacher and painter. She was one of the first women who completed normal school in Argentina. She started with publishing textbooks and other books on geography, promoted education for women and gave advice to indigenous people who were defending land claims. She took the initiative for the foundation of the Geographical Society of Argentina and was its first president. She participated in many international scientific congresses and was invited by the Argentinean government to represent the country at the IGC in Cairo in 1925 (https://en.wikipedia.org/wiki/Elina_Gonz%C3%A1lez_Acha_de_ Correa_Morales). A few women participated in the IGC in 1904 in Washington (Close 1928, 111). The list of participants of the 1913 IGC in Rome includes hundreds of male geographers and only six women (Rössler 1996, 260).

After the First World War, representatives of the Academies of Sciences of the Allied Powers took the initiative for an International Research Council and the creation of disciplinary international unions, one of them being the IGU (ARH 1922; Robic 1996). The IGU is the community of geographers worldwide. However, at the time of its origin IGU was mainly a European project. The founding countries were six European countries (Belgium, France, Italy, Portugal, Spain and the United Kingdom) and Japan. Membership was growing gradually and became more and more international: IGU had 21 members in 1931, including South Africa, Argentina, Egypt, the United States, Morocco, Cuba and New Zealand (Volle 1996, 43). After the Second World War, IGU membership grew from 31 members in 1949 to 89 members in 1984. IGU has currently 110 members, representing all continents (www.igu-online.org).

An analysis of the position of women in the IGU is complicated, because of the specific membership structure of IGU (Volle 1996; Droogleever Fortuijn 2019). Formal members are not people but national IGU committees that represent the academic geographers in a country. The chairs of the national committees form the General Assembly that decides about the election of president, secretary-general and vice-presidents and the creation and continuation or dissolving of Commissions and Task Forces. IGU has more than 40 thematic Commissions and Task Forces that organize scientific meetings and sessions at the IGC and IGU Regional Conferences and publish scientific articles and books. Commissions have members, with a total of about 14,000 from more than 100 countries. The majority of the Commissions and Task Forces publish the number of members per country, but data on the gender of the commission members are not available. The analysis in this chapter is therefore based on the complete list of presidents, secretaries general and vice-presidents in 1922–2022 and a list of steering committee members of the Commissions and Task Forces between 2004 and 2022.

Women in geography: the IGU Executive Committee 1922–2022

The first decades of its existence, IGU was not exclusively a community of academic geographers, but a mixture of military, civil service and academic geographers, all men. Four of the first five IGU presidents were high-ranked military men: general Roland Prince Bonaparte, general Nicola Vacchelli, general Robert Bourgeois and commander Charles Close. From 1938 onwards, all presidents were academic geographers. In the 100 years of its existence, IGU had 26 presidents, only one of them being a woman: the Irish Anne Buttimer who was president from 2000 to 2004. Anne Buttimer was one of the most famous humanistic geographers in the world, with an exceptional career. After graduation from University College in Cork, she became a nun in Seattle where she completed a PhD in geography. Her cosmopolitan career took her to Belgium, France, Canada, UK and Sweden before she became full professor in Dublin in 1992 (Ferretti and Jones 2018).

The first woman in the IGU Executive Committee (EC) was elected in 1938: the Belgian Marguerite Lefèvre, who became IGU secretary-general jointly with Paul Michotte, professor in geography at the Catholic University of Louvain. Michotte passed away in 1940 and Lefèvre remained IGU secretary-general until the first post-war election in 1949 and became vice-president until 1952. Her career was unlike careers of male academic geographers, but – as Janice Monk (2004) demonstrated – in line with the careers of many American women geographers in the first half of the 20th century. She was educated in normal school and became a teacher before she was appointed as secretary of Paul Michotte who was director of the Institute of Geography. After some years she took courses in geography in Louvain and Liège and finally went to Paris where she completed a PhD in geography at the Sorbonne University. She returned to Louvain and became director of the Institute of Geography after the death of Paul Michotte. Although she was an internationally recognized researcher, a committed teacher and manager of the institute, it was not until 1960 that she was promoted to full professor, the first woman to become full professor at the Catholic University of Louvain (BESTOR 2021).

As I reported in an article on Women geographers and the IGU in *Boletín de la Asociación de Geógrafos Españoles* (Droogleever Fortuijn 2019), no women were represented in the EC between 1949 and 1984 when Maria Gutiérrez de Macgregor from Mexico was elected as vice-president. With the exception of Marguerite Lefèvre and Anne Buttimer, the first women vice-presidents were from outside Europe: the Nigerian Folassade Iyun, elected in 1992, the Brazilian Bertha Becker, elected in 1996, the Mexican Irasema Alcantara-Ayala and the Australian Ruth Fincher, both elected in 2008. From 2012 onwards more European women were elected as vice-presidents: in 2012 Joos Droogleever Fortuijn from the Netherlands, in 2014 Elena dell'Agnese from Italy and in 2016 Nathalie Lemarchand from France. The current EC is the first one with four women vice-presidents: Elena dell'Agnese, Nathalie Lemarchand, Céline Rozenblatt from Switzerland and Holly Barcus from the United States.

The roll of honour of the IGU includes two awards: the Planet and Humanity Medal to honor individuals who have made outstanding contributions to peace, human welfare, or sustainability and the Lauréat d'Honneur to recognize individuals who have achieved particular distinction or who have rendered outstanding service in the work of the IGU or in international geography (https://igu-online.org/about-us/roll-of-honour/). A total of 11 people received the Planet and Humanity medal. Two of them were women: the Norwegian Gro Harlem-Brundtland in 1996 and the Irish Mary Robinson in 2000. Seven of the 48 Lauréat d'Honneur awardees were women: Jacqueline Beaujeu-Garnier (1988), Yola Verhasselt (1996), Janice Monk (2012), Maria Dolors Garcia Ramon (2016), Robyn Longhurst (2018), Joos Droogleever Fortuijn (2020) and Helen Kerfoot (2021). Four of them were founders and chairs of the IGU Commission on Gender and Geography.

Women in geography: the IGU Commissions and Task Forces steering committees, 2004–2022

Between 2004 and 2022 the share of women in the steering committees of the IGU Commissions and Task Forces increased from 25.0 to 34.6 percent (Table 6.1). The representation of women geographers is different in the different parts of the world: the share of women from European and Latin American countries in the current steering committees is higher than from Asia, North America, Africa and Oceania (Table 6.2). East and South European and Latin-American countries in particular are countries with an equal number or majority of women steering committee members (Table 6.3). Human geography Commissions have in general higher numbers of women steering committee members (Figure 6.1) and more often a female chair or co-chair (Table 6.4) than physical geography Commissions.

Four Commissions and Task Forces have no women steering committee members and five have only one woman in their steering committee. Thirteen Commissions and Task Forces have 50 percent or more women steering committee members. Only one Commission, the Commission on Gender and

Table 6.1 Percentage of women and men in the IGU Commissions and Task Forces steering committees, 2004–2022*

	Women	Men	All
2004–2008	98 (25.0%)	294 (75.0%)	392 (100%)
2008–2012	102 (25.9%)	292 (74.1%)	394 (100%)
2012–2016	108 (27.1%)	290 (72.9%)	398 (100%)
2016–2020	141 (31.4%)	308 (68.6%)	449 (100%)
2020–2022	163 (34.6%)	308 (65.4%)	471 (100%)

* Data are missing of three Commissions and Task Forces in 2004–2008, two in 2008–2012 and three in 2012–2016. Gender unknown of one steering committee member in 2008–2012.
Sources: Lists of steering committee members provided by the President of the IGU; Annual Reports and websites of the IGU Commissions and Task Forces.

54 *Joos Droogleever Fortuijn*

Table 6.2 Percentage of women and men in the IGU Commissions and Task Forces steering committees by continent, 2020–2022

	Women	Men	All
Europe	83 (42.3%)	113 (57.7%)	196 (100%)
Asia	28 (25.2%)	83 (74.8%)	111 (100%)
Latin America	17 (38.6%)	27 (61.4%)	44 (100%)
North America	15 (31.3%)	33 (68.8%)	48 (100%)
Africa	13 (29.5%)	31 (70.5%)	44 (100%)
Oceania	7 (25.0%)	21 (75.0%)	28 (100%)
All	163 (34.6%)	308 (65.4%)	471 (100%)

Source: List of steering committee members 2020–2022 provided by the President of the IGU.

Table 6.3 Countries with an equal number or majority of women steering committee members of the IGU Commissions and Task Forces, 2020–2022

Argentina	Latvia
Bolivia	Malaysia
Bulgaria	Namibia
Cabo Verde	Netherlands
Czechia	Nigeria
Ecuador	Peru
Estonia	Portugal
France	Romania
Ghana	Serbia
Greece	South Korea
Hungary	Spain
Ireland	Taiwan
Kenya	UK
Kyrgyzstan	Ukraine

Source: List of steering committee members 2020–2022 provided by the President of the IGU.

Geography, has no male steering committee members. This – a 100 percent female steering committee – was an issue in 1988 when the General Assembly of the IGU approved a new Study Group (later Commission) on Gender and Geography. As reported by Janice Monk (2008; see also Huang et al. 2017), the Study Group resulted from an informal meeting of feminist geographers in some backroom during the IGC in Paris in 1984. Janet Momsen, Janice Monk and Maria Dolors Garcia Ramon took the initiative for the Study Group on Gender and Geography which was reluctantly approved by the General Assembly under the condition that the steering committee should have at least one male member. The Japanese Isama Ota has been the only male steering committee member of the Commission: from 1996 onwards only women were chair or steering committee members. Now and then the issue is discussed in the EC in the same way in which other Commissions are urged to expand female membership.

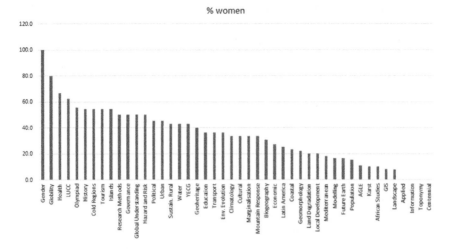

Figure 6.1 Percentage of women in the IGU Commissions and Task Forces steering committees, 2020–2022.

Source: List of steering committee members 2020–2022 provided by the President of the IGU.

Table 6.4 IGU Commissions and Task Forces with a woman as (co-)chair, 2020–2022

Climatology
Cold and High Altitude Regions
Gender and Geography
Geography of Tourism, Leisure and Global Change
Geoheritage
Geomorphology and Society
Global Change and Human Mobility
Health and Environment
History of Geography
Landscape Analysis and Landscape Planning
Land Use and Land Cover Change
Marginalization, Globalization and Regional and Local Responses
Mediterranean Basin
Political Geography
Research Method in Geography
Sustainability of Rural Systems
Urban Commission
Olympiad Task Force
Young and Early Career Geographers Task Force

Source: List of steering committee members 2020–2022 provided by the President of the IGU.

In a short time, the Commission on Gender and Geography was acknowledged to be one of the most active and productive IGU Commissions. In 2004, when I finished my term as Commission chair, IGU President Anne Buttimer complimented the Commission for its academic performance in a meeting of Commission chairs during the Congress in Glasgow. And in 2014, the Commission on Gender and Geography was the first one to be awarded the IGU Commissions' Excellence Award.

In the years of my vice-presidency (2012–2020), I was looking for activities that directly or indirectly stimulated the participation and visibility of women geographers. I chaired the subcommittee for the IGU Commissions Excellence Award. Part of the award was an invitation to give a keynote lecture at the IGC or IGU Regional Conference. The awards between 2014 and 2020 resulted in an increase in women keynote speakers, as six of the seven awarded Commissions were chaired by women.

I was responsible for the IGU travel grant program in which around 25 geographers, mainly young geographers from low-income countries, received a grant that enabled them to participate in the IGC or IGU Regional Conference. Although no more than one third of the applicants were women, half of the grants were awarded to female applicants. I remember an email from a Romanian man who was furious because he was denied a grant, while a female colleague was one of the awardees.

Conclusions

Geography was and still is a male-dominated discipline worldwide and this male domination is reflected in the global community of geographers: the International Geographical Union. The representation of women geographers, however, has improved substantially in the 100 years of its existence, particularly in the past decades.

In the period before the Second World War, women geographers were almost absent in IGU, as Mechtild Rössler (1996) demonstrated. No women were represented in the IGU Executive Committee until 1938; many women were present during International Geographical Congresses, but mainly as wives, daughters or secretaries, participating in the 'ladies programs' of the congresses. Only a handful of women presented papers in the scientific programs.

The first woman in the EC was the Belgian Marguerite Lefèvre, who was secretary-general between 1938 and 1949. Her career – as teacher, secretary, director and finally full professor – was very different from the academic careers of her male colleagues, but very similar to the careers of women geographers in the United States at that time, as Janice Monk (2003, 2004) has reported.

Nowadays, many women from all parts of the world are active in the IGU and one-third of the current EC members, IGU Commission and Task Force (co-)chairs and steering committees members are women. This is similar to the share of women members in the American Association of Geographers (Droogleever Fortuijn 2019) and much higher than in many other parts of the world.

Women geographers in the IGU are more often from Europe and Latin America than from the other world regions. It is remarkable that the women

EC members in the period between 1984 and 2008 were mainly from outside Europe, while in recent years the majority of the women EC members are European.

The analysis in this chapter focuses mainly on numbers, absence and presence of women geographers. Janice Monk has convincingly demonstrated how important it is to give face and voice to the increasing number of women geographers in all parts of the world. The increasing number of women geographers is at least partly the result of her never-ending effort to support women geographers by collaborating, mentoring, writing thousands of letters of endorsement and other ways to including women geographers from under-represented regions in international networks such as the IGU.

Acknowledgement

I would like to thank Bruno Schelhaas for his support in compiling the list of members of the IGU Executive Committees 1922–2022.

References

ARH. 1922. "The International Geographical Union." *The Geographical Journal* 60 (4): 291–294.
Awumbila, Mariama. 2007. "Challenging contexts: gender studies and geography in Anglophone African countries." *Belgeo* 3: 261–274.
Bagheri, Nazgol. 2019. "Avoiding the 'F' word: feminist geography in Iran." *Gender, Place and Culture* 26 (7-9): 1128–1136.
Bauriedl, Sybille, Nadine Marquardt, Carolin Schurr, and Anne Vogelpohl. 2019. "Celebrating 30 years of feminist geographies in the German-speaking countries Germany, Switzerland and Austria." *Gender, Place and Culture* 26 (7-9): 1049–1063.
BESTOR. *Lefèvre, Marguerite (1894-1967)*. https://www.bestor.be/wiki_nl/index.php/Lef%C3%A8vre,_Marguerite_(1894-1967). Accessed on 6 March 2021.
Blidon, Marianne. 2019. "Still a long way to go: gender and feminist geographies in France." *Gender, Place and Culture* 26 (7-9): 1039–1048.
Blidon, Marianne, and Sofia Zaragocin. 2019. "Mapping gender and feminist geographies in the global context." *Gender, Place and Culture* 26 (7-9): 915–925.
Buehler, Elisabeth, and Karin Baechli. 2007. "From 'Migration der Frau aus Berggebiete' to 'gender and sustainable development': dynamics in the field of gender and geography in Switzerland and in the German-speaking countries." *Belgeo* 3: 275–300.
Caretta, Martina A., Danielle Drozdweski, Johanna C. Jokinen, and Emily Falconer. 2018. "'Who can play this game'? The lived experiences of doctoral candidates and early career women in the neoliberal university." *Journal of Geography in Higher Education* 42 (2): 261–275.
Chiang, Lan-Hung Nora, and Ying Chun Liu. 2011. "Feminist geography in Taiwan and Hong Kong." *Gender, Place and Culture* 18 (4): 557–569.
Chiang, Lan-Hung Nora, and Rebecca A. Stephenson. 2019. "The challenges of feminist geography in Taiwan." *Gender, Place and Culture* 26 (7-9): 1280–1287.
Close, Charles. 1928. "Address at the Anniversary Meeting of the Society held on 18 June 1928." *The Geographical Journal* 72 (2): 97–116.

Creton, Dominique. 2007. "Gender issues in French geography." *Belgeo* 3: 313–322.

Datta, Anindita. 2019. "'But this is not geography...' of ontological circumcisions and writing feminist geographies from India." *Gender, Place and Culture* 26 (7-9): 1103–1110.

Diaz Cortés, Fabia, Maria Dolors Garcia Ramon, and Anna Ortiz. 2007. "Engendering Spanish geography." *Belgeo* 3: 323–334.

Domosh, Mona. 2000. "Unintentional transgressions and other reflections on the job search process." *The Professional Geographer* 52 (4): 703–708.

Droogleever Fortuijn, Joos. 2004. "Gender representation and participation in Dutch human geography departments." *Journal of Geography in Higher Education* 28 (1): 133–141.

Droogleever Fortuijn, Joos. 2019. "Women geographers and the International Geographical Union." *Boletín de la Asociación de Geógrafos Españoles* 81 (2819): 1–16.

Duplan, Karine. 2019. "A feminist geographer in a strange land: building bridges through informal mentoring in Switzerland." *Gender, Place and Culture* 26 (7-9): 1271–1279.

Falconer Al-Hindi, Karen. 2000. "Women in geography in the 21st century. Introductory remarks: structure, agency and women geographers in academia at the end of the long twentieth century." *The Professional Geographer* 52 (4): 697–702.

Fenster, Tovi. 2011. "Teaching gender in Israel: experiences at Tel Aviv university." *International Research in Geographical and Environmental Education* 20 (3): 195–197.

Ferretti, Federico, and Alun Jones. 2018. "Anne Buttimer. 1938-2017. Geography and biography." *Geographers Biobibliographical Studies* 37 (37): 13–40.

Garcia Ramon, Maria Dolors, and Janice Monk. 2007. "Gender and geography: world views and practices." *Belgeo* 3: 247–260.

Garcia Ramon, Maria Dolors, Margarida Castañer, and Núria Centelles. 1988. "Women and geography in Spanish universities." *The Professional Geographer* 40 (3): 307–315.

Gilmartin, Mary, Claire McGing, and Kath Browne. 2019. "Feminist and gender geographies in Ireland." *Gender, Place and Culture* 26 (7-9): 1111–1118.

Hall, Jennifer, Brenda L. Murphy, and Pamela Moss. 2002. "Focus: equity for women in geography." *Canadian Geographer* 46 (3): 235–240.

Huang, Shirlena, Janice Monk, Joos Droogleever Fortuijn, Maria Dolors Garcia Ramon, and Janet Henshall Momsen. 2017. "A continuing agenda for gender: the role of the IGU Commission on gender and geography." *Gender, Place and Culture* 24 (7): 919–938.

Kaplan, David H., and Jennifer E. Mapes. 2016. "Where are the women? Accounting for discrepancies in female doctorates in U.S. geography." *The Professional Geographer* 68 (3): 427–435.

Kinyanjui, Mary. 2019. "A lone ranger: my journey towards becoming a feminist geographer in Nairobi, Kenya." *Gender, Place and Culture* 26 (7-9): 1159–1169.

Kish, George. 1992. "International Geographical Union: a brief history." *GeoJournal* 26 (2): 224–228.

Lee, D. R. 1990. "The status of women in geography: things change, things remain the same." *The Professional Geographer* 42 (2): 202–11.

Longhurst, Robyn. 2011. "Teaching gender and geography in Aotearoa New Zealand." *International Research in Geographical and Environmental Education* 20 (3): 179–183.

MacKenzie, Susan. 1989. "The status of women in Canadian geography." *Operational Geographer* 7 (3): 2–8.

Maddrell, Avril, Kendra Strauss, Nicola J. Thomas, and Stephanie Wyse. 2016. "Mind the gap: gender disparities still to be addressed in UK higher education geography." *Area* 48 (1): 48–56.
McDowell, Linda. 1979. "Women in British geography." *Area* 11(2): 151–154.
Momsen, Janet. 1980. "Women in Canadian geography." *The Professional Geographer* 32 (3): 365–369.
Monk, Janice. 2003. "Women's worlds at the American Geographical Society." *Geographical Review* 93 (2): 237–257.
Monk, Janice. 2004. "Women, gender and the histories of American geography." *Annals of the Association of American Geographers* 94 (1): 1–22.
Monk, Janice. 2006. "Changing expectations and institutions: American women geographers in the 1970s." *Geographical Review* 96 (2): 259–277.
Monk, Janice. 2008. *Connecting people, places and ideas: reflections on the history of the International Geographical Union Commission on Gender and Geography.* https://igugender.wixsite.com/igugender/publications.
Robic, Marie-Claire. 1996. "La naissance de l'Union Géographique Internationale." In *Géographes face au monde. L'Union Géographique Internationale et les Congrès Internationaux de Géographie*, edited by Marie-Claire Robic, Anne-Marie Briend, and Mechtild Rössler, 23–39. Paris: Histoire de Sciences Humaines.
Rössler, Mechtild. 1996. "From the ladies' program to the feminist session." In *Géographes face au monde. L'Union Géographique Internationale et les Congrès Internationaux de Géographie*, edited by Marie-Claire Robic, Anne-Marie Briend, and Mechtild Rössler, 259–267. Paris: Histoire de Sciences Humaines.
Timár, Judit. 2007. "Gender studies in the gender-blind post-socialist geographies of East-Central Europe." *Belgeo* 3: 349–370.
Veleda da Silva, Susana, and Diana Lan. 2007. "Geography and gender studies: the situation in Brazil and Argentina." *Belgeo* 3: 371–382.
Villagrán, Paula Soto. 2019. "Geographies of gender and feminism in Mexico: a field in construction." *Gender, Place and Culture* 26 (7-9): 1170–1181.
Voiculescu, Sorina. 2011. "Teaching gender and geography in Romanian universities." *International Research in Geographical and Environmental Education* 20 (3)1: 189–193.
Volle, Dominique. 1996. "La carte des états: vers la couverture du monde?" In *Géographes face au monde. L'Union Géographique Internationale et les Congrès Internationaux de Géographie*, edited by Marie-Claire Robic, Anne-Marie Briend, and Mechtild Rössler, 41–62. Paris: Histoire de Sciences Humaines.
WGGRN (Women and Gender Geographies Research Network of Aotearoa New Zealand), Gail Adams-Hutcheson, Ann E. Bartos, Kelly Dombroski, Erena Le Heron, and Yvonne Underhill-Sem. 2019. "Feminist geographies in Aotearoa New Zealand: cultural, social and political moments." *Gender, Place and Culture* 26 (7-9): 1182–1197.
Wrigley-Asante, Charlotte, and Elizabeth Ardayfio-Schandorf. 2019. "The emergence and institutionalization of feminist geography in Ghana." *Gender, Place and Culture* 26 (7-9): 1064–1072.
Zelinsky, Wilbur. 1973. "The strange case of the missing female geographer." *The Professional Geographer* 25 (2): 101–105.
Zelinsky, Wilbur, Janice Monk, and Susan Hanson. 1982. "Women and geography: a review and prospectus." *Progress in Human Geography* 6 (3): 317–366.

Part II
Career Trajectories of Women Geographers
Strategies to Survive and Thrive

7 "Making Zonia Known"
Discussing Baber's "Peace Symbols" (1948)

Marcella Schmidt di Friedberg

A three-way encounter

In 2007, while teaching a geography course to students of Primary Education, I was researching a book on critical geography teaching in the 19th and 20th centuries and had already identified a number of critical voices who had dissented from a myopic and arid geography – from Reclus to Kropotkin and Geddes to Tolstoy – but I had only managed to include one woman: Emma Willard (dell'Agnese 2010, 47–62). Yet in practice, geography in schools has mainly been taught by women: an invisible majority including "many others who played little-noticed, but pivotal, roles in the development of geography as a professional discipline" (Pittser 1999, 302). Nevertheless, it remains difficult to find documentary evidence of these women's efforts. So, I turned to Janice Monk. Since I first met Janice, I have learned a lot from her, beginning with her kindness and courtesy. Janice always responds and finds time to share all kinds of resource materials. On this occasion too, her reply came swiftly, with a name – Zonia Baber – and a set of materials about this woman geographer.

That was the beginning of our three-way encounter with Zonia Baber, who, as Janice Monk notes: "is a very interesting character and deserves more visibility than she has enjoyed to date" (Monk, private communication, in Schmidt di Friedberg 2010, 11). Together, we presented *Zonia Baber: Following her Moral Compass* to the Commission on Gender and Geography *(Hamburg, August 2012)*. We also jointly compiled the entry *Mary Arizona (Zonia) Baber (1862–1956)* (Monk and Schmidt di Friedberg 2011) in the *Geographers Bibliographical Studies*. In 2013, I presented *Women, Geography, and Education: André Léo, Ellen Churchill Semple, Zonia Baber* at the IGU Regional Conference in Kyoto. In the meantime, I had managed to get hold of a copy of the book *Peace Symbols* (Baber 1948), on which this chapter is based. In sum, the commitment I share with Janice Monk is that "We have to keep making Zonia known" (private communication May 20, 2017).

It is 40 years since Janice Monk with Susan Hanson (1982) first proposed "not excluding half of the human in human geography", a discipline that "through omission of any consideration of women, most geographic research has in effect been passively, often inadvertently, sexist" (Monk and Hanson

DOI: 10.4324/9781032275611-9

1982, 11). Since then many things have changed. Monk, with her extensive and continuous work, has been a pioneer in the production of a history of feminist geography and the development of a feminist perspective in the discipline (Silva 2010). Through her work and that of others, the landscape of the history of geography has begun to repopulate with female scholars, educators, and travellers and has opened up to a feminist gaze on the world. Mary Arizona (Zonia) Baber, in turn, entered the *Geographers Biobibliographical Studies*, and it can no longer be said today that she is "almost unknown by contemporary American geographers and not visible in histories of the discipline that address the late nineteenth and early twentieth centuries" (Monk and Schmidt of Friedberg 2011, 68).

An outstanding teacher

The American geographer and geologist, Mary Arizona (Zonia) Baber (1862–1956) devoted her life to reforming geography education and working as an activist in feminist, anti-racist, anti-imperialist, and environmental organizations. "Zonia Baber made her mark as an outstanding teacher" (Pittser 1999, 305). Following Parker and Dewey, she promoted a progressive pedagogy, centred on the needs of the child and responsive to social issues. Her pedagogical endeavours began with the attempt to get teachers to engage more deeply with geography education. On 12 January 1889, she first floated the concept of a geographical society for Chicago, which she eventually set up herself in 1898:

> I suggest the founding of a Geographic Society in Chicago, similar to the National Geographic Society in Washington, which will bring together not just professional geographers, but all those who travel and study for pleasure. With lectures and field excursions, the public may be brought to understand the importance of geography.
>
> (Baber in Hunter 2013)

In 1899, Baber went on an 11-month post-graduate tour of the world, sponsored by the Chicago Institute, gathering information for future teaching, and traveling by all possible means of transport, "from rail, boat, camel, elephant, donkey, horse, jinrikisha, palanquin and ox-cart" ("Zonia Baber Circles Globe", *Chicago Tribune*, 1900, 8).

In addition to calling for a more progressive pedagogy (Baber 1901, 1905, 1907), Baber addressed in detail the methodological and practical aspects of teaching. She organized field trips for her students and theorized their importance as a key component of the school curriculum, recognizing that "[t]he measure of progress in teaching geography is nowhere more strongly marked than in the use of fieldwork" (Baber 1904, 261). She even patented a school desk "for such schools where geography and kindred sciences are taught objectively by advanced methods" (Letters Patent No. 563,688, dated July 7 1896). Baber came to see geography as the instrument *par excellence* for educating people to respect human rights:

Race prejudice must be eliminated. [...] In perplexity we turn to the school for help. Here we find the geography teacher more than any other has the opportunity to erase racial prejudice. This is because geography is the only subject that brings one into contact with all the living peoples of the world.

(Baber 1916, 295)

Zonia Baber, activist and feminist

The few notes held in the archives of the Society of Woman Geographers (SWG) provide us with some insight into Baber's busy and eventful life. "Baber challenged the norms throughout her life" (Monk 2008), declared Janice Monk in an opening address to the SWG. Indeed Zonia was an active member of various political organizations whose causes included international peace, disarmament, the rights of minorities and women, and the fight against imperialism. "She was a prominent figure [...] – a valiant champion of peace – that balanced state of consciousness in mankind where race prejudices and national hatred are sublimated in love and humanity. Such, at least, is the ideal" (Fitzgerald 1929, 89).

Baber was also an active environmentalist who assisted in the founding of Indiana Dunes National Park (Baber 1913). In the project proposal for the Park, she wrote: "We must begin with the children, and teach them to read nature just as we teach them to read books; and it is much more difficult to read nature than it is to read books" (Baber in Mather 1917, 49). Janice Monk inquires: "Did other early 20th century geographers share Zonia Baber's commitments to peace, antiracism, and conservation, evident in her writing on goals in the teaching of geography (Baber 1916) and in her public lectures on such topics as "Disarmament', 'Philippine Islands: Desire for Independence', 'Work of the Women's International League for Peace and', 'Freedom', 'Conditions for a Durable Peace', 'The Price We Pay for the Color Line', 'The Superior Race', 'Myth', and 'The Protection of Wild Flowers in South Africa'? An active organizer, founder of the Chicago Geographical Society for which she sought women speakers, Baber also chaired the Race Relations Committee of the Chicago Woman's Club, was a member of the Executive Committee, Chicago Branch of the National Association for the Advancement of Colored People, and worked with the *Asociación Puertorriqueña de Mujeres Sufragistas* and the *Liga Social Sufragista*, Puerto Rico (Baber File Society of Woman Geographers Collection Library of Congress)" (Baber File, Society of Woman Geographers Collection, Library of Congress) (Monk 2004, 17).

Zonia Baber was committed to the women's rights movement and played an active part in feminist associations, both inside and outside the United States. Her involvement came at the height of the suffragist movement's success. In a letter to Harriet Chalmers Adams, Baber explored the possibility of having a panel of women geographers at the 1927 Chicago Geographic Society conference. She wrote "Male speakers are invariably chosen in the first place out of ignorance because nobody knows that women geographers exist, and in the second place based on prejudice" (Zonia Baber to Harriet Chalmers Adams, President, Society of Woman Geographers, Feb. 17, 1927). She next spoke critically about male aggression, which she defined as

> the savage instinct of man for the war [...] Men are not particular upon which side they fight as long as they are fighting. The only superiority men have is in brute strength, and they must satisfy their desire to fight [...] If there are no wars they invent sports that are as near like war as possible.
> ("Knife in Hand Pacifist Chides Man as 'Savage'", *Chicago Tribune* 1917, 14)

From 1927 until the end of her life, Zonia was an active member of the SWG, an association aimed at connecting women from all over the world engaged in work across a range of disciplinary fields, but all "explorers at heart". During World War II, Baber's peace activism intensified and she gave frequent lectures on peace and the eradication of prejudice, apart from working for numerous human rights associations. In 1929–1930, she went to South Africa to monitor the work of the British Association for the Advancement of Science (BAAS), and from there to East Africa and the Far East. Her travel memoirs were published in 1930 under the title *Impressions of Africa*, in a series of articles carried by the leading African-American newspaper, the Chicago Defender.

Throughout her life, she would be an active and committed member of the 'Women's International League for Peace and Freedom (WILPF) (Vellacott 1993; Plastas 2011), the oldest international 'women's peace organization, founded in 1915, to bring together "women of different political views and philosophical and religious backgrounds determined to study and make known the causes of war and work for a permanent peace". As chair of WILPF's Pan-American Committee, with *the Asociacion Puertoriquena de Mujeres Sufragistas* and the *Liga Social Subaristas* of Puerto Rico, in 1926, Baber was in Puerto Rico, fighting to obtain the right to vote for the women of the island. Also, in 1926, she was a member of the Balch Mission to Haiti, which led to the end of U.S. military occupation there (Balch 1927). Baber became president of the Chicago section of the WILPF and the Peace Symbols Committee, to which she dedicated her book *Peace Symbols*. In 1951, at the age of 89 years, she was still committed to the peace movement and actively involved in WILPF.

Peace Symbols (1948)

"My major interest is in 'Peace' and 'Justice for the Colored Races" stated Baber (Zonia Baber to Harriet Chalmers Adams, President, Society of Woman Geographers, 17 February 1927). Born during the American Civil War, Baber lived through two world wars and up to the beginning of the Cold War, leading her to develop profoundly anti-war and anti-imperialist views. The material remembrance of peace was a constant theme in her work. Baber

"*Making Zonia known*" 67

asked herself, "Since all human intercourse must be through symbols, is it not strange we have not erected monuments to peace as we have to war? War symbols are scattered throughout all so-called civilized countries but peace monuments are rare" (Baber 1937, 151). In 1948, she published a small book with the WILPF entitled *Peace Symbols*. The work offers descriptions and images of 40 peace monuments. In the author's own words: "In comparison with memorials celebrating war, monuments dedicated to peace may seem few in number. Nevertheless, the wide chronological and geographic distribution of peace symbols attests to the persistence and universality of mankind's desire for lasting peace on earth" (Baber 1948, 6). The book also includes, among the "Supplementary Materials" (section V), a list of the "Early Peace Treaties made by the U.S. Government" (Ibid., 89–93) and two poems on racial equality (Ibid., 94–95).

For each of the 40 peace symbols selected via a careful research process, Baber provided a brief description with annotations, comments, and an image. She divided the 40 symbols into four spatial categories, arranged in chronological order: (I) *Historical and Foreign* (19); (II) *United States Monuments* (7), (III) *United States and Canada* (10), (IV) *United States and Mexico* (4). As she selected them, Baber marked their positions on a map of the world. Today some of them no longer exist as a result of vandalism or neglect (Figure 7.1).

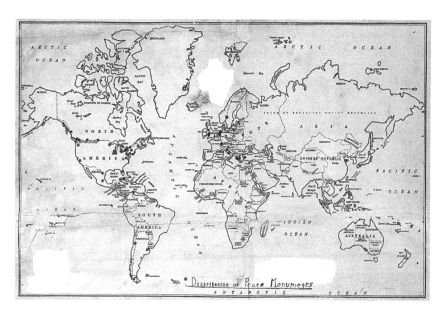

Figure 7.1 Map (with annotations). Distribution of peace monuments, Zonia Baber (1937–1949 ca.), part of material gathered for the Peace Symbols Committee of WILPF, 1937–1949, Oversized Documents collection, Swarthmore College Peace Collection. https://digitalcollections.tricolib. brynmawr.edu/object/sc93762. The 39 points marked on the map correspond to the monuments listed in this book.

The theme of peace and the production of the material symbols celebrating it cannot be separated from the historical, political, and ethical context. Zonia Baber's collection spans different thematic areas. First, that of heritage, or artefacts and ancient monuments selected on account of their artistic value. Assigned to this first category were both classical works (*Irene, Greek Goddess of Peace, Athens, Greece, IV century B.C., Pax, Roman Goddess of Peace, Medallion, Asia Minor, 28 B.C., PAX, Ambrose Lorenzetti, Peace Hall, Siena, Italy, 1339, Ara Pacis Augustae, the "Altar of Augustan Peace", Rome, 9 BC)*, and historical emblems such as the American Statue of Liberty and a small Japanese temple (no longer in existence) in Chicago.

Another key theme is religion. As Appelbaum explains: "Religious pacifism between World War I and the Vietnam era had a distinctive vocabulary of visual and material images. [...] Pacifist culture incorporated narratives of heroes and saints, iconography, metaphors for peace, and representations of other nations and peoples" (Appelbaum, n.d., *Material Pacifism*). The religious theme recurs in the statues of martyrs and heroes, in the languages, messages, and styles of many monuments that were built with political or celebratory aims. Also of religious origin is "the earliest of the modern peace emblems" (Baber 1948, 18), the peace plough, made of weapons refashioned into everyday objects, in light of the biblical principle "they shall beat their swords into ploughshares, and their spears into pruning hooks" (Isaiah 2:3–4). Baber's inventory includes two versions of the peace plough (see pages 18 and 24), one which had been exhibited at the Centennial International Exposition in Philadelphia (1876), and the other which had been on show in Chicago at the World's Columbian Exposition in 1893. Another significant contribution to the celebration of peace, according to Baber, came from Fraternal Organizations of freemasons or other groups. In particular, "Kiwanis International has excelled all other groups in this country in the number of peace symbols they have established" (Baber 1948, 76).

In representing world peace, another frequent theme, which also bears echoes of Christian spirituality, is that of nature and gardens, "The garden is the Edenic beginning" (Appelbaum 2009, 101). Baber included in her collection a number of peace gardens located along the border between the United States and Canada. Two international border parks – Waterton-Glacier International Peace Park set up in 1932 between the United States and Canada and the International Peace Park in Big Bend, on the border with Mexico, proposed by Rooswelt in 1944 and still the object of debate today – are also dedicated to peace. The nature theme meanwhile was also present in the commemoration of trees of great symbolic value, such as the elm (which fell in 1810) under which William Penn had signed the Peace Treaty of Shackamaxon in 1682, and the Pan-American Fraternity Tree, planted in 1928 in Havana, in soil collected from all the countries of North and South America.

Like religion, patriotism – which was understood by Baber as "a zealous, continued effort to have your country right, and yourself right" (Bainbridge in Baber 1937, 158) – is a further theme running through the book. Most of the symbols selected by Baber (24 out of 40) are located in the United States, with a particular focus on the neighbouring country to the north. In the period between the two world wars, the symbols of peace – Baber listed 14 of them (1937) – located along the Canadian border, were of particular significance (Baber 1948, 60). The first of these was the Peace Arch, inaugurated in 1921 to celebrate over 100 years of peace between Canada and the United States, following the Treaty of Ghent (1814). Kuenker critically analyses the significance of shared identity and the rhetoric associated with such border monuments:

> In the post-World War I context, Americans and Canadians witnessed the creation of a series of symbolic monuments to commemorate a century of peaceful relations along the U.S./Canadian border. Analyzing the language and symbols used to describe these events, one finds several common threads. Newspapers, dedication speakers, and commemorative ceremonies cast these monuments as visual symbols of two peoples bonded by a common language and racial heritage and linked by parallel histories. The advancement of both countries into modernity and their friendly relationship along the border were held up as markers of racial superiority and instructive examples for the world to follow. These notions of a shared transnational identity made the U.S./Canadian border unique in the public imagination.
>
> (Kuenker 2011, 113)

Many monuments, such as the earlier mentioned Christ of the Andes at La Cumbre Pass, between Chile and Argentina, or the *Fredsmonument* (1914) between Sweden and Norway, marked the end of border disputes. In some cases, pacifism blended with nationalism, such as at the Flemish Peace Shrine (1930), whose inscription *AVVKV* in Flemish stands for "all for Flanders and Flanders for Christ". Military commemoration, on the other hand, is the leitmotif of numerous monuments that celebrate the end of a war (American Civil War, World War I), while honouring its heroes and fallen. Baber commented that "In peace celebrations war symbols too often prevail [...]. But recently the celebration through the erection of peace monuments is a salutary prediction of a higher future in international good will" (Baber 1937, 151).

The meaning of commemoration

Peace Symbols speaks to "Baber's commitment to peace, and stands testimony to her geographical heritage, one inspired by the diversity of landscapes and places as a means to deepen understanding and widen appreciation" (Monk and Schmidt di Friedberg 2011, 76). While in some respects, the book may not always appear critical in relation to some of the issues we have reviewed, it is crucial to situate it in its own historical period. Baber dedicated *Peace Symbols* to the cause of world peace and gifted it to the WILPF in 1948 at the age of 86 years. This was a more extensive version, enriched with photographic illustrations and annotations of the collection of peace-themed monuments, works, and gardens that she had already presented in an article of the same title published in 1937. And indeed, the period between the two wars was the key focus of Baber's inquiry. Fifteen of her 40 selected symbols date to the 1930s, while only four are later than 1940, the latest being the park in Big Bend (1944). The collection contains no comments or memories relating to World War II. Zonia Baber's activism and her peace campaigning were particularly intense in the immediate aftermath of World War I, the dramatic impact of which helped to shape her pacifist ideas. Hence her efforts to collect material signs of peace, with which to build a better world based on brotherhood and far removed from the horrors of the Great War. The largest number of peace symbols is concentrated in 1936. "It is a pleasure to report that 1936 recorded the erection of more peace symbols than any preceding year. This method of expressing an ardent desire for international peace was indulged in by people of various walks of life" (Baber 1937, 158).

Baber's optimism was not shaken by the outbreak of World War II, which played a background role in her work. In section V, she lists the peace treaties of which the United States is a signatory, calling them "gestures of conciliation and goodwill which indicate the progress of people's faltering steps towards peace" (Baber 1937). In particular, she touches on the Kellogg-Briand pact (1928), in which the parties agreed to forego war as an instrument of national politics, and which had been celebrated by the pacifist movement as the dawn of a new era. Baber summed up the failure of the pact in a terse few words: "Sixty-two nations signed the Pact. (It is now obsolete.)" (Baber 1948, 93). The 1920s and 1930s were the key periods framing her positive emphasis on peace and untiring activism: "Before and after that date (about 1930), as in earlier periods, this will to peace has vacillated or failed, and the blood and slaughter of two world wars have dashed their hopes" (Baber 1948, 88). After World War II, the identity of the pacifist movement changed, as did its material symbols, which were now more likely to represent new themes, such as opposing nuclear arms, or honouring deserters, conscientious objectors, and all those who refuse to take part in wars. Baber did not have enough time left to continue her fight for peace by extending it to new issues, although she did view the founding of the United Nations in 1945 as raising the prospect of "the achievement of a peaceful world in which to live" (Id).

Materially speaking, "memory matters" (Drozdzewski and Monk 2020, 254): peace monuments are not just neutral elements of a landscape, but rather are laden with meaning and bear a clear educational and communications function, which at times can be ambiguous. Zonia Baber, did not analyse the contradictions surrounding commemorations or the counter-narratives associated with the individual monuments she catalogued. Rather, as a true educationalist, she intended her collection of peace symbols to convey a strong message of peace and brotherhood and to demonstrate the geographical dissemination of this message: "Though such monuments might seem to function largely as backdrops in daily life, they are intended to commemorate what we value and to instruct us in our heritage through visible expressions on the landscape" (Monk 1992, 124).

After the paper "Zonia Baber: Following Her Moral Compass" (Monk and Schmidt of Friedberg), presented in Hamburg, August 2012 at the IGU Commission on Gender and Geography, Janice Monk asked:

> To conclude we would like you to reflect on why a geographer such as Baber has become unknown in the history of geography, – masculine hegemonies? privileging of theories over education and activism? Should we pay more attention to excavating the place of our foremothers?

Certainly much remains to be done. We need to follow Janice 'Monk's invitation "to keep making Zonia known"; Zonia as well as many other women geographers need to be brought back into the limelight for their work and proposed to the academic community and students. I would conclude with Janice's proposal for a new geography:

> My hope is for a geography that is enriched by and more responsive than it has historically been to diversity. To attain that future, we need ways in which conjunctions and divisions are created, sustained, and challenged, to bring our energies and talents to bear on fostering institutions and knowledge that are consciously inclusive
>
> (Monk 2004, 18)

References

Appelbaum, P. 2009. *Kingdom to Commune. Protestant Pacifist Culture between World War I and the Vietnam ERA*. Chapel Hill: The University of North Carolina Press.
Appelbaum, P. n.d. "Material Pacifism", *The Material History of American Religion Project*. http://www.materialreligion.org/journal/appelbaum/appelbaum.html
Baber, Z. 1901. "The Course of Study." *Journal of Geography* 5 (1): 409–412.
Baber, Z. 1904. "The Scope of Geography." *The Elementary School Teacher* 4 (5): 257–270.
Baber, Z. 1905. "Field Work in Elementary School." *Journal of Geography* 1 (4): 386–396.
Baber, Z. 1907. "A Lesson in Geography: From Chicago to the Atlantic.." *The Elementary School Teacher* 8 (7): 458–473.
Baber, Z. 1913. "Conservation of Important Geographical Areas for Educational Purposes." *Journal of Geography* 9 (11): 287–290.
Baber, Z. 1916. "Lost Opportunities in Teaching Geography." *Journal of Geography* 14 (8): 295–298.
Baber, Z. 1937. "Peace Symbols." *Chicago Schools Journal* 18: 151–158.
Baber, Z. 1948. *Peace Symbols*. Chicago: Women's International League for Peace and Freedom.
Balch, E. G., 1927. *Occupied Haiti*. New York: The Writers Publishing.
dell'Agnese, Elena 2010. " Per una riforma della didattica della geografia: William C. Woodbridge, Emma Willard e Samuel G. Goodrich". In *Che cos'è il mondo? È un globo di cartone. Insegnare geografia fra Otto e Novecento*, edited by M. Schmidt di Friedberg, Unicopli, Milano, pp. 47–64.

Drozdzewski, D., and J. Monk. 2020. "Representing Women and Gender in Memory Landscapes." In *Routledge Handbook of Gender and Feminist Geographies*, edited by A. Datta, P. Hopkins, L. Johnston, E. Olson, and J. M. Silva, 254–270. London: Routledge.

Fitzgerald, H. 1929. "All Humanity Her Kinsfolk." *The Brooklyn Daily Eagle*. Brooklyn, New York, October 20, p. 89.

Hunter, D. 2013. "Zonia Baber: The Public May Be Brought to Understand the Importance of Geography." *Scientific American*, 29 March. https://blogs.scientificamerican.com/rosetta-stones/zonia-baber-the-public-may-be-brought-to-understand-the-importance-of-geography/

"Knife in Hand Pacifist Chides Man as 'Savage'." 1917. *Chicago Tribune*. Chicago, Illinois, December 7, p. 14.

Kuenker, P. 2011. "One Hundred Years of Peace: Memory and Rhetoric on the United States/Canadian Border, 1920-1933." *Hemisphere: Visual Cultures of the Americas* 4 (1): 94. https://digitalrepository.unm.edu/hemisphere/vol4/iss1/2

Mather, S. 1917. *Report on the Proposed Sand Dunes National Park Indiana*. Washington Government Printing Office.

Monk, J. 1992. "Gender in the Landscape: Expressions of Power and Meaning." In *Inventing Places: Studies in Cultural Geography*, edited by K. Anderson and F. Gale, 123–138. Melbourne: Longman Cheshire.

Monk, J. 2004. "Women, Gender, and the Histories of American Geography." *Annals of the Association of American Geographers* 94 (1): 1–22. DOI: 10.1111/j.1467-8306.2004.09401001.x.

Monk J. 2008. "Practically All the Geographers Were Women." *Presentation at Society of Woman Geographers Triennial*, May 2. www.iswg.org

Monk, J., and M. Schmidt di Friedberg. 2011. "Mary Arizona (Zonia) Baber (1862–1956)." *Geographers Biobibliographical Studies* 30: 68–79.

Monk, J., and S. Hanson. 1982. "On Not Excluding Half of the Human inHuman Geography." *The Professional Geographer* 34: 11–23. DOI: 10.1111/j.0033-0124.1982.00011.x.

Pittser, S. E. 1999. "Early Women Geography Educators, 1783-1932." *Journal of Geography* 6 (98): 302–307.

Plastas, M. 2011. *A Band of Noble Women: Racial Politics in the Women's Peace Movement*. New York: Syracuse University Press.

Silva, J. M. 2010. "On Not Excluding Half of the Human in Human Geography: Interview with Janice Monk." *Revista Latino-americana de Geografia e Genero* 1 (1): 153–156. DOI: 10.5212/Rlagg.v.1.i1.153156.

Schmidt di Friedberg, M. 2010 (ed.) *Cos'è il mondo? È un globo di cartone. Insegnare geografia fra Otto e Novecento*. Milano: Unicopli.

Vellacott, J. 1993. "A Place for Pacifism and Transnationalism in Feminist Theory: The Early Work of the Women's International League for Peace and Freedom." *Women's History Review* 2 (1): 23–56. DOI: 10.1080/09612029300200021.

"Zonia Baber Circles Globe". 1900. *Chicago Tribune*, Chicago, Illinois, 19 June, p. 8.

8 Janice Monk and Evelyn Stokes
Two Women Geographers from Down Under Break New Ground

Robyn Longhurst and Lynda Johnston

This research uses a life course approach to examine differences, but mainly commonalities, in the careers of two influential women geographers from Down Under (Aotearoa New Zealand and Australia). It begins with a discussion of Janice Monk's, and Evelyn Stokes' individual journeys from Down Under to the United States as young women committed to studying geography. This is followed by an examination of the commonalities that emerged in their stories of engaging with geography, including that: each wanted something more than what was usual for women in their own country; throughout their careers they lacked women role models; they worked long and hard in order to succeed; they showed huge resilience in the face of setbacks; their career aspirations developed slowly over time; and, both broke new disciplinary ground. The chapter concludes that Monk and Stokes both helped shape the field of critical geography. Although Monk focused primarily on gender and Stokes focused primarily on Māori, both commonly looked beyond one single axis of identity, instead paying attention to mutually constitutive and intersectional forms of social oppression. We remain appreciative to both women for their mentoring and for all the other work they carried out over the course of their extensive and impressive careers.

Introduction

When the idea of a *Festschrift* to celebrate Emerita Professor Jan Monk's ground-breaking contributions to feminist geography was first mooted we were keen to contribute. Both of us have had a long and rich association with Monk and with the IGU Commission on Gender and Geography that Monk was instrumental in setting up along with Janet Momsen in 1992. In addition, we recently wrote a biographical essay about another influential geographer from Down Under – Professor Dame Evelyn Stokes (nee Dinsdale) – with whom we have also had a long and rich association (Johnston, Longhurst and Roche, forthcoming). Stokes, like Monk, devoted her career to addressing issues of inequality. A number of publications document separately Monk's and Stokes' contribution to the discipline of geography but none so far have discussed these two influential women together.

DOI: 10.4324/9781032275611-10

Both these remarkable women have had a huge influence on our careers. We continue to be influenced by the scholarship and mentoring we received from them over a period of decades. Monk and Stokes shaped our early work in feminist geography, as well as our commitment to building and leading gender and geography networks. Sadly, Stokes passed away in August 2005 (see Bedford and Longhurst 2005 for a *Festschrift* issue of the *New Zealand Geographer* published the same week Stokes died).

As far as we know, the two women never met in person. Monk, with Frances Slater, visited the University of Waikato in Aotearoa New Zealand in 1997 to attend GeoEd'97 / Kaupapa Aro Whenua Conference, but we do not think she met Stokes. Around the same time, Monk was the Erskine Fellow at the University of Canterbury. Waikato and Canterbury are located in different islands, though, and travel between the two is costly and time consuming. During this period Monk, as far as we know, remained in the South. Much earlier, in 1976, Stokes enjoyed a period of study leave in North America working with colleagues involved in environmental impact assessment in Alaska, Ontario and Arizona but she did not meet Monk. We know from our conversations with both Monk and Stokes that the women knew of each other and of their work. There was undoubtedly mutual respect, but we do not think they ever met in person.

We begin this chapter by outlining our approach to the task of examining the careers of these two influential geographers from Down Under. Second, we chart both Monk's and Stokes' journey from Down Under to the United States as young women committed to studying geography at the post-graduate level – Monk to enter a Master's programme and Stokes to enter a Doctoral programme. Third, we discuss the commonalities that emerged in the stories of these two women from Down Under paying attention to what these tell us about the exclusionary nature of the discipline of geography in the early 1960s. Finally, we conclude that the way Monk and Stokes over four decades brought their social concerns 'to the table' helped shape not only the discipline at the time but also an entire generation of critical – gender, feminist, anti-racist, Māori – geographers who came after.

Life course approach: examining 'the careers of women geographers'

Monk (2004, 1) argues: 'Histories of American geography have tended to concentrate on geographical thought and on the men who have been seen as major figures in research'. She chooses, in contrast, to examine 'the careers of women geographers' (Monk 2004, 1). In this chapter we take the opportunity to turn our attention towards her own pioneering and impressive career (e.g. producing more than 100 scholarly books, journal articles and chapters including landmark pieces such as Monk and Hanson 1982; Norwood and Monk 1987; Katz and Monk 1993; Monk 1995) alongside that of Stokes.

We adopt an approach that Monk (2004, 2) herself used when examining the careers of women geographers, that is to acknowledge 'the existence of multiple histories' and the importance 'of recognizing differences among women as gender intersects an array of other distinctions, among them race and ethnicity, class, place, and time'. In *Full Circles: Geographies over the Life Course*, Katz and Monk (1993, 4) make a case for describing and interpreting:

> the geographies of women's lives in an array of settings from the perspective of the life course, hoping that in this way [they] could extend understanding of the diversity and commonalities of women's experiences and of the roles of space and place in shaping those experiences.

We do not consider Monk's and Stokes' entire life courses here but instead focus attention on their *academic* lives and the way these are intersected by gender, race, ethnicity and class. We seek to understand some of the differences and commonalities in their experiences and the roles of space and place in influencing these experiences.

We consider a number of points frequently made by scholars who adopt a life course approach (see Elder, Kirkpatrick Johnson and Crosnoe 2003) including that: people's development occurs throughout their lives; people have agency within particular structural constraints; place and time matter; the timing of life transitions has an impact on how they are experienced; and lastly, people are not self-contained but exist in relationship with others. These ideas – threaded through the stories we offer here about Monks' and Stokes' lives – are partial. They are our memories of interactions we have had with our colleagues/mentors, Jan and Evelyn, and our interpretation of texts that each of these women has written and that have been written about them over a period of four decades.

Journeying from Down Under to the United States

As stated earlier, Monk and Stokes are both from Down Under and as Monk (1994, 289) argues: 'Place matters'. It matters that both these women were raised in countries that sit at the bottom of the map, in the 'Global South' (Sparke 2007, 117). It matters that Monk was born in 1937 and Stokes in 1936 and that both grew up in working class families. Monk (2007, 107) explains: 'The family finances always had to be watched very carefully'. Stokes was 'the eldest of five children [three sisters and brother]. Her father was a garage proprietor and motor mechanic' (Johnston, Longhurst and Roche, forthcoming).

Both women to some degree followed in the footsteps of their families but in other ways, they charted their own path. Monk comments:

> Like my great-grandmother, I moved across the world, though as a single woman, at the age of twenty-four. Unlike my forebears, I obtained considerable education, the beneficiary of a variety of state scholarships and institutional support from the age of eleven. Like them, I married in my late twenties. Unlike them, I had no children. Also unlike them, I support myself financially, now live alone, and travel widely nationally for work and pleasure.
>
> (J.M. in Katz and Monk 1993, 2)

Monk and Stokes were both the first in their families to go to university. Most Pākehā/white settler women born to working class families in the 1930s in Aotearoa New Zealand and Australia imagined their futures as housewives, or if they were to work outside the home it would likely be as teachers, nurses or clerical workers. 'It was a period when job advertisements in newspapers were categorized separately for men or women, the governmentally established basic wage levels were higher for men than for women' (Monk 2007, 110). Most people did not imagine that young Antipodean women would travel abroad alone, especially to North America rather than to the 'home' country (United Kingdom) to study for a higher degree in geography, but this is exactly what both Monk and Stokes did (see King 2007 for stories of other Antipodean geographers whose careers were also shaped by their experiences in North America). It has become a truism in Aotearoa New Zealand and Australia that a 'can-do' attitude pervades, that individuals find a way to overcome challenges and that is exactly what both Monk and Stokes did. One such way was to secure a scholarship.

In 1961, Monk took up an offer for funding from the University of Illinois in Chicago. One year earlier Stokes was awarded a Fulbright grant from Syracuse University in the state of New York. Both women set sail. Study awaited them but so too did the beginning of many life-long international adventures. Monk (2007, 115) writes:

> I booked passage in a four-berth cabin on a P.&O. liner that was on a round-the world cruise. It called at Manila, Hong Kong, Kobe, Yokahama (I travelled on land to Kyoto and Tokyo with shipmates between those ports), Honolulu, then Vancouver ... I disembarked at Vancouver, took the Canadian Pacific train, stopping off in Banff, then on to Winnipeg, Minneapolis and Chicago ... It was a five week adventure, and my first alone.

Stokes (2005) too documented her journey to the United States, in a collection titled *Evelyn's Letters from America 1960–1963*. These letters reveal Stokes' passion for adventurous travel. Her journey to the United States began in late May 1960 when she boarded the SS *Oronsay* in Auckland stopping along the way at Suva, Fiji, Honolulu, Hawaii, and Vancouver, before finally disembarking in San Francisco.

In bringing together Monk's and Stokes' journeys to the United States to study geography, we are not meaning to suggest they were the same. One important difference is that following their respective journeys, Monk spent the duration of her career researching and teaching in the United States while Stokes returned home to Aotearoa New Zealand in 1963, shortly after beginning work at the University of Auckland – Waikato Branch (later the new University of Waikato) where she spent her entire career. Leaving Syracuse was not easy for Stokes (2005, 182), as she writes in a letter dated 26 March 1963:

It was hard to say good-bye to all those guys in the Geography Department, professors and students. I cannot quite realise I am leaving permanently yet. I am still thinking in terms of hopping on the bus back to Syracuse. But when the ship sails tomorrow I guess it will be final. Ed Soja (grad student) is going to help me take my stuff from the Greyhound Station to the boat in the morning.

Monk did not return home to Down Under, remaining at the University of Illinois from 1961 to 1980. She writes:

I was undertaking work of a kind [in education and social geography] then not widely included in Australian institutions. I liked what I was doing, the people I was meeting, and the continuing appointment. I did not look seriously for any opportunities to return to Australia.

(Monk 2007, 118)

In 1980, Monk arrived at the University of Arizona to take up the position of Associate Director of the Southwest Institute for Research of Women (SIROW) where she remained until retirement.

Although Monk spent her entire career in the United States and Stokes spent hers in Aotearoa New Zealand, both women continued for many decades to be keen and engaged travellers connecting with people from all walks of life across the globe. A great pleasure and privilege for us has been connecting with Monk and other members of the International Geographical Union's Commission on Gender and Geography at conferences in an array of places – between us these include Hungary, Romania, Brazil, Israel, Tunisia, Taiwan, Germany and United States. We also hosted a meeting of the IGU Commission on Gender and Geography in 2006 in Hamilton, Aotearoa New Zealand which Monk attended. These deep personal connections that we developed and intellectual exchanges we engaged in, often spending whole days and evenings together face-to-face, we value even more now in light of the COVID-19 global pandemic. They enabled us, often with Monk leading discussion, to explore our rich differences and to deepen our understanding of issues of gender, culture, ethnicity, nationality, class, economic status, age and ability/disability.

In piecing together fragments of Monk's and Stokes' academic lives as Australasian women geographers, there are important differences, for example, Monk not having any children and Stokes having two. Also, Monk focused her teaching and research on women and minority groups in the United States and Mexico while Stokes focused hers on Māori in Aotearoa New Zealand. As we have suggested though there are also many commonalities and connections, and it is on these that we focus in the next section of this chapter since it tells us something important about the academic lives of women geographers from Down Under from the 1960s onwards and about the discipline of geography.

Commonalities and connections

The first commonality that emerged from interacting and reading Monk's and Stokes' work over a long period (and from reading what others have written about them) is that both women wanted something more than what was usual or expected in the societies into which they were born and grew up. Both had an appetite for independent travel. Both from a young age were highly committed to learning about people, place and power relations. Both defied the gender norms of their time in their countries of origin, travelling overseas alone to attend university and study geography instead of staying home, getting married and tending to home and family which was the norm for Pākehā/white settler women of the time.

Stokes (2005, 1) explains that she remembers being 'a young, naïve, New Zealand female geographer in 1960' who challenged conventions. There were members of her extended family who did not think that as a young woman she should travel overseas alone or attend university. The expectation was that she would stay at home and get married. Stokes ignored this advice but was thankful for her father's support, illustrated in one of his letters to her: 'Personally, I think anyone marrying at 20 is nuts: it is a life sentence and there is plenty of time after you have done some the things you want to do and gained a bit more experience in life' (Arthur to Evelyn, Stokes 2005, 2).

While both Monk and Stokes left Australasia in order to explore wider horizons, there were also other women in the 1950s and early to mid-1960s from outside the United States who entered graduate geography programmes but for other reasons: 'there were differences among the women of this period [they came] from Taiwan, Trinidad, England, Ireland, France, Poland, Thailand, New Zealand and Australia' (Monk 2004, 12). Some were leaving political disruption, others were seeking training in order to teach geography in Catholic women's colleges, while still others were joining their male partners in graduate school. As is suggested by a 'geographies over the life course' approach, there is both diversity and commonalities in women's experiences and these are shaped by time, space and place.

The second theme that emerged as we read work by Monk and by Stokes, as well as by those who have written about them, is that neither, as they began their careers, or progressed through their careers, had many women role models. Monk (2004, 10) notes, in the 1950s and early to mid-1960s: 'Masculinity prevailed in the daily culture of [geography] departments – the red-checked flannel shirts, knee-high boots, and hairy chests that Fraser Hart described as the 1950s uniform'. While the reference here is to culture in universities in the United States, it was not dissimilar in Aotearoa New Zealand (see Nairn 1999 on fieldwork in geography).

It seems, however, that having themselves had few opportunities to be mentored, as they progressed in their careers, both took every opportunity to mentor and support the careers of other women. Richard Bedford (2005, 243) comments: 'One of the most enduring features of Evelyn's academic career was the intellectual stimulation and scholarly empowerment she gave to her female and Māori colleagues and students'. We – Lynda and Robyn – both know from personal experience that Monk was also a dedicated mentor, especially to those who needed her most. One can only imagine throughout their lives how many hours Monk and Stokes have each spent writing letters of support for students, colleagues and others, for job applications, tenure, promotions, grant applications and awards. Having been the beneficiaries of this on a number of occasions, we always do everything we can to 'pay it forward' to those who now approach us to undertake such tasks.

A third theme that became apparent as we undertook this research was that both women proved themselves over and over again by working harder, longer and more effectively than many male colleagues. Both worked tirelessly as rigorous researchers, as effective supervisors and as engaging teachers. Interestingly, in relation to teaching, both women were not only always keen to progress their knowledge but also share it and so made important contributions to the field of geographical education. Stokes, having trained as a teacher and taught at secondary school, was a keen educator (Burridge and Stokes 1974). She served on the National Geography Curriculum Committee from 1976 to 1987, noting: 'I recall the surprise of some members when the small female minority ... stubbornly insisted that we talk about the earth and our environment as the home of people, not man alone' (Stokes 1986, 4). Monk published extensively on geographical education and comments:

> Much of my work in geography education has been concerned with university teaching and graduate education. I have contributed to the Geography Faculty Development Alliance, which mentors early career faculty, and currently co-principal investigator for the Association of American Geographer's (AAG) EDGE projects that are researching career opportunities and professional development for MA and PhD students.
> (School of Geography, Development and Environment, University of Arizona, 2021)

A fourth commonality that emerged was resilience which both Monk and Stokes displayed particularly at the beginning but also throughout their careers. Although in the 1970s and early 1980s the conservative context began to change with social movements and political activism impacting organizations such as the Association of American Geographers (AAG) and New Zealand Geographical Society, it would have still been very difficult to challenge the sexism inherent in geography departments a decade earlier in the 1960s. Monk (2004, 13) notes: 'For those [women] who did obtain positions in the late 1960s, what often followed were absent or slower promotions, tenure denials, inequities in salaries, and year-at-a time appointments. Some had heavier teaching or service loads imposed upon them'. Despite this, Monk and Stokes endured, often making do, working around and sometimes using humour to make things work or to get a point across. For example:

In 1985 when the Waikato Branch of the New Zealand Geographical Society hosted the 13th New Zealand Geography Conference, Stokes delivered the presidential address. Five of the seven women academic geography staff out of 67 across the six New Zealand universities were then at the Waikato Geography Department ... After recalling humorously that her horoscope for the week warned her not to force her views on other people, Stokes reflected on gender, language, social inequality, and homes, as well as wilderness and scenery. She declared her positionality as a 'working class kid who had succeeded in climbing over the academic hurdles'.

(Johnston, Longhurst and Roche, forthcoming)

A fifth commonality in Monk's and Stokes' stories is that their aspirations developed gradually over the duration of their careers. Neither set out to 'conquer the world' and yet both by the end of their career had achieved extraordinary things. Both developed a capacity to astutely read and understand power relations. Along with this came an ability to work from 'the inside', that is, from within various offices and institutions to bring about positive change. For Monk, this was often but certainly not solely, positive change for women. For Stokes, it was often positive change for Māori.

An excellent example in relation to Monk is that she was for many years actively engaged with the AAG (an educational society founded in 1904 with members from close on 100 countries). Monk (2007, 119) writes:

In the AAG's Committee on the Status of Women in Geography, political activity rose with efforts to advance women in the discipline and in AAG leadership. One outcome of this was my nomination and election as a national councillor of the Association.

(1978–1981)

Several decades later, Monk served as President of the AAG 2001–2002 and as Former President 2002–2003. Her list of successes, contributions and recognitions is long and impressive (see Wikipedia, 2021).

Stokes also made an impressive contribution to various organizations including the New Zealand Geographic Board Ngā Pou Taunaha o Aotearoa (established in 1946 to assign and alter place names in New Zealand – see Stokes 1994) and the Waitangi Tribunal (a permanent commission of inquiry that makes recommendations on claims brought by Māori relating to alleged breaches by the Crown of the promises made in the Treaty of Waitangi). Stokes' work for the Tribunal meant she played a key role in some of Aotearoa New Zealand's most historically and politically important defining moments (Johnston, Longhurst and Roche, forthcoming).

Both Monk and Stokes worked tirelessly over decades, from within different institutions, often finding themselves at loggerheads with colleagues resistant to change. Our conversations with both women, however, indicate that this rarely fazed them. Maybe it was because both during their careers prompted new insights that were qualitatively different from many of their colleagues (mainly Pākehā/white settler men). Perhaps they grew used to holding oppositional positions.

This leads us to the sixth theme that emerged when comparing and contrasting Monk's and Stokes' stories, and this is, that they both continually pushed disciplinary, social and political boundaries. Monk and Stokes were pivotal in generating new geographical perspectives – gender, feminist, Māori, indigenous, anti-racist and intersectional – in an attempt to bring about a more equitable, just and inclusive society. Sometimes these perspectives are broadly captured under the umbrella term 'critical geographies'. While at many points during their life courses this must have felt like a struggle, history has proven itself to be on their side. The aforementioned perspectives or 'critical geographies' are now commonly used in teaching and research. It is interesting that both women, despite early setbacks in their careers such as Monk being denied tenure in 1979 for lacking 'potential' in the University of Illinois' Geography Department's programs (Monk 2007, 119) and Stokes after completing her PhD being unsuccessful in her application for a lecturer position in the Geography Department at the University of Auckland, received prestigious accolades for their outstanding work.

Monk in 2012 was awarded the Lauréat d'Honneur, an award established in 1976 by the International Geographical Union. It was 'established to recognize individuals who have achieved particular distinction or who have rendered outstanding service in the work of the IGU or in international geography and environmental research' (IGU Online – The World in Geography – Roll of Honour, 2021). Monk was one of the first women, if not *the first* woman, to ever be awarded this honour. In 2008, she received the Outstanding Achievement Award from the Society of Woman Geographers and also in the same year, the Enhancing Diversity Award by the AAG. Earlier, in 2000, Monk was awarded the Lifetime Achievement Honors by the AAG and in 1999 by compatriots in her country of birth, the Australia-International Medal, Institute of Australian Geographers. She has also received many other awards.

Stokes too has had her efforts recognized, but as was typical for many women, and 'others' such as Māori, of her generation, quite late in her career. She was presented the Distinguished New Zealand Geographer medal in 2001. One year earlier, 2000, Stokes was appointed Dame Companion of the New Zealand Order for Services to education and Māori. Her response was characteristically modest. In a conversation we had with Stokes soon after the announcement, she expressed her incredible (and very genuine) disbelief at receiving the award when so many others would have been more worthy recipients.

Conclusion

Monk's and Stokes' academic life courses share much in common and when brought together illustrate that while for most of their careers they occupied different geographical contexts, their shared values such as a belief in the importance of equity, fairness, justice and learning for all resulted in each producing ground-breaking geographical research that pushed for a more socially just society. The subject areas they addressed were similar including gender, ethnicity, culture, social class, history, geographical education and indigeneity (Monk focusing on aboriginal communities, Stokes focusing on Māori communities). Both were hugely influential in shaping critical geography (Monk in shaping gender geography and Stokes in shaping Māori geography). Also, both, throughout their careers looked beyond one single axis of identity to instead focus on mutually constitutive and intersectional forms of social oppression – again breaking new ground. Both, in many ways, were ahead of their time, engaging such an approach and playing a major role in shaping much of the debate in contemporary critical geography that came to follow.

Finally, we continue to be inspired by Janice and Evelyn and thank them for their profound contribution to the discipline geography and beyond. We feel privileged that both played such an important role in our own scholarly journeys, through their mentorship and through their work. For us bringing their contributions together for this *Festschrift* has been an honour.

Acknowledgements

We would like to thank the reviewers and editors for their feedback. Some of the material in this chapter was presented at the Institute of Australian Geographers Conference, Sydney, 9 July 2021. We are grateful for the discussion at this conference which helped us refine our ideas. Special thanks goes to Professor Michael Roche (Massey University) who invited us into a collaborative biobibliography project about Evelyn Stokes (forthcoming, https://www.bloomsbury.com/uk/geographers-9781350203419/). This project prompted us to consider the similarities and differences between Jan and Evelyn. Finally, we thank Jan for her unwavering support of women, feminist and queer geographers.

Disclosure statement

No potential conflict of interest was reported by the authors.

References

Bedford, Richard. 2005. "Obituary – Evelyn Mary Stokes (née Dinsdale) DNZM, MA (NZ) PhD (Syr) 5 December 1936 – 11 August 2005." *New Zealand Geographer* 61 (3): 242–249.

Bedford, Richard and Robyn Longhurst. 2005. "Evelyn Stokes and Geography at the University of Waikato." *New Zealand Geographer* 61: 87–88.

Burridge, Geoffrey and Evelyn Stokes. 1974. "Student Needs and Syllabus Revision." *New Zealand Journal of Geography* 57: 20–24.

Elder, Glen H. Jr., Monica Kirkpatrick Johnson and Robert Crosnoe. 2003. "The Emergence and Development of Life Course Theory." In *Handbook of the Life Course*, edited by Jeylan T. Mortimer and Michael J. Shanahan, 3–19. New York: Kluwer Academic/Plenum.

IGU Online – The World in Geography – Roll of Honour. 2021. https://igu-online.org/about-us/roll-of-honour/, accessed 8 June 2021.

Johnston, Lynda, Robyn Longhurst and Michael Roche. Forthcoming. "Evelyn Mary Stokes (1936-2005)." In *Geographers: Bibliographical Studies*, Vol. 41, edited by Elizabeth Baigent and André Reyes Novaes.

Katz, Cindi and Janice Monk, eds. 1993. *Full Circles: Geographies of Women over the Life Course*. London and New York: Routledge.

King, Leslie J., ed. 2007. *North American Explorations: Ten Memoirs of Geographers from Down Under*. Victoria, BC, Canada: Trafford.

Monk, Janice. 1994. "Place Matters: Comparative International Perspectives on Feminist Geography." *The Professional Geographer* 46 (3): 277–408.

Monk, Janice (Executive Producer). 1995. *The Desert Is No Lady* with Shelley Williams, Producer/Director. Arts Council of England/Arizona Board of Regents. Distributed by Women Make Movies, New York.

Monk, Janice. 2004. "Women, Gender, and the Histories of American Geography." *Annals of the Association of American Geographers* 94 (1): 1–22.

Monk, Janice. 2007. "Navigating Uncharted Waters." In *North American Explorations. Ten Memoirs of Geographers from Down Under*, edited by Leslie J. King, 107–124. Victoria, BC, Canada: Trafford.

Monk, Janice and Susan Hanson. 1982. "On Not Excluding Half of the Human in Human Geography." *The Professional Geographer* 34 (1): 11–23.

Nairn, Karen. 1999. "Embodied Fieldwork." *Journal of Geography* 98 (6): 272–282.

Norwood, Vera and Janice Monk, eds. 1987. *The Desert Is No Lady: Southwestern Landscapes in Women's Writing and Art*. New Haven: Yale University Press (re-published University of Arizona Press).

School of Geography, Development and Environment, University of Arizona. 2021. "Janice Monk." https://geography.arizona.edu/people/janice-monk, accessed 17 June 2021.

Sparke, Matthew. 2007. "Everywhere but Always Somewhere: Critical Geographies of the Global South." *The Global South* 1 (1): 117–126.

Stokes, Evelyn. 1986. "The Presidential Address." In *Proceedings of the 13th New Zealand Geography Conference, Hamilton, August 1985*, edited by Ann Magee and Lex Chalmers, 1–9. Hamilton: New Zealand Geographical Society, Conference Series No. 13.

Stokes, Evelyn. 1994. "Geographic Naming in New Zealand: The Role of the New Zealand Geographic Board." *New Zealand Geographer* 50: 51–54.

Stokes, Evelyn. 2005. *Evelyn's Letters from America 1960–1963*. Hamilton: Department of Geography, University of Waikato.

Wikipedia. 2021. "Janice Monk." https://en.wikipedia.org/wiki/Janice_Monk, accessed 18 June 2021.

9 The 'Excluded Half of the Human' in Brazilian Geography

The Life Course of Women in a Scientific Field

Joseli Maria Silva, Marcio Jose Ornat and Tamires Regina Aguiar de Oliveira Cesar

Introduction

As one of the most influential feminist geographers, Janice Monk has greatly impacted work on the geographies of gender and sexualities by the Grupo de Estudos Territoriais (GETE) of the State University of Ponta Grossa (UEPG). We first met Janice Monk in Brazil in 2011 at the First Geography and Gender – Space, Gender and Power Latin-American Seminar in Rio de Janeiro. She gave the opening lecture called 'Placing Gender in Geography: Politics and Priorities' and fascinated the Brazilian audience with her intellectual skills and rich background in the construction of feminist geographies.

As access to papers and books on the feminist geographies of the 1980s and 1990s could only be found in large Brazilian universities, it was only in 1998 that we could access the seminal paper 'On Not Excluding Half of the Human in Human Geography' (Monk and Hanson 1982). Even sixteen years after its publication, the ideas expressed in that paper were unimaginable for those on the scientific periphery in Brazil. In the same year, we read 'Full Circles: Geographies of Women Over the Life Course' (Katz and Monk 1993) which inspired us to build a research agenda exploring the women's scientific trajectory in Brazilian geography, their life courses and the relation between scientific production and their daily domestic space.

This chapter analyzes how women who have achieved academic recognition in Brazilian geography understand gender as a component of their scientific trajectory. We carried out a survey of quantitative information in the Plataforma Sucupira[1] and interviewed nine women[2] who are positioned at top levels of the 'h' index. In the group 7 were aged between 60 and 70 years, one of them was 53 and the other 74 in 2017, when the interviews were carried out. They were all white women in heterosexual relationships, and only two of them had no children. The interviews were transcribed and systematized using content analysis and processed using network analysis methodology (Newman 2011), assisted by the software Gephi 0.8.

DOI: 10.4324/9781032275611-11

We found that there was an increase in the number of women in Brazilian geography, but this did not lead to a growth in the study of gender relations. Women generally publish less than men and in lower-ranking journals. Secondly, women who achieved academic success varied between alliances with and in opposition to feminist geographies. The concealed presence of women and mechanisms of maintenance of male epistemic ideas predominated Brazilian geography.

The increase in number of women in Brazilian universities is recent (Veleda da Silva and Lan 2007). In geography, the feminization occurred more recently, as shown in Cesar and Silva's (2021) analysis of 60 existing geography graduate courses in Brazil in 2017. They reported 49.8% women and 50.2% men in Master's programs, and 45% women and 55% men in doctorate courses. Regarding professors/advisors in the geography graduate courses in Brazil, 38.6% were women, while 61.4% were men. The coordinator positions in Brazilian geography graduate courses were mostly occupied by men at 68.8%, while 31.2% were women.

Despite the importance of administrative and teaching structures for women's achievements at universities, academic recognition occurs as a result of scientific publications and citations in higher-ranking scientific journals in the Qualis System[3], created and kept by the Coordenação de Aperfeiçoamento de Pessoal de Nível Superior – CAPES (Coordination for the Improvement of Higher Education Personnel) of the Brazilian government.

The analysis of the research output, in terms of publication of scientific papers by gender, by Cesar and Silva (2021) revealed that of the 17,636 papers published between 1974 and 2015 in 90 online geography journals in Brazil, women were authors in 39.8%, while male authors comprised 60.2%. When the distribution of publications was examined by quality according to the rank set by the Qualis System in the period 2013–2015, women authors were fewer than men at all levels and their representation was even lower in higher-ranking journals. The highest level, classified as 'A1', had 30% women and 70% men as authors. At level, 'A2', women authors represented 37%, while men were 63%. At 'B1' level, 39% women were found, compared to 61% men. The 'B2' level showed 43% women and 57% male authors. The 'B3' level showed 42% women and 58% male authors while the 'B4' level had 41% female and 59% male authors. Finally, at the 'B5' level, the papers had 38% women and 62% male authors. The analysis of editorial board members in the 90 journals (Ibid) also revealed a male majority of 62%, against 38% women.

This difference in scientific production between men and women cannot be explained by the time they spend developing research and teaching activities. Pinto and Silva (2016) analyzed time management by 10 men and 10 women scientists considered high-performance professionals due to their level of productivity and impact of their theories on geography[4]. Adapting the time-management methodology used by the *Instituto Brasileiro de Geografia e Estatística* – IBGE (Brazilian Institute of Geography and Statistics), they carried out a survey of activities performed by each person each hour of the day from Monday to Friday and over weekends. The activities reported were classified by sex and the presence of children and were grouped into five types, namely, (1) research and teaching activities (hours spent teaching classes, in laboratory experiments, giving advice and in administrative meetings); (2) personal care (hours spent with hygiene, eating, physical exercises and beauty care); (3) leisure (hours spent with entertainment, parties, cinema, outings and watching TV); (4) idleness (hours spent relaxing or taking a nap); (5) family care (hours dedicated to household chores, cooking and taking care of other members of the family).

The results revealed that women reported 64.9 hours of activities, while men were involved in activities 60.0 hours from Mondays to Fridays. When the activities were compared taking into consideration the groups formed, the authors found that women dedicated 55 hours to teaching, while men spent 50.5 hours of their time on this activity. In the group 'personal care', women spent 1.2 hours, while men spent 1.5 hours. Women dedicated 1.2 hours to 'leisure' activities, while men had 5 hours for this. In the 'idleness' group, women did not report any hours dedicated to this activity, while men spent one hour a day on this. Women spent 7.5 hours on family care, while men dedicated only 2 hours to their families.

On weekends, their time management repeated this picture with women reporting 18 hours of activities against 16.6 hours spent by men. Women dedicated 8 hours to teaching, while men used 5.2 hours of their weekend on this activity. This difference shows that women faced greater difficulty in completing their workload during the week and so had to perform some of their professional activities during the weekend. When 'personal care' was analyzed, both women and men dedicated 2 hours. However, in the 'leisure' group, women spent 3 hours, while men dedicated 5.6 hours. In the 'idleness' group, both women and men spent 1 hour. Regarding 'family care', however, women spent 4 hours, while men dedicated 2.8 hours of their weekend to it. Among women and men, the difference between the total number of hours spent in activities on weekends was just over 2 hours. Mainly, women reported higher number of hours spent in 'teaching activities' and 'family care', while men had more hours dedicated to 'leisure' activities.

The flexibility of work conditions in Brazilian universities led professionals to take academic activities into their private space. This worsened women's disadvantage as the demands on their time in domestic spaces is more intense than for men, making it more challenging to increase their work productivity. Intellectual activities depend on concentration and, many times, this becomes impossible for women in the domestic space, especially with small children. Women's huge domestic workload is hidden and appears in scientific statistics as low productivity, heightening women's frustration and low self-esteem.

Cesar and Silva (2021) reported an analysis of the curricula of the 60 geography graduate courses and focused their discussion on the programs of epistemology in geography. This subject is relevant because it is important to discuss the understanding of the discipline, its development and fundamental concepts, and also because it is in this sphere that the content of the geography curriculum is set. In addition to the subject content, the main works and authors indicated in the references were listed. The sum of bibliographic references of the 60 programs of the epistemology of geography resulted in 1,804 references. Out of those, 90.3% referred to male and 9.70% to women authors. The 1,804 references were grouped according to the frequency they were cited in the programs, and out of the 10 works mostly cited, there was only one woman author mentioned as in the 8th position. The contents of the epistemology paper in different programs shared some characteristics. The subject is usually presented as a historical narrative, in which one paradigm succeeds another, in a sequential and evolutive way, in addition to portraying an array of male heroes. The way these epistemology narratives of Brazilian geography are built up sets the boundaries of thought developed by the scientific community, creating more obstacles to women occupying central roles in the production of geographical knowledge. The narrative of what 'real geography' is becomes the truth through repetition, associated with the teaching authority of the men performing such narratives.

This investigation, inspired by Monk and Hanson (1982), demanded great effort to state what we already knew: in Brazilian geography, women's scientific production is disseminated in journals of lower academic prestige, thus rendering their research output having a lower ranking than that of male academics (Silva, Cesar and Pinto 2015). Thus, even though women work more hours than men, they obtain less recognition for the work done (Zelinsky, Monk and Hanson 1982; Johnston and Brack 1983). The problems and obstacles faced by women in geography highlighted by our study have been pointed out in the literature for decades (Berman 1977; Tivers 1978; Momsen 1980; Berman 1982; Bowlby, Foord and Mackenzie 1982; Monk and Hanson 1982; Bowlby and McDowell 1986; Garcia Ramon, Castener and Centellers 1988; Bowlby and Peake 1989; Chiang 1989; McDowell and Peake 1990; Garcia Ramon and Monk 2007; Karsten 1989; Little 2007). A special issue to celebrate the 25th anniversary of the journal '*Gender, Place & Culture: A Journal of Feminist Geography*', discussed the development of feminist geographies in the world (Blidon and Zaragocin 2019) describing an advancement of gender and feminist geographies worldwide. However, it also showed that even in the twenty-first century these knowledge perspectives face obstacles and several forms of oppression.

The near universality of the situation is sometimes tiring and discouraging. Even though, the academic contexts of knowledge production might seem similar, each epistemological context has its own power geometries (Massey 1999). It is necessary to understand the powers that organize and configure the places of scientific activity, and how they position individuals into different hierarchies and enable certain trajectories at the cost of others (Massey 1994). We, feminist geographers, must continue to understand the scientific histories of each place to learn how absences and silences are created at universities by the imposition of hegemonic groups. This process of enabling also includes an internal criticism of feminist geography hierarchies among women geographers (Browne 2008, 2015). Women in geography do not constitute a homogeneous group, even though they comprise a group that experiences structural disadvantage when compared to men (Garcia Ramon, Ortiz and Pujol 2011). Women's existence in the field of geographical production is marked by differences of race, sexuality, social class, age, access to economic resources and membership in academically prestigious networks (Rose 1993; McDowell 1999).

The 'greatest women' in Brazilian geography: life courses, resignifications and the construction of alliances with feminist geographies

Despite the aura of science as higher knowledge, unaffected by mundane issues, scientific knowledge is created by ordinary people in a concrete and daily routine, taking time and space into consideration. In the previous section, we reported on the hierarchies between women and men, together with the male-oriented symbolic and conceptual superiority of the production of geographic knowledge in Brazil. However, reality is not simply women and men in an oppositional relationship but requires understanding asymmetric relations when researchers are separated by sex. In institutional contexts, it reveals power limits, gaps and resistances that are developed by the disadvantaged group of scholars. Several women have managed to tackle male power and stand out as important names in Brazilian geography, even in a field in which female disadvantage is explicit and undeniable.

Out of the 52 Brazilian geographers with the highest 'h' index, 23 are women. From this group, nine agreed to participate in this research. The interviewees were asked to develop a narrative of their life course and the paths that led them to a career in geography as well as their evaluation of the advances and limits faced by them in their intellectual career. Next, they evaluated their position as women in the scientific arena, and finally, they were asked to give their opinions on the graphs and statistics comparing women and men's scientific productivity. Their responses were analyzed and a network was built (Figure 9.1). Circles of different sizes were used to represent discursive categories in which sizes vary according to the frequency of mediation between the categories. The circles represent the communities formed by greater proximity between the discursive categories. The lines connecting the categories reflect their frequency.

The life courses narrated by the participants intertwine with phases of their life course within social structures of each time and space (Katz and Monk 1993). These well-known Brazilian geographers presented the trajectory of different phases of their life course in which their careers were woven into their interpretation of the sociopolitical relations in the country, and simultaneously memories and emotions related to building up their families. The interdependence between their professional choices and family constitution became clear in their life course narrative that connected scientific production and family reproduction, public and private spaces, reasoning and emotion. Their passion for geography and the satisfaction from professional

The 'Excluded Half of the Human' in Brazilian Geography   89

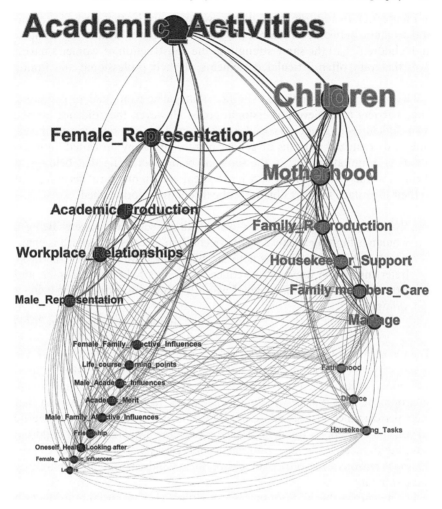

Figure 9.1 Structure of a general network of women's discourse on their scientific trajectories.

Source: Interviews carried out with nine women of high academic performance in Brazilian geography 2017.

accomplishments became evident in their narratives. The development of their careers was intertwined in a visceral way with their family relations. The important landmarks of their academic life were expressed in the women's narratives through links with family events such as the birth of a child, difficulties of balancing mothering with their professional development and so forth.

The women's description of their experience of research resulted in a complex network, showing their bridging of the false duality between what belongs to the private space and what is part of the public space. The connections created tensions between the two communities (shown in black and gray in Figure 9.1). In addition, both discursive communities that formed the general semantic network, structured around the categories 'academic activities' and 'children', had the same strength in the construction of women's narratives that very often articulated elements of their professional and family lives.

The narratives also revealed the fact that participants had to overcome huge barriers to achieve professional goals. However, they did not ascribe their difficulties to gendered social structures and the way science and universities are organized in terms of gender hierarchies. They presented 'motherhood' as a limitation, but in the sense of being something that belongs to 'being a woman', with which they had to deal with in private at certain point in their lives. Jade's report illustrates the discursive trend verified.

> Evidently, the fact of being a woman limits scientific careers. Being a woman is limiting because you have children, because the world is chauvinist, but I think that the activism with which we approach the tasks [referring to the university], reduces a bit this fight between men and women. I was never, or maybe I was a few times overlooked for being a woman.
>
> (Interview with Jade in 2017)

The recognition of a 'chauvinist world' occurred in family relations, but due to participant's competence it did not affect them at university. Motherhood and taking care of their children was reported as being part of the private environment, and that it was the mother's task to find alternatives so that their performance in research activities would not be affected by domestic responsibility. Reports involving the pain of being away from their children, traveling to meet academic requirements and periods of absence due to professional reasons even during illness of their children were also shared by these women.

The narratives thus did not present a political view on social reproduction and the sexual division of labor and family care. On the contrary, participants faced motherhood to become academically successful in very individual ways, often relying on the work of other women, including their own mothers or housekeepers, with whom they developed strong bonds of trust. They recognized the role of other women as accomplices of their academic success, remembering with great fondness the women who often substituted for them in taking care of their children.

The participants recalled their performance as mothers as imperfect, as if there existed a maternal ideal that they could not reach due to their investment into their careers. Ametista's voice reflects this trend:

> Well, I became a mother and (my children) do not complain about the mother they had. They were raised by a working mother, looking after them, and struggling with that. Working and not complaining about this or that. That's why nowadays I ask ... I tell them 'I don't know how I

managed to bring you up, or even if I did it well, I don't know'. There are things that they remember that I used to do, but I cannot remember. I say 'look, I really don't know'. When I look back to what my life was like when doing master's and doctorate courses, working at the university, and with [number of children], I don't know, and I don't even know if it really worked. Because I never advised them. I had no time to give them advice. You know, those mothers who sit and advise their children? I never did that.

(Interview with Ametista in 2017)

Only one of the women in our study mentioned the role of the father or husband as important in the tasks of bringing up their children during crucial moments of her academic career. Fatherhood and marriage were most of the time reported as an element that was more negative than positive in the development of their academic career.

Our participants' narratives show that they built up the ideas of themselves as strong women, able to carry out multiple tasks simultaneously and surrounded by other women who helped them to keep the family structure without letting it become a barrier to their professional achievements. In fact, these women managed to contest academic positions in an arena in which male hegemonic rules required that academic production remain unaffected by domestic routines, seen only as women's responsibility. This idea was internalized as something natural by the women as they had to show the same performance as men, preventing domestic problems from affecting their professional image.

Their narratives show that they lived by the rules dictated by male logic, without reflecting on the gender relations that disadvantaged them in research. This group of academically successful women felt that gender relations did not affect them when they were asked to evaluate their own condition as women in the scientific arena. For them, gender relations mean having suffered attacks, aggressions, harassment or demonstrating fear to face academic debates. Diamante's speech exemplifies this.

Look, from the gender standpoint, as I said before, I myself did not suffer any attack. I've never had any type of problem in my academic life, which is long, I am (telling her age). It is a long academic life and I have never had any gender problems.

(Interview with Diamante in 2017)

Ametista's report also shows an interpretation of gender relations that seems to be an individualized experience, distinct from the gendered social structure.

I'm not afraid of discussing academically or positioning myself next to a man. I don't know if that was the reason, or if I was lucky. But if I had to report discrimination episodes, prejudice because I'm a woman, I had one or two. I cannot say it never happened. (...) I never gave much importance to it, I said something and moved on.

(Interview with Ametista in 2017)

When reflecting upon gender relations in her scientific trajectory, Pérola followed the same interpretive path, saying:

... the fact that I'm a woman is a detail that might have had some importance at a certain point. But I never bothered about that. I never gave visibility to it, I never nurtured that. I feel as if I speak equally to any person, no matter whether it is a man or a woman, a minister, governor, or rector. (...) I've never noticed restrictions because I'm a woman. Maybe because I never paid attention to that, because it did not matter to me if it matters to other people. Whatever I have to say I say, to anyone and anywhere. (...) I see it like that, in my work environment I think of people as asexual, do you understand? I know they are men, women, or of the male or female gender, and so many other possibilities. It's none of my business. What matters to me is what I have to say about something, my specialty. Then, that's it! I never gave much space to that. This does not mean it never happened, I just never saw it as a priority, or saw myself as a victim.

(Interview with Pérola in 2017)

Esmeralda's narrative, in addition to being similar, claimed the need to think about scientific production as the work of individuals who do not have specifically sexed bodies.

I would say that the gender issue has to do with thinking the person more as related to their social function, their function as a person, as subject, and an individual. When speaking of sex, you refer to being a man or women or other sexes. There are many discussions that also lead..., talking about gender is talking about feminism, feminist women, etc. All this in relation to women, I kind of disagree with this biased view. To me, discrimination would be when talking about a feminist, I think, particularly regarding my gender, I am a person who has a social role relating to both, to the work of both, women and men. I work in society in a way that what gives me visibility is not the fact that I'm a woman, but the fact that I have a function, I'm committed to society, mainly, with the university.

(Interview with Esmeralda in 2017)

The narratives show the conception of an academic production space in which gender relations made no difference, and the academic merit resulted from work. All the women remembered their sources of intellectual inspiration, all of whom were men. They made no reference to women intellectuals who had influenced them. The rules of the game that keep male hegemony in scientific production had not been questioned until the last moment of the interviews when they were asked to give their opinion about the graphs and statistics comparing differences in male and female scientific output.

When analyzing the graphs, a resignification of their trajectories was clear and their narratives of women's representation in scientific production activities were redirected. Aspects that had been disregarded up to that point became the focus of their narrative. The women who initially did not consider that gender issues impacted their lives as researchers started to talk about male advantages in academic writing due to the unequal division of household work. At the same time, they were able to go beyond their initial individualized perspective of their own experiences to reach an interpretation that acknowledges the disadvantaged position of women in an academic world structured by male hegemony and the relations between academic tasks and male and female representations.

> Well! The male figure is still very important, it is still dominant, so I mean important as dominant. (…) Most of those concluding doctorate programs were men. Many women have no help at home enabling them to study, and to be able to apply for a vacancy in a graduate program. Then, that is why men dominate here and everywhere else, I can see that the most remarkable presence is the male presence. Men tend to follow a career. I think this has to do with this horrible thing [referring to the graphs of the data presented].
>
> (Interview with Rubi in 2017)

Esmeralda's speech shows the same understanding of gender relations in the configuration of the gender hierarchies in academic spaces.

> Yes! I looking at the scientific production of men and women, I admit that men have more time to write than women. Women have multiple tasks to accomplish, they get involved in household chores, and with children. Tasks that make them busier than men. I would say that while men are more tranquil to stay at the university, working at the office, researching at home, women must manage to deliver their research while accomplishing other tasks as well. (…) It is just as I say, this is not about women being lesser than men and producing work of poorer quality, but this is what they manage to do!
>
> (Interview with Esmeralda in 2017)

The change provoked in the interpretation of the participants about the importance of gender in their life course, after seeing the quantitative data related to the differences in women's and men's productivity, shows the relevance of and need for this research. It creates the basis for dialogue with social groups that are not used to feminist discussions or do not understand the meaning of feminism. Monk (2011) insists that the growth of a gendered approach in geography depends a lot on our actions regarding the construction and maintenance of support organizations, promotion of changes in the classroom and relations within the community. In Brazil, an expansion in the number of research groups in which gender is an element of approach and inclusion of specific subjects or topics on the theme have been a source of disputes. Meanwhile, we as feminist geographers have tried to broaden the dialogue with varied groups, even those that are resistant to feminism, showing through our research inspired by Janice Monk that gender is a founding element in social relations.

Conclusion

Through our research we demonstrated Janice Monk's legacy that has inspired feminist geographies in Brazil and stimulated us to know more about our epistemological context, its limits and possibilities of advancement in gender studies. Although this research has revealed that the landscape of Brazilian geography keeps male privilege alive in the production of knowledge, it was also possible to show that currently women are questioning the power structures that produce male hegemony.

Our research also revealed that the results of an investigative process might result in resignification of one's reality and produce alliances to struggle for the dismantling of gender inequalities in scientific research. This can make the epistemological space of Brazilian geography more plural and welcoming of the multiple possibilities to become a part of the process. This research also opens up the possibility of transformation in the production of scientific knowledge within Brazilian geography.

Notes

1 The Plataforma Sucupira (https://sucupira.capes.gov.br/sucupira/) is a data repository of all the existing graduate programs in Brazil based on information provided by universities.
2 All the names adopted in this chapter are fictitious.
3 The Brazilian government created a national scientific production evaluation system called 'Qualis System' in which scientific journals are classified as per area of knowledge and ranked from the highest to the lowest position as follows: A1, A2, B1, B2, B3, B4, B5.
4 Productivity measured by the number of papers published annually and impact measured by the 'h' index.

References

Berman, Mildred. 1977. "Facts and attitudes on discrimination as perceived by AAG members: survey results". *Professional Geographer* 29 1: 70–76. doi: 10.1111/j.0033-0124.1977.00070.x.
Berman, Mildred. 1982. "On being a woman in American geography: a personal perspective". *Antipode* 6 (3): 61–66. doi: 10.1111/j.1467-8330.1984.tb00073.x.
Blidon, Marianne and Sofia Zaragocin. 2019. "Mapping gender and feminist geographies in the global context". *Gender, Place & Culture* 26 (7–9): 915–925. doi: 10.1080/0966369X.2019.1636000.

Bowlby, Sophie and Linda McDowell. 1986. "The feminist challenge to social geography". In *Social Geography: Progress and Prospects* edited by Micheal Pacione, 295–322. Sussex: Croom Helm.
Bowlby, Sophie and Linda Peake. 1989. "The challenge of feminist geography". *Journal of Geography in Higher Education* 13 (1): 104–106. doi: 10.1080/03098268908709063.
Bowlby, Sophie J. Foord and Suzanne Mackenzie. 1982. "Feminism and geography". *Area* 14 (1): 19–25.
Browne, Kath. 2008. "Power and privilege: (re)making feminist geographies". In *Feminisms in Geography: Rethinking Space, Place, and Knowledges*, edited by Pamela Moss, 140–149. Maryland: Rowman & Littlefield Publishers Inc.
Browne, Kath. 2015. "Contesting Anglo-American privilege in the production of knowledge in geographies of sexualities and genders". *Revista Latino-Americana de Geografia e Gênero* 6 (2): 250–270. doi: 10.5212/Rlagg.v.6.i2.0015.
Cesar, Tamires R. A. de Oliveria and Joseli Maria Silva. 2021. "Geografia brasileira, poder, gênero e prestígio científico". *Revista da Anpege* 17 (32): 244–258. doi: 10.5418/ra2021.v17i32.12473
Chiang, Nora. 1989. "The challenge of feminist geography". *Journal of Geography in Higher Education* 13 (1): 94–96. doi: 10.1080/03098268908709065.
Garcia Ramon, Maria Dolors and Janice Monk. ed. 2007. "Feminist geographies around the world". Special issue, *BELGEO* 3. doi: 10.4000/belgeo.11103.
Garcia Ramon, Maria Dolors, Margarida Castener and Núria Centellers. 1988. "Women and geography in Spanish universities". *Professional Geographer* 40 (3): 307–15. doi: 10.1111/j.0033-0124.1988.00307.x.
Garcia Ramon, Maria Dolors, Ana Ortiz and Hermínia Pujol. 2011. "Universidade e gênero na Espanha: trajetórias acadêmicas de docentes na geografia". In *Espaço, gênero e feminilidades ibero-americanas*, 43–63. Ponta Grossa: Todapalavra.
Johnston, Ron J. and E. Brack. 1983. "Appointment and promotion in the academic labour market: a preliminary survey of British university departments of geography 1933-1982". *Transactions, Institute of British Geographers* 8: 100–111. doi: 10.2307/622280.
Karsten, Lia. 1989. "The challenge of feminist geography." *Journal of Geography in Higher Education* 13 (1): 104–106. doi: 10.1080/03098268908709071.
Katz, Cindi and Janice Monk. 1993. *Full Circles: Geographies of Women over the Life Course*. London: Routledge.
Little, Jo. 2007. "Gender and geography in the United Kingdom, 1980-2006." *Documents d'Anàlisi Geogràfica* 49: 57–72.
Massey, Doreen. 1994. *Place, Space and Gender*. Minneapolis: University of Minesota Press.
Massey, Doreen. 1999. "Imagining globalization: power-geometries of time-space". In *Global Futures: Migration, Environment and Globalization*, edited by Avtar Brah, Mary J. Hickman and Máirtín Mac an Ghaill, 27–44. London: Macmillan Press Ltd.
McDowell, Linda. 1999. *Gender, identity and Place: Understanding Feminist Geographies*. Minneapolis: University of Minnesota Press.
McDowell, Linda and Linda Peake. 1990. "Women in British geography revisited: or the same old story". *Journal of Geography in Higher Education* 14 (1): 19–30. doi: 10.1080/03098269008709094.
Momsen, Janet. 1980. "Women in Canadian geography". *Canadian Geography* 24 (2): 177–183. doi: 10.1111/j.0033-0124.1980.00365.x.
Monk, Janice. 2011. "Colocando gênero na geografia: política e prioridades". In *Espaço, gênero e poder: conectando fronteiras*, 75–89. Ponta Grossa: Todapalavra.

Monk, Janice and Susan Hanson. 1982. "On not excluding half of the human in human geography". *The Professional Geographer* 34 (1): 11–23. doi: 10.1111/j.0033-0124.1982.00011.x.

Newman, Mark E. J. 2011. *Networks: An Introduction*. Oxford: Oxford University Press.

Pinto, Vagner A. M. and Joseli Maria Silva. 2016. "Produção científica e geografia: devassando o poder da invisibilidade de gênero do fazer científico". *Terra Livre* 47 (2): 52–78.

Rose, Gillian. 1993. *Feminism and Geography: The Limits of Geographical Knowledge*. Cambridge: Polity Press.

Silva, Joseli Maria, Tamires Regina A. de Oliveira Cesar, Vagner André Morais Pinto. 2015. "Gênero e geografia brasileira: uma análise sobre o tensionamento de um campo de saber". *Revista da Anpege* 11 (15): 185–200. doi: 10.5418/RA2015.1115.0007.

Tivers, Jacqueline 1978. "How the other half lives: the geographical study of women". *Area* 10: 302–306.

Veleda da Silva, Susana Maria and Diana Lan. 2007. "Geography and gender studies: the situation in Brazil and Argentina". *BELGEO* 3 (3): 371–382. doi: 10.4000/belgeo.11227.

Zelinsky, Wilbur, Janice Monk and Susan Hanson. 1982. "Women and geography: a review and prospectus". *Progress in Human Geography* 6: 317–366. doi: 10.1177/030913258200600301.

10 Being (From) There

Antipodean Reflections on Feminist Geography

Ruth Fincher, Katherine Gibson and Louise C. Johnson

In the discipline of geography Jan Monk has been a quiet (and sometimes not so quiet) revolutionary who has extended the feminist tenet 'the personal is political' to 'the personal (is political) is professional'. As fellow geographers whose academic careers intersected with and followed in her wake, we are deeply grateful for the pioneering work she did to alert our chosen discipline to the value of 'not excluding half of the human in human geography'. Our career paths were made all the easier because of Jan's efforts, and it is for this reason that we came together to write this appreciative reflection.

Jan's interest in the personal/political/professional led her to explore ethnographies of women geographers and included a willingness to venture into auto-ethnography, as she did in her wonderful Barcelona lecture and subsequent paper "Braided streams: spaces and flows in a career" (Monk 2015). As only a geographer who has been trained in both physical as well as human geography could do, in that paper Jan traces convergences and divergences of the metaphorical rivulets that have plaited together to form the strongly flowing river of thought and practice that constituted her body of work. In this chapter we pick up on this metaphor of braiding to show how Jan's career and concerns intersected and influenced our own careers, helping us to survive and thrive in our chosen discipline of human geography.

We trace aspects of our collective auto-ethnographies that we share with Jan—those origins in the wetlands of Australian undergraduate training in geography, those peripheral subjectivities swimming in the side streams of Northern Anglospheric academic geography, those diversions into fields of study other than geography when barriers to career development stood in the way and those joyful recombinations of force and flow in international collaborative networks of feminist geographers. Without wanting to push the metaphor too far, we are interested in how the braided streams of Jan's career and those of our own careers have been shaped by the Australian/Antipodean topography from which our collective attraction to geographic study sprang. We identify the pull of the field, that is, the practicalities and power of 'being there' in place and in person, as one strong element and we play around with the notion of 'being there' as we constitute our collective account.

DOI: 10.4324/9781032275611-12

Being *from* there

As someone who never totally lost her Aussie accent despite living most of her life in the USA, Jan Monk has been identifiable to those of us in the know as 'from Australia'. But has she been an *Australian geographer*, that is, is her scholarship in any way distinctively Australian? While we reject the jingoistic overtone of this question, we are interested to explore how 'place' has mattered in our collective experiences. Certainly, we are all 'from there' and gained our original geographic education in Australia, so we felt it worth dwelling on some of the aspects of this foundation.

Academic Australian geography was institutionalised at the University of Sydney with the formation of a Department of Geography in 1921. It was here, more than three decades later, that Jan graduated with a BA (honours) in 1957. Presumably as one of the leading students, she was invited to come on staff as a demonstrator in 1959, a position she held till 1961. Some years later, Ruth completed honours in geography at the University of Melbourne in 1972 and Louise and Katherine graduated in the honours cohort of 1975 from the same department as Jan. Like Jan, Louise and Katherine were invited onto the staff as tutors.

The bulk of students studying geography at university from the 1950s onwards were training to be high school teachers supported by Department of Education scholarships. Being a demonstrator or tutor meant supervising three-hour practical classes; conducting tutorials on selected readings; and organising and monitoring week-long student field excursions. During Jan's tenure as a student and demonstrator, Scotsman Professor James Macdonald Holmes headed up the Department. He strongly supported an honours program, that is, a fourth research-oriented year of study at the end of the three-year undergraduate degree. It was during this honours year that a taste for being a researcher (rather than a high school teacher) was fostered, where research methods were taught, and where students were required to conduct an independent research project and write a thesis.

It is hard to imagine what undergraduate life was like for Jan in the 1950s. We do know that Prof Macdonald Holmes worked at the interface of human activity and geomorphology and was an enthusiastic field excursioner. He helped to establish the Royal Flying Doctor Service (to provide medical care to the outback) and was a supporter of the Sydney University Settlement, a neighbourhood outreach to the poor working class and Aboriginal residents living in the vicinity of the University (Maze et al. 1967). It was during her time after graduation in 1957 that Jan spent a summer volunteering her labour to construct a house for an Aboriginal family in a white neighbourhood in a small rural town and it was this experience that led to her subsequent and path-breaking PhD research on the socio-economic characteristics of six Aboriginal communities in rural New South Wales (Monk 1972). It must be remembered to our shame that in Australia at this time Aboriginal people were not counted in the census, something that was not remedied until after a national referendum held in 1967 to modify the Constitution. Given this context, and from these scattered facts, it seems plausible that the study of geography at Sydney University was engaged with real world issues, with some concern for, maybe un-theorised or un-articulated, social justice.

In the 1970s, just as Louise's Dad had warned her, the Sydney University campus was awash with Marxists and feminists disrupting the Economics and Philosophy Departments. In contrast, the Geography Department appeared to be calm, civilised and apolitical. There were very few women on academic staff (only one lecturer), except as tutors and demonstrators, and lots of resources devoted to heroically physical field work. No geographical teaching mentioned women much at all, with the exception of the demographic studies of 'natural increase' and debates around family vs single person migration. It didn't mention men either, though text-books like *Man's role in changing the face of the earth* (1956) did give a clue to those who had the political lens to see.

Nevertheless, as honours students, we were encouraged to engage with real world issues, to get out and 'be there' with hobby farmers on the rural-urban fringe (Louise) or inner city residents facing gentrification (Katherine). Katherine remembers meeting Jan in 1975 during this honours year when Jan was visiting the Sydney Department. With some tentative thoughts about proceeding to study a higher degree overseas, Katherine remembers the encouragement Jan gave to apply to departments in the USA, as she had done. The very next year the Department was joined by US geographer and ex-Detroit Geographical Expeditioner, Ron Horvath, and it was not long before a chapter of the Union of Socialist Geographers was formed in Sydney with many early career researchers and postgraduate students explicitly taking on more radical topics engaged with social and racial justice. For Katherine, this meant orienting her sights towards US and Canadian Geography Departments that were at the forefront of the radical turn.

In the University of Melbourne Geography Department Ruth recalls an older, male undergraduate-honours supervisor advising her that women (he probably said 'girls') didn't do PhDs as they were incapable of this. Fortunately, Jack Massey, a younger member of the faculty from the USA, encouraged her to explore the North American opportunity to study and earn a teaching stipend at the same time. Following in Jan's footsteps, both Katherine and Ruth ventured abroad to North America in the mid-1970s to embark on graduate study.

It is interesting to hear Jan reflecting on her momentous move in the early 1960s in the context of an interview question from Joseli Maria Silva:

> To some extent I attribute [my interest working with geographers beyond my own milieu] to having grown up in Australia, outside the British-American "heartlands", in a lower-income family in a place and time where non-British immigrants were arriving in substantial numbers and we became aware of the "other". Also, it was a time and place of being in an educational system that was making resources available for youth who might otherwise have lacked opportunities. Additionally, young

> Australians, especially women, seeing ourselves on the peripheries and not yet ready to settle in being wives and mothers, were attuned to international travel, or "going overseas" (even if temporarily). By comparison, young men were more likely to remain at home for their careers. Because my father also had interests in other parts of the world, though not the resources to travel abroad, I grew up with awareness of the non-local. So we come back to the intersections of gender, class, what education offers and rewards, and place and time.
>
> (Silva 2010, 56)

In the 1950s the only Australian university to offer a PhD in geography was the Australian National University in Canberra in the newly established Department of Geography under the leadership of Professor Oskar Spate (Gibson-Graham 2020). For most Australians seeking a higher education in the 1950s to 1970s, Britain, or 'home' as some still referred to it, was the preferred option. But Jan was one of a new breed of students (such as Reg Golledge, Mal Logan and Bob Smith, see King 2007) who, in 1961, sought the opportunities of a graduate program in North America. That very same year Spate travelled to the USA to visit geography departments to see what was happening in the context of a vibrant university sector that was well-funded by the Office of Naval Research and other defence agencies. He writes in his 1961 Study Leave report on the unintended impact of the 'munificent activities' of the Office of Naval Research (ONR) and other defence agencies:

> The ONR, in particular, seems to subsidise _anything_; the ostensible objective is to build a pool of trained researchers, able to study anything needed in an emergency (whether anything will be left of the pool in the event of a real "emergency" is not considered). However, it seems to me that what is needed is not so much people trained in the more or less mechanical assembly of data… but critical minds. And what seems like a rather uncritical shovelling out of money _ad lib_ is more likely to produce the former.
>
> (Spate 1961, emphasis in the original)

We can read into Spate's comments a precursor of the kinds of criticisms of mainstream geography that were to emerge at the end of the 1960s and early 1970s when those, such as David Harvey, trained in techniques associated with the 'quantitative revolution' turned their backs on 'status quo' data gathering and number crunching.

This divergence into a parallel stream of experience alongside Jan's in the early 1960s serves partly to illustrate the context into which she was catapulted when she landed at the University of Illinois, Urbana-Champaign to take up a teaching assistantship and begin graduate study. As Ruth and Katherine also found, the graduate education on offer at McMaster (Ruth) and Clark Universities (Ruth and Katherine) was daunting, challenging and invigorating.

Interestingly, being 'from there', that is Australia, served Jan well in being able to maintain focus on a PhD topic that was highly original and socially significant, not only at the time, but to this day. For her dissertation, she returned to Australia to conduct field research into the lives and housing conditions of Aboriginal Australians living in the towns of New South Wales. Along with another notable woman geographer, Fay Gale, she was one of the first researchers to shed light on 'urbanised' (albeit in rural towns) First Nations communities, working with community members to record stories of their lives and families (Monk 1972). Decades later that work was re-visited with colleague Richie Howitt when they re-engaged with present-day members of the communities in which she conducted interviews so long ago. An Australian Research Council grant allowed Jan to reconnect and leave her old notes and photos in the possession of family members.

The grounding Jan received in geography in Australia guided some of the streams of her career. Certainly, her continued interest in Indigenous communities can be traced back to her earliest research channels. And how did our early Australian training in geography influence we three women geographers? It is hard to pin down how 'place' has mattered, but part of what we share by having grown up Antipodean is a slightly disrespectful attitude to academic hierarchy, especially that of the British-American academic heartland and, through our undergraduate honours experience, a love of the practice of geographic research and touch of adventurousness.

Not being there

As much as the streams of our careers have found nourishing wetlands and easy slopes, there have been significant pinch-points and barriers that have forced diversions into unexpected channels leading in seemingly different directions. Cracking the employment market, making a disciplinary mark, finding a convivial intellectual home proved not to be easy within geography. All of us have been forced outside our chosen discipline to advance our academic careers. This is the sense in which we have learnt from *not* being there in geography.

After graduating with her PhD at the University of Illinois in 1972, Jan assumed the position of Assistant Professor in the Department of Geography where she had worked as a Teaching Assistant in the early phases of her graduate career. After eight years in this role from 1972 to 1980 she was denied tenure. Her research on geographic education and teacher training and her dissertation research on Australian Aboriginal communities were not appreciated by the all-male committee. Katherine remembers Jan recounting her story of inner turmoil and triumph as, many years later and as President of the Association of American Geographers (AAG: later renamed American Association of Geographers), she had to make some kind of award to the male geographer who had been head of the tenure committee that refused to endorse her tenure application! Facing unemployment, it was at this point that Jan was recruited to the position of Associate Director (and later Executive Director) of the Southwest Institute for Research on Women (SIROW) at the University of Arizona.

Leaving geography to lead a Women's Studies program was a major career channel change that had the unexpected effect of unleashing a torrent of creativity and discipline-shaping scholarship. Just two years after this move in 1982 Jan and Susan Hanson published their landmark paper in *The Professional Geographer* 'On Not Excluding Half of the Human in Human Geography' and Jan, Susan and Wilbur Zelinsky published 'Women and Geography: Review and Prospectus' in *Progress in Human Geography* (Zelinsky et al. 1982). The most important aspects of these two essays were in a way their most banal—the counting of women and men in geography departments, as undergraduate and then graduate students, as editors and contributors to academic journals. But these simple head counts affirmed the vital importance and power of 'being there'; of women being within (or more usually not within) the academy. The power of such descriptions and the implicit demand for inclusion was profound. Such observations had not been made so publicly before, let alone in some of the most prestigious journals. Further, the analysis in these essays was of a discipline that concerned itself primarily with the worlds of men, a focus that not only excluded half of the world's population, but which meant that studies of, for example, the journey to work, were seriously partial and inaccurate. Any idea that women's experiences might have been different, let alone limited by the very transport systems that were being described, was extraordinarily radical.

With these revolutionary interventions out in the world, Jan turned herself to redressing 'the dearth of attention to women's issues, explicit or implicit [that] plagues all branches of human geography' (Monk and Hanson 1982, 11). Meshing feminist theory, politics and a focus on women's experiences into the core of human geography was to be one of the major intellectual contributions Jan made. Her two landmark co-edited collections *The Desert is No Lady: Southwestern Landscapes in Women's Writing and Art* (1987) and *Western Women: Their Land, Their Lives* (1988) brought to light, for example, new perspectives on how landscape is understood and represented drawing on cultural data including women's writing, art works and travel accounts.

All of us share this experience of channel switching into other disciplines to continue an academic career. In a sense we have all found ways of 'working around' institutional sexism. Like Jan, we have found that the time 'not there' in geography has enriched our geographic research. So, while entering these cross-cutting streams may not always have been a desired course, they have been extremely stimulating.

In the early 1990s the Monash University Department of Geography and Environmental Science was a male bastion. With no new resources to work with, the newly appointed Head and Aussie returnee from the USA, Professor Gordon Clark, cooked up the plan to advertise a joint appointment with the Centre for Women's Studies and gained approval from a supportive Faculty of Arts. Katherine jumped in, moving from the University of Sydney where she had been lecturing from 1984 to 1991 in her 'old' Department. With some trepidation, she joined a high-powered Women's Studies team, including poststructuralist feminist theoreticians Elizabeth Grosz and Terry Threadgold, as Director of the Centre. This 50/50 appointment was shared with Geography and Environmental Science. At an early workshop to introduce the idea of feminist geography to the Department (including as speakers Ruth Fincher, Hilary Winchester, Jane Jacobs, Robyn Dowling, Gabrielle Meagher, Lauren Costello and herself) she came across one of her senior male colleagues 'jokingly' attempting to burn the sign indicating what room the session was in—and he was one of the friendly ones! The extensive education in feminism gained by having to teach a Master's Women's Studies program alongside some world leading scholars at Monash over seven years had a lasting impact on her thinking. It was during this time that she and Julie Graham, as J.K. Gibson-Graham, published *The End of Capitalism (As We Knew It): A Feminist Critique of Political Economy* (1996).

For Louise reading the now iconic piece 'On not excluding half the human in human geography' (1982) in the early 1980s was earth shattering. At last, so much of her earlier experience in academia could be seen for what it was—a highly structured system that marginalised women and their experiences from the discipline. Louise stayed on at the University of Sydney after completing her honours degree to undertake a Research Masters in phenomenology and Historical Geography. When she applied to upgrade this to a PhD, she was blocked by the very male academic she tutored for. It was a different senior male who did not extend her contract, as was done for her male colleagues in a similar situation. A frantic search for other employment ensued.

Louise subsequently moved to Deakin University in Geelong, Victoria, an institution that was boldly exploring the real possibilities offered by interdisciplinarity. As a Human Geographer she joined historians, sociologists, literary and fine arts scholars in defining and teaching Australian Studies. It was here too and with a comparable sense of innovation—but also before rabid opposition—that Women's Studies came into being in the mid-1980s. Like Katherine, Louise was introduced to feminist scholars, theory and politics by this experience. She found the challenge of merging geography with Socialist Feminist thinking critical to her understanding of the shifting sexual division of labour in Australia's collapsing textile industry, a process she documented for her PhD (Johnson 1990a). It was as a result of this knowledge and related publications, including replicating Jan's head counts of Australian geography (Johnson 1985), that the University of Waikato in Aotearoa New Zealand approached Louise to teach feminist geography, which she did from 1988 to 1990 (Johnson 1990b) before returning once more to Australian Studies at Deakin. While over the next 30 years Louise either taught, fought to maintain, or (re)introduced geography at Deakin, her forced departure in 2020 means that the discipline will cease to exist there from 2022. This recent history is a reminder that what Jan fought for needs to continue, when maintaining gains is as difficult as securing them in the first place, be it women's employment or our very discipline itself.

Ruth's early academic career was spent working as an Assistant Professor in geography departments at McGill and McMaster Universities in Canada before returning to Australia and the University of Melbourne in the mid-1980s. She also navigated career obstacles in geography and spent a decade outside the discipline in a Faculty of Architecture and Urban Planning and in two research centres of Australian Studies and Migration Studies. In the early 1990s she was the only woman on the academic staff in the Melbourne Geography Department and remained on a contract. It seemed to be taking a long time to get a permanent position compared to what was happening with her male colleagues.

With an avid interest in public policy, she accepted the invitation for a secondment to become a Manager of Research at the federal government's Bureau of Immigration Research. There, she remembers fondly working with two other (non-geographer) colleagues to successfully propose a government-funded research program on women in migration. This resulted in the co-authored book *Gender Equity and Australian Immigration Policy* (Fincher et al. 1994; and see Fincher 1997). Collaborating across the 1990s with fine feminist scholars from the built environment disciplines, history and migration and multicultural studies has had a lasting impact on Ruth's writing and intellectual pursuits. Working with other feminist academics from across Melbourne University, Ruth helped to develop seminars, share research and make curriculum and committee structures more gender-inclusive. Seeing the ways that feminism threaded through other disciplines and inter-disciplines was helpful to her thinking about the possibilities of feminism in geography. Like Jan, she has always published in geography's journals, even when she worked formally outside the discipline.

There is another sense in which *not* being there has featured in Jan's scholarship, and this is in her attention to women geographers who were largely denied positions in academic, i.e. university-based, geography. She gained great pleasure in

> excavating the histories of women geographers in the US from the late nineteenth century and continuing into the 1970s. How did they envision their work? What challenges did they face, especially from male-dominated universities, and how did they contribute to education and society?
>
> (Monk 2015, 17)

Through archival documents, correspondence and interviews in the 1980s when some women geographers who had worked in the 1930s were still alive, Jan documented the circumstances and contributions of women geographers working in universities (not many), those in teacher-training institutions (far more) and women employed in US government agencies in Washington. Her interest in the teaching of geography teachers, and who these teachers were, is another of those streams that connects back to her work from 1967 to 1971 in the Office of Instructional Resources at the University of Illinois and perhaps even further back to her fellow undergraduate students at Sydney University training to head off into high school teaching.

Being there *together*

Geography will never be the same, never as sexist, as it was up until the 1980s. This is because Jan forced a wide and inclusive channel through the male terrain of academic geography righting the gender balance in the discipline and creating space for women geographers to be there *together*, feeling legitimate, in joyful, supportive and increasingly powerful networks. Single-handedly she improved the head count in geography for women scholars by writing countless letters of reference or assessing applications for promotion for geographers all over the world. She put women geographers' names forward for awards with organisations like the AAG and International Geographical Union (IGU), so they were visible when the awards were made. She took on leadership roles in the organisations she was involved in—as President of the AAG and Vice-President of the IGU—and exercised her principles there in how she performed in those roles.

A strong principle of Jan's strategic actions to transform geography has been the practical importance of being there *together*. To this point, Ruth remembers her first contact with Jan well. It was on the wintery day of her wedding (!) in Canada in the early 1980s, when Jan phoned her at home to discuss what they could do to help another Australian woman geographer living in North America who was in difficulty. Since then, for nearly 40 years, they have kept in touch. Jan involved Ruth in her plans and activities for women in international geography, especially in the IGU's Gender and Geography Commission, wrote references for her when she needed them and helped her chart out a career amongst the feminist geographers of the world.

We have all benefitted from Jan's constant presence in leading women and feminist geographers from around the world and setting up institutional forums for their networking and discussions. Jan saw clearly the ways that institutions like the IGU could provide accessible pathways for women to be affiliated with major and respected international institutions. In the workshops and conferences of the Gender and Geography Commission, often preceding a major IGU Congress, Jan lent her support to local organisers to create lively and enjoyable events at which participants learned a great deal about local geographies and local places (see Figure 10.1). Katherine remembers very well attending with Julie Graham the workshop organised by the IGU Commission on Geographical Perspectives on Women at Rutgers University, New Brunswick in 1992 after the IGU Congress meeting in Washington, with Jan in attendance. It was here in a dorm room on the campus that the joint authorial persona of J.K. Gibson-Graham was 'born' in post-modernist inspired hilarity and dawning seriousness, sometime before going on to present a paper on 'Mining town women and the ambiguities of political activism' (a precursor to Gibson-Graham 1994).

Jan's attendance at these events was always accompanied by strategy sessions, to plan for what the Gender and Geography Commission would do next. Over the years, feminist geographers from numerous nations who were

Figure 10.1 Janice Monk (USA), Saraswati Raju (India), Maria Dolors Garcia Ramon (Spain), IGU Gender and Geography Conference, Jerusalem, 2010.

(Photo: Ruth Fincher)

setting up gender and geography organisations or panels in their own countries could count on connection to the IGU body to publicise their efforts and support them intellectually.

With Jan as a role model, Ruth has participated actively in national and international organisations of geography including on the executives of the Canadian Association of Geographers, the Institute of Australian Geographers, the IGU Gender and Geography Commission and the IGU itself. She has endeavoured to be a voice of (feminist) geography on the executives of broader-focused organisations—the International Social Science Council and the newly formed International Science Council. In Australia, Louise went on to not only emulate the head counts of women in the discipline (Johnson 1985, 2000) but also learnt from Jan the power of the collective voice as she encouraged Louise and others (including Ruth) to set up the Gender and Geography Group within the Institute of Australian Geographers. Acting as a support network, the group also convened sessions on gender and sexuality at the annual conferences, while individuals provided mentoring and guidance to younger women to assist in completing higher degrees, juggling home and professional lives, getting and keeping jobs, attending local and international conferences, publishing and being promoted. Jan had not only taught us through her writing but had demonstrated through her actions that supporting other women was fundamental to an inclusive discipline.

Over the last three decades the Gender and Geography Commission of the IGU has dramatically increased the visibility of feminist and gender geography in the Anglo world and, with much effort and increasing success, has developed alliances between geographers from different countries interested in questions of gender and place (Huang et al. 2017). Jan's work with Spanish speaking geographers started to break down another fundamental intellectual as well as political barrier in the discipline—its anchoring in the Anglosphere and quiet insistence that anything worth reading has to be in English—and to ensure through her roles within the professional associations and on editorial boards that her seniority and power were indeed used for good, to internationalise as well as include and practically support huge numbers of female geographers. Certainly, there remain regional variations in participation of the work of the Gender and Geography Commission, usually for institutional reasons and academic politics (see Monk 2018), and '… considerable barriers and uneven power relations remain, including colonial biases, the marginalization of LGBTQ issues, as well as uneven progress and the racialization of the discipline in different parts of the world' (Huang et al. 2017, 933).

Drawing others in, collaborating and partnering with them, is what doing science is all about. Place matters in all things, as does the perspectives of those from different places. Jan put this into practice in her own working life. She found it important to be there in person in places (sometimes overseas from where one mostly is resident), to be 'in the field' and displacing oneself from one's normal milieu. Grounding one's own scientific research in being there in places is the basis of most geography, as she had learned as an undergrad. Jan has embodied that understanding. But she has also demonstrated that going out and looking at other researchers' field and research places aids our learning and development as researchers in our own places. Furthermore, of course, it is great fun and builds a lifelong network of colleagues and friends. It is a source of great happiness for Katherine to remember the day trip Jan took her and Julie on to visit the Arizona-Sonora Desert Museum outside of Tucson, just two days before Julie died (See Figure 10.2). J.K. Gibson Graham was visiting to give the Jan Monk lecture at the University of Arizona (Gibson-Graham 2011). Jan insisted on us seeing some desert landscapes and, though Julie was quite weak, she was a huge lover of plants and couldn't resist the offer. What a great benefit of our discipline it is to be so centred on being in the field and observing aspects of environment and place closely. In her work and institutional practice Jan took full advantage of this!

We regard this work of Jan's with many, many contemporary women and feminist geographers, and her creation of institutional supports for them, as far more than 'service'. She did much more of it, and more imaginatively, than the word 'service' could ever conjure. She made her own home available for travelling geographers who needed to be in Arizona and who would be helped by her accommodation, guidance and company when they were there. Ruth recalls a wonderful stay in the little guesthouse at the back of Jan's home in Tucson, when visiting the University of Arizona (like

Figure 10.2 Janice Monk, Vincent Del Casino, Paul Robbins, Sarah Moore, Katherine Gibson, Sallie Marston, Julie Graham, and Daoquin Tong at dinner after presenting the Jan Monk Lecture, Tucson, 2010.

(Photo: J.P. Jones III)

Gibson-Graham) to deliver the annual Jan Monk Distinguished Lecture (Fincher 2007). The visitor's book that Jan kept there in her guesthouse indeed lists a formidable array of geographers from around the world! Jan regularly attended colleagues' conference presentations and set up conference sessions to showcase feminist geographers. She was always there at conferences and the fieldtrips they offered and these, under her watch, became sites of networking and encouragement for women, especially more junior women. Louise fondly remembers the salons Jan held in her rooms at the AAG when she would invite all and sundry for drinks, warmth and good conversation, an offer enthusiastically accepted by many female geographers overwhelmed by the scale and anonymity of the event.

Conclusion

The braided streams of Jan's professional career have been path-breaking and agenda-setting. She sought to transform the practice and content of contemporary geography to ensure that women's presence and voices are recognised and that the work of feminist geographers in the discipline is recorded and appreciated. Following in her wake, our careers have been shaped by some of the similar forces and obstacles that Jan encountered, but our professional life courses have been made all the smoother because of her actions. As fellow feminist geographers hailing from Australia (some people's Antipodes) we are proud of Jan. While in some ways an outsider, as a woman and an Australian she became a central figure in the international discipline of geography. She and we believe in the importance of being there to get things done, not just being there ourselves but together with women and feminist geographers from all over the world, being there in geography's central activities. We see only a positive future of further disciplinary braiding inspired by this work and led by many of those women Jan has supported.

References

Fincher, Ruth. 1997. "Gender, ethnicity and age in immigration for an Australian nation." *Environment and Planning A* 29: 217–236.

Fincher, Ruth. 2007. "Space, gender and institutions in processes creating difference. The Jan Monk Distinguished Lecture 2006." *Gender, Place and Culture* 14 (1): 5–27.

Fincher, Ruth, Lois Foster, and Rosemary Wilmot 1994. *Gender Equity and Australian Immigration Policy*. Canberra: Australian Government Publishing Service.

Gibson-Graham, J. K. 1994. "Stuffed if I know: reflections on postmodern feminist social research." *Gender, Place and Culture* 1 (2): 205–224.

Gibson-Graham, J. K. 1996. *The End of Capitalism (As We Knew It): A Feminist Critique of Political Economy*. Oxford, UK and Cambridge, USA: Blackwell. (Republished in 2006 with New Introduction by University of Minnesota Press).

Gibson-Graham, J. K. 2011. "A feminist project of belonging for the Anthropocene." *Gender, Place and Culture* 18 (1): 1–18.

Gibson-Graham, J. K. 2020. "Reading for difference in the archives of tropical geography: imagining an(other) economic geography for beyond the Anthropocene. The 2016 Neil Smith Lecture." *Antipode* 52 (1): 12–35.

Huang, Shirlena, Janice Monk, Joos Droogleever Fortuijn, Maria Dolors Garcia Ramon, Janet Henshall Momsen. 2017. "A continuing agenda for gender: the role of the IGU Commission on gender and geography." *Gender, Place and Culture* 24 (7): 919–938.

Johnson, Louise C. 1985. "Gender, gene(r)ics and the possibility of feminist geography." *Australian Geographical Studies* 23 (1): 161–171.

Johnson, Louise C. 1990a. "New patriarchal economies in the Australian textile industry." *Antipode* 22 (1): 1–32.

Johnson, Louise C. 1990b. "New courses for gendered geography: teaching feminist geography at the University of Waikato." *Australian Geographical Studies* 28: 16–28.

Johnson, Louise C. with Jane Jacobs and Jackie Huggins. 2000. *Placebound: Australian Feminist Geographies*. Melbourne: Oxford University Press.

King, Lesley J. 2007. *North American Explorations: Ten Memoirs of Geographers from Down Under*. Vancouver BC: Trafford Press.

Maze, Wilson H., Eric R. Woolmington, and Kenneth W. Robinson. 1967. "James Macdonald Holmes obituary" *Australian Geographer* 10 (3): 220–222.

Monk, Janice. 1972. *Socio-Economic Characteristics of Six Aboriginal Communities in Australia: A Comparative Ecological Study*. PhD Dissertation, University of Illinois, Urbana-Champaign.

Monk, Janice. 2015. "Braided streams: spaces and flows in a career." *Documents d'Analisi Geografica* 61 (1): 5–20.

Monk, Janice. 2018. "Placing gender in geography: directions, challenges and opportunities, Finisterra Annual Lecture." *Finisterra* 108: 3–14.

Monk, Janice, and Susan Hanson. 1982. "On not excluding half of the human in human geography." *The Professional Geographer* 31 (4): 11–23.

Silva, Joseli Maria. 2010. "On not excluding half of the human in human geography: interview with Janice Monk". *Revisto Latino-americana de Geografia e Genero, Ponta Grossa* 11: 153–156.

Spate, Oscar H. K. 1961. *Study Leave Report to the Australian National University Council Unpublished typescript*. Spate Archives, National Library of Australia.

Zelinsky, Wilbur, Janice Monk, and Susan Hanson. 1982. "Women and geography: review and prospectus." *Progress in Human Geography* 6: 317–366.

11 Valuing Mentoring

Jan Monk's Role in Creating a Community of Support for Early Career Researchers

Michael Solem and Ken Foote

During Jan Monk's tenure as President of the American Association of Geographers (AAG), she published a column in the AAG newsletter entitled "Valuing Service" (Monk 2004). Jan was motivated to change the narrative around service, which is often presented to early career academics and considered by many senior faculty as a mundane chore that geographers must endure as a rite of passage. As Susan Hanson noted,

> Jan Monk has made service central to her academic career ... Jan's service work demonstrates not only how service is central to a vibrant, meaningful, and rich academic life; it is also an essential vehicle for creating change within, as well as outside of, the academy.
>
> (2007, 29)

Fundamental to Jan's commitment to service was her tremendous skills as a mentor. Here, we consider the deep impact of Jan's work on creating a community of support of early career researchers. Few people will ever be able to match Jan's ability to encourage individuals forward in their careers in ways that have supported major advances in feminist geography, the geographies of gender, and, indeed, the entire discipline of geography. The result has been enduring systemic change in academic culture away from a "sink or swim" view of academic life to one that is increasingly supportive of early career geographers, both women and men, all around the world.

Several papers in this festschrift focus on the impact that Jan's mentoring has had on the development of feminist geography and the geographies of gender, as well as on encouraging international collaborations and research. In this chapter, we focus on Jan's contributions to the support of early career geographers both through workshops, such as those held as part of the Geography Faculty Development Alliance (GFDA), and publications such as *Aspiring Academics* (2009) and *Practicing Geography* (2013). We also reflect on our own experiences working with Jan over many years and invited several of Jan's other research collaborators to share their experiences. We stress Jan's continuing efforts to improve mentoring practice in graduate programs, particularly in the United States, through research projects such as the

DOI: 10.4324/9781032275611-13

Enhancing Departments and Graduate Education (EDGE) in geography project discussed below.

Mentoring qualities and values

To understand Jan's impact, it is important to highlight her qualities as a mentor. In the research literature, mentors are sometimes described as advisors, sponsors, coaches or guides for early career colleagues. Perhaps a better description of Jan's style is as that of a caring friend – a person who listens carefully, asks the right questions, offers the right sort of feedback at just the right moment, and serves as a role model. In the research literature, this is a perfect description of an effective mentor (Foote and Solem 2009, 54–57; Hardwick 2005; Moss et al. 1999; Nakamura, Shernoff, and Hooker 2009, 119–186).

In our experience, and in comparing notes with others who have benefitted from working with Jan, she is an excellent listener. Her style is best described as *active listening*, a term used to describe deep engagement with conversational cues, both verbal and non-verbal, while ignoring distractions. As Professor Richie Howitt (2021) mentioned to us, "Jan has taught so many of us the importance of simply offering a listening ear to young scholars as they find their way." In doing this, Jan seems to completely set aside other work and distractions to focus exclusively on the conversation at hand. This ability to listen actively wasn't confined solely to early career colleagues. Professor Howitt was already a well-established figure when he began to work with Jan on reassessing some of her research on Aboriginal communities and families in Australia. Jan's abilities as a mentor have been valuable to colleagues at all career stages: early, middle, and late. This point was seconded by Professor Antonio Luna Garcia (2021) who mentioned that Jan played the strongest role "as a mentor is with professors in the early stages of their careers … [but], to be honest, also after getting tenure."

Jan has also always been good at asking questions and drawing out details that help to define the situation being discussed. Never one to jump ahead to offer advice or suggestions prematurely, Jan is particularly skilled at paraphrasing key points to make sure she has a full picture of a problem or issue before discussing options. We think that too often senior scholars tend to jump ahead too quickly, with a "This is what you should do" approach, sometimes missing nuances that can matter to the mentee. She never seems to provide feedback in this way, but instead offers suggestions, options or possibilities.

Sometimes these suggestions are what is termed "task" feedback, simply sharing information of which someone may be unaware. In describing her mentoring relationship, Professor Ellen Hansen (2021) noted that Jan did this, on many occasions, by passing along information that paid off in a big way, for example, by suggesting the name of someone Professor Hansen might benefit from contacting, a professional meeting worth attending or a job worth considering for an application. As Professor Luna notes, another important aspect of Jan's mentoring is her support and advice in academic conferences, at the AAG, the IBG, or the IGU. She always had time for you, even as a grad student, to introduce you other scholars, or give you some advice where to send your manuscripts. I remember that even the year she acted as President of the AAG she had time to help the Spanish/Catalan group of geographers that attended the conference.

Jan is also an expert at offering "process" feedback, the sorts of "what-if" questions that encourage mentees to think through all possible options in a given situation. Above all else, Jan was skilled at helping her friends change the ways they approached their work and career choices – what is psychologists call "self-regulation." This is the way she helped so many colleagues improve their ability to monitor their own work and decision making in the same wholistic way that Jan did. To Professor Rickie Sanders (2021) this involved recognizing that

> we shared a special bond likely because she and I were both outsiders – treading unfamiliar waters. In her case, she knew that she was doing work, though important, was very new to the field at the time and took a backseat to the tyranny of grand theorizing.

Mentoring, for Jan, also included whole-hearted, unconditional support. Professor Sanders again highlights this quality in mentioning that "Jan welcomed me and as only a handful of others in the field had done, she recognized that I would 'stay the course' and work hard. She gifted me always with good insights, advice, ideas, and support." Or, as Professor Ann Oberhauser (2021) explains,

> Jan was an enthusiastic and tireless advocate … always encouraging me and many others to advance and contribute in different ways to the field … She gave me invaluable professional advice about navigating departmental politics and personalities in an era when women and people of color were minorities and often overlooked and marginalized … I have learned from and make every effort to emulate her example and commitment to mentoring early career, international, and women faculty and students.

Her mentoring went beyond the professional "and the lines between private and public became blurred, a truly gender approach to mentoring," as Professor Luna observed.

Both these points are mirrored in Professor Howitt's observation that

> She has also taught me to remind our mentees that we are a network of scholars whose ideas give our communities the tools to make a better world. I've deeply admired her modelling of professional generosity, integrity, and service throughout her life.

Building community, changing culture

In many ways, Jan's mentoring transcends her skill at helping friends and students. Her work has helped to build a sense of community within geography and gender studies that has improved the academic climate and culture for women, international academics, and marginalized groups. As Professor Oberhauser notes,

> Jan was especially adept at and committed to working with early career women and geographers from around the world in the field of gender and feminist geography. Jan's networks were intentionally global and built on her interest in indigenous and marginalized groups within the discipline of geography. She demonstrated these areas of focus in her wide-spread and ongoing participation in international workshops, conferences, organizations, teaching, and research projects.

Professor Hansen reaffirms this point in that

> Jan has been such an important part of geography worldwide for so many years. I'm always moved by the number of people who would say the same thing ... that she had a significant impact on their outlook and careers, even more, perhaps, than their actual advisors. I am grateful that I worked so closely with her over the years of graduate school, and that we have maintained a friendship since then.

And the importance of Jan's international work has always shone through in her mentoring. As Professor Howitt again points out, "Her life exemplifies formidable professionalism, and her networking is so generously marshalled to help connect people across institutional and national boundaries."

Jan's mentoring was impactful outside the United States as she reached out to early career feminist geographers in underrepresented regions. She has been instrumental to introducing them to supportive networks and has on occasion taken care of their expenses during conferences, paid membership fees, and provided constant encouragement and inspiration. This assumes even more significance because these were country contexts where raising issues related to gender within set human geography syllabi has proved difficult; funding has been hard to secure; and the overall climate for pursuing gender-themed research is challenging.

Research and mentoring for early career faculty

Late in her career, Jan continued to invest a massive amount of energy in changing disciplinary culture by strengthening support and professional development opportunities for graduate students and early career geographers pursuing both academic and non-academic careers. For well over a decade, we worked closely with Jan on research, workshops, and publications associated with two such projects, both funded by the U.S. National Science Foundation: the GFDA and the EDGE in Geography project.

The GFDA originated out of the concern that, for many aspiring faculty members, the first years of academic life are the most stressful of their entire career. Having focused for years on refining the research skills needed to complete a doctoral dissertation, new faculty often find themselves almost immediately overwhelmed by an array of responsibilities, opportunities, and choices rarely discussed explicitly in their graduate training. Prior to the GFDA, the weight of learning the unwritten rules of academic life as a geographer was the burden of the individual. This self-help approach to professional development appeals to some, but all too easily discourages many highly talented scholars who are marginalized by lack of access to the insider knowledge they need to succeed.

Since the first workshop in 2002, the GFDA program has been trying strategically to assist early career faculty with the well-documented problems experienced by many new scholars transitioning into faculty positions. Working through the AAG, the GFDA aims to change the culture of geography in higher education so that academic geographers come to view and understand faculty development as a community-based responsibility.

By "community-based" faculty development, we mean moving away from the self-help approaches that have typified the preparation of future faculty in many disciplines toward more systematic dialogue and sharing of resources involving the full participation of graduate students, junior and senior faculty, department chairs, and academic administrators. Community-based faculty development, moreover, recognizes the totality of faculty aspirations, talents, and professional expectations across all types of academic institutions and demographic contexts. New hires who are able to identify and quickly meet the expectations for their work are more likely to succeed than those who cannot; and the difference between success and failure is often defined by the amount and type of support received by scholars in their formative professional preparation.

In addition to serving for several years as a workshop leader for the GFDA program, Jan took the lead on several studies conducted for the EDGE project. Jan liked to refer to EDGE as a "research and action" project, placing the focus on policy-relevant questions that advance knowledge of how systemic change in graduate education is conceptually achievable. Her work highlighted the influence of the overall social and academic dynamics of departments on the experiences and professional development of graduate students and early career faculty, an influence that much of the available literature at the time tended to overlook while focusing on the attributes and abilities of individual scholars.

Yet, as we discovered with Jan in our research with graduate students and early career faculty, there is little consistency in the ways various graduate programs prepare individuals for academic careers. Some departments and institutions offer structured mentoring programs and certificate programs for graduate teaching assistants. Others provide graduate students with opportunities to develop grant proposals and guidance on academic publishing. Still others offer internship programs linking the graduate curriculum with community service or work with private and public sector employers. But few graduate programs do all of these things, leaving many faculty members underprepared for their jobs.

Compounding this situation are the internal relations in some departments that result in "chilly" climates, divisive politics, and bitter infighting that can marginalize individuals from each other and departments from the broader academic community on campus and beyond. Even the most talented scholars find it difficult to do good work, let alone persevere in such conditions. These key insights came from a major data collection effort led by Jan and Beth Schlemper in 2006 and 2007. They visited 10 academic geography departments randomly selected to represent a range of master- and doctoral-level programs. Collectively, Jan and Beth interviewed 10 department chairs, 10 graduate program coordinators and directors, 62 faculty members, 121 graduate students, 18 university administrators, and 3 administrative staff members (Monk, Foote, and Schlemper 2012a; Schlemper and Monk 2011). Follow-up studies considered other issues facing geography graduate programs, particularly the rapid rise of master's and certificate programs in geographic information science, supporting international students in geography, and increasing the representation of women in higher education as both students and faculty (Lukinbeal and Monk 2015; Monk, Foote, and Solem 2012b; Monk and Foote 2015), interests reflected also in some of Jan's earlier work (Foote et al. 2008, 2012; McEwen et al. 2008; Monk, Droogleever Fortuijn, and Raleigh 2004).

Putting research into practice

The summative external evaluations of GFDA and EDGE pointed to the growing recognition among geographers of the need to change approaches to graduate education and faculty development in ways that extend the timing and scope of professional development while simultaneously engaging multiple stakeholders in the process. Academic associations like the AAG have a unique and far-reaching role in reforming the preparation of future faculty, while encouraging healthy dynamics that benefit all members of an academic department. These discipline-based programs complement the efforts by interdisciplinary professional development providers on many campuses.

Two book publications co-edited by Jan put the GFDA and EDGE research into action. In 2009, Pearson Prentice Hall published *Aspiring Academics: A Resource Book for Graduate Students and Early Career Faculty* (Solem, Foote, and Monk 2009). Whereas many graduate programs in geography and related disciplines provide excellent research training and some form of teaching apprenticeship, most new scholars begin faculty positions with little or no preparation in course design, time management, professional ethics, academic publishing, interdisciplinary collaboration, grant writing, and teaching diverse students (to name just some of the topics addressed in

Aspiring Academics). Rather than viewing these aspects of academic work as separate and unrelated, *Aspiring Academics* aims to help graduate students and faculty understand teaching, research, service, outreach, and personal lives intersect and interconnect – and how they can use this knowledge productively in the pre-tenure years of their academic appointment.

Aspiring Academics was written for an audience of doctoral students planning academic careers as well as faculty who are getting started at 2-year, 4-year, and graduate-degree institutions. The book is aimed at scholars in geography and related disciplines, reflecting the diverse research interests of the authors who contributed chapters. We also solicited formative reviews from faculty development professionals affiliated with the Professional and Organizational Development (POD) Network in Higher Education. The intent was to produce a book rooted in faculty development theory while offering accessible, forward-looking advice undergirding the needs of academic geographers.

In keeping with a philosophy of community-based professional development, each chapter in *Aspiring Academics* is supported by materials for professional development workshops, graduate seminars, faculty mentoring programs, as well as more informal settings such as departmental colloquia and brown-bag socials. The book and activities are now open access on the AAG website to provide universal access to resources that can promote reflective dialogue while helping graduate students and faculty test new practices in their own professional work.

Jan also helped with the organizing of professional development sessions and workshops at AAG regional and annual meetings. Readings and activities from *Aspiring Academics* were featured in these sessions and workshops, which attracted large numbers of graduate students and early career faculty. Student-led organizations such as the AAG Graduate Student Affinity Group and the Supporting Women in Geography group advised these outreach efforts, thereby participating directly in our shared efforts to promote change in the discipline.

The second AAG book publication, *Practicing Geography* (Solem, Foote, and Monk 2013), aimed to help the career advancement of geographers seeking positions in business, government, and nonprofit organizations. Because few U.S. employers put out "help wanted" ads for a "geographer" per se, many geography students need help finding the occupations where their geographic knowledge, skills, and perspectives can make a difference, from improvements to corporate logistics and sustainability practices to the effectiveness of government and nonprofit programs for the environment and society.

Instead of another nuts-and-bolts guide to writing resumes and how to prepare for a job interview, *Practicing Geography* applies the results of EDGE research in chapters that take students on a data-driven journey into the professional positions and workplace cultures that broadly define the field of professional geography. Each chapter features vignettes based on interviews with professional geographers who discuss their career paths and reflect on the value of their geography education and training for preparing them in their chosen career. Much like *Aspiring Academics*, *Practicing Geography* addresses some of the themes that are central to Jan's life work – such as professional identity, the importance of work-life balance, workplace ethics, and the contributions of women geographers – so that readers come away with a holistic understanding of what it's like to be a geographer in the world of work.

Practicing Geography is part of a larger ecosystem developed to support students who aspire to enter non-academic professional careers. The AAG maintains a wide array of data, resources, and outreach materials to support career advising and mentoring. Each year, the AAG Annual Meeting features a Jobs and Careers Center that attracts hundreds of students to mentoring sessions and panels of professional geographers who share their advice, experiences, and perspectives on a changing job market and the opportunities available to geography students. It is another example of the community-driven mentoring that Jan's work has helped to solidify in the culture of the discipline.

Continuing legacies

The work that Jan began continues on many fronts. The AAG annually sponsors the GFDA early career workshops and has extended them to include monthly webinars, thereby broadening access to the professional development that is so important for supporting faculty. This also creates more opportunities for people in the discipline to give back and contribute to the GFDA mission in a way that honors the spirit of Jan's call for geographers to value service and mentoring.

Many of the themes Jan pursued in her research on graduate education continue to be discussed by AAG leadership as well as through the annual AAG workshops for emerging leaders. These workshops are planned together with the early career workshops so that both groups have opportunities to exchange perspectives on ways of making geography a more diverse and inclusive discipline, among other major challenges.

Although the representation of women has improved in our graduate programs, Jan remained concerned about the lack of progress in broadening participation at the undergraduate level. Prior to becoming AAG President in the early 2000s, Jan and her associates pioneered a geography curriculum entitled *Finding a Way* aimed at encouraging young female students and students of color. Jan noted at the time how the topics and concepts from research in feminist geography and racial and ethnic geographies were practically invisible in the school geography education reforms that started in the mid-1980s (Monk 1997). Her concern was the geography curriculum in schools did not reflect the experiences and communities of women and people of color.

Finding a Way was a visionary effort to foster gender and racial equity in geography classrooms, yet it was never brought to the scale needed to improve student outcomes in the nation's schools. Recent research has confirmed what

Jan and her *Finding a Way* collaborators anticipated: disparities in geography achievement in the United States are enduring and systematically associated with gender, race, and other student characteristics (Solem et al. 2021). Changing this will require an unwavering commitment by geographers and geography organizations to prioritize educational equity in our research and teaching practices. Bringing attention to this issue is yet another example of how Jan has led the way. It is now up to geographers to respond accordingly.

Jan's legacy as a mentor to early career geographers will continue long into the future. She has been instrumental in establishing professional development innovations that have helped an entire generation of early career geographers succeed in their careers, and the programs she has helped establish will continue these efforts. The international collaborations she supported to advance feminist geography and the geographies of gender have enriched our discipline through better mentoring worldwide. In spotlighting the need for better mentoring, Jan has been fearless not only in questioning how academic culture perpetuates unhealthy and unwelcoming climates but also by taking actions that have helped to create a diverse and inclusive global community of support for early career researchers.

Acknowledgements

We wish to thank Maria Dolors Garcia Ramon, Ellen Hansen, Richie Howitt, Antonio Luna Garcia, Ann Oberhauser, and Rickie Sanders for their reflections on Jan's mentoring. We would also like to thank Professor Oberhauser and two reviewers for their suggestions for strengthening this chapter.

References

Foote, Kenneth E., and Michael N. Solem. 2009. "Toward better mentoring for early career faculty: results of a study of U.S. geographers." *International Journal for Academic Development* 14 (1): 47–58.

Foote, Kenneth E., Wei Li, Janice Monk, and Rebecca Theobald. 2008. "Foreign-born scholars in U.S. universities: issues, concerns, and strategies." *Journal of Geography in Higher Education* 32 (2): 167–178.

Foote, Kenneth E., Sarah W. Bednarz, Janice J. Monk, Michael N. Solem, and Joseph P. Stoltman. 2012. "Rethinking postgraduate geography education in the USA: issues and concerns." *Journal of Geography in Higher Education* 36 (1): 57–64.

Hansen, Ellen. 2021. Personal communication.

Hanson, Susan. 2007. "Service as a subversive activity: on the centrality of service to an academic career." *Gender, Place & Culture* 14 (1): 29–34.

Hardwick, Susan. 2005. "Mentoring early career faculty in geography: issues and strategies." *The Professional Geographer* 57 (1): 21–27.

Howitt, Richie. 2021. Personal communication.

Lukinbeal, Chris, and Janice J. Monk. 2015. "Master's in geographic information systems programs in the United States: professional education in GIS and Geography." *The Professional Geographer* 67 (3): 482–489.

Luna Garcia, Antonio. 2021. Personal communication.

McEwen, Lindsey, Janice Monk, Iain Hay, Pauline Kneale, and Helen King. 2008. "Strength in diversity: enhancing learning in vocationally-orientated, master's level courses." *Journal of Geography in Higher Education* 32 (1): 101–119.

Monk, Janice J. 1997. "Finding a way." *New Zealand Journal of Geography* 104: 7–11.

Monk, Janice J. 2004. "Valuing service." In *Presidential musings from the meridian*, edited by M. Duane Nellis, Janice Monk, and Susan Cutter, 69–71. Morgantown: West Virginia University Press.

Monk, Janice J., and Kenneth E. Foote. 2015. "Directions and challenges of master's programs in geography in the U.S." *The Professional Geographer* 67 (3): 472–481. doi: 10.1080/00330124.2015.1006537.

Monk, Janice, Joos Droogleever Fortuijn, and Clionadh Raleigh. 2004. "The representation of women in academic geography: contexts, climate and curricula." *Journal of Geography in Higher Education* 28: 83–90.

Monk, Janice J., Kenneth E. Foote, and M. Beth Schlemper. 2012a. "Graduate education in U.S. geography: students' career aspirations and faculty perspectives." *Annals of the American Association of Geographers* 102 (6): 1432–1449.

Monk, Janice J., Kenneth E. Foote, and Michael N. Solem. 2012b. "Rethinking postgraduate education in geography: international perspectives on improving practice." *Journal of Geography in Higher Education* 36 (1): 25–27.

Moss, Pamela, Karen J. Debres, Altha Cravey, Jennifer Hyndman, Katherine K. Hirschboeck, and Michele Masucci. 1999. "Toward mentoring as feminist praxis: strategies for ourselves and others." *Journal of Geography in Higher Education* 23 (3): 413–427. doi: 10.1080/03098269985371.

Nakamura, Jeanne, David J. Shernoff, and Charles H. Hooker. 2009. *Good mentoring: fostering excellent practice in higher education*. San Francisco: Jossey-Bass.

Oberhauser, Ann. 2021. Personal communication.

Sanders, Rickie. 2021. Personal communication.

Schlemper, M. Beth, and Janice J. Monk. 2011. "Discourses on 'diversity': perspectives from graduate programs in geography in the United States." *Journal of Geography in Higher Education* 35 (1): 23–46.

Solem, Michael N., Kenneth E. Foote, and Janice J. Monk, ed. 2009. *Aspiring academics: a resource book for graduate students and early career faculty*. Upper Saddle River, NJ: Prentice-Hall.

Solem, Michael N., Kenneth E. Foote, and Janice J. Monk, ed. 2013. *Practicing geography: careers for enhancing society and the environment*. Upper Saddle River, NJ: Pearson.

Solem, Micheal, Phillip Vaughan, Corey Savage, and Alessandro De Nadai. 2021. "Student- and school-level predictors of geography achievement in the United States, 1994-2018." *Journal of Geography*, Forthcoming.

12 Students' Evaluation of Instruction
A Neoliberal Managerial Tool Against Faculty Diversity

Martina Angela Caretta and Federica Bono

Foreword

Janice Monk is a beacon of feminist mentoring in and beyond geography. Her work on the representation of women in academia (Monk 2004, 2006, 2010; Monk et al. 2004; Jöns et al. 2017), the emergence of gender studies in geography (Monk and Hanson 1982; Garcia Ramon and Monk 2007), the importance of teaching about gender and critical thinking (Wellens et al. 2006; Monk 2011), as well as her activism and feminist mentorship in many national and international geographic associations (Huang et al. 2017) have been of great inspiration and guidance for us. This chapter draws on her specific work on diversity and on the issues that foreign-born scholars face when teaching gender and critical geography in the United States (Foote et al. 2008; Monk 2011, 2017).

With this self-reflective commentary, we aim to contribute to the crucial discussions that Janice started in the 1980s. We discuss our experience as two European female geographers coming to terms with the neoliberal academic system and particularly its most managerial tool, the student evaluation of instruction (SEI). While Janice Monk advocates for a socially inclusive geographic education aimed at social transformation that challenges 'students' preconceived perceptions of the economy, society, environment and politics constructed through social structures' (Wellens et al. 2006, 121; see also McEwen et al. 2008), we argue that SEIs undermine this goal. After setting the stage and explaining the environment in which we operated as junior faculty, we present original data from the evaluations we received from our students and, with Janice Monk's work in mind, discuss how these evaluation tools effectively work against diversity in academia.

Setting the stage

In recent decades, the discipline of geography has been part of a broader trend in Western academia where precarization, adjuntification, intensification, and increasing demands on tenure-track faculty in relation to publications and external funding have become the norm. This neoliberalization of academia has generated a lively and widespread debate within the discipline,

DOI: 10.4324/9781032275611-14

highlighting how far-reaching managerial and accountability metrics have consequences for early career, untenured, and contingent faculty and researchers (Vajoczki et al. 2011; see also Caretta et al. 2018; Webster and Caretta 2019).

Feminist, cultural, and critical geographers in particular have explored how these challenging and demanding labor market conditions negatively affect women's ability to stay and progress in academia (Collective FemMentee et al. 2017; Manzi, Ojeda, and Hawkins 2019). For women, entering the job market, working in precarious temporary teaching positions, or being pre-tenure often corresponds with the time that they start a family. This situation results in stressful and insistent demands on women's time on both the home and job front (Klocker and Drozdzewski 2012; González Ramos and Bosch 2013; Peake and Mullings 2016).

Under the guise of efficiency and accountability, performance measurements related to publications, research funding, graduation rates, and teaching evaluations constitute the backbone of advancement in neoliberal academia. By putting in place these requirements, administrators ensure that faculty teaching and research activities can be packaged and sold as part of the brand they market to student-consumers (Butcher 2018). In this commentary, inspired by Janice Monk's (2017) writing on diversity, we focus on teaching evaluations and their implicit bias. We do this from our perspective of pre-tenure, female, foreign-born geography faculty employed at universities at some point in our careers.

'Students as consumers' ratings of instruction

At a time when diversity and inclusion are at the forefront of ongoing academic and societal debates, many universities remain predominately white and male. Male networks have a strong and rooted history in the discipline of geography (McDowell 1992; Monk 2017). Likewise, whiteness pervades geography and is manifested in toxic working environments for colleagues of color and minorities (see e.g. Peake 2011; Mahtani 2014; Faria et al. 2019).

The neoliberalization of academia has enabled and reinforced the success of those living in white and male bodies (Kobayashi, Lawson, and Sanders 2014). Productivity metrics, coupled with rising expectations for publication and grant-funded research, are modeled around individuals without care responsibilities. Men are often surrounded by strong family and professional support networks that allow for this lack of care responsibility. Women and people of color, however, are more likely to be primary caregivers and less likely to find a suitable mentor that can help them navigate the homosocial and white academic labyrinth (Monk 2011; Bonds and Inwood 2015). As a result, women and minorities in academia report feelings of not belonging and are hindered in their institutional progress by daily macro- and micro-aggressions (Kobayashi, Lawson, and Sanders 2014; Faria et al. 2019).

SEIs are widespread measures in neoliberal academia that play a crucial role in hiring and tenure and promotion decisions (Boring 2017). This is particularly problematic given the implicit biases present in SEI surveys. In general, researchers have demonstrated consistent student bias against women (Centra and Gaubatz 2000; Mitchell and Martin 2018), racial and ethnic minorities (Smith and Hawkins 2011; Chávez and Mitchell 2020), and faculty that challenge mainstream worldviews (Wahl et al. 2000; Wilkerson 2017), often in intersecting ways. Even when controlling for different classroom settings, teaching styles, materials, and student performance, women's capacities as instructors are judged more strongly based on personal characteristics and in line with gendered stereotypes (MacNell, Driscoll, and Hunt 2015; Mengel, Sauermann, and Zölitz 2017). Students more often challenge the authority of women and faculty of color regarding their teaching competency and scholarly expertise (Pittman 2010; MacNell, Driscoll, and Hunt 2015). Finally, classes on race or gender relations are consistently rated lower, something that is aggravated even more when faculty teaching these courses belong to a 'non-normative' racial or gender group (Schueths et al. 2013; Tolia-Kelly 2017; Young and Hines 2018).

Along with rising competition for decreasing tenure-track positions and funding for critical scholarly research, higher education is becoming more of a service industry that sells a 'brand' to student-consumers. In this context, teaching evaluations are particularly useful to rate student satisfaction of the product they paid for (Butcher 2018). This trend shifts pedagogical authority from the faculty to the student-consumer, thereby threatening academic freedom (Titus 2011). Moreover, student surveys allow for the quantifiable data necessary to implement quality control of education that must be increasingly standardized and homogenized in order to market and sell the university brand (Butcher 2018). In sum, while the discussion on implicit bias in SEIs is not new, they are an additional stress-factor for women and minority faculty in an already demanding work environment.

Evaluating the instructor, not the instruction

Grounded in our lived experience as two untenured, white, female and foreign-born geography faculty in the United States, we illustrate how SEIs are designed to enable and maintain a white, masculine academic structure. Using an autoethnographical qualitative approach (Ellis et al. 2011), we present several quotes from our SEIs of both lower- and upper-level undergraduate classes that we taught at three different institutions between 2016 and 2019. Our SEIs illustrate (1) bias against diverse faculty; (2) resistance to faculty that teach critical content, including critical geographers; and (3) the power of the student-consumer's non-expert opinions on the overall quality of instruction. As such, SEIs risk to undermine the goals of bringing diversity, including gender, and social justice in geography education (Wellens et al. 2006; Monk 2017). While acknowledging our privileged positions as white women, we present our experiences as additional illustrations for the homogenization and managerialism of higher education.

The comments that students made were often deeply personal and focused on us as foreigners, rather than on our capability of instructing them in geography (see also Bono et al. 2019):

> I think she is a great professor. All of her weaknesses were because of her lack of understanding of how our educational culture worked.
>
> While Professor (…) is new and is not used to the education system here, she truly is trying to change her style of teaching to be more like the system is here and help her students understand the material. I know she will improve as a teacher throughout her time here as she gains more feedback from students.

Both statements depict us as good instructors, but also note that we are foreign to the American education system. This difference is clearly perceived by students as a weakness. Striving to teach in a different way and learning the system's culture as we went was our shortcoming and something that could be rectified and improved with students' help and feedback.

The perception that we did not understand the American educational systems, according to our students, resonates with the work done by Janice Monk and her colleagues (Foote et al. 2008) that shows how foreign-born scholars are faced with unique issues. Our testimonies contribute to the continuing gap in the literature about the cultural and institutional challenges that foreign faculty face in the United States, highlighted by Janice Monk and colleagues (Ibid). Additionally, these students' quotes show that SEIs are often directed at the instructor's identity (e.g. Kierstead, D'Agostino, and Dill 1988) rather than at their pedagogical skills. There is also the expectation among students – who often self-identify as customers – to be provided a uniform service by the professor, the service provider. Hence, diversity of instruction is perceived as something abnormal and negative, as Janice Monk highlighted in several of her writings (Foote et al. 2008; Monk 2011, 2017), rather than as an opportunity to be exposed to new approaches and cultures (Bono, De Craene, and Kenis 2019).

Geography as a discipline aims to expose students to a range of different cultural, social, and economic phenomena. Likewise, we emphasize critical perspectives on global issues in our courses (Wellens et al. 2006). For example, Latin American Geography, taught by Caretta, cannot be understood without examining the role that colonialism, imperialism, and racism have played in the geopolitical order of this region. In the Introduction to Human Geography and Geography of Food courses, taught by Bono, students gained a critical perspective on gender and race relations, including urban segregation and the role of neoliberal corporations and institutions (IMF, World Bank, USAID) in global development and the global agricultural system.

Our students' responses show the opposing outcome of SEIs to ensure that all professors teach in the same way. This desire for uniformity also emerges in statements about courses that challenge mainstream world views:

> Everything we read and discussed came back to sexism, racism, or imperialism and while that's interesting, it didn't really help my understanding of Latin American geography.

> The instructor could have been more fair when talking about sexes, races and countries. The instructor made white men and America out to be evil and everything else to be pure. The instructor tried to force these ideas and did not say anything about the bad side of the different countries, races or sexes.

> I think including some articles that are pro-neoliberalism could give the "other side" of the issue could help everyone better understand what neoliberalism is and if they support or don't support it *(sic)*.

In these quotes, students negatively assert how we exposed them to critical readings about sexism, racism, and neoliberalism. Monk (2011, 2017), Wellens et al. (2006), and Kobayashi, Lawson, and Sanders (2014) encourage geographers to teach with diversity in mind and present students with a range of authors and arguments, particularly enriching students' perspectives beyond dominant white, cisgender, and capitalist views. However, faculty striving to put these recommendations into practice are more likely to receive pushback from students.

These statements illustrate how current SEIs reproduce the wider US anti-critical studies climate, also enabled by the controversial proposal and passage of state bills (Schwartz 2021), where professors and teachers are accused of indoctrinating students with radical left thinking and have become victims of targeted harassment campaigns (Freedberg 2020; see also AAUP n.d.). SEIs are one of the mechanisms through which conservatism, racism, and white supremacy are embedded and reproduced in academic institutions (Apple 2013; Johnson, Joseph-Salisbury, and Kamunge 2018). Accordingly, we have been singled out as socialists – both in SEIs and directly in the classroom – and challenged to present 'the other side of the story'. Certainly, our European background as well as our positionality as female junior faculty played a role in students' perceptions of our expertise as showed elsewhere in our SEIs through comments on our accent, looks, and teaching style (Bono, De Craene, and Kenis 2019).

In these course evaluations, students question our pedagogical choices and fundamentally, the critical nature of our discipline. This feedback is reviewed by the university administration and may ultimately impact decisions about tenure and advancement. Despite debates on increasing diversity in academia, emphasizing diversity in teaching is at odds with students' preferences and can thus weaken our tenure case. Additionally, for administrators with a managerial mindset, standardized SEIs are very convenient as they help to provide a consistent, sellable, and educational product.

Challenging neoliberal academia through alternative evaluation of instruction

In this commentary, we argue that standardized course evaluations are a managerial and biased tool working against the retention and promotion of a diverse faculty body, reproducing the neoliberal ideal of white masculinity in academia and impacting negatively the current and future diversity of geography as a discipline. SEIs are fundamental to maintaining neoliberal managerialism in academia and, consequently, support the homogenization of higher education in terms of curriculum and faculty demographics. SEIs are counteractive to diversity and inclusion frameworks that institutions of higher education are adopting across the United States. It is nearly impossible to achieve diversity and inclusion in the current context of a market-based, academic environment. As noted by Monk (2017), our experiences with the student biases on course evaluations contradict the goals of achieving diversity and social justice in academia.

Toxic work environments, micro-aggressions towards minority colleagues, and neoliberal metrics have historically promoted those that have been socially and culturally bred in the white-maleness of academia (Mahtani 2014; Faria et al. 2019). SEI course evaluations, coupled with publishing and funding managerial accountability metrics, have contributed to the lack of diversity in our discipline and the dominant figure of a white male geographer (Herschberg et al. 2014).

These issues of whiteness and masculinity in academia have long been problematic and are particularly timely in the midst of ongoing racial reckoning in the United States. Neoliberal metrics and forms of evaluation ultimately maintain the status-quo and do not challenge traditional value systems in hiring committees and in the classroom. This, as well as a tenure system that does not account for the time it takes to socialize into a predominantly white and male environment, for the overburdening service and care tasks that fall on the shoulders of female and minority faculty, and for how consuming it is to work in an environment with micro-aggressions against faculty of color, thus results in a non-diverse faculty (Mahtani 2014). This is counterproductive to equitable and inclusive educational opportunities as students will not enroll in programs where they cannot see themselves (Foote et al. 2008; Monk 2017). At the same time, institutions enforcing heavily-biased productivity metrics like SEIs towards women, people of color, and immigrant scholars are less likely to successfully train geography PhDs as future faculty (MacNell, Driscoll, and Hunt 2015; Tolia-Kelly 2017).

Providing diverse and critical research and educational content is crucial if we want to challenge structural racism and gender-inequality in academic and societal institutions. In the spirit of feminist pedagogy this allows us to integrate different epistemologies, including embodied, affective, and qualitative research methods, in our teaching activities (Danvers 2018). Importantly, we exercise a counter-politics of citation by striving to include scholars that identify as female or non-binary and are people of color (The Athena Collective 2018). By adopting such teaching approaches, we show our students that the critical geographer is not just the white male academic (Danvers 2018) and that critical thinking is not only happening within Western universities, but that it is also practiced and published in other languages and in other continents (de Araújo and Germes 2016).

Janice Monk (2017) raised a relevant question about how our discipline will attain diversity and inclusion and uphold feminist pedagogies in the current neoliberal university context. We contend that one answer is for geographers to push for a transformation of the way teaching is evaluated. In particular, we call for alternative ways of evaluating teaching that reward critical, inclusive, and effective pedagogies over a particular homogenized ideal. First, several universities across the United States have already removed student surveys from their evaluation measures (Doerer 2019). In many cases, these evaluations merely reflect student opinions and satisfaction ratings and do not actually evaluate teaching effectiveness and whether learning objectives have been met (Boring et al. 2016). The only way to evaluate effective teaching is through peer-review of syllabi, teaching materials, and class observations (Hornstein 2017).

Second, if evaluation data is collected from students, they should focus on pre- and post-assessment of learning goals, while also including a self-reflection on their own engagement with the course (see e.g. Stark-Wroblewski, Ahlering, and Brill 2007). These approaches shift pedagogical authority back to the instructors and provide opportunities for exchanging teaching practices and ideas among faculty in order to improve students' and faculty learning experience and to diversify the pedagogical range evaluated by tenure committees. Additionally, they emphasize student responsibility in the learning process, rather than reproducing the idea of students as clients who can decide what and how they are taught.

Our emphasis and goal of achieving diversity and inclusion is imperative to confront the managerial tools that sustain neoliberalism in academia. Alternative, more qualitative, ways of evaluating teaching that make it impossible to package teaching activities into a single, commodified product are one way through which the neoliberal managerialism in academia can be challenged. With this critical commentary on high quality, feminist, and critical teaching, we hope to continue advancing the work that Janice Monk has set out for us to do.

References

AAUP. n.d. Faculty Are under Attack. Accessed on August 7, 2020. https://onefacultyoneresistance.org/faculty-attack-fighting-targeted-harassment/

Apple, Michael W. 2013. "Audit Cultures, Labour, and Conservative Movements in the Global University." *Journal of Educational Administration and History* 45 (4): 385–394. DOI: 10.1080/00220620.2013.822349.

Araújo, Shadia Husseini de, and Mélina Germes. 2016. "For a Critical Practice of Translation in Geography." *ACME: An International Journal for Critical Geographies* 15 (1): 1–14.

Bonds, Anne, and Joshua Inwood. 2015. "Beyond White Privilege: Geographies of White Supremacy and Settler Colonialism." *Progress in Human Geography* 40 (6): 715–733.

Bono, Federica, Valerie De Craene, and Anneleen Kenis. 2019. "My Best Geographer's Dress: Bodies, Emotions and Care in Early-Career Academia." *Geografiska Annaler: Series B, Human Geography* 101 (1): 21–32. DOI: 10.1080/04353684.2019.1568200.

Boring, Anne. 2017. "Gender Biases in Student Evaluations of Teaching." *Journal of Public Economics* 145 (January): 27–41. DOI: 10.1016/j.jpubeco.2016.11.006.

Boring, Anne, Kellie Ottoboni, and Philip B. Stark. 2016. "Student Evaluations of Teaching (Mostly) Do Not Measure Teaching Effectiveness." *ScienceOpen Research*, 1–11. DOI: 10.14293/S2199-1006.1.SOR-EDU.AETBZC.v1

Butcher, Ian. 2018. "Student Evaluations, Neoliberal Managerialism, and Networks of Mistrust." *Workplace: A Journal for Academic Labor* 30: 234–250.

Caretta, Martina Angela, Danielle Drozdzewski, Johanna Carolina Jokinen, and Emily Falconer. 2018. "Who Can Play This Game? The Lived Experiences of Doctoral Candidates and Early Career Women in the Neoliberal University." *Journal of Geography in Higher Education* 1–15. DOI: 10.1080/03098265.2018.1434762.

Centra, John A., and Noreen B. Gaubatz. 2000. "Is There Gender Bias in Student Evaluations of Teaching?" *The Journal of Higher Education* 71 (1): 17–33. DOI: 10.1080/00221546.2000.11780814.

Chávez, Kerry, and Kristina Mitchell. 2020. "Exploring Bias in Student Evaluations: Gender, Race, and Ethnicity." *PS: Political Science & Politics* 53 (2): 270–274. DOI: 10.1017/S1049096519001744.

Collective, Fem-Mentee, Alison L. Bain, Rachael Baker, Nicole Laliberté, Alison Milan, William J. Payne, Léa Ravensbergen, and Dima Saad. 2017. "Emotional Masking and Spill-Outs in the Neoliberalized University: A Feminist Geographic Perspective on Mentorship". Journal of Geography in Higher Education 41 (4): 590–607. DOI: 10.1080/03098265.2017.1331424.

Danvers, Emily. 2018. "Who Is the Critical Thinker in Higher Education? A Feminist Re-Thinking." *Teaching in Higher Education* 23 (5): 548–562.

Doerer, Kristen. 2019. "Colleges Are Getting Smarter About Student Evaluations. Here's How." *The Chronicle of Higher Education* 65 (18): A8.

Ellis, Carolyn, Tony E. Adams, and Arthur P. Bochner. 2011. "Autoethnography: An Overview." *Historical Social Research/Historische Sozialforschung*, 12(4): 273–290. DOI: 10.2307/23032294.

Faria, Caroline, Bisola Falola, Jane Henderson, and Rebecca M. Torres. 2019. "A Long Way to Go: Collective Paths to Racial Justice in Geography." *The Professional Geographer* 71 (2): 364–376. DOI: 10.1080/00330124.2018.1547977.

Foote, Kenneth E., Wei Li, Janice Monk, and Rebecca Theobald. 2008. "Foreign-Born Scholars in US Universities: Issues, Concerns, and Strategies." *Journal of Geography in Higher Education* 32 (2): 167–178. DOI: 10.1080/03098260701731322.

Freedberg, Louis. 2020. "President Trump Accuses Schools of 'Extreme Indoctrination' of Children." *EdSource*. Accessed on August 5, 2020. https://edsource.org/2020/president-trump-accuses-schools-of-extreme-indoctrination-of-children/635299

Garcia Ramon, Maria Dolors, and Janice Monk. 2007. "Gender and Geography: World Views and Practices." *Belgeo* 3: 247–260. DOI: 10.4000/belgeo.11162.

González Ramos, Ana M., and Nuria Verges Bosch. 2013. "International Mobility of Women in Science and Technology Careers: Shaping Plans for Personal and Professional Purposes." *Gender, Place & Culture* 20: 613–629. DOI: 10.1080/0966369X.2012.701198.

Herschberg, Channah, Yvonne Benschop, and Marieke van den Brink. 2014. "Gender Practices in the Construction of Excellence." *GARCIA Working Papers* no 10. http://garciaproject.eu/wp-content/uploads/2014/07/GARCIA_working_papers_n.10.pdf

Hornstein, Henry A. 2017. "Student Evaluations of Teaching Are an Inadequate Assessment Tool for Evaluating Faculty Performance." *Cogent Education* 4 (1): 1304016. DOI: 10.1080/2331186X.2017.1304016.

Huang, Shirlena, Janice Monk, Joos Droogleever Fortuijn, Maria Dolors Garcia Ramon, and Janet Henshall Momsen. 2017. "A Continuing Agenda for Gender: The Role of the IGU Commission on Gender and Geography." *Gender, Place & Culture*. DOI: 10.1080/0966369X.2017.1343283.

Johnson, Azeezat, Remi Joseph-Salisbury, and Beth Kamunge. 2018. *The Fire Now. Anti-Racist Scholarship in Times of Explicit Racist Violence*. London: Zed Books Ltd.

Jöns, Heike, Janice Monk, and Innes M. Keighren. 2017. "Introduction: Toward More Inclusive and Comparative Perspectives in the Histories of Geographical Knowledge." *The Professional Geographer*. DOI: 10.1080/00330124.2017.1288572.

Kierstead, Diane, Patti D'Agostino, and Heidi Dill. 1988. "Sex Role Stereotyping of College Professors: Bias in Students' Ratings of Instructors." *Journal of Educational Psychology* 80 (3): 342–44. DOI: 10.1037//0022-0663.80.3.342.

Klocker, Natascha, and Danielle Drozdzewski. 2012. "Commentary". *Environment and Planning A* 44 (6): 1271–1277. DOI: 10.1068/a4547.

Kobayashi, Audrey, Victoria Lawson, and Rickie Sanders. 2014. "A Commentary on the Whitening of the Public University: The Context for Diversifying Geography." *The Professional Geographer* 66 (2): 230–235. DOI: 10.1080/00330124.2012.735943.

McEwen, Lindsey, Janice Monk, Iain Hay, Pauline Kneale, and Helen King. 2008. "Strength in Diversity: Enhancing Learning in Vocationally-Orientated." *Master's Level Courses, Journal of Geography in Higher Education* 32(1): 101–119, DOI: 10.1080/03098260701731579.

MacNell, Lillian, Adam Driscoll, and Andrea N. Hunt. 2015. "What's in a Name: Exposing Gender Bias in Student Ratings of Teaching." *Innovative Higher Education* 40 (4): 291–303. DOI: 10.1007/s10755-014-9313-4.

Mahtani, Minelle. 2014. "Toxic Geographies: Absences in Critical Race Thought and Practice in Social and Cultural Geography." *Social and Cultural Geography* 15 (4): 359–367. DOI: 10.1080/03098260701731322.

Manzi, Maya, Diana Ojeda, and Roberta Hawkins. 2019. "Enough Wandering Around!': Life Trajectories, Mobility, and Place Making in Neoliberal Academia." *The Professional Geographer* 1: 1–9.

McDowell, Linda. 1992. "Towards an Understanding of the Gender Division of Urban Space." *Environment and Planning D: Society and Space* 1: 59–72.

Mengel, Friederike, Jan Sauermann, and Ulf Zölitz. 2017. "Gender Bias in Teaching Evaluations." *IZA Institute for Labour Economics Discussion Paper Series* no. 11000.

Mitchell, Kristina, and Jonathan Martin. 2018. "Gender Bias in Student Evaluations." *PS: Political Science & Politics* 51 (3): 648–652. DOI: 10.1017/S104909651800001X

Monk, Janice. 2004. "Presidential Address: Women, Gender, and the Histories of American Geography." *Annals of the Association of American Geographers* 94 (1): 1–22.

Monk, Janice. 2006. "Changing Expectation and Institutions: American Women Geographers in the 1970s." *The Geographical Review* 96 (2): 259–277.

Monk, Janice. 2010. "Time, Place, and the Lifeworlds of Feminist Geographers: The US in the 1970s." *Gender, Place & Culture: A Journal of Feminist Geography* 17(1): 35–42.

Monk, Janice. 2011. "Politics and Priorities: Placing Gender in Geographic Education." *International Research in Geographical and Environmental Education* 20 (3): 169–174.

Monk, Janice. 2017. "Geography Education: Promoting Diversity and Broadening Participation." In Richardson, Douglas, Castree, Noel, Goodchild, Michael F., Kobayashi, Audrey, Liu, Weidong and Marston, Richard A. (eds.) *The International Encyclopedia of Geography The International Encyclopedia of Geography: People, the Earth, Environment, and Technology*, Hoboken: John Wiley & Sons, Ltd: 2731–2739.

Monk, Janice, and Susan Hanson. 1982. "On Not Excluding Half of the Human in Human Geography." *The Professional Geographer* 31 (1): 11–23.

Monk, Janice, Joos Droogleever Fortuijn, and Clionadh Raleigh. 2004. "The Representation of Women in Academic Geography: Contexts, Climate and Curricula." *Journal of Geography in Higher Education* 28 (1): 83–90. DOI: 10.1080/0309826042000198657.

Peake, Linda. 2011. "In, Out and Unspeakably About: Taking Social Geography beyond an Anglo-American positionality." *Social & Cultural Geography* 12 (7): 757–773. DOI: 10.1080/14649365.2011.610245.

Peake, Linda, and Beverley Mullings. 2016. "Critical Reflections on Mental and Emotional Distress in the Academy." *ACME: An International E-Journal for Critical Geographies* 15 (2): 253–284.

Pittman, Chavella T. 2010. "Race and Gender Oppression in the Classroom: The Experiences of Women Faculty of Color with White Male Students." *Teaching Sociology* 38 (3): 183–196. DOI: 10.1177/0092055X10370120.

Schueths, April M., Tanya Gladney, Devan M. Crawford, Katherine L. Bass, and Helen A. Moore. 2013. "Passionate Pedagogy and Emotional Labor: Students' Responses to Learning Diversity from Diverse Instructors." *International Journal of Qualitative Studies in Education* 26 (10): 1259–1276. DOI: 10.1080/09518398.2012.731532.

Schwartz, Sarah. 2021. "8 States Debate Bills to Restrict How Teachers Discuss Racism, Sexism." *Education Week*, 15. April 2021, avs. States. https://www.edweek.org/policy-politics/8-states-debate-bills-to-restrict-how-teachers-discuss-racism-sexism/2021/04

Smith, Bettye, and Hawkins, Billy 2011. "Examining Student Evaluations of Black College Faculty: Does Race Matter?" *The Journal of Negro Education* 80 (2): 149–162.

Stark-Wroblewski, Kimberly, Robert F. Ahlering, and Flannery M. Brill. 2007. "Toward a More Comprehensive Approach to Evaluating Teaching Effectiveness: Supplementing Student Evaluations of Teaching with Pre-Post Learning Measures." *Assessment & Evaluation in Higher Education* 32 (4): 403–415. DOI: 10.1080/02602930600898536.

The Athena Co-Learning Collective. 2018. Intervention – "A Femifesto for Teaching and Learning Radical Geography." AntipodeFoundation.org. Accessed on August 27, 2021. https://antipodefoundation.org/2018/11/27/a-femifesto-for-teaching-and-learning-radical-geography/

Titus, Jordan J. 2011. "Pedagogy on Trial: When Academic Freedom and Education Consumerism Collide." *Journal of College and University Law* 38: 107.

Tolia-Kelly, Diyyva P. 2017. "A Day in the Life of a Geographer: 'Lone', Black, Female." *Area* 49 (3): 324–328. DOI: 10.1111/area.12373.

Vajoczki, Susan, Tamara C. Biegas, Melody Crenshaw, Ruth L. Healey, Tolulope Osayomi, Michael Bradford, and Janice Monk. 2011. "Professional Development in Teaching and Learning for Early Career Academic Geographers: Contexts, Practices and Tensions." *Journal of Geography in Higher Education* (35) 3: 395–408. DOI: 10.1080/03098265.2011.563380.

Wahl, Ana-Maria, Eduardo T. Perez, Mary Jo Deegan, Thomas W. Sanchez, and Cheryl Applegate. 2000. "The Controversial Classroom: Institutional Resources and Pedagogical Strategies for a Race Relations Course." *Teaching Sociology* 28 (4): 316–332.

Webster, Natasha A., and Martina Angela Caretta. 2019. "Early-Career Women in Geography. Practical Pathways to Advancement in the Neoliberal University." *Geografiska Annaler: Series B, Human Geography* 101 (1): 1–6. DOI: 10.1080/04353684.2019.1571868.

Wellens, Jane, Andrea Berardi, Brian Chalkley, Bill Chambers, Ruth Healey, Janice Monk, and Jodi Vender. 2006. "Teaching Geography for Social Transformation." *Journal of Geography in Higher Education* 30 (1): 117–131. DOI: 10.1080/03098260500499717.

Wilkerson, Wade R. 2017. "Review of Teaching Controversial Issues, The Case for Critical Thinking and Moral Commitment in the Classroom." *Journal of Political Science Education* 13 (4): 483–485. DOI: 10.1080/15512169.2017.1337581.

Young, Jemimah L., and Dorothy E. Hines. 2018. "Killing My Spirit, Renewing My Soul: Black Female Professors' Critical Reflections on Spirit Killings While Teaching." *Women, Gender, and Families of Color* 6 (1): 18–25.

Part III
Gendered Geographies of the Life Course
Work and Everyday Life

13 Migrant Women's Everyday Lives and Work Burdens

Insights from Kusumpur Pahari, Delhi

Swagata Basu

Situating migrant urban women's altered geographies: reading Janice Monk's contributions to feminist geography

Professor Janice Monk's research has profoundly influenced women geographers at various stages of their careers even in India. As a post-graduate student, her clarion call to geographers in "On Not Excluding Half of the Human in Human Geography" acted as an eye-opener on the politics of knowledge creation within the disciplinary boundaries of geography (Monk and Hanson 1982). Their argument resonates with Datta's then-recent report in which she laments about the subfield not deepening in India referring to her earlier reports: 'On not holding half the sky' and 'Claiming the dawn sky'; pointing to the sameness that plagued the sphere of Indian geographical research and the need to address the erasure of women's role in producing geographies (Datta 2016). A deeper engagement with Professor Monk's work helped identify the existing 'sexist biases' inherent in geographical research and veering my research interests towards feminist geography. Professor Monk's subsequent publications on the influence of landscape on women's life and work continued to inspire me, and I felt deeply about the meaningful outcomes research in feminist geography would lead to.

In my research on migrant women's lives in large cities, Monk's contribution to women's geographies over life course began resonating with the voices from the field. In the context of her seminal work *Full Circles: Geographies of Women over the Life Course* (Katz and Monk 1993) and the intergenerational experiences that are shaped by changing geographies, the experiences documented by Monk echo in cities located far away from her region of research, even decades later. This chapter is framed on Jan Monk's work on women's geographies over the life course as described in *Full Circles* to draw out variations in the way same aged women build their lives with changing geographies.

Recent feminist geographical interventions on gendered right to the city, questioning the assertion that women's lives improve with urbanization (Peake 2020, 285) and centering "role and relation of social reproduction" to understand through whose labor the urban emerges, have also provided a theoretical lens for this study (Peake et al. 2021, 22). The chapter highlights

DOI: 10.4324/9781032275611-16

variation in the experiences of migrant women in terms of their family life, work and economic security as they contribute to life-making processes that reproduce urban life.

Through this work, I feel deeply honored to be able to pay tribute to Professor Monk's writings which have shaped my research, helped uncover the intensive nature of women's role in the production and social reproduction process and document the invisible care work women perform daily over their life course.

Contextualizing migrating bodies: family and work from a life course perspective

The intensity of the work burdens of poor migrant women in large cities in India goes beyond the household into the waged labor market to support rising household expenses. Drawing from Katz and Monk (1993), the chapter delves into the work and rest pattern of migrant women in metropolitan cities in India by documenting their struggles through the lens of the life course.

Pioneering the incorporation of life course in the study of women's geographies, Katz and Monk "charted new territory" in exploring women's influence in creating new geographies (Katz and Monk 1993, 17). Delving into the lives of migrant women in a metropolitan city offers immense scope for mapping their changing geographies through their life course by documenting biological ruptures and discontinuities. Their experiences along such turning points in life reflect how women negotiate with such events and how geographies are participative of life transitions (Hörschelmann 2011, 378). Recently, studies of everyday lives have helped salvage the invisible work that women perform, highlighting women's contribution to the work domain and labor history (Ramaswamy 2016, xxxiii).

Urban women's life courses are controlled by rhythmic interactions between paid and unpaid work, which women carry out 'without recompense or recognition' (Ferguson 2020, 9). In South Asian contexts, women's social value is derived from the work they perform (Datta 2013, 29) and their entry into the workforce is shaped by gender and the social group they belong to, determining the kind of work offered (Neetha 2021, 85) and stage within the life course (Sen and Sengupta 2016, 7). Women work before marriage, marry at a younger age, leave work and eventually return to it after childbirth, raising the children until their school-going age. As mentioned by Mazumdar (2007) and Swaminathan (2012), dual structures of patriarchy and capitalist production shape working women's experiences of oppression in private, as well as public domains, perpetuated through reorganizing and devaluing their life-making activities, confirming the assertion that patriarchy and global capitalism together exploit women's labor in both realms (Katz and Monk 1993). As noted by Neetha and Mazumdar (2010), the neo-liberal regime in India renders a variety of women's wage work as casual, thus strengthening patriarchal forces within the household. As quoted by Sinha (2020), in Delhi paid domestic work is a "necessity as in the process of transformation in class relations and development of new lifestyles". The National Sample Survey (NSSO, 68th Round, 2011–2012) estimated the number of domestic workers in India as 3.9 million while 6.7 million in Census 2001.

The participants of the study are residents of Kusumpur Pahari, a working class locality that is home to multiple streams of migrants from different regions of India. Located between two affluent neighborhoods and girdled by high-end shopping malls, residents remain assured of steady employment in the upper- and middle-class homes as house-helps, drivers, guards, among others. Women resort to domestic service for income, making it the commonest occupation of poor and marginalized women who play an active role in "reproducing the worker through food and physical care to become ready for the next day of work" at both her workplace and at her home (Bhattacharya 2017, 73).

From a pool of thirty participants, six women were invited to participate in the study based on the region they migrated from. Three women pseudonymized as Kalavati, Manju and Geeta belong to the neighboring state of Uttar Pradesh, and three others named Debi, Mina and Jaba in the study hail from West Bengal, located almost 1500 km away. All have been living in Delhi for more than fifteen years except one participant who migrated to the city on marriage. Three participants, Kalavati, Manu and Geeta live with their spouses and children, while the other three, Debi, Mina and Jaba, were abandoned and are single mothers. All participants are in their forties, belong to scheduled caste groups and are 'live out' or part-time helpers who work in different households but live at their own residences. Though they earn lower wages than a live-in domestic help, they can be with their families for some part of the day (Neetha and Mazumdar 2010, 64–75). The residents of the neighborhood lead precarious lives in illegal housing colonies which are often associated with threats of slum demolition and evictions (Datta 2012, 4). In such an event, displacement to peripheral areas would increase the intervening distance between workplace and home to further 'destroy their relations to social reproduction' (Chaudhary 2021, 213).

Turning points and trajectories: entering realms of waged work

Katz and Monk noted that changes in spaces and places in women's life course play a significant role in how women construct their lives (Katz and Monk 1993, 265). This section explores the life histories of migrant domestic workers who travel to the city in search of better livelihoods after marriage – the first turning point of their lives. The participants recounted their excitement to live in a city away from the drudgery of poorly paid work they performed as field-hands with their parents and siblings. "Dearth of food, clean water and liquid money" in the rural hinterland prompted Kalavati's family to arrive at the city while for Mina it was her deep desire to "*see Delhi*" apart from dreams of "happy married life". When Jaba was abandoned by her husband, she had entrusted her two infants to her mother's care to work in

Kolkata for nine long years as a domestic help, until a relative helped her migrate to Delhi for better paying jobs. As discussed by Hapke and Ayyankeril (2004), their experiences reiterate earlier studies on women entering remunerative work from different positions and contexts that reflect notions of gender and socialization experiences into a gendered economic role. Participants with no family support settled for home-based employment to supplement their family income since stepping out of home involves transgression of social and material boundaries of home and locality (Sharma 2016, 205). Also, integrating productive and reproductive activities for women with young children remains a significant concern in cities since men join temporary jobs which places the balance of work on the women (Monk and Alexander 1986, 395).

Kalavati and Manju initially did embroidery at home while their children were young – implementing 'value choices about family and work life' (Katz and Monk 1993, 269). They began looking for outdoor work near their homes once the workshop closed down. By then their children had begun going to school, validating that 'greater concern for home and family' determined women's choices while looking for employment. In the Global South, unpaid household labor and peasant labor on farms is difficult to distinguish (Hopkins 2017, 134), so women who had worked as farmhands before marriage appeared to have been aware that just as they had struggled to eke out a living *by* toiling on fields in their village, life in the city would be equally tough and through "*sangharsh*" (struggle) they would make ends meet.

Mina, on the other hand, was unprepared for employment outside her home. A few years into her marriage, her husband began extra-marital affair(s) and stopped providing for her and her children. As she was skilled in tailoring and possessed a sewing machine, she began working as a home-based tailor. Even though she had completed school she could only communicate in *Bengali*, her mother tongue. This rendered her skills and education ineffectual in obtaining a 'white-collar job'. Her tailoring did not assure a steady income so she wanted a job outside her home to ensure food security for her children. When her neighbor suggested working as a nanny nearby, she readily accepted it but had to counter aggression from her husband for leaving her own children at her young sister-in-law's care. Geeta began working recently, after fifteen years of marriage when her husband lost his job during the COVID-19 lockdown. Her husband initially resisted by finally relenting due to their extreme financial crisis.

From their accounts one may conclude that spaces accessible to married women for employment are constrained by enduring family commitments with more "contingent" relationships to work than men. Trapped between paid and unpaid work; they have little time for leisure and self-care. Their lives follow a clockwork pattern from the time they wake at wee hours to avoid queueing at shared mobile toilets and bathing cubicles, cooking and cleaning in their own homes before they leave for waged work to service other homes outside their neighborhoods. They return home to tend to their children, cook and clean again to settle for less than six hours of sleep. Thus, women's altered geographies help create new geographies and improved quality of life in terms of monetary liquidity and availability of basic amenities. The following section maps their journeys beyond their households.

Spatial mobility: negotiating the city streets and reaching new destinations

Mobility provided "greater autonomy" for the women participating in this study; but their "geographies remained tied to the constraints of their gender roles ... their reproductive work" (Katz and Monk 1993, 271). Daily travel to work in the city is fraught with issues of safety, cost and confidence. For a migrant woman from the rural hinterland, walking through unfamiliar spaces with no experience of use of public transport can cause grave anxiety, fear and distress. Reaching one's workplace while breaking out of the cocoon of domesticity is fraught with difficulties in the initial phase. All participants recollected feeling fear and anxiety during their initial journeys to and back from work. Manju recounted "*I had got lost on my way back from work, I wept for a while when I realized that. When the feeling of shock ebbed, I composed myself, wiped my tears, began asking passersby and found my way back*". Mina was chaperoned by the same lady who had helped her find her first job. She remembered

> every morning Malti didi would pick me up from my home and both of us would walk together to my place of work and in the evenings, I would wait at my workplace till she finished her work and reached my employer's home ... then we would walk back home together; I wouldn't have been able to manage without her help as during those days I was petrified by the sight of a man walking towards me.

Kalavati's fears stemmed from stepping into rich people's homes, "what if I made a mistake? What if someone scolded me?" It took years for all the participants to shed off the apprehensions of working in other's homes; identify their capabilities and teach themselves the skills to negotiate their remunerations. Over time, traversing through the alien urban space has instilled confidence in them. As Manju quipped, "now I don't feel scared to venture out ... I can even take a bus ride to my sister's home".

Closely linked to the issue of women's mobility is the subject of home-based care work that women perform. Separation of home and workspace heightens women's burden of tending to care work at home and paid work outside. Those who held jobs "close to their homes" validate the fact that they prioritized their responsibilities at home over their roles at their workplaces (Katz and Monk 1993, 269). Each of the participants worked in places located within 20–30 minutes walking distance, reiterating the difficulties women workers experience due to physical distance between their homes and places of work. Working in the vicinity of their homes ensures that women spend the least time in travel and can return home quickly if needed.

The women also reported sharing a part of the responsibility of care work with other woman in their household to balance both roles. For Kalavati, as her daughter grew up, she took care of cooking and cleaning, and Manju had to wait for her eldest son to get married and her daughter-in-law managed the household while she ventured out for employment. This arrangement didn't work for the participants who are single with small children, so their mothers took care of their children when they entered waged work. The inevitability of a female family member taking over the care work highlights the responsibility placed on women and the devaluation of life-making work in a patriarchal ethos that keeps men in the family from sharing household chores and childcare.

Intergenerational experiences aren't starkly different for women who migrated to the city. Participants recollected their mothers having worked equally hard all day at agricultural lands followed by their household chores. Yet, they felt that they were better off in the city as "at least the payment for the work you do is assured". Single mothers averred that their mothers too toiled as much but were happier since "my father was a good man, so at the end of the day she had a partner to share her life with, which I miss. I feel lonely with no one to share my pains and fears ...". Debi shares her fears, "my elder son is a special child and I worry for his future ... who would take care of him later in life?" The concerns exemplify a heightened sense of anxiety single women experience regarding their own and their family's health in the absence of support from their partners.

Strategies deployed by women to balance their homes and waged work vary geographically by class cohort, ethnic group and across time. The following section examines the solidarities and resistances as coping strategies for survival and work among the women.

Resistances and solidarities: towards survival with dignity

Patrilineal-patrilocal households in South Asia help consolidate authority among male members, compelling women to deploy strategies within the household to "maximize their life chances" (Kandiyoti 2012, 82). Within the patrilocal household, women bring into play coping mechanisms with which they resist accommodate and adapt to hostile conditions. The participants recounted their acts of 'defiance' when they decided to find paid work outside their household resisting the men's ire. They also felt that the anonymity the city offered facilitated their struggle, and being away from their kin in the village helped them to negotiate with and convince their partners. Once they began supplementing their family incomes, their work outside the household received acceptance with the partners. At the personal level, those participants who were single, i.e., abandoned by their husbands, continued to wear markers of marriage like the *'sindoor'*(vermillion), *'pola'* (coral bangles) even after decades of separation while going to work. In Mina's opinion, the markers "often shield me from unsolicited advances from men", while Jaba argued that "since he fathered my children, and my children use his family name, there is no way that I can give up on wearing those markers".

'Mutual aid relationships' (after Kropotkin 1904) exist not just within family members but also among neighbors (Katz and Monk 1993, 274). Women help each other locate employers and work as substitutes to retain the job for friends and family who take temporary leave from their jobs. Research on creation and perpetuation of agential spaces within low-income neighborhoods of Delhi has been well documented (Magar 2007; Grover 2017; Basu 2021). This study also highlights the diverse experiences of neighborhood-based solidarities among women living in the same residential zone. Kalavati, Manju and Geeta, from Uttar Pradesh, living in a caste- and region-based cluster within the neighborhood, narrated that elderly women of the neighborhood took care of the children left behind by working mothers ... "even though they stay in their own homes or play outside, women keep a vigil; if they hear a child crying, they go and pacify him/her ...and why won't they? The children are all own, from the same biradari (caste/sub-caste)". Similarly, when Geeta's nine-year-old son suffered head injury while she was at work, she remembered "my neighbours rushed my child to the hospital". On the other hand, Mina, Debi and Jaba from West Bengal complained, "no one would take care of left behind children regularly ... we have to fend for ourselves" highlighting the absence of a cohesive care network for children living outside a caste or region based cluster.

As mentioned by Ray and Seemin (2009), beyond the neighborhood, formation of feminist solidarities across upper-class employers and their economically vulnerable domestic servants was observed in the study when the common-place understanding of relationships between "Maids and Madams" (employer and employees across class divide) is fraught with antagonism, with the employer's homes turned into the location for paid work and a site of power and control, and where the domestic help became virtually invisible as an individual (Sinha and Prabhat 2021, 3). Confrontations between domestic workers and the employers have lately begun appearing in the public domain (Chaudhary 2020); in this context, the experiences of the participants of this study are heartening.

Class barriers do not come in the way of realizing how one's work/service is invaluable to the other and necessary for both the employer and the employee. Debi narrates "my madam makes me accompany her to her friends and relatives' homes and also to shopping malls; she ensures that I wear good clothes so, she buys clothes and make-up for me". This goes on to enhance rather than restrict the domestic help's visibility in public spaces. Geeta narrates, even within home space, "when guests arrive, it is me who takes care of their food and other needs. Since my 'madam' is a working lady, she instructs me to look after her guests in her absence". It appears that "redemptive" amends are being made to the long history of invisibilizing the work of domestic help, especially in some middle-class households where their labor and care is being appropriated and acknowledged.

An alternate reading of this practice may also be interpreted as an employer's efforts to 'sanitising/sanskritising' her help to fit into the ethos of the household (Pallavi 2017). Changes are perceptible in efforts made by employers in facilitating leisure time and providing care. Most of the participants complete the assigned duties and return home for lunch, rest and spend time with their children before they walk back to work for the evening. Those who had grown up children stay back at the place of work for lunch like Debi whose 'madam' tells her "to take a nap till tea time" post-lunch. Jaba realizes, "it is during those two hours that I sleep peacefully; at home I can never get uninterrupted rest". When Geeta's son suffered a head injury, her madam told her "… don't come for work till your son recovers" apart from helping her monetarily for his treatment.

Such solidarities, mutual dependence and empathy between the employee and her employer, neighbors and family, assist in creating caring geographies through their life courses.

"Making connections": adding channels to the braided streams

This study built on Janice Monk's theoretical contributions offers scope for "new ways of knowing" women's efforts to build their lives and contribute to the city-making process in the Global South. Through a re-reading of the lives of migrant women living in Kusumpur Pahari, Delhi along their life course, with special attention to their life-making activities, this chapter brought out the trajectories and turning points women encounter during their life that determine their choices in terms of the work they perform, the way they organize their family life and connect with people and spaces in the new/altered geographies they are located in. Despite remaining entangled in "extensive webs of care" (Katz and Monk 1993, 275) these women forge mutual aid relationships within and across class barriers to improve their quality of life. Single women were found to shoulder greater responsibilities underlining the fact that different stages in the life course and diverse life conditions hold out varied challenges to women in cities.

In Professor Monk's words, she wished to "illustrate how time and place were important in women's lives" and document "emotions that are intertwined with experiences of and shaping of spaces and places" (Silva 2010, 153–154). As a feminist geographer, building on Monk's contribution to exploring women's geographies is a rewarding experience and feels like having added new channels to the mesh of "braided streams" Monk has created through her research, writing and professional engagement with geography (Monk 2006, 226).

All names have been anonymized.

Acknowledgement

I am grateful to the Institute for Eminence, University of Delhi, for supporting this collaborative research through a generous grant under the Faculty Research Programme, 2021.

References

Basu, Swagata. 2021. "Mahila Panchayats of Delhi: Scripting Agency within Low-Income Urban Neighbourhoods." In *Gender, Space and Agency in India: Exploring Regional Genderscapes*, edited by Anindita Datta, 77–91. Oxon: Routledge.

Bhattacharya, Tithi. 2017. "Introduction: Mapping Social Reproduction." In *Social Reproduction Theory: Remapping Class, Recentering Oppression*, edited by Tithi Bhattacharya, 1–20. London: Pluto Press.

Chaudhary, Tanya. 2020 "From 'Spaces of Work' to 'Spaces of Struggle'." *City, Culture and Society* 20: 1–6.

Chaudhary, Tanya. 2021. "Engels' 'Proletarisation' and 'Great Towns' vis-à-vis Dispossession, and Gendered Work in an Informal Economy." *Human Geography* 14 (2): 212–226.

Datta, Ayona. 2012. *The Illegal City: Space, Law and Gender in a Delhi Squatter Settlement*. Farnham: Ashgate. (Published in 2016 by Routledge).

Datta, Anindita. 2013. "Work, Gender and Social Value: Conceptual Links and Field Insights". In *Gender and Human Development in Central and South Asia*, edited by Mondira Dutta, 26–31. New Delhi: Pentagon Press.

Datta, Anindita. 2016. "Geography of Gender." In *Progress in Indian Geography* edited by R. B. Singh, 141–148. New Delhi: Indian National Science Academy.

Ferguson, Susan J. 2020. *Women and Work: Feminism, Labour, and Social Reproduction*. London: Pluto Press.

Grover, Shalini. 2017. *Marriage, Love, Caste and Kinship Support: Lived Experiences of the Urban Poor in India*. London: Routledge.

Hapke, Holly M., and Devan Ayyankeril. 2004. "Gender, the Work-Life Course, and Livelihood Strategies in a South Indian Fish Market." *Gender, Place & Culture* 11 (2): 229–256.

Hopkins, Carmen Teeple. 2017. "Mostly Work, Little Play: Social Reproduction, Migration, and Paid Domestic Work in Montreal." In *Social Reproduction Theory: Remapping Class, Recentering Oppression*, edited by Tithi Bhattacharya, 131–147. London: Pluto Press.

Hörschelmann, Kathrin. 2011. "Theorising Life Transitions: Geographical Perspectives: Theorising Life Transitions." *Area* 43 (4): 378–383.

Kandiyoti, Deniz. 2012. "Bargaining with patriarchy." In *Feminist Theory Reader: Local and Global Perspectives*, 4th ed.. edited by Carole M. McCann and Seung-Kyung Kim, 80–88. London: Routledge.

Katz, Cindi, and Janice Monk. 1993. *Full Circles: Geographies of Women over the Life Course*. London: Routledge.

Kropotkin, Petr A. 1904. *Mutual Aid: A Factor of Evolution: Revised and Cheaper Edition*. New York: Heinemann.

Magar, Veronika. 2007. "Empowerment Approaches to Gender Based Violence: Women's Courts in Delhi Slums." In *Urban Women in Contemporary India*, edited by Rehana Ghadially, 118–136. New Delhi: Sage Publications.

Mazumdar, Indrani. 2007. *Women Workers and Globalization: Emergent Contradictions in India*. Kolkata: Stree publications. (Distributed by Bhatkal Books International).

Monk, Janice. 2006. "Spaces and Flows." In *Approaches to Human Geography*, edited by Stuart Aitken and Gill Valentine, 226–32. London: Sage Publications.

Monk, Janice, and Charles S. Alexander. 1986. "Free Port Fallout: Gender, Employment, and Migration on Margarita Island." *Annals of Tourism Research* 13 (3): 393–413.

Monk, Janice, and Susan Hanson. 1982. "On Not Excluding Half of the Human in Human Geography." *The Professional Geographer* 34 (1): 11–23.

Neetha, N. 2021. "Crisis in Female Employment: Analysis across Social Groups." In *Women in the Worlds of Labour*, edited by Mary John and Meena Gopal, 84–110. Hyderabad: Orient Blackswan.

Neetha, N., and Indrani Mazumdar. 2010. *Study on Conditions and Needs of Women Workers in Delhi*. New Delhi: Centre for Women's Development Studies.

Pallavi. 2017. "Politics of the Intimate Pt 3: The Brahmin Mistress and the Bahujan Maid."*The Medium*.December27.https://pallavir.medium.com/politics-of-the-intimate-pt-3-the-brahmin-mistress-and-the-bahujan-maid-6becf6e2fbcb

Peake, Linda. 2020. "Gender and the City." In *International Encyclopaedia of Human Geography*, edited by Audrey Kobayashi, 281–292. Amsterdam, Netherlands: Elsevier.

Peake, Linda, Elsa Koleth, Gokboru Sarp Tanyildiz, and Rajyashree N. Reddy. 2021. *A Feminist Urban Theory for Our Time: Rethinking Social Reproduction and the Urban*. Oxford, UK: John Wiley & Sons.

Ramaswamy, Vijaya. 2016. *Women and Work in Precolonial India: A Reader*. New Delhi: SAGE Publications India.

Ray, Raka, and Qayum Seemin. 2009. *Cultures of Servitude: Modernity, Domesticity and Class in India*. Standford, CA: Stanford University Press.

Sen, Samita, and Nilanjana Sengupta. 2016. *Domestic Days: Women, Work, and Politics in Contemporary Kolkata*. India: Oxford University Press.

Sharma, Sonal. 2016. "Housing, Spatial-Mobility and Paid Domestic Work in Millennial Delhi: Narratives of Women Domestic Workers." In *Space, Planning and Everyday Contestations in Delhi*, edited by Surajit Chakravarty and Rohit Negi, 201–217. New Delhi: Springer.

Silva, Joseli Maria. 2010. "On Not Excluding Half of the Human in Human Geography: Interview with Janice Monk." *Revista Latino-Americana de Geografia E Genero* 1 (1): 153–156.

Sinha, Nitin. 2020. "Between Welfare and Criminalisation: Were Domestic Servants Always Informal." *The Wire*. March 20. https://thewire.in/labour/domestic-servants-informal-workforce.

Sinha, Nitin, and Kumar Prabhat. 2021. *Lesser Lives: Stories of Domestic Servants in India*. New Delhi: Pan Macmillan India.

Swaminathan, Padmini. 2012. *Women and Work*. Hyderabad: Orient Blackswan.

14 Challenging Instability

Women's Multigenerational Narratives of Work in the Margins of Central and Eastern Europe

Doris Wastl-Walter, Ágnes Erőss and Monika Mária Váradi

Introduction

Jan Monk's work has been praised for its emphasis on diversity and collaboration (Fenster 2007), as well as its global influence outside the English-speaking context (Garcia Ramon and Luna-Garcia 2007). Some of this research focuses on migrant or minority women at work as academics or transnational caretakers (see among others, the collection edited by Garcia Ramon and Monk 1996). Jan's commitment to including perspectives from beyond the Anglophone world has inspired us to examine the spatial context of women's work in the rural periphery of Hungary and Transcarpathia, the westernmost region of Ukraine. The precarious economic situation of families in these rural areas has either induced women's labor migration (e.g. as care workers or assembly line workers) to the European Union or constrained them to stay put, looking after the household and relatives and earning supplementary income through low-paid, often informal jobs (Erőss, Váradi and Wastl-Walter 2020; Németh and Váradi 2018).

Feminist geographers emphasize the experiences of women migrants and how they negotiate spaces and subject positions (Kofman and England 1997). In particular, feminist scholars have studied the lives, challenges, power relations, and experiences of domestic workers in the global north (see Salazar Parreñas 2015 for Philippinas in Los Angeles and Rome), as well as global geographies of care (see Pratt 2012; Pratt and Yeoh 2003; Pratt, Johnston and Banta 2017). Kofman and Raghuram (2020) emphasize the importance of place in the research on gendered migration. A recent comprehensive publication about intraregional migration is the Palgrave *Handbook of Gender and Migration* (Mora and Piper 2021) which adopts intersectionality to further the understanding of gender and migration by drawing on global examples. This chapter builds on these studies and focuses on the transformative power of both mobility and immobility on women's work history and career prospects over time in rural areas.

According to Janice Monk and Cindi Katz (1993, 1) "generation and historical context, changing fertility patterns, class positions and class mobility, state policies and personal motivations intersect with the geographies of

DOI: 10.4324/9781032275611-17

women's lives, constraining choices and providing options." Intrigued by the interconnectedness of personal life, macroeconomic, and political contexts that influence women's choices and narratives, we explore if and how those macro processes and migration influence women's notions of 'work' and 'job' among different generations. By analyzing the experiences of three generations of women, our study extends the existing literature by adding temporality to the analysis. We interpret temporality first as the shifts in individual work-narratives of women throughout the course of their lives. Second, we illustrate how the meaning of work has significantly changed from one generation to another as the region of Central and Eastern Europe has been restructured politically and economically. The analysis of women's work narratives allows us to examine their downward social mobility in the rural peripheries of the post-Socialist countries, where once reliable and secure jobs have become more unstable, leaving the middle-aged and younger generation in precarious working conditions in their homelands and abroad.

After introducing the political and economic context of the research areas, we follow a biographical approach and analyze semi-structured interviews of three generations of women. The interviews focus on the work biographies of exemplary women, the stories of mobility in their life course (Katz and Monk 1993, 266) and the sometimes transnational and cross-generational strategies to make a living and navigate through rigid gender boundaries in their families. This discussion focuses on women who built a successful career and to whom work means self-fulfillment.

Background to case study and geopolitical context

This analysis is based on data gathered from in-depth interviews since 2015. One of our projects examined female live-in care migration from a peripheral municipality of southern Hungary (Poppyfield) to Germany and Austria. The other project focused on minority Hungarian communities in peripheral settlements in Transcarpathia, Ukraine (Knightfield and Oakpark). In this region, men often migrate to foreign countries while women stay at home. One similarity in the two projects is that labor migration as a strategy among these women and their families has either forced them to rearrange their lives to be able to migrate or to stay and support family members who migrate. Second, the historical and political macro events in the last thirty years impacted many women in Central and Eastern Europe (CEE) peripheries regarding their job opportunities and lived experience as well as their ideas about work. Third, irrespective of their age or the country where they were born, their situation was both economically and socially precarious (Standing 2011).

Based on conversations with women in the research sites, four macro processes or historical events stand out as impacting their lives. First, the post-Socialist transition brought high unemployment, especially in peripheral regions where thousands of people were left without 'proper work' that is formalized, legal employment with a valid contract and regular payment

(Ferguson and Li 2018). Second, the CEE countries joined the European Union (EU) in 2004, which opened up new geographical pathways and job opportunities in the EU job market. The third macro process included the 2008 global economic crisis and especially the following debt trap. In Hungary, including our research site, record numbers of out-migration were registered in the post-2008 period (Hárs 2016; Németh and Váradi 2018). Finally, the devastating economic and social consequences of Euromaidan and the Donbas conflict in Ukraine boosted out-migration after 2014, especially among men who wanted to avoid conscription. Since 2011 the out-migration from Transcarpathia has increased because of the streamlined naturalization process introduced by Hungary which allows those whose ancestors were once citizens of Hungary to obtain citizenship. This has allowed tens of thousands to enter the EU job market (Tátrai, Erőss and Kovály 2017).

Women's work stories and narratives of instability in the CEE

Women who were born and worked during the Socialist era in Central and Eastern Europe often had jobs which provided low, but regular incomes. Many of these women are currently either elderly pensioners or middle-aged full-time workers in dual-earner households socialized according to state-Socialist model of the 1950s (see Table 14.1). While women had relatively high labor force participation, they often received lower salaries and were excluded from certain positions while they continued to be responsible for domestic chores and care work (Gal and Klingman 2000). As a result, rather than emancipating women, Socialism produced a 'failed emancipation' (Kiczková and Farkasová 1993). Nevertheless, the women who had jobs during Socialism and now are pensioners might describe their work history as *safe* (or secure) jobs. The following descriptions of and stories from women who participated in this research illustrate the generational differences and impact of spatial mobility on employment and household roles.

Mária was born during World War II in Oakpark (Transcarpathia, Ukraine) and worked in the local factory for 40 years. The factory provided jobs to generations of families living in Oakpark and in nearby villages. She remembers that '... life was better back then. Because we had a proper salary, which we received every second week.' Additionally, under Socialism in rural settlements, factory workers like Mária managed a small backyard farm. Since it was subsidized by the factory, they could 'do some business' with their produce. Women of this older generation admit that their proper job was often physically demanding, boring or pointless, but it provided a regular income and, importantly, the status of being employed. Having a proper job and a workplace was a central part of life, and it was taken for granted. These women were employed in a 'proper job,' as well as were the prime caretakers of their family and also worked in their small subsistence farms, thus we realize that they had not only a double (Monk and García Ramon 1996), but a triple burden.

Table 14.1 Background of the research participants

Name	Date of birth	Work history	Social mobility	Geographical mobility	Meaning of work
Mária	1937	Worked as administrator in the local factory for 40 years	No career	Immobile, lived and worked in the same municipality	Safety, predictability, 'proper job,' locally available
Róza	1961	Shoe factory → unemployed → seasonal work in Germany, → migrant care worker in Austria and Germany	Immobility (unskilled job in Hungary and as care worker)	Temporary and circular cross-border mobility	Uncertainty (lost certainty), precarity, informality
Ilona	1963	Library seasonal agricultural jobs → unemployed, but informal work as housekeeper; elected representative (voluntary, unpaid position) for the village	Downward mobility	Temporary, circular cross-border mobility in the past, now: micro mobility in the region	Informal + voluntary work = important in her self-esteem. 'proper job' locally unavailable
Emilia	1993	Teacher (6 months) → migrant, temporary physical jobs in Germany, later in Czechia	Downward mobility	Temporary and circular cross-border mobility	Necessary for survival, periodic, available outside of the country
Eva	1991	School leaving exam → could not begin university → migrant care worker → unemployment → social-shop employee	Blocked upward mobility 'precarity of future'/ dead end so far	Temporal circular mobility (from native town to Germany → return), planned migration to Western Europe	Necessary for survival, periodic, available outside of the country

(*Continued*)

Challenging Instability 149

Table 14.1 (Continued)

Name	Date of birth	Work history	Social mobility	Geographical mobility	Meaning of work
Emma	1993	School leaving exam → migrant work in a meat processing factory → unemployment → social-shop employee	Immobility (neither profession, nor degree) 'precarity of future'/ dead end so far	Temporal circular mobility, Planned migration to Western Europe	Necessary for survival, periodic, available outside of the country
Kinga	1983	Accountant → project manager → director of HR + president of local political organization	Upward mobility, synergy of educational, professional, and geographical mobility	Trainee in Ukraine, Canada → project leader in Sweden → employed by a global company, works in Transcarpathia, travels regularly	Self-fulfillment, power, security, career
Ida	1970	Headmistress → vice-mayor, national expert for Sure Start program	Upward social mobility without geographical mobility	Immobility, but success in the local community and nationwide recognition as expert	Self-fulfillment, power, security, career

Note: The names of the research sites and participants have been anonymized and some narratives of their life stories have been modified to maintain confidentiality.

The sense of economic stability and job security evaporated under the post-Socialist transition. With the collapse of factories like the one in Oakpark, not only families, but whole settlements and regions were shaken. The new, capitalist labor conditions offered less stability and reliability. These situations intensified in peripheral, rural settlements in post-Socialist Central and Eastern Europe where selective labor migration has become the common way of securing family income and often embodies the only way out of social and spatial marginality (Nagy et al. 2015). A large proportion of women perform live-in care work for the elderly in other countries, in a rotation system of two, four, or six-week shifts (see Gábriel 2020; Marchetti 2013; Palenga-Möllenbeck 2013). In Poppyfield, Hungary, for women of the middle-generation, live-in care work in Austria and Germany became the dominant livelihood strategy after the 2008 economic crisis fueled by a lack of legal job opportunities, low wages, and family indebtedness.

For example, Róza's work trajectory changed dramatically as a consequence of the 2008 global economic crisis. This low-skilled woman lost her last formal employment when the shoe factory in a nearby town was closed. Unemployed,

Róza could only find occasional jobs at local entrepreneurs, and for six years, she spent two months every summer as a seasonal agricultural worker in Germany. Recalling these times, she said it 'was cruel, like in a camp.' Her uncertain prospects for earning a livelihood forced her to go abroad to work. When we met, she had been working as caregiver for seven years without any formal contract Table 14.1. Róza complained about the harsh situation of her workplace and the worsening physical and mental health (dementia) of the woman for whom she cared. In addition, the woman's son was condescending toward Róza, treating her 'as an uncivilized woman from the underdeveloped East. I used to say to him that I also have washing machine or microwave oven at home. I have everything except a workplace and money.'

Róza's story exemplifies the precarity of care migration in many ways (Silvey and Parreñas 2019). She is completely dependent on informal recruitment agents, who arrange the work abroad, transport the women back and forth, and negotiate women's salaries and working conditions. Care work, especially in the informal segment of the care labor market, means precarious conditions in terms of low salaries, an asymmetric relationship between employers and caregivers, low job prestige, and lack of personal recognition of care workers themselves. In sum, Róza and other women who perform live-in care work abroad find themselves facing permanent uncertainty: They are in a precarious situation both in the receiving country's labor market and in the sending society due to their economic and social status (Gábriel 2020; Silvey and Parreñas 2019).

The condition of middle-generation women who do not migrate across borders but stay at home is precarious in a different way, as the case of Ilona shows. She is about the same age as Róza but was born and lives in Knightfield and worked as a librarian in a nearby town Table 14.1. On returning from maternity leave in 1991, the library refused to re-employ her. She has not been able to find any formal, legal employment since then. Ilona realized that 'I could not even bear the idea of sitting all day at home and watching TV,' so she has been working as a housekeeper in wealthy families' homes six days a week while her husband and two sons work abroad. Additionally, she was an elected representative in the municipal council for ten years, which partially rehabilitates her status as a white-collar working woman and trusted member of the local community.

The third age group, the younger generation, refers to those who were born in the 1980s or after and raised in the post-transition period in rural regions in CEE. For this generation, work is often something which is necessary for survival, but periodic, unpredictable, and often informal. Notably, work is not scarce; it is 'just' far away from home, geographically distant, often available in a different country. As Emilia, a young woman born in Knightfield in 1993, noted: 'Here this is what you hear: there are jobs, you can earn money, you just need to travel abroad to work.' Emilia graduated as an English teacher in 2016 and happily accepted a part-time teaching position in a good high school. She soon realized, however, that her monthly salary of 1500 hryvna (about 40 EUR) was totally inadequate, so she left for Poland with her fiancé. For two years they had worked in two countries, in half a dozen workplaces for a few months each (restaurant, warehouse, vegetable farm, bakery, meat-processing factory, assembly line). In general, they worked 12–16 hours, seven days a week for periods of three to five months. The only experience she labeled as *'bad'* highlights the extent of their self-exploitation:

> 'They did not offer enough work hours. Meaning that we could only work for 8 hours a day, which is [financially] not sufficient for us. Plus, we had lots of free days. But if we travel abroad to work and stay far from our family, we do not go there to relax, but to earn money.'

All her former classmates also work abroad. Emilia's story exemplifies that earning a diploma guarantees neither employment nor the chance of social mobility.

Moreover, fewer and fewer families in rural CEE can afford to support their children's higher education. After graduation, Eva was admitted to college, but she could not even begin her studies: 'my mother [who was a care worker in Germany] told me she couldn't support me [financially], I should go and work abroad.' For a short time, she worked as a live-in care worker but could not handle the precarious work conditions, especially in terms of the psychological and emotional burdens inherent to this kind of job. She complained about isolation, solitude, and disgust at the sick bodies of the elderly she cared for. 'I am young, and I don't want to do this anymore,' concluded Eva and did not return. Back home, she worked in the social shop of the municipality for an amount lower than the minimum wage Table 14.1. Meanwhile, she and her colleague, Emma, were steadily searching for jobs abroad on the internet. 'Anywhere but here.' The migratory aspirations of the two women in their twenties exemplify the 'precarity of future' (Silvey and Parreñas 2019) in terms of structurally constrained livelihood and mobility perspectives. For Eva and Emma, as for other young women in Poppyfield, the social mobility path through higher education is impossible. Moreover, they have little opportunity in these marginal regions that would provide them stable work in the formal labor market with enough income to start and build up a secure life on their own. They planned to migrate, but with neither profession nor knowledge of a foreign language, they could only hope to get unskilled and underpaid work somewhere abroad. From their point of view, labor migration – even under such circumstances – is the sole escape from the precarity of their present situation at home.

Successful women's careers in the periphery

Several women from these regions have built a successful career in which their work is fulfilling. Kinga was born in the 1980s in Knightfield, Ukraine to a Hungarian family and at the age of 14 was enrolled in a prestigious high school in Hungary. From the age of 16, she worked part time to be able to pay her college tuition fee in Transcarpathia. She obtained a university degree in Kyiv, which gave her a grant with a paid internship in the USA (N.B. as a

Hungarian minority). She built strong relationships with the host organization, which recommended her for a temporary job in Sweden where she was responsible for the recruitment of logging workers from Ukraine and organized their work on site. As Kinga recalls, it was a huge challenge: 'You can imagine, it was not easy at all, me, twenty-something-year old girl ordering men twice my age.' Before her thirtieth birthday, she returned to Knightfield, married a local man, and started to work for an international company that has a factory in the nearby town. She climbed the career ladder and eventually became the deputy director of the company. Kinga still regularly travels for work with the support of her husband (who is a farmer) and mother who looks after the children and the household. She is also one of the leaders of the local community life and charity programs.

Ida from Poppyfield, Hungary was born in 1970. She began to work in local childcare, and after her graduation from college, she became the head of local childcare (between 1996 and 2007) Table 14.1. Ida worked throughout her studies (her mother was divorced and could not help to pay for her studies). Since 2006, she has been the vice-mayor of the village. Ida is married to an agricultural entrepreneur, and they have two children. As vice-mayor, she has overseen local social issues and has launched several projects aimed at alleviating (children's) poverty (e.g., Sure Start program). As a result of her local project experience, she has become a national expert for the Sure Start program.

The work histories and life stories of Kinga and Ida represent upward mobility in terms of intergenerational educational, social, and professional mobility. Kinga's social mobility was intertwined with geographical mobility which helped her to accumulate strong skills in networking and transnational cultural and social capital. Although she could easily have stayed in Sweden (she had a job and a partner), she returned to Knightfield, as she could not imagine her life elsewhere, or without her mother and sister. Ida has been immobile and never aspired to leave the village or the country. Once she was offered a job in the county seat, but refused it, stating 'We were considering it, but we decided to stay because of our parents.'

Both Kinga and Ida nurture strong emotional ties to their homeland. This strong place attachment is one of the main drivers of their public activity, which is additionally enhanced by their embeddedness in the local society and their access to (rare) local resources in terms of real estate, a 'proper job', wide social network, recognition, and respect, to put it simply: social and symbolic capital. Both women have a safe and supportive family network, which helps them in successfully balancing their ambitious workload, their household chores, and childcare. In addition to childcare, they both voiced the moral obligation to care for elderly family members, which they understand as a woman's task – independently of their career advancement or position.

Concluding remarks

According to Monk and Garcia Ramon (1996, 13), "While women's employment is likely to continue growing, especially in the service sector, growth will probably occur in jobs that are insecure and low-paying." Our findings confirm that the neoliberal agenda and the single European labor market would worsen the already disadvantaged economic position of women and further deepen the gender-based inequalities in the labor market.

This situation is particularly evident in the semi-peripheral, rural regions presented here. For the majority of women in these regions, only low-paid and low-prestige, precarious jobs are available, predominantly in the informal sector both at home and abroad. Hence, labor migration rarely provides social mobility, but is a way to improve living conditions and to stabilize the family budget, often at the price of self-exploitation.

Jan Monk and others (Monk 1978; Monk 1983; Zelinsky 1973; Zelinsky, Monk and Hanson 1982) highlight the invisibility of women and argue for emancipation and justice, especially in regions where very few women have been able to overcome obstacles and build a career. The cases of Kinga and Ida illustrate how they could thrive because of personal aspirations, a good education, and a strong and supportive family network. Nevertheless, they did not reflect on advancing their career or shifting the roles in their families toward more gender balance as examples of emancipation. Kinga and Ida, and most women we encountered believed that in addition to the work performed in formal or informal jobs, it remains a woman's duty to take care of household chores, including care for elderly family members. If a family member needs care, these women would rather leave their job abroad and return home because in many CEE rural contexts, families can neither afford to pay for care workers nor overlook their social responsibility as caregivers. Hence, our findings align with Gregor and Kováts (2019) who noted that in these rural, marginalized spaces, labor market participation of lower-class women is far from full emancipation.

The multigenerational narratives of work in this research show that women's emancipation was neither achieved during Socialism nor under the given circumstances of global capitalism. In fact, Jan Monk's insight of a 'double day' has often worsened alongside their mobility. This was particularly salient in the work stories and narratives of middle-aged generation women, who worked during Socialism and in the subsequent capitalist, neoliberal economy. The experiences of women like Róza or Ilona illustrate how rapidly job security and predictability have evaporated and given way to instability. Importantly, given the post-Socialist transition and the EU membership of CEE countries access to the EU job market expanded the spatial frames and geographical trajectories of people's lives. During Socialism, as Mária explained, work was available locally, but this changed after 1990 in rural peripheral areas in Transcarpathia, while in Hungary the situation turned following the 2008 economic crisis.

Consequently, work in jobs which provide a decent income is almost exclusively found abroad and forces hundreds of thousands of people from these rural regions to travel to foreign countries on a regular basis. This migration is especially common among the young generation who, like Emma, Eva, or Emilia, were raised amidst unstable economic circumstances, often by one parent while the other worked abroad. Additionally, the previously existing channels of social mobility (e.g., free higher education) have evaporated; thus, many feel trapped by the constraints of local conditions. The work they perform abroad, however, barely sustains their precarious circumstances. Spatial mobility seems the only way to overcome the precarious circumstances; although, work abroad does not secure social mobility because the women lack skills and (access to) education. Spatial mobility can rather be understood as an attempt to escape from the present precarious circumstances at home to an equally precarious future in a foreign country. Nevertheless, research should now begin to observe whether and how this generation can cope with being caught between two such precarious situations.

During the fourth wave of SARS-COVID-19 in Europe, transnational travel and work have changed dramatically. The situation of women in precarious living and working conditions in CEE has become even more challenging and unstable. Thus, it is vital to research the situation of these women under the new circumstances and their strategies to cope with them.

Finally, temporality and spatiality are important to understand the geographical expansion of work and life in these rural regions. Expanding spatial mobility is linked to more frequent travel (e.g., rotation system) and reaches areas that were inaccessible to the grandparents' generation, and some of today's middle-aged generation. Increased geographic mobility also allows families to make a living in these rural areas; however, it is also a constraint that has fundamentally changed the lives of many generations. As illustrated in our research, geographical mobility offers the opportunity for some women to temporarily step out of traditional female roles to achieve upward social mobility.

Acknowledgements

We dedicate our chapter to Jan Monk whose outstanding research and publications based on her warm interest in women's work encouraged and stimulated our own academic life in many ways. Jan Monk's work emphasizes diversity and collaboration beyond the Anglophone world. Her commitment to include narratives beyond these contexts inspired us to examine the spatial context of women's work in Central and Eastern Europe. Motivated by her and Janet H. Momsen's book series *International Studies of Women and Place* and Jan's impressive and wonderful collection of representations of women at work in her home, we have focused here on precarious working situations in three generations of women in the rural periphery of Hungary and Transcarpathia, the westernmost region of Ukraine.

This chapter is based on the results of 'International Migration from Hungary and its Impacts on Rural Society' (2015–2018) funded by NFKI/OTKA (K111 969) in Hungary and on 'Studying the assimilation of the Transcarpathian Hungarian Diaspora Community' financed by Bethlen Gábor Fund in Transcarpathia, Ukraine.

References

Erőss, Ágnes, Monika Mária Váradi, and Doris Wastl-Walter. 2020. "Cross-Border Migration and Gender Boundaries in Central Eastern Europe – Female Perspectives." *Migration Letters* 17 (4): 499–509. doi: 10.33182/ml.v17i4.700.

Fenster, Tovi. 2007. "Reinforcing Diversity: From the 'inside' and the 'outside'." *Gender, Place and Culture* 14 (1): 43–49. doi: 10.1080/09663690601122234.

Ferguson, James, and Tania Murray Li. 2018. "Beyond the 'Proper Job:' Political-Economic Analysis after the Century of Labouring Man." *Working Paper 51*, Cape Town: PLAAS, UWC.

Gábriel, Dóra. 2020. "Negotiating Working Conditions – Hungarian Care Workers in the Austrian Live-in Care Sector." In *Towards a Scarcity of Care? Tensions and Contradictions in Transnational Elderly Care Systems in Central and Eastern Europe*, edited by Noémi Katona and Attila Melegh, 115–143. Budapest: Friedrich Ebert Stiftung.

Gal, Susan, and Gail Klingman. 2000. "Introduction." In *Reproducing Gender, Politics, Publics, and Everyday Life after Socialism*, edited by Susan Gal and Gail Klingman, 3–20. Princeton, NJ: Princeton University Press.

Garcia Ramon, Maria Dolors, and Tony Luna-Garcia. 2007. "Challenging Hegemonies through Connecting Places, People and Ideas: Jan Monk's Contribution to International Gender Geography (with Particular Reference to Spain)." *Gender, Place & Culture* 14 (1): 35–41. doi: 10.1080/09663690601122200.

Garcia Ramon, Maria Dolors, and Janice Monk. 1996. *Women of the European Union: The Politics of Work and Daily Life*. London and New York: Routledge.

Gregor, Anikó, and Eszter Kováts. 2019. "Work-life Balance? Tensions between Care and Paid Work in the Lives of Hungarian Women." *Socio.hu*. doi: 10.18030/socio.hu.2019en.91.

Hárs, Ágnes. 2016. "Nemzetközi vándorlás, migrációs válság" (International Mobility, Migratory Crisis). In *Társadalmi Riport 2016*, edited by Tamás Kolosi and István Gy. Tóth, 351–372. Budapest: TÁRKI.

Katz, Cindi, and Janice Monk. 1993. "Making Connections. Space, Place and Life Course." In *Full Circles. Geographies of Women over the Life Course*, edited by Cindi Katz and Janice Monk, 264–278. London: Routledge.

Kiczková, Zuzana, and Etela Farkasová. 1993. "The Emancipation of Women: A Concept That Failed." In *Gender Politics and Post-Communism. Reflections from Eastern Europe and the Former Soviet Union*, edited by Nanette Funk and Magda Mueller, 303–312. London: Routledge.

Kofman, Eleonore, and Kim England. 1997. "Citizenship and International Migration: Taking Account of Gender, Sexuality and Race." *Environment and Planning A* 29 (2): 191–248. doi: 10.1068/a290191.

Kofman, Eleonore, and Parvati Raghuram. 2020. "Geographies of Gendered Migration: Place as Difference and Connection." In *Routledge Handbook of Gender and Feminist Geographies*, edited by Anindita Datta, Peter Hopkins, Lynda Johnston, Elizabeth Olson, and Joseli Maria Silva, 244–53. Abingdon: Routledge.

Marchetti, Sabrina. 2013. "Dreaming Circularity? Eastern European Women and Job Sharing in Paid Home Care." *Journal of Immigrant & Refugee Studies* 11 (4): 347–63. doi: 10.180/15562948.2013.837770.

Monk, Janice. 1978. "Women in the Geographical Games." *Journal of Geography*, 77 (5): 190–91. doi: 10.1080/00221347808980117

Monk, Janice. 1983. "Integrating Women into the Geography Curriculum." *Journal of Geography* 82 (6): 271–273. doi: 10.1080/00221348308980417.

Monk, Janice, and Maria Dolors Garcia Ramon. 1996. "Placing Women of the European Union." In *Women of the European Union: The Politics of Work and Daily Life*, edited by Maria Dolors Garcia Ramon and Janice Monk, 1–30. London: Routledge.

Monk, Janice, and Cindi Katz. 1993. "When in the world are women?" In *Full Circles. Geographies of Women over the Life Course*, edited by Cindi Katz and Janice Monk, 1–26. London: Routledge.

Mora, Claudia and Nicola Piper. 2021. *The Palgrave Handbook of Gender and Migration*. Cham: Palgrave Macmillan. doi: 10.1007/978-3-030-63347-9.

Nagy, Erika, Judit Timár, Gábor Nagy, and Gábor Velkey. 2015. "The Everyday Practices of the Reproduction of Peripherality and Marginality in Hungary." In *Understanding Geographies of Polarization and Peripheralization: Perspectives from Central and Eastern Europe and Beyond*, edited by Thilo Lang et al., 135–155. Basingstoke: Palgrave Macmillan.

Németh, Krisztina and Monika Mária Váradi. 2018. "Development in the Context of Care Migration from Rural Hungary: An Agency-Based Approach." *Review of Sociology* 28 (4): 88–110.

Palenga-Möllenbeck, Ewa. 2013. "New Maids – New Butlers? Polish Domestic Workers in Germany and Commodification of Social Reproductive Work." *Equality, Diversity and Inclusion: An International Journal* 32 (6): 557–574. doi: 10.1108/EDI-10-2012-0086.

Pratt, Geraldine. 2012. *Families Apart: Migrant Mothers and the Conflicts of Labor and Love*. Minneapolis: University of Minnesota Press. doi: 10.5749/minnesota/9780816669981.001.0001.

Pratt, Geraldine, and Brenda Yeoh. 2003. "Transnational (Counter) Topographies." *Gender, Place and Culture* 10 (2): 159–166. doi: 10.1080/0966369032000079541.

Pratt, Geraldine, Caleb Johnston, and Vanessa Banta. 2017. "Lifetimes of Disposability and Surplus Entrepreneurs in Bagong Barrio, Manila." *Antipode* 49 (1): 169–92. doi:10.1111/anti.12249.

Salazar Parreñas, Rhacel. 2015. *Servants of Globalization: Migration and Domestic Work*, 2nd ed. Stanford: Stanford University Press.

Silvey, Rachel, and Rhacel Salazar Parreñas. 2019. "Precarity Chains: Cycles of Domestic Worker Migration from Southeast Asia to the Middle East." *Journal of Ethnic and Migration Studies* 46(16): 3457–71. doi: 10.1080/1369183X.2019.1592398.

Standing, Guy. 2011. *The Precariat. The New Dangerous Class*. London: Bloomsbury.

Tátrai, Patrik, Ágnes Erőss, and Katalin Kovály. 2017. "Kin-State Politics Stirred by a Geopolitical Conflict: Hungary's Growing Activity in Post-Euromaidan Transcarpathia, Ukraine." *Hungarian Geographical Bulletin* 66 (3): 203–218. doi: 10.15201/hungeobull.66.3.2.

Zelinsky, Wilbur. 1973. "Women in Geography: A Brief Factual Account." *The Professional Geographer* 25 (2): 151–165. doi: 10.1111/j.0033-0124.1973.00151.x.

Zelinsky, Wilbur, Jan Monk, and Susan Hanson. 1982. "Women and Geography: Review and prospectus." *Progress in Human Geography* 6 (3): 317–366. doi: 10.1177/030913258200600301.

15 Life Course in the New Processes of Re-Ruralization in Spain

Mireia Baylina, Maria Dolors Garcia Ramon, Montserrat Villarino, Mª Josefa Mosteiro García, Ana Mª Porto Castro and Isabel Salamaña

Re-ruralization through young adult entrepreneurs

The global economic and financial crisis of the 2010s has significantly impacted rural areas. Given the regional inequalities in Spain, the poverty triggered by the crisis is concentrated in the more disadvantaged urban neighborhoods and rural areas (Méndez 2014). Despite this context of recession, many rural settings with good transport networks in Spain have attracted young women and men who wish to develop their own professional activities (Salamaña et al. 2016; Recaño 2017). The current COVID-19 pandemic has increased these urban-rural residential movements, as some people seek a better quality of life closer to nature. In any case, this transformative process in rural communities is not exclusive to Spain but is evident in other parts of Europe alongside residential growth and tourism (Wiest 2016).

Although re-ruralization of country spaces is emerging throughout Europe, there have been few published studies about this process (Woods 2016). Much of the literature that is available tends to focus on labor migration to areas with an established labor market or to create small businesses in the traditional services sector, or migration to return home. A gender-based perspective is largely absent in these analyses (Hedberg and do Carmo 2012; Monllor and Fuller 2016). Moreover, the literature that does focus on the return to the countryside from a gender perspective tends to discuss lifestyles and social and environmental matters (Bonifacio 2014) or emphasizes men or women (Grimsrud 2011; Schmidt 2016) instead of addressing financial issues.

This chapter contributes to recent work on women's entrepreneurship in rural areas that emphasizes the business processes implemented by women who have returned or moved to the country following urban life experiences. Porto et al. (2015) argue that education and university training are empowering factors for start-up businesses and building new rural feminine identities in Spain. This research also explores multifunctional entrepreneurship among women who incorporate knowledge, behavior and emotional learning (Seuneke and Bock 2015). These processes take place in sectors and areas such as the agricultural and livestock sector and family farming where women have been socially and economically undervalued and underrepresented. Some scholars state that progress is being made by women business leaders in

DOI: 10.4324/9781032275611-18

the rural agrarian economy largely due to the adoption of new entrepreneurial dynamics in family farming (Warren-Smith and Jackson 2004; Heikkila 2009). Various studies have dealt with how gender is treated in rural entrepreneurship as a way to highlight the potential challenges in gendered relations. Most of this research, however, is not related to the current re-ruralization processes (Pettersson and Cassel 2014) and/or does not relate the experience of the two genders to the entrepreneurial process (Laszlo Ambjörnsson 2020).

This chapter examines the entrepreneurial activities of women and men who have decided to settle in the countryside from a gender perspective. We focus on the startup of their professional activities (beginnings and proposals) taking into account that the women and men in this study have similar training and are in the same life stage. According to Monk and Katz (1993), behaviors we associate with a specific life stage rather than biological age may more accurately reflect the conditions through which a group has lived collectively, such as the group's access to education. As life course mediates everyday life, it is important to examine different experiences. The authors state that under similar circumstances, there are some problems that confront females at the beginning of the life course in the contemporary world that intersect with cultural ideologies, specific socio-spatial patterns and the gender division of labor at all scales (Monk and Katz 1993). This group's decision to launch entrepreneurial projects in a rural setting after a period of deep economic crisis in Spain indicates that new socio-economic dynamics are being triggered by agents that share training, fresh outlook and original ideas with a long-term perspective. The analytical category of gender is critical to examine the power relationships underlying these dynamics.

Methodology and subjects

Our study employs a qualitative methodology based on in-depth interviews and field notes in order to get rich understandings and insights. Qualitative methods remain a dominant mode of doing gender and feminist research. In-depth interviews respond to a theoretically motivated research question that seeks to illustrate how people make sense of their own experiences (Monk 2001a; Monk and Allen 2021). We advocate talking to people in their own territory because participants might feel more comfortable and more can be learned about their own place-specific contexts and spatial routines. This facilitates ability to get information from the study context and gather it through field notes. We take short notes during the event, after the conversation ends and later on, when additional critical reflection can be included (Phillippi and Lauderdale 2018).

Important findings have emerged from this work on agricultural activities such as the division of labor in the farm, the household and the community; degrees of authority, decision-making and empowerment; and time allocation (Tickamyer 2021). Participants in this study are young adult women and men who decided to move to the countryside with a professional and life project and with university studies. Some of them have been living before in the rural, others are new dwellers. The interviewees were contacted based on personal

Life Course in New Processes of Re-Ruralization in Spain 159

acquaintance through third parties and via information available online. The interviews lasted approximately two hours each and covered several aspects of the entrepreneurs' daily lives, focusing on key points in their professional project and personal life in a rural setting. There were also wide-ranging questions about new socio-economic dynamics of the rural environment and gender roles and relationships within these contexts (Baylina et al. 2017). In this chapter, we have focused on the origins of their projects (motivation, opportunities and difficulties) and the impact of their activities on the local area. The interviews were recorded, transcribed and coded to facilitate analyzing the discourse.

This research is based on the experiences of 12 young adults (6 men and 6 women with an average age of 36 and all with university studies) who have chosen to settle in the countryside of Catalonia and Galicia (Spain) between 2008 and 2015 to carry out their professional and personal life projects (Table 15.1). Ten of the interviewees are of rural origin. Six have gone back to work on an earlier family project, while the other six have launched a new project. Four began their project with a partner or sibling. Six are engineers (four in agronomy) and the others have degrees in political science, economics, tourism, chemistry, biology and business management. Most of them also have a master's or postgraduate degree [mainly in business administration (BA) and marketing], and one has completed his doctorate (in chemistry). No gender

Table 15.1 Young women and men entrepreneurs. Basic information

Name	Rural origin	Type of projects	Family business continuation	Place (county, province and region)	Training	Personal situation
Xulio	No	Organic production of autochthonous hens & organic meet	No	Ferrol (A Coruña, Galicia)	Political science. Master's in management and international cooperation	With heterosexual partner. 1 daughter (7 years old)
Gustavo (& sister)	Yes	Organic cheese production	Yes	Deza (Pontevedra, Galicia)	Technical Engineering - Agri-food Industry.	No partner, no kids
Lois	Yes	Wine producer	Yes	Chantada (Lugo, Galicia)	Economic sciences. Master's in commercial management and marketing of wineries.	No partner, no kids

(*Continued*)

Table 15.1 (Continued)

Name	Rural origin	Type of projects	Family business continuation	Place (county, province and region)	Training	Personal situation
Sofía (& partner)	Yes	Organic Dairy producer	Yes	Deza (Pontevedra, Galicia)	Industrial Engineering. Master's in business administration	With heterosexual partner. No kids
Leonor	Yes	River tourism manager	No	Chantada (Lugo, Galicia)	Tourism	With heterosexual partner. No kids
Alicia	Yes	Organic cattle farm and yoghourt producer	Yes	A Ulloa (Lugo, Galicia)	Biology. Course on business training	With heterosexual partner. No kids
Gabriel	No	Organic olive oil producer	No	Baix Ebre (Tarragona, Catalonia)	Agronomist Engineering	With heterosexual partner. 1 son (3 years old)
Tomàs	Yes	Organic olive oil producer	No	Terra Alta (Tarragona, Catalonia)	PhD in chemistry	With heterosexual partner. 1 daughter (1.5 years old)
Pere	Yes	Cider producer and other apple derived products	Yes	Baix Empordà (Girona, Catalonia)	Aeronautical Engineering Studying business management	With heterosexual partner. No kids
Carina (& brother)	Yes	Rural houses (for tourists) manager	No	Pla de l'Estany (Girona, Catalonia)	Business management Postgraduate in marketing	No partner, no kids
Magalí (& partner)	Yes	Organic authoctonous pig producer	No	Solsonès (Lleida, Catalonia)	Agronomist Engineering	With heterosexual partner. 1 son (4 years old)

(*Continued*)

Table 15.1 (Continued)

Name	Rural origin	Type of projects	Family business continuation	Place (county, province and region)	Training	Personal situation
Mariona	Yes	Wine producer, fruit producer	Yes	Baix Empordà (Girona, Catalonia)	Agricultural Technical Engineering. Oenology	With heterosexual partner. 1 son (3 years old)

Source: Authors

differences were observed in the interviewees' educational achievements, and there was a break with stereotypes in terms of the university courses studied by the women (three are engineers, one has a science degree in biology and the other two have social science and juridical degrees in BA and Tourism). Nine of the interviewees have a heterosexual partner; seven live with their partner full-time and two only partially. Five have a child (aged between 1 and 7 years old). Five of the entrepreneurial projects revolve around organic farming: dairy and autochthonous pig and hen farms. Two of the projects are dedicated to producing olive oil, two projects to winemaking and one project to producing cider. The tourism projects concern river tourism and promoting and managing rural holiday homes. All are dedicated to high-quality local production for the regional, national or international market.

The impact of life course and the financial crisis on rural entrepreneurship

Social and cultural ideas and expectations surrounding the life course mediate the gendered experiences of individuals (Monk and Katz 1993). Young adult entrepreneurs are part of the transformation of rural settings through expectations linked to a re-evaluation of territory and identity. New activities are being created and farms are being overhauled to add value, quality and singularity to their production. The social group of young professionals represents a radical turnaround in the sociodemographic trends observed in rural settings in previous decades. This change is primarily the result of the generalization of basic services and communication infrastructures; of the "expulsion" of city dwellers in times of crisis (the strong pressure on the housing market and the loss of employment cause an expulsion of metropolitan population to some rural areas); and of the urban construction of idyllic representations of the countryside (Baylina and Berg 2010). Social constructionism has provided rurality with a discussed and lived meaning, particularly idealized and with strong links between rurality, nature and the community (Cloke 2006). They are biased meanings that promote a country vision that favors certain social groups and ideologies (Baylina and Berg 2010).

Many of these new rural residents are capable of creating their own life journeys based on imaginary constructs (mainly around food and environmental safety and quality) onto which they project their abilities (Camarero 2013). Women and men entrepreneurs, on average in their mid-30s, share understandings of how their lives "should" unfold with age, such as owning a house, getting married, having children or starting a professional project. In their life stage the creation of a professional project coincides with the long-term expectations of a life project. These two aspects merged in most of the interviews: commitment to a professional challenge was matched by consolidation of a personal relationship, the desire to have or not have offsprings and their enjoyment of independence. All of these factors were connected to a specific place.

However, the rural newcomers rarely idealize country life or a reality that they wanted to transform. In their interviews, they mixed commercial interests with values connected to the land and/or the family in a very natural way and with great conviction. These emotional links would not have led them to start businesses without the education that enabled them to see opportunities and carry out projects: Magalí (organic pig producer) states that she strongly disagrees with the way food is being produced, the way the land is being worked, and with many other aspects of the primary sector and the agri-food industry. "I knew how to do it very well and so I thought to myself, why not do it?"

Notwithstanding the interviewees' specific life circumstances, the context of economic crisis in Spain often triggered their entrepreneurial initiatives. "There came a time when my means of earning a living disappeared and there was no expectation or prospect of any job with a salary. After one crisis, another one came along. So, we decided to take the plunge..." (Xulio). Most of the interviewees started off with few financial resources, and with a business that had to be overhauled or that needed investment from the outset. Many of the participants in this study asked for bank loans and some sought subsidies from the authorities, who prioritized projects developed by women. These public subsidies are welcome but have no bearing on the launching of a project, as most are granted later on.

Funding was not the only difficulty involved in starting up a project. Local power structures show that women faced discrimination in the farming profession and highlight the ways in which rural space is male dominated (Donkersloot 2012). Gabriel asserts that "it is easier being a man farmer as people have more confidence in you; when people look at a woman farmer, they look at her saying 'let's see how this'll turn out'". The constructions and transformations of gendered rurality intersect with other identities, such as age, that have implications for everyday lives. Carina remembers business meetings (as a rural tourism manager) where she was always being questioned by older men. "Do you know how it feels to be totally belittled? When somebody with such relevance is questioning you, it makes you doubt yourself".

Women stand out for their interest and aptitude in social networks, which require substantial personal resources such as cultural capital and organizational skills.

> If, as a woman, I settle down here, I'm not going to be able to do it on my own. So, let's try to give this potential a stronger argument. The first thing is to get to know the area and then try to set up networks.
>
> (Alicia)

Networks and cooperation are an innovative formula in entrepreneurship (Berg 1997; Hanson 2009). Alicia's statement also underlines a need to increase visibility, empowerment and overcome male symbolic power (Pallares-Barbera and Casellas 2019).

Dedication to their project took up most of the time of both male and female interviewees. Sofia expressed openly that "I'm available 24 hours a day, 365 days a year" and this marks a very significant advance with respect to women's personal priorities, strengths and concerns. Actually, this finding raises important questions about how work and other parts of life come together (Monk 2012). Both the women and men entrepreneurs recognized that it is difficult to find a balance between work and family at this point of life. The men clearly expressed support for gender equality (another novelty), but this was often full of contradictions. Tomàs recognized "the difficulty for women to reconcile work and family" and expressed that "men don't have to do that". Lois referred to his static position of privilege when he associated his desire to have children with the "traditional" model of fatherhood:

> If I make that decision [to have a child], I can throw myself into the projects, but I think that a woman, even when she makes that decision, can't devote herself 100%. So it's simpler for me.
>
> (Lois)

There is no guarantee that the fact of being young son of a generation born with gender equality laws, makes a man aware of the social construction of gender. A very young man of our sample stated, "I know there are differences [in gender roles] but maybe it's ultimately a question of genetics. It's not for nothing that men are more enterprising than women. Maybe it's not a cultural question but rather one of genetics" (Pere). In the light of such comments, it is hardly surprising that men do not always understand that a woman can devote most of her time to a profession, and that women's professional activities give rise to social expectations. This illustrates how patriarchy is interwoven with a place's historical processes:

> Being a woman, I attracted a lot of attention from the press, which ended up publishing lots of articles about me and giving me great publicity… If I had been a man, perhaps it wouldn't have been such a big deal…
>
> (Leonor)

In effect, the media have placed the spotlight on these initiatives, several of which have won awards. This attention has undoubtedly given the interviewees a high profile and recognition which, in the case of the women, are still not matched by any profound changes in the gender systems.

The introduction of creative economic activities in rural areas

Young women's and men's agency has introduced new elements into their professional activities, whether in the form of their product, production process, management, marketing or ethical relationship with respect to their production methods and the environment. The interviewees have mobilized themselves to find a distinctive niche in the global economy by emphasizing local resources and making connections with markets beyond their territory. For example, Carina stated that through her managerial and booking system for rural holiday homes she has "merged the rural world with the online world, and with foreign countries." These entrepreneurs spoke of the relationship between the rural and the global, while omitting references to the city as a counterpoint to the countryside, as a way to overcome rural-urban dichotomies.

Many of the interviewees base their unique singularity on the production of high-quality foodstuffs as a local specialty. Magalí, Alicia and Xulio have focused on autochthonous breeds of Gascon pigs, Friesian and Pardo-alpina cows, and Mos and Piñeira hens, respectively (Table 15.1). These animals have links with the local culture and landscape, and therefore these entrepreneurs are involved in the constructive production of the specific rural setting (Jones 2003). Mariona emphasizes that the traditional *country* wine she makes is not only organic but also represents "the work involved, its additional value in cultural terms, the fact that a tradition is being preserved, and that we're working with local varieties of grapes…".

Some of the interviewees were proud of the history (context) of their project or product. They position their product in a unique and specific rural context, and they imbue it with positive ideas about the setting. Leonor considers that her innovation in river tourism has been to steer her local area, the *Ribeira Sacra del Miño*, towards high-end tourism. Tomàs chose the brand name *Identidad* (Identity) to convey both his own experience and heritage and those of his area, *Terra Alta*, when announcing his oil to the world; while Sofía opted for *Kalekói* (a word used by the original inhabitants of Galicia for their land, as recorded in Strabo's *Geography* in the 1st century AD) to identify her yoghurts and place them in a specific territorial context.

Alicia talked about the connection between the cooperative movement and innovation. She took it for granted that women, due to the roles they play, had greater difficulties in moving forward on an individual basis in any field (Ní Fhlatharta and Farrell 2017) and clearly saw cooperation between women as the way forward:

> lots of women in Galicia have lots of good ideas but they don't have either the time or the support in terms of human resources to get them off the ground. And the cooperative model is what makes this possible.

She also believes that innovation can transform a place by creating an impact on its community (Hanson 2009), "when women run a business project, they put much greater emphasis on its social development and so, obviously, overall, it's a lot more positive for the area" (Alicia). In this regard, Monk (2012, 177) states that

> women usually see work as a place for forming friendships, enhancing their sense of personal identities and offering opportunities for engagement in the community service activities that they value. This community work, in turn, enhanced their careers, developed their skills, and contributed to the goals of their companies.

Further, all the entrepreneurs are aware of the economic impact of their work and their contribution to the upkeep of a population. The fact that "tourism has a multiplying effect on society: on the hotels, restaurants, wineries…" (Leonor), exemplifies that creative economic and social dynamics introduced by young women and men entrepreneurs have given value to the romantic view of country life, at least in financial terms. These new country dwellers embody a return to a vision of the rural environment as a place of production and as a space in which to earn a living.

Conclusions

This chapter has addressed processes of re-ruralization in Spain based on men and women who create economic activities, from a gender and a life course approach. The return of young women and men to the countryside as entrepreneurs is the result of the economic crisis, a university education, a specific time in their life course, the possibility of credit and family links with a particular place. They form a highly distinctive group that they have collectively experienced as a generation, with training and values related to food safety, environmental management and work self-sufficiency. These entrepreneurs are also more aware of gender inequalities; although, their experiences are very different so that in the daily life men still enjoy the privileges while women bear the oppressions.

Young, highly educated women's entrepreneurship is an innovation in the rural settings under discussion due to the nature of their projects, the effect that they have on generations of younger women, and the new representation of femininity that they are constructing, far removed from the rural idyll that placed them at the center of the traditional family and community values (Little 2015). Starting a family is generally not a priority for women who combine work and life to advance in their career (Monk 2012). This trend is relatively new in the rural communities in this study.

In general, men and women have the same relationship and level of dedication to their professional project. Women's overt and explicit verbalization of the desire to devote themselves fully to a profession, however, is a clear illustration of a generational change. A life course perspective will provide a framework for understanding the work–life relations (Monk 2012) of these young women and men with the advent of more dependents. As Monk (2001b) observes when studying the lives of women geographers, it is impossible that women could have described their professional careers without referring to their personal lives. It may not be so clear in men. Additionally, women have to deal with questions in the professional sphere because of their gender. Their roles as female entrepreneurs often do not fit in the rural environment of male dominance. This situation leads them to work out defensive and resistance strategies which, despite being empowering, reveal a situation of gender subordination and emotional discomfort. When women identify this discomfort, it leads them to change; they attempt to bring their project to fruition and are prepared to overcome any social pressure to achieve their goal.

The re-ruralization processes carried out by young women and men with higher education in the form of a project of their own and at a life stage in which they are creating their life project are evidence of new social and economic dynamics in rural areas. The analytical category of gender makes it possible to visualize oppressions and situations of change. It is also essential to evaluate the continuity of these economic projects and determine whether women stay in rural areas. As noted by Monk and Katz (1993), the intersection between gender and age has made specific problems visible in a white, middle-class rural environment. These findings encourage further research into rural gender and power relations beyond these categories in different contexts.

Funding

This research has been supported by the Ministry of Economy and Competitiveness, Spanish Government (Refs. CSO2015-63913-R and PID2019-105773RB-100).

Acknowledgments

Our gratitude to the reviewers and editors for their useful comments to improve this chapter.

References

Baylina, Mireia, and Nina Berg. 2010. "Selling the countryside: representations of rurality in Norway and Spain." *European Urban and Regional Studies* 17 (3): 277–292.

Baylina, Mireia, Maria Dolors Garcia Ramon, Ana María Porto, Maria Rodó, Isabel Salamaña, and Montserrat Villarino. 2017. "Work life balance of professional women in rural Spain." *Gender, Place and Culture* 24 (1): 72–84.

Berg, Nina. 1997. "Gender, place and entrepreneurship." *Entrepreneurship & Regional Development* 9: 259–268.

Bonifacio, Glenda Tibe. 2014. *Gender and rural migration. Realities, conflict and change*. London: Routledge

Camarero, Luis. 2013. "Espacios Rurales, ¿Crisis sistémica o brotes verdes? Entrevista con Luis Camarero. Encrucijadas." *Revista crítica de Ciencias Sociales* 6: 6–17.

Cloke, Paul. 2006. "Conceptualising rurality". In *Handbook of rural studies*, edited by Paul Cloke, Terry Marsden and Paul Mooney, 18–28. London: Sage.

Donkersloot, Rachel. 2012. "Gendered and generational experiences of place and power in the rural Irish landscape." *Gender, Place and Culture* 19 5: 578–599.

Fhlatharta, Aoife M. Ni, and Maura Farrell. 2017. "Unravelling the strands of patriarchy in rural innovation: a study of female innovators and their contribution to rural Connemara." *Journal of Rural Studies* 54 (2017): 15–27.

Grimsrud, Gro Marit. 2011. "Gendered spaces on the trial: the influence of regional gender contracts on in-migration of women to rural Norway." *Human Geography* 93B (1): 3–20.

Hanson, Susan. 2009. "Changing places through women's entrepreneurship." *Economic Geography* 85 (3): 245–267.

Hedberg, Charlotta, and Renato Miguel do Carmo, eds. 2012. *Translocal ruralism*. Dordrecht: Springer.

Heikkila, Katariina. 2009. "Farm space as an arena for female entrepreneurship." In *Gendered rural spaces*, edited by Pia Olsson and Helena Ruotsala, 51–69. Helsinki: Finnish Literature Society.

Jones, Owain. 2003. "The restraint of beasts: rurality, animality, Actor Network Theory and dwelling." In *Country visions*, edited by Paul Cloke, 283–307. Harlow: Prentice Hall.

Laszlo Ambjörnsson, Emmelie. 2020. "Performing female masculinities and negotiating femininities: challenging gender hegemonies in Swedish forestry through women's networks." *Gender, Place and Culture* 28 (11): 1584–605. doi: 10.1080/0966369X.2020.1825215.

Little, Jo. 2015. "The development of feminist perspectives in rural gender issues." In *Feminisms and ruralities*, edited by Barbara Pini, Berit Brandth and Jo Little, 107–118. Lanham: Lexington books.

Méndez, Ricardo. 2014. "Crisis económica y reconfiguraciones territoriales." In *Geografía de la crisis económica en España*, coordinated by Juan Miguel Albertos Puebla and Jose Luis Sánchez Hernández, 17–38. Valencia: PUV.

Monk, Janice. 2001a. "Continuidades, cambios y retos de la geografía contemporánea en los Estados Unidos." *Documents d'Anàlisi Geogràfica* 39: 75–95.

Monk, Janice. 2001b. "Many roads. The personal and professional lives of women geographers." In *Placing autobiography in geography*, edited by Pamela Moss, 167–187. Syracuse: SUP.

Monk, Janice. 2012. "Work and life: crossing boundaries of time, space and place." In *Practicing geography: careers for enhancing society and the environment*, edited by Michael Solem, K. Foote and Janice Monk, 174–186. Washington: American Association of Geographers and Pearson.

Monk, Janice, and Cassey D. Allen. 2021. "The deviant geographer." *The Geographical Bulletin* 62 (1): 43–44.

Monk, Janice, and Cindi Katz. 1993. "When in the world are women?" In *Full circles. Geographies of women over the life course* (pp. 1–26). London: Routledge.

Monllor i Rico, Neus, and Anthony M. Fuller. 2016. "Newcomers to farming: towards a new rurality in Europe." *Documents d'Anàlisi Geogràfica* 62 (3): 553–567.

Pallares-Barbera, Montserrat, and Antònia Casellas. 2019. "Social networks as the backbone of women's work in the Catalan Pyrenées." *European Urban and Regional Studies* 26 (1): 65–79.

Pettersson, Katarina, and Susanna Heldt Cassel. 2014. "Women tourism entrepreneurs: doing gender on farms in Sweden." *Gender in Management: An International Journal* 29 (8): 487–504.

Phillippi, Julia, and Jana Lauderdale. 2018. "A guide to field notes for qualitative research: context and conversation." *Qualitative Health Research* 28 (3): 381–388.

Porto, Ana María, Montserrat Villarino, Mireia Baylina, Maria Dolors Garcia Ramon, and Isabel Salamaña. 2015. "Formación de las mujeres, empoderamiento e innovación rural." *Boletín de la Asociación de Geógrafos Españoles* 68: 385–406.

Recaño, Joaquín. 2017. "La sostenibilidad demogràfica de la España vacía." *Perspectives Demogràfiques* 7: 1–4.

Salamaña, Isabel, Mireia Baylina, Maria Dolors Garcia Ramon, Aría Porto Castro, and Montserrat Villarino. 2016. "Dones, trajectòries de vida i noves ruralitats." *Documents d'Anàlisi Geogràfica* 62 (3): 661–681.

Schmidt, Susanne. 2016. "Women in creative jobs and living in rural areas. A contradiction? In *Women and migration in rural Europe: labour markets, policies and imaginaries*, edited by Karin Wiest, 131–149. London: Palgrave Macmillan.

Seuneke, Pieter, and Bettina Bock. 2015. "Exploring the roles of women in the development of multifunctional entrepreneurship on family farms: an entrepreneurial learning approach." *Wageningen Journal of Life Sciences* 74-75: 41–50.

Tickamyer, Ann R. 2021. "Feminist methods and methodology in agricultural research." In *Routledge handbook of gender and agriculture*, edited by Carolyn Sachs et al., 239–250. London: Routledge.

Warren-Smith, Izzy, and Catherine Jackson. 2004. "Women creating wealth through rural enterprise." *International Journal of Entrepreneurial Behaviour & Research* 10 (6): 369–383.

Wiest, Karin. 2016. *Women and migration in rural Europe: labour markets, policies and imaginaries*. London: Palgrave Macmillan.

Woods, Michael. 2016. "International migration, agency and regional development in rural Europe." *Documents d'Anàlisi Geogràfica* 62 (3): 569–93.

16 Independence and Entrepreneurship Among Arab Muslim Rural and Bedouin Women in Israel

Ruth Kark, Emir Galilee and Tamar Feuerstein

Over the last 40 years, Janice Monk dedicated some of her research effort to the study of geography and gender and women. The main topics dealt with in her studies were the exclusion of women in human geography, women geographers, feminist geography, women and landscape and geographic education and gender (papers from 1982 to 2021). As a feminist geographer, she writes on issues related to the history of women in the discipline, comparative international perspectives, landscape and geographic education. As a Research Professor at the Southwest Institute for Research on Women (SIROW) she has developed and participated in projects focusing on women's employment, education, health and culture, emphasizing the diversity of women in the Southwest.

Especially interesting and relevant to this chapter was the film by Susan Palmer (writer) and Shelley Williams (director), *The Desert is No Lady* (1995), which Monk helped produce and to which Ruth Kark was exposed, when Janice visited Israel in 1998. The film was based on a book edited by Vera Norwood and Janice Monk: *The Desert is No Lady: Southwestern Landscapes in Women's Writing and Art* (Yale UP 1987 & Arizona UP 1997), containing ten papers. Kark was struck by the similarity in Israel of the desert theme in Arizona, the "otherness," as well as the women and gender issues. The film deals with the "other" in the border territory of the US Southwest, collaborating with women artists, philosophers, ecologists, dancers, writers and neuroscientists.

Introduction: theory and comparative context—keeping women "in their place": the situation in the Middle East

According to Seager: "Women worldwide live with *de facto* restrictions on their movement, public presence, dress, and public and private behavior ..." (Seager 1997, 108).

The situation of women's rights to real estate (or land) is bleak. The Global Land Tool Network estimated that only 2% of women in developing countries own real estate. In 2008, the network researched gender issues in the Muslim world, which constitutes 20% of the world population (WUNRN, 2008).

DOI: 10.4324/9781032275611-19

Suppression of and discrimination against Arab women in the Middle East has been noted by various scholars in the humanities and social science fields. Lewis (2004) discussed the history of the low status of women in the Islamic world since the eighth century, to modern times, and Starr (1984) mentions the almost total exclusion of women from land inheritance in the Ottoman Empire. Other researchers argue against a monolithic definition regarding the status and equality of women in the Middle East and North Africa. Women's situations are closely allied to the social, economic and political situations (Roded 2001; Efrati 2004). They bring examples of women's activity in the public, economic and social activity in the Muslim world. Finally, Cooke (2000) and Taraki (1995) researched Islam and feminism and Islamic feminists. Bengio claimed that Islamic law and its differing interpretations constitute simultaneously a stumbling block and a key to changing women's status (Bengio 2004).

Kark and Fischel's study on women in Palestine/Israel revealed the need to re-examine the current conceptions of the socio-economic situation of Arab women in Palestine/Israel in the different types of settlement, leading to the initiative to undertake the study presented here (Kark 1992, 2005; Kark and Fischel 2012). It is against these understandings that the present chapter is framed.

Methods and background

This chapter addresses, through interviews and questionnaires, the extent of independence and entrepreneurship among rural and Bedouin Muslim Arab women in Israel today. Nineteen in-depth interviews were conducted with Muslim Arab-Israeli women in Arab villages near Jerusalem and in Bedouin settlements in southern Israel in February–September 2007. The respondents were recruited through the "snowball" technique. Most of the questions were closed. Additionally, we carried out a number of general interviews using a personal questionnaire with women who were Arab and non-Arab scholars in the fields of history of the Middle East, sociology and anthropology, education and Islamic religious law.

The aim was to examine family, educational and professional backgrounds; the extent of economic independence in the management of the respondents' home and family; and the extent of their initiative and independence along with their share in holding and managing family assets, with the emphasis on real estate and geographic components. The ensuing discussion presents our initial results.

Personal data

Of the 19 Muslim women, aged between 20 and 50, interviewed in this study, 42% were from villages around Jerusalem, 53% Bedouins from Negev cities, 5% originated from villages in the north and are now living in Negev. Twelve of them were married; four were unmarried; and three were divorced.

The personal interviews began with gathering details about the interviewee, her family status, education and family member details (parents, spouse, children, etc.). The average marriage age was 19.5 years, lower than that of Muslim brides in Israel, which was 22.3, and of Jewish brides, 26.6 in 2006 (Israel Statistical Yearbook 2008, issue 3.6). The marriage age of Bedouin women was the lowest, followed by women of the Jerusalem region; the highest was of women from northern villages who live in the Negev. Marriage age increased in correspondence with the rise in educational level. Moreover, one can see the maintenance of endogamy through marriage within the family.

In 2021, the Total Fertility Rate (TFR) for Arab woman in Jerusalem district decreased to 3.00 and in the southern district increased to 4.92 (Israel Statistical Yearbook 2021, issue 2.39). Apparently, the respondents' fertility rate was higher than the general average in their districts; secondary or non-secondary education did not result in a significant decline in the number of children born.

We found that women's education constituted one of the most important instruments which provided knowledge to cope with challenges. Notably, an intergenerational change was clear: the women interviewed were more educated than the generation of their mothers and the range of their professions and opportunities therefore broader. They also hoped for their daughters' advancement in this sphere and offered them actual support.

Most respondents had post-high school education. Yet, no link was found between education and the nature of some interviewees' activity. We found that the respondents dealt with management of educational institutions, administration of businesses and "business entrepreneurship," Prominent among the southern women was activity in non-profit organizations and women's associations as well as public and political party activity.

Most spouses of respondents, married or divorced, had high school and academic education. As a rule, the spouses' support for their wives becomes important for the chances for her success. The husband's education was a common denominator regarding the geographic cross-section, marital status and sphere of vocation.

Legal concepts: respondents' awareness of women's rights to property and land in differing family situations

The interviewees' attitudes toward women's ownership of property and assets according to Islamic religious law, civil law and the customary situation in Arab society were examined. This included women's ownership of assets in general, women's inheritance, ownership of assets within the marital framework and in the case of divorce and a women's ownership of her profits. The results proved an awareness by most respondents of their rights to be owners of real estate and other assets. W. B., an educator from the Jerusalem district emphasized that "I know what my rights are. I know what part I deserve from the property." Most of the woman interviewed did know the rights provided by the different laws. S. A. Sh, an entrepreneur and owner of bridal salon in a Bedouin city emphasized that: "By the religious law, the boys (men) always get more then the girls (women)."

Most interviewers were aware of a woman's reduced inheritance in case of the death of a father, or husband, according to Muslim religious law by half, quarter, or eighth. According to civil law, women are eligible to equal inheritance, but actually receive less, or waive it in line with cultural practice even though they know they are qualified to receive it by religious and civil law. As they see it, differences exist between religious-civil-customary law even in the instance of the death of a son or daughter. In practice, from most of the interviewees' responses we see that daughters either do not receive or relinquish their portion of the inherited property.

Inconsistency or lack of familiarity appeared regarding the ownership of property that each side brought to the marriage. Yet, some answered that according to religious law the property belonged to the person who brought it to the marriage (the wife or the husband). Most thought that the property that accrued during the marriage was to be registered in equal form in the name of both members of the couple.

Most respondents thought that the profits of a working woman belong to them and are intended for their use, the home and the children. They assumed they had coverage and backing from religious law, civil law and customary practice as well.

From recent scholarly literature, one learns that despite religious and state laws allowing women to inherit from their parents, only a few "dare" to demand their portion in the inheritance after parents' death. Their refraining from claiming their inheritance also derives from fear of disputes with other family members (Layish 1995; Halichel 2008).

Women's entrepreneurship and economic independence

Successful women entrepreneurs and initiators in the southern region were in the feminine spheres of weaving, crafts, sewing, cosmetics, hairdressing and quasi-establishment NGO empowerment activities as well as small businesses. In the Jerusalem area, however, prominent initiatory activity is in branches of education (management and teaching), small businesses, restaurants and catering, as well as medicine and psychology.

Development of women's entrepreneurship encountered many obstacles; while those working with education and businesses received support from family. Despite the financial difficulties, entrepreneurship proved itself as worthwhile, profitable and contributed toward maintenance of the family. Independent working women contribute to the family economic status. The women claimed that their entrepreneurial activity had a positive influence on their lives and their familial and social standing. All expressed support for the idea of advancing the education and professionalism of the next female generation.

Entrepreneurship and management by women—general perceptions

Most interviewees were aware of other entrepreneurial women—owners of businesses or in a profession, including the free professions. But no spontaneous social networks of entrepreneurial women were noticeable. Activities for empowering women in the southern region were noticeable. Various internal and external motives for action could be identified.

Most interviewees distinguish between the country's different regions regarding the attitude toward women with initiative and capabilities; some even discern a sub-regional division on this issue. H. A-R., director of a Jerusalem region community center explains: "In our region there are differences between villages. Women run businesses and go out working in certain villages. In others the men are more 'aristocrats'. They do not give the women opportunities to get outside and build a career." On the larger scale, most of the interviewees distinguished between North and South, between urban settlements and rural settlements, and center and periphery.

An improvement of social status, among the respondents in terms of their immediate surrounding and within Arab society in Israel, was noticeable. This provided encouragement to other women.

Scholarly literature has scarcely discussed women's entrepreneurship in Arab or Bedouin settlements. It primarily foregrounds the problems of low employment rates among Arab women. (Standel 1975; Kama 1984; Shay 2004; Miari 2008).

Assets and financial administration of the family and woman

Women's increasing independence is expressed in management of family expenses and independence in making decisions related to management of the household, the children's education, purchases, etc. Most of the women have bank accounts, separate or joint, and they use credit cards and checkbooks. Seemingly, this is a clear channel of independence, providing the woman with a position of authority in the family unit. Conversely, the question arises as to whether this entrepreneurship or activity of such type is an impetus toward making the woman more dominant not only within the family unit but also outside of it?

Rise in the age of marriage: a social phenomenon of financial and real estate significance

The continuous rise in marriageable age is one of the important phenomena in the Arab world. In various places within it, there is a salient growing percentage of older unmarried men and women who find other venues for solving the marriage problem or remain unmarried (Tzoreff 2004). According to Halichel (2008), this phenomenon is likely to lead to a reversal of gender roles and result in a change of patterns in marriage, residence and fertility rate, a rise in their participation in the labor force, increased support of the family and inheritance patterns.

From the interviews, a different pattern is evident: daughters remaining unmarried inherit their parents' house or a certain portion of their parents' assets. In other cases, the married siblings help support the unwed sister.

Socially and economically a new phenomenon may emerge. A working unmarried woman can considerably reduce such a burden or, perhaps, need not have recourse to the inheritance. From a real estate perspective, in the foreseeable future, an increasing trend may arise of unmarried women owning land and other assets gained as inheritance, leading to accumulation of assets, capital and property by unmarried women.

Assets and financial administration of the family and of the woman—general concepts

According to most women, a trend of cancelling customs of bride price and dowry prior to the marriage has emerged. Others, however, think that for reasons of maintenance of tradition and religion, these customs should be continued. Some feel that the change should be toward legal agreements and totally shared, egalitarian life.

Most respondents agree that the process of extended family disintegration reinforced the woman's status and independence and raised her level of her control over assets. As opposed to vehicles and real estate, home contents do not constitute a collection of negotiable items.

Empowerment activities

Group activities in the area of empowerment in non-profit associations, organizations, workshops and interest groups, partially based on traditional activities, are prominent mainly among the Bedouin women in the south and less among rural women around Jerusalem. The motivation for these entrepreneurial breakthroughs is a clear distress of triple marginality—in the sectorial, accepted and gender aspects. We noticed that women in the Bedouin sector depart from traditional functions and social traditions which restrict her to the home.

To a great extent the entrepreneurs needed to find solutions integrating maintenance of tradition with characteristics of modernization and independence. Some women from among the Bedouin sector who were interviewed for the study are active in sewing and embroidery associations. A woman from the Jerusalem area told the story of two women from her village who wanted to work in a nearby McDonald branch. In the past the family would have objected, including violence by men, but at the time of our interview, they received the support of the family and the village society.

From the advancement of these organizations into the awareness of Israeli society, it appears that the unique position of Bedouin society in the south of the country is one that preserves traditional characteristics yet undergoing changes which have resulted in various, and sometimes contradictory, challenges for the population of women. Interviews with women from villages in the Jewish area show that they encountered fewer barriers in gaining an education, a professional career and entrepreneurship.

Geographic and patrilocal mobility

The institution of patrilocality (moving into residence with the husband's family) has been described in classic scholarly literature as one of the foundational elements of traditional family structure in Arab society (Rosenfeld 1958, 1960; Marx 1967; Cohen 1972). Despite the disintegration of the extended family described above, one can see that the institution of patrilocality has not suffered serious damage and that the woman, upon her marriage, moved to live in her husband's settlement and near his family. This is especially indicative of marriages of Bedouins from the south with northern non-Bedouin Arab women, more open to the possibilities of entrepreneurship and independence.

Conclusion

This study attempted to estimate the degree of independence and entrepreneurship among groups of rural and Bedouin Muslim women in Israel. The discussion also examines their personal their personal opinions on independence, entrepreneurship, economic involvement, legal and social status against the background of gender inequality among Arab women in the country and a changing world economy. The study shows the importance of education and involvement in organizations and associations in the women's empowerment and entrepreneurial activity as well as the gap between civil and Sharia law versus tradition on the issue of women's inheritance. Among the salient changes observed among them, the weakening of the extended family and the clan and the rise in marriageable age, along with the increase of unmarried women, are likely to lead to a boost the participation of women in entrepreneurship and the labor force and expand their control over real estate. Their support for entrepreneurial women in family economics contributes to their independence, change in their family, social and economic status, and in the traditional patterns of inheritance.

This study's findings support Abu-Baqer's 2008 conclusions concerning gender inequality in Israeli Arab society and the inability of pioneering Arab women who attained striking achievements in education and employment to circumvent tradition, the patriarchalism, and the double yoke they suffer under, and transform their mental–social well-being in their home and in the bosom of the family (Abu-Rabia-Queder 2007; Abu-Baqer 2008).

Researchers of Israeli Arab society highlight gender inequality among the country's Arab women and the difficulty of making a breakthrough in this sphere by the first and second generation of educated women. Yet, one may conclude from this study that the ongoing changes in the main social structures in Arab society will have a decisive influence on the economic situation of the women and the unique situation of women who are trying to gain independence. Seemingly, the shift to an economy more reliant on the nuclear family and less on the extended family enhances the woman's value as a component in family economics and allows her independent initiative and ownership of different types of assets. Still, the belief is that a large part of a woman's support at crucial times is the extended family, whose weakening may pose consequences for the woman's security to contribute to the perpetuation of tradition and limit the process of "freeing" women.

References

Abu-Baqer, Haula. 2008. "Welfare, Modernity and Tradition: The Coping of Palestinian Women in Israel with Changes in the Frameworks of Their Lives." In *The Book of Arab Society in Israel: Population – Society – Economics 2*, edited by Adel Manaa and Ramsis Gera, 359–384. Jerusalem: Van Leer Institute; Tel Aviv, Hakibbutz Hameuchad.

Abu-Rabia-Queder, Sarab. 2007. "Permission to Rebel: Arab Bedouin Women's Changing Negotiation of Social Roles." *Feminist Studies* 33 (1): 161–187.

Bengio, Ofra ed. 2004. *Women in the Middle East: Between Tradition and Change*. Tel Aviv: Moshe Dayan Center.

Cohen, Avner. 1972. *Arab Border Village in Israel*. Manchester: Manchester University Press.

Cooke, Miriam. 2000. "Women, Religion, and the Post Colonial Arab World." *Cultural Critique* 45: 150–184.

Efrati, Noga. 2004. "The Study of Women and Gender in the Middle East: The Development of the Field and Its Directions." In *Women in the Middle East: Between Tradition and Change*, edited by Ofra Bengio, 29–37. Tel Aviv: Moshe Dayan Center.

Halichel, Ahmad. 2008. "Unmarried Women among Arab Women: Causes of the Expansion of the Phenomenon in Central and Northern Israel." In *The Book of Arab Society in Israel: Population – Society – Economics 2*, edited by Adel Manaa and Ramsis Gera, 312–383. Jerusalem: Van Leer Institute; Tel Aviv, Hakibbutz Hameuchad.

Israel Statistical Yearbook 2021, issue 2.39

Kama, Blansh. 1984. "The Status of the Arab Women in Israel." Prime Minister's Office, Jerusalem.

Kark, Ruth. 1992. "Land-God-Man: Concepts of Land Ownership in Traditional Cultures and in Eretz Israel." In *Ideology and Landscape in Historical Perspective*, edited by A. Baker and G. Biger, 63–82. Cambridge: Cambridge University Press.

Kark, Ruth. 2005. "Land-God-Women: Women, Land and Property in Traditional and Modern Societies – The Case of Africa." In *Gender in Agriculture and Technology*, edited by Finite Tanzarn and Gendered Worlds Series edited by Bantebya Kyomuhendo, 27–43. Kampala, Uganda: Women and Gender Studies.

Kark, Ruth, and Roy Fischel. 2012. "Gendered Space: Palestinian Women in the Public Domain during the Late Ottoman and Mandate Periods, 1831–1948." In *Gendered Space in Middle Eastern Societies and Cultures. Hawwa* Special Issue edited by R. Roded and I. Greenberg, 129–166. Leiden: Brill.

Layish, Aharon. 1995. "The Status of the Moslem Woman in the Sharia Court in Israel." In *Women's Status in Law and Society*, edited by Frances Raday, Carmel Shalev and Michal Liban-Kobi, 364–397. Jerusalem: Schocken.

Lewis, Bernard. 2004. "Gender and the Clash of Civilizations." In *Women in the Middle East: Between Tradition and Change*, edited by Ofra Bengio, 15–27. Tel Aviv: Moshe Dayan Center, Tel Aviv University.

Marx, Emmanuel. 1967. *Bedouin of the Negev*. Manchester: Manchester University.
Miari, Sami. 2008. "The Dynamics of Unemployment among Arabs in Israel: Evidence from Panel Figures." In *The Book of Arab Society in Israel: Population – Society – Economy 2*, edited by Adel Manaa and Ramsis Gera, 313–358. Jerusalem: Van Leer Institute; Tel Aviv, Hakibbutz Hameuchad.
Roded, Ruth. 2001. "Mainstreaming Middle East Gender Research: Promise or Pitfall?" *Middle East Studies Association Bulletin* 35: 21–22.
Rosenfeld, Henry. 1958. "Processes of Structural Change within the Arab Village Extended Family." *American Anthropologist* 60 (6): 1127–1139.
Rosenfeld, Henry. 1960. "On Determinants of the Status of Arab Village Women." *Man* 60: 66–70.
Seager, Joni, 1997, *The State of Women in the World: Atlas, Penguin reference books*. London: Penguin Group.
Shay, Tamar. 2004. "The Women in the Arab Village.' Seminar Paper, The Hebrew University of Jerusalem.
Standel, Uri. 1975. "The Status of the Arab Women in Israel, 1976." *Social Security* 10: 137–143.
Starr, June. 1984. "The Kegal and Social Transformation of Women in the Aegean Turkey." In *Women and Property: Women as Property*, edited by Renee Hirschon. New York: St. Martin's Press.
Statistical Abstract of Israel. 2008. https://www.cbs.gov.il/en/publications/Pages/2008/Statistical-Abstract-of-Israel-2008-No59.aspx
Taraki, Lisa. 1995. "Islam Is the Solution: Jordanian Islamists and the Dilemma of the 'Modern Women'." *The British Journal of Sociology* 46 (4): 643–661.
Tzoreff, Mira. 2004. "The Others' of the Others: Women, Gender and Nationalism in Palestinian Society in the Shadow of the Intifadas." In *Women in the Middle East: Between Tradition and Change*, edited by Ofra Bengio, 109–138. Tel Aviv: Moshe Dayan Center, Tel Aviv University.
WUNRN. 2008. http://www.iwpr.net/?p=syr&s=f&o=347082&apc_state=henh (We thank Prof. Ruth Roded for assistance with this reference).

Part IV
Gender and Environmental Concerns
Change, Crisis and Recovery

17 Social Change in Griffith, NSW, Australia

Discourses of Indigeneity, Identity, Justice and Well-Being over Fifty Years

Janice Monk, Richard Howitt, Claire Colyer, Candy Kilby, Lynette Kilby, Stephen Collins, Bev Johnson, David Crew and Roger Penrith

Tensions, contradictions and inconsistencies are woven into the highly racialised landscapes and social dynamics of the rural towns of Australia. This chapter focuses on Griffith, a planned city in rural south-eastern New South Wales (NSW) proclaimed in 1916. It lies in the southern area of Wiradjuri Country, the customary territory of the Wiradjuri First Nation encompassing the riverine region of the western slopes and plains of southern NSW. Griffith was named after the then NSW Minister for Public Works and designed by Walter Burley Griffin as a major service centre for the state-supported Murrumbidgee Irrigation Area (MIA) established in 1912.

A particular assemblage of moments has shaped Griffith as a successful, modern, multicultural city whose economy and social fabric reflects the manipulation of land and water for agricultural and industrial production, alongside the rich Wiradjuri cultural landscapes and the lives of the Wiradjuri people who occupied this region for more than 40,000 years.

When the MIA and Griffith were established, Wiradjuri people were not recognised as stakeholders. Recent legislative concessions of Aboriginal land rights and Native Title,[1] and the resilient presence of Aboriginal people and their cultural landscapes have done little to reorient dominant settler narratives to recognise that places like Griffith existed before "settlement". In Aboriginal narratives of place, deeper connections to Country constantly break through more recent layers in the palimpsests of local geographies. Our discussion privileges Wiradjuri narratives in Griffith's stories of place.

Griffith's Settlement Imaginary

Reflecting on her experience of the vast, sparsely populated regions of Central Australia, Robyn Davidson (2017, 97) says Australian landscapes should be understood as narratives that stretch into the "deep time" of human presence on the continent. This understanding is also true for "settled Australia", where colonial narratives dominate representations of place. In the settler imaginary stories of a named (and venerated) colonial figure

DOI: 10.4324/9781032275611-21

crossing hostile, apparently empty, unknown and un-named terrain mark the local beginning of history, and that beginning comes to define place. In these stories of settlement, deeper histories of Aboriginal presence – if acknowledged– are typically silenced as an irrelevant preface to the story of settling.

The opening act in these local settler dramas thus focuses on colonisation. Tropes of prior emptiness (Howitt 2012) are mobilised to affirm that what was unowned is now owned: the colonisers' expertise imagined the "wasteland" transformed into a homeland through successful possession in the face of environmental adversity. Histories of "dispersal" – genocidal erasures and policies to separate families, extinguish languages and annihilate cultures (Read 1983, 1984, 1998) – are rendered invisible in these dominant narratives of places brought into existence by the act of settlement.

Such triumphalist colonial discourses of place create halls of mirrors (Rose 1999) and echo chambers that valorise the colonisers' self-proclaimed achievement. According to the conventional settler narrative, the area that became Griffith lay in a barren region rarely visited by its traditional owners – prior to "the 19th century... westward movement of settlers who utilised the semi-arid plains as massive sheep stations" (Griffith Visitors Information Centre 2010, 4). Treating abundant Wiradjuri cultural landscapes and waters as *terra nullius*, colonial occupation of southern NSW initially reinscribed them as grazing lands. In time, irrigation transformed the region into a patchwork of canals and small farms for horticultural production and intensive agriculture. The region's pastoral wealth was created in the primitive accumulation of squatters,[2] including Irish-born grazier Sir Samuel McCaughey,[3] who experimented with canals to channel water onto North Yanco station in 1900 and made windfall profits from government resumption of "his" property (Cowper 1987).[4]

The dominant settler narrative is that McCaughey's success inspired national and state government cooperation to construct the MIA (Griffith Visitors Information Centre 2010, 4), but the MIA actually developed through a complex history of colonial rivalries between large-scale landholders and smaller scale settlers, political corruption, incompetence and bureaucratic inertia (Cowper 1987). The creation of irrigation farms and closer settlement after World War I recruited demobilised Australian and British soldiers as new settlers; however, misrepresentation of the opportunities for prosperity in the region saw many soldier settlers abandon their farms, burdened with crippling debt (Ibid. Chapter 10).

In contrast to settler society's commodification of water, Wiradjuri narratives value water, rivers and landscapes as parts of a fragile balance of forces in which humans had responsibilities shaped by stewardship, mutuality and care.[5] Conflicts over water management across the Murray-Darling Basin[6] (Hartwig et al. 2021; Jackson and Head 2020; Walker 2019) and elsewhere (Poelina 2020; Taylor et al. 2016) highlight tensions between an understanding of water as a sacred element in a fragile landscape rather than a commodity "more precious than gold" (Jeffcoat 1988; McHugh 1991).

The Wiradjuri Nation's history of dispersal, exclusion and exploitation (Bamblett 2013; Macdonald 1998; Read 1984) is deeply scarred into the landscape. Macdonald's work (1998, 2013), challenges the widely held settler assumption that colonial occupation of NSW's western riverine region erased Wiradjuri identities. While Wiradjuri people were profoundly affected by colonial Governor Macquarie's military expansion into the riverine slopes, they resisted strongly. They maintained strong links between people and Country throughout the colonial period. Their experiences mark local histories and geographies across this part of "settled Australia" and even when silenced by representations that celebrate and promote tourism, pastoralism and developmentalism (Bamblett 2013), First Nations' narratives of deep connection are the foundational layers of the palimpsests of southern NSW.

Griffith in Regional Context

Like every rural town, Griffith today is a unique assemblage. It is a regional service and economic centre, a planned city built on hydraulic engineering. Its town plan drew on coloniser visions of a region similar to the irrigated regions of the Punjab in British India (Cowper 1987; McKillop 2016). Contemporary Griffith is now acknowledged as a Wiradjuri place, with a range of markers of their continuing presence such as strong Aboriginal organisations and services, public artwork and routine acknowledgement at public events. Aboriginal families were always part of the MIA's seasonal workforce, moving throughout Wiradjuri Country for work and increasingly settling in and around Griffith from the 1940s (Figure 17.1). Some moved to Griffith because

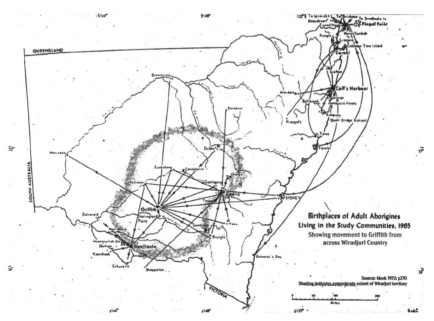

Figure 17.1 New South Wales showing the birthplaces of adult Aboriginal people living in the communities in Monk's PhD study in 1965 and indicating the movement of people to Griffith from across Wiradjuri Country.

of conflict with the managers of the Erambie Aboriginal Reserve at Cowra, NSW, and many families were also linked to the former Warangesda Mission near Darlington Point which closed in the 1920s (Howitt et al. 2016, 26).

Griffith is also remarkably multicultural, famous for its multicultural festivals, hospitality and cuisine. Griffith became a focus for chain migration from Italy between the 1920s and the mid-1950s, with 85% of horticultural farms in the area held by people of Italian descent by 1969 (Huber 1981, 52). By 2016, census data showed that people with Italian ancestry represented 25.1% of the Griffith population (compared to just 4.3% of the total Australian population); people with South Asian and Pacific Islander ancestry were also over-represented compared to the national data. Griffith has also established a strong reputation for welcoming refugees, with the 2016 Census identifying 98 Hazaragi speakers from Afghanistan compared to none in 2011 (https://profile.id.com.au/griffith). Griffith is also home to Aboriginal people from many other First Nations.

Methods and Data – Two Projects, 50 Years Apart

Janice Monk's Project, 1965

Monk's 1960s PhD project collected data about the socio-economic circumstances of Aboriginal communities in six towns across rural NSW – Griffith, Cowra, Deniliquin and Coffs Harbour, now cities, and two smaller communities at Fingal Point and Coraki (Figure 17.2) – with a view to explaining differences between the Aboriginal communities and differences between Aboriginal and non-Aboriginal communities (Monk 1972). Her work received support from and contributed directly to Rowley's seminal Social Science Research Council of Australia project (Rowley 1971, 142–159).

In contrast to most early anthropological work, Monk's study rejected the prevailing typologies that viewed differences between Aboriginal communities as degrees of "acculturation", reflecting either "stage[s] in a continuum between traditional Aboriginal and European cultures" where time was "the major variable accounting for differences"; or the type of residential setting that might reflect "varying positions on Redfield's folk-urban continuum"; or, Gale's (1964) approach which examined "types of Aboriginal assimilation from a regional viewpoint" (Monk 1972, 347–348). Rather, her study aimed to show that differences in the socio-economic characteristics of the communities were expressions of a complex interplay of the characteristics of Aboriginal life in each place with influencing variables such as government policy and the history of Aboriginal-White contact in each town (Monk 1972, 354).

The towns selected for Monk's PhD study had different economic contexts but similar demographic structures and residential patterns. Each of the larger towns had a population of 5,500–7,500 people, with Aboriginal people comprising 2–2.5% of the local population. In each, new public

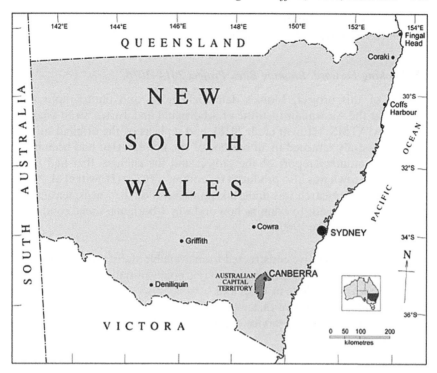

Figure 17.2 New South Wales, showing the six towns included in Monk's PhD.

housing had recently been allocated to Aboriginal people – typically on the edge of the town and often separated from the town by infrastructure – and each had nearby government Aboriginal reserves or mission stations, or reserves that had been recently closed. About one-third of Aboriginal households in each town were interviewed, completing a detailed survey that documented housing conditions, economic resources, employment, education, health, migration history and social networks. The households were selected randomly with the aim of reflecting the community, ensuring equal representation of people living on Aboriginal reserves, in public social housing in town, or camping / living in makeshift homes in informal settlements. Surveys were completed for each member of every household.

Monk's research was distinct from previous geographical and anthropological work in NSW. Rather than reducing the towns and their people to figures collected in the survey, it focused on conditions in these rural towns, incorporating local, qualitative observations, conversations and information into its interpretation of quantitative data. Her study recognised diversity within Aboriginal populations, but also identified poverty as the key issue for all the Aboriginal families in the study. It found that past government policies, isolation of Aboriginal people on reserves, limited education and prejudice continued to have a major impact on their well-being, work opportunities and incomes. Other factors, such as the local economy and availability of work in the area, were also very important.

The Looking Forward, Looking Back Project 2014–2016

As part of this project, Monk's data, field notes and photographs were archived at the Australian Institute of Aboriginal and Torres Strait Islander Studies (AIATSIS) (Howitt et al. 2018), and replicas of the original surveys were successfully returned to all but one of the families that had been interviewed. A summary report of the project and the changes that had taken place in each town was also produced for community use (Howitt et al. 2016).

In 2015, new research was undertaken in several of the towns, teasing out three narrative threads to examine how and why Aboriginal social conditions had changed since the 1960s:

- a statistical narrative constructed from available statistical sources;
- a policy narrative considering the major policy initiatives since the original surveys were done in 1965; and
- a community narrative that would draw on interviews with a range of community members, service organisations and government agencies in the towns.

Fifty years on, these towns were remarkably different (Table 17.1), with Coffs Harbour increasing its population more than tenfold, Griffith more than threefold, Cowra doubling and Deniliquin – formerly the wealthiest – remaining relatively stable in population but reduced in wealth and employment opportunities (Howitt et al. 2016). An important development was that in each town, the Aboriginal population increased as a proportion of the total population by between 3.6% and 6.5%, significantly higher than for the state and national populations.

Griffith

Before commencing the new research activity in Griffith, several meetings were held with the Griffith Aboriginal Working Group. After consideration, a local group of Aboriginal community leaders established the *Yamandhu Marang* Social Research Reference Group.[7] The role of the Reference Group was to oversee the research and hold the university-based researchers accountable under a governing cultural protocol (Appendix 17.1), which was also approved by the Macquarie University Human Research Ethics Committee. The aim of the research was to document community experience of the significant changes of the 50 years since Monk's 1965 research. With the assistance of Western Riverina Community College, local Aboriginal people were trained in interviewing, undertaking 17 community interviews

Social Change in Griffith, NSW, Australia   187

Table 17.1 Key community statistics 1965, 2011 and 2016

	Coffs Harbour			Deniliquin			Griffith			Cowra			
	1965	2011	2016	1965	2011	2016	1965	2011	2016	1965	2011	2016	
Total Population	6,996	68,414	72,944	5,472	7,122	7,434	7,590	24,363	25,641	6,407	12,147	12,460	
No. of Aboriginal People	159	2,817	3,643	114	257	340	165	1,001	1,226	149	793	984	
Ratio of Aboriginal people to non-Aboriginal people	1:44	1:24	1:20	1:48	1:28	1:22	1:46	1:24	1:21	1:43	1:15	1:13	
Indigenous persons as % of total persons	2.27	4.12	4.99	2.08	3.61	4.57	2.17	4.11	4.78	2.33	6.53	7.89	
Most important industries	Timber, Agriculture, Tourism	Services (Education, Health, Retail, Welfare), Tourism	Services Health, Retail, Education) Tourism	Pastoral production	Services (Education, Retail), Cereal Processing, Sheep, Beef, Grain Farming	Services (Welfare, Retail, Education, Health), Meat Processing	Irrigated Agriculture	Wine, Fruit Growing, Meat Processing, Services (Education)	Poultry, Wine, Services (Retail, Health, Education)	Service town (wheat and sheep)	Sheep, Beef and Grain Farming, Services (Education, Retail, Welfare, Local Government)	Sheep and Beef Farming, Meat Processing, Services (Welfare, Local Government, Education, Retail)	

Figure 17.3 An information table about the Monk Archive at the Griffith Family History Day in May 2014 received a very positive reception. Left to right: Janice Monk, Gloria Goolagong, Bev Johnson and Melissa Carberry.

(Photo: C Colyer)

with 19 Aboriginal community members. At the request of the Reference Group, the university-based researchers interviewed 22 selected community leaders who held a range of leadership roles in both Aboriginal and non-Aboriginal community or business organisations (Figure 17.3).

Participants in the community interviews were asked to reflect on a set of overlapping issues that have influenced Aboriginal experience and outcomes in Griffith since the mid-1960s. The community interviewers were almost exclusively women, and the Aboriginal community interviewees were also largely women. It is notable that two of the men interviewed as community members were also interviewed separately as community organisational leaders. This reflects both the circumstances of our research and the tendency for some activities to be gender sensitive (i.e., women preferring to conduct interviews and be interviewed by other women) (see, e.g., Fredericks 2008), and also something important about the historical and contemporary community leadership provided by women (Behrendt 2005; Cohen and Somerville 1990; Gale 1983, 1990; Locke 2018; Moreton-Robinson 2011; Tynan and Bishop 2019), both in senior roles and in youth and emerging roles. As Monk had in interrogating her data in the 1960s, the community and organisational interviewees reflected on gender issues.

Discussion

Our Griffith interviews drew out community narratives of change. The interplay of racism, education, employment, the health and judicial systems and experiences of family fragmentation were common across many of the interviews, echoing Monk's 1965 findings. Much had changed at state and federal level in the 50 years since Monk's study. A national referendum in 1967 overwhelmingly approved constitutional change to empower the national government to make laws for Aboriginal people and include them in the national Census. Following the election of a progressive federal Labor government in 1972, the overarching policy of "assimilation" of First Nations peoples gave way to a national policy of "self-determination"; recognition of Aboriginal rights to land followed, enacted by the Commonwealth in Australia's Northern Territory in 1976 and then by the state government in NSW in 1983. In 1992, the Australian High Court *Mabo* decision rejected the foundation myth of "terra nullius" and recognised the concept of Native Title. Such changes specific to Aboriginal people were accompanied by changes to welfare support, changes in education, labour rights and many other domains of policy and social values.

Policies and Their Consequences on the Ground

Mainstream literature on Indigenous issues in Australia focuses on the development, implementation and failure of government policies intended to affect the lives of Indigenous Australians (Dillon and Westbury 2007; Ford and Rowse 2013; Hocking 2018; Rowley 1986; Rowse 2010). On the ground in Griffith, however, even major policy changes were perceived to have little positive impact to achieve better outcomes.

> **Are there any major events that happened in your life that have impacted on you or your family… changes in employment, health or government policies?**
> The Land Rights Act, I suppose; that was a big one. [thinking] But then they had stereotyping there with blackfellas. Everybody around here was panicking: "They're going to take our land, they're going to take our land", all this crap.
> (Community Participant Interview GC11, May 2015)

> In terms of policy… you know, the Land Rights Act [NSW, 1983] – has had a positive effect, in terms of potential economic use of land assets and housing. Although, I think Griffith hasn't done so well out of it, because the assets that the Land Council got through the Land Rights Act aren't high-value assets, particularly the dry area of farming tracts of land that the Land Council has …
> (Senior Commonwealth Public Servant Interview GO14, October 2015)

> The Land Rights Acts, [and] Mabo [decision], saying that we weren't deserted country, we were actually invaded – those have been major events in the life of us as a people. But they haven't really impacted on us, because there are only certain people that get any benefit from those changes.
> (Community Participant Interview GC1, April 2015)

Lack of confidence in government's ability to deliver intended policy targets was reflected in both community and organisation interviews. Participants expressed concern about how well-intentioned policies transitioned into complex, fragmented, poorly delivered and inadequately funded programmes. A different funding approach had been implemented in 2014 when a unified policy framework, the Indigenous Advancement Strategy, was intended to secure outcomes prioritised in the national government's Closing the Gap strategy.

> That was very competitive – very. And of a thousand successful applications, less than half were Aboriginal organisations, so it's all the mainstream organisations, now, getting the funding to deliver programs for us, on the ground …
> (Community Participant Interview GO3, October 2015)

This shift proved to be flawed when a 2016 audit of the process concluded:

> The way [the Government] did that, according to the independent watchdog, was a textbook case of how not to implement policy.
> (Conifer 2017)

Many community participants reflected on how previous policy regimes impacted their families and constrained opportunities in ways that continue to influence their lives, particularly the trauma arising from long-entrenched government policies of removing children from their families:

> … I think the other psychological impact, also, was the fear: fear of the Welfare, fear of the kids being taken, and told what to do, when to come, when to go, who to marry, and when you could go off the Mission … they escaped that sort of regime and came over to Griffith, and we see that as an escape from that tyranny.
> (Community Participant Interview GC2, April 2015)

> The forced removal of children also affected a lot of local families. The ongoing effects of transgenerational trauma are evident within our communities. The unemployment rates, feeling of hopelessness, drug & alcohol misuse and domestic violence continue to be issues that … the AMS[8] are dealing with every day.
> (Community Participant Interview GO3, October 2015)

> ... back then you couldn't miss school, because the Welfare would be straight down if you missed one or two days, and they didn't muck around too much, because they'd just grab the kids and send them off to the homes ... my grandmother, she spent a bit of time at Cootamundra Girls' Home, she was a Stolen Generation[9] ... Yeah, the chain was broken.
> (Community Participant Interview GC15, August 2015)

Identity, Mobility and Attachment to Place

The memories of today's Elders recall the lives of the families Janice Monk recorded in the 1960s. Many remembered an itinerant childhood of moving around Wiradjuri Country with their parents in search of work. For many, these experiences and narratives of mobility and connection to Country and extended family are part of their Wiradjuri identity and culture.

> My father, who was a railway worker [in Tumut] and every holiday that he got on the railway we used to come to Griffith and do the fruit-picking. We did that itinerant kind of work so the family can earn some extra income, and the kids had to help out ... we used to come during the orange season during the winter, and during the summer we used to do the grapes ... I spent a lot of time here doing that kind of work, seeing the cousins and getting to know Griffith, and it was just like a second home to my family.
> (Community Participant Interview GO2, October 2015)

> [W]e just mainly travelled most of the time ... we did a lot of fruit picking. So that's how we lived, travelling; a lot of schools, different towns ... we'd go sort of a circle ... we'd catch the goods train from Griffith to Hillston or Roto, we'd stay there overnight, we'd just make up a camp ... get up early in the morning, catch the other train going back up the line to Condo[10] ... following the fruit picking ... Did a lot of fruit picking here in Griffith ... whatever was in season we'd pick it.
> (Community Participant Interview GC11, May 2015)

Experiences of disconnection and reconnection are part of that identity and the culture that has evolved, despite the losses and impacts of previous policies.

> The Aboriginal Welfare Board ... days, left a psychological impact on my family, because ... Grandfather was the last initiated man in our family. He was a 'clever man',[11] so he carried that responsibility. But living on the Mission in Condobolin ... they had to do [language and cultural business] in secret ... a lot of our language was lost ... the impact is not only the loss of a lot of the cultural ways, but also the singing and the dancing. And he wouldn't pass on any of the knowledge of the clever man knowledge; he said it just stopped with him.
> (Community Participant Interview GC2, April 2015)

> We do have [our own culture here in Griffith], and we still do. Unfortunately, it's changed because of some government policies that were dished out earlier on, and that was around the assimilation policies and all that there, and the start of the Stolen Generation era – which took our language, our culture, and took people away from their traditional land – and unfortunately, we're still dealing with it today.
> (Community Participant Interview GC4, April 2015)

> I'm proud to be an Aboriginal. I wish that I knew my language … I am proud now, you know. But knowing my own language, I would've been very happy. That's one thing we missed out on, we missed out on our language.
> (Community Participant Interview GC16, Interview, August 2015)

> I'm Wiradjuri, darling. I'm not Aboriginal or Torres Strait Islander, I'm Wiradjuri; I live in Wiradjuri Country, that's it.
> (Community Participant Interview GC11, May 2015)

Education and Opportunity

For many families, access to education was highly valued but for older participants, barriers to education included not only family mobility but also the sense that Aboriginal children were out-of-place in schools – particularly in local secondary schools.

> I really liked school, just to get away from down there – and learning… I only went to Year 8, because at that time everyone was leaving school; you turned 15, you had to leave school or stay in school… all of my friends ended up leaving, all my Koori friends, and I was only left there with the white, so I thought: 'What's the point of me staying here? There's no one there,' where I should've stayed at school.
> (Community Participant Interview GC7, May 2015)

> The teachers couldn't be bothered. Well, their attitude was: 'They're black, they're not going to amount to anything; they're only just going to leave school and have kids anyway, so why teach them?'.
> (Community Participant Interview GC14, June 2015)

Although there have been improvements, similar barriers remain. At the time of the 2015 study, the rate of school completion for the Griffith population was well below the state average and for Aboriginal people was still less than half that of the non-Indigenous population.

> I can only speak for me and my immediate children – they're better off; they did their schooling, they did their education, and like all Koori kids, they weren't always angels. But yeah, it was just a matter of teaching them to grow up with respect, and to find their way in the world. And to

do that, they needed their education, and I kind of pushed that on them, but I think it's worked out; they seem to be pretty okay at the moment – so most of them are working.
(Community Participant Interview GC1, April 2015)

Employment

Despite hard conditions in the 1960s, many community participants recalled that seasonal labouring and other jobs were relatively easy to come by. Fifty years later, many of those jobs no longer existed and very few Aboriginal people worked in the primary industries that had been the major employers of Aboriginal people in the 1960s (Howitt et al. 2016, 31):

> I've done heaps of jobs in Sydney. Back then, you could just walk out of one job and into another ... Didn't need any qualifications. I never had any qualifications, anyway, just labour. And there were heaps, just jobs everywhere, back then. Not like now, you battle to get a job.
> (Community Participant Interview GC14, August 2015)

> I think what's changed here is those [labouring] positions no longer being available on the farms, and that's due to a lot of the small orchards ... a lot of those smaller plots where they used to do a lot of employment of Aboriginal staff, and they were just pulled out of the ground because it wasn't viable anymore.
> (Community Participant Interview GC2, April 2015)

In 2015, the rates of Aboriginal children completing high school were still low, and there were barriers to employment even in unskilled jobs due to competitive demands for higher qualifications and the cost of meeting mandatory requirements such as a NSW "white card"[12] or driver's licence.

> Some of the barriers here with Aboriginal people applying for positions is ... they don't have the qualifications. And for general ... labouring work and roadworks operations and that type of role, the qualifications that they request there are just ... over the top, and makes [it] even more difficult for those Aboriginal people coming in and applying.
> (Community Participant Interview GO3, November 2015)

Employment and short-term training programmes aimed to increase Aboriginal employment have not overcome structural disadvantage and discrimination in local labour markets.

> [I]t's only Aboriginal-identified positions that you can get. It's horrible here; it's a real racist town ... They say it's multicultural; it's multicultural

in applying for funding and whatever so that they can put this pretty picture out of Griffith and whatever, but when it comes down to it, when you look in the shops, the shops aren't multicultural. You won't see very many people in the shops ... that are not Anglo-Saxon.
(Community Participant Interview GC11, May 2015)

There's a lot of racism, still racism, but I think we can overcome that; we don't have to accept that sort of treatment. But at the same time, they need to open up their businesses, too, to employ our people, and not just shove us into, okay, six months here, six months there, get some training, and then you're still queuing up at Centrelink for the dole. It's not the way it's supposed to work. You need some real employment.
(Community Participant Interview GC2, April 2015)

In the wider community, there is often both hostility towards and misunderstanding – and even misrepresentation – of Aboriginal employment policies:

[We see] that generational disadvantage ... in some of our low socioeconomic groups, and people are saying, 'Well, they should've just changed.' You know: 'They've got all this money and access to all this training and welfare and things just don't change.' But they don't understand the complexities of some peoples' lives ...
(Organization Leader Interview GO1, October 2015)

Experiences of Racism

The town's multicultural demography means that issues of race, ethnicity and identity are not simply polarised around "black" and "white" positionalities. The non-Wiradjuri Aboriginal population, its large and longstanding Italian population, the diversity of faith communities and the continued economic and political privilege of some community sectors makes Griffith's experience of racism complex.

Griffith was a great town growing up here. There was very little racism when I was at school. It has become worse as I grew up ... Griffith likes to claim we're a multicultural community and we're all accepting of all races, but it's not the case. Racism is alive and well in Griffith – in my opinion ... back when I first left school, I tried to get a flat in Griffith ... the real estate told [my sister] straight out: 'No, the landlord, the owner won't rent to Aboriginal people.' ... It's getting better, but I can say there's a long, long way to go.
(Community Participant Interview GO3, October 2015)

There was racism at school. Yeah, there was a lot of that at school, and you just learnt to protect yourself, to fight against them ... Yeah, I got

notes sent home, then, and I was expelled from school, and then I just ended up going out carrot-picking with my father.
(Community Participant Interview GC13, June 2015)

There's still a sense of, I guess, racism that you sense, and that could be when you walk into a shop and people think you're going to steal and follow you around, or they don't even bother about giving you service, or they don't look you in the eye when they're dealing with you, and all that stuff.
(Community Participant Interview GC3, April 2015)

For non-Aboriginal locals, racial attitudes can be quite confronting:

I think there's a real attitude in Griffith ... I think that bias exists and is even stronger now. I actually had someone from an Italian background say this really horrible comment that 'the Aboriginals and the Muslims are going to kill Australia' ... I want[ed] to say, 'But look at all the crime these families brought to Griffith. Look at all the drug-laundering money that you brought to Griffith.' And we showcase that and we pat them on the back, and we say, 'look what they've built,' knowing full well it came from corruption and crime.
(Organization Leader Interview GO1, October 2015)

Conventional discourses of settler colonialism emphasise the privilege created by the so-called primitive accumulation by dispossession; however, this region's later transformation through state investment in water control, closer settlement and migration has created an extraordinarily diverse community. There are continued uneven patterns of misunderstanding, marginalisation and judgement of Indigenous experience amongst settler groups, but despite entrenched racism, there are foundations for a diverse and potentially inclusive future. That ambiguity is reflected in different perceptions of racism amongst our participants.

I think non-Aboriginal people in Griffith have good intentions ... Some of them are very missionary thoughts, that they think that they're doing good for Aboriginal people, but really don't know the grassroots of what Aboriginal people lived through, because they're not Aboriginal themselves, so it's hard to engage non-Aboriginal people.
(Community Participant Interview GC8, April 2015)

... there's still a lot of harassment going on out there. But there's a lot of new [police] officers coming through, also, that think they're: 'I'm the law, you do as I say'. They've got attitudes. Which is creating havoc ... So, I don't see a lot of change there, although it's the way they're doing it now, is different [chuckles]. But it's still ending up with our mob being locked up.
(Community Participant Interview GC1, April 2015)

Better-off-ness

Fifty years after Monk's original work concluded that poverty, poor housing conditions and uncertain employment characterised Aboriginal social conditions in Griffith, the community participants recognised ambiguity as to whether they were "better off". Monk had identified the Save The Children Preschool as providing important opportunities for families, and many of its graduates were amongst our participants. As discussed above, education was valued highly, but often marred by racism. Achieving change has been hard won and slow within the Aboriginal community.

> You can change it. Like we grew up in ... we were living in this little tin house, down the backyard there was heaps of us living there, we had no electricity and stuff like that, and we've all got that picture on our wall, so that we always remember where we came from. Our parents didn't have a lot, growing up, but they made sure we got the best education we could get, they made us go out and do the work in summertime. So we went through school and we didn't want to do paddock work like they had to. We all own our homes now.
> (Community Participant Interview GO3, October 2015)

> I think there are a lot more opportunities now ... than what there were in the 1960s. I think, because there were limited opportunities for Aboriginal people, our Aboriginal people did stay with the seasonal work and labouring sort of jobs. And also, we've heard the stories that people tell about their experiences of school: it wasn't that good, and they were rushed out with limited education. So today is a bit different, we're trying to keep people in the schools ... and providing other opportunities that are out there: you're having opportunities with scholarships and stuff like that, get to go into university – the opportunities are there. So I think, yeah, there's a bit more opportunities.
> (Community Participant Interview GC4, April 2015)

> Absolutely, they're better off now. My parents both lived up on the hill ... in the '60s, and lived in little shacks. There was no welfare at that stage, so they couldn't depend on welfare agencies to support them, as far as food, feeding and clothing, and so no electricity; you had a fire, candles ... and there was no water, so you had to walk to the channel and take your water back up to the hut, which was probably about four or five kilometres .... things have changed now. And the employment opportunities are absolutely better now, because my family, they were all pickers, as most Aboriginal people were back then. So, they all have job opportunities now that they wouldn't have had back then. So, standard of living has increased ... you know, no one had a car when

we were a kid, for instance. And it's funny, nowadays, my kids couldn't imagine not even having a car, and they ask me why it took me so long to get my license, and I say, 'Because no one had a car to teach me how to drive'.

(Community Participant Interview GC8, April 2015)

My family is better off ... The standard of living is better ... but the opportunities for employment – no. No, I don't believe that it's changed from what I'm seeing with the employment. And the majority of people that are employed, are employed from a government bucket specified for Aboriginal people. There's not a lot of mainstream-employed.

(Community Participant Interview GC1, April 2015)

Oh, I guess my family is better off now, because we both had the opportunity to work and I only have the one daughter. So whilst I hear a lot of stories about how people, or the mob [community], struggled back in the 1960s, I think they were more closer – and maybe that was due to hard times and that – they all gelled together, and it was real happy, and they used to enjoy each others' company, whereas, today, the communities are fractured and split and that kind of stuff. So yeah, it's good and bad opportunities.

(Community Participant Interview GC3, April 2015)

Conclusion

The period since Monk's PhD research encapsulates iconic shifts in policy settings, and more broadly in the relationships between First Nations people and the wider Australian population. The statistical narrative has refined over time (Rowse 2006) and revealed gaps at the national scale between Indigenous and non-Indigenous Australians on most social indicators. However, it is important to recognise that numbers don't tell any particular truth until they are contextualised by understanding the lived experiences of the people they concern. Despite substantial government intervention targeting specific indicators since 2002, those gaps have persisted and even widened (Commonwealth of Australia 2020). The ghosts of earlier policies that targeted racialised "protection" and "assimilation" continue to haunt policy debates and community experience on the ground. At the local scale, major policy developments, the shift in policy rhetoric towards self-determination, the passage of a national *Racial Discrimination Act* in 1975, land rights legislation and judicial and legislative recognition of Native title (1992), a decade of national reconciliation and a national apology for the policies that produced the Stolen Generations, have been rendered locally marginal by the interplay of history and the social, economic, cultural and environmental contexts in which First Nation lives are lived.

In Griffith, the transformation of the landscape through irrigation simultaneously relied on and marginalised Aboriginal people. Their labour was often undervalued, but essential to the developmentalist vision. In the 1960s, employment, albeit in precarious seasonal employment, made a difference to many Aboriginal families, but did not move them out of poverty. Poverty and prejudice persist. Poverty restricts access to housing. Prejudice restricts access to education and employment. Griffith's exceptional ethnic diversity, challenges of restructuring its irrigation-reliant rural industries in response to changing environmental, labour and global trade conditions, along with the complex dynamics of relationships between community groups, their leaders and local institutions, all influence socio-economic outcomes for local Aboriginal people.

In understanding the interplay of statistical, policy and community narratives in Griffith, our key learning is that people and place matter. While social policy is inevitably top down, it will not support change if it is deaf to lived experience at local scales and fails to address the structural, historically embedded impediments to justice. Listening to the cultural narratives of belonging and becoming; understanding the cultural landscapes and relationships that underpin the narratives of place; and recognising that building change from the bottom-up through changed access to education, health, employment and respect (inter alia) will all reshape how top-down policies are understood and practised in Griffith – and elsewhere in "settled Australia"– to the betterment of future generations.

Acknowledgement

The research was supported by the Australian Research Council (Grant No. ARCDP110101721). We acknowledge Yamandhu Marang Griffith Social Research Reference Group in Griffith, Yarkuwa Indigenous Knowledge Centre Aboriginal Corporation in Deniliquin, Ngurrala Aboriginal Corporation in Coffs Harbour, Macquarie University and the American Association of Geographers. We also thank the generous engagement with our work from Indigenous families in Coffs Harbour, Deniliquin and Griffith; the Australian Institute of Aboriginal and Torres Strait Islander Studies; and colleagues in various conferences (Institute of Australian Geographers, American Association of Geographers and International Geographical Union). Our work was approved under Macquarie University Human Research Ethics Committee approvals 52014000647, 5201200210 and 5201500110. With the kind permission of his family, the authors acknowledge the contribution of the late Roger Penrith who passed away during preparation of this chapter.

Appendix 17.1

Yamandhu Marang Research Project Principles
Cultural Protocol Governing the Macquarie University Research Project
Social and economic conditions of Aboriginal people in rural NSW
Formally adopted by *Yamandhu Marang* Reference Group 15 January 2015

Purpose and aims of the *Yamandhu Marang* project
The project is a collaborative research activity between members of the Griffith Aboriginal community and Macquarie University (MQ) researchers from the Department of Geography and Planning. It is part of a larger research project about the social and economic circumstances of Aboriginal people in NSW, in the context of policy change over the past 50 years.

The project aims to:
1. Document and analyse the experience of people in the Griffith Aboriginal community in the context of policy changes since 1965 by investigating the following broad themes:
    - What were the most significant changes?
    - How has the community fared socially and economically?
    - How have policies affected the community - what worked or failed?
2. Develop an evidence-based framework for community discussion, action and policy change that addresses the following question:
    - What are key issues, challenges and priorities for the community in 2015?

Purpose of this Cultural Protocol for research collaboration
This protocol sets out the principles for
- An ethical and culturally respectful framework to guide the project and the development of relationships between the University and Aboriginal community organisations in Griffith
- Guidance for researchers, community organisations, reference group members and participants about how the research activities should occur.

What are Cultural Protocols?
Protocols specify the ethical principles and practices that will guide behaviour in a particular situation. This Cultural Protocol is designed to protect the Griffith Aboriginal community's cultural and intellectual property rights in conducting the *Yamandhu Marang* project.

Cultural and intellectual property rights include the right for the Griffith Aboriginal community to:
- own and control their cultural and intellectual property
- ensure that any means of protecting cultural and intellectual property is based on the principle of self-determination
- be recognised as the primary guardians and interpreters of culture and so regulate how stories and information are presented
- authorise or refuse the use of cultural and intellectual property according to appropriate customary law as agreed by the *Yamandhu Marang* Reference Group.
- maintain the confidentiality of any sensitive cultural knowledge and information about other cultural practices that are seen as sacred or requiring protection by members of the *Yamandhu Marang* Reference Group.
- be given full and proper attribution for sharing our heritage
- control the recording, documentation and storage of cultural customs and expressions.

Collaboration
This protocol acknowledges that local Aboriginal people will direct and make decisions about research affecting them, including this research project. This is a fundamental principle underpinning the project.
The aim of our collaboration is to work together in ways that support the Griffith Aboriginal Community and its organisations to draw on and benefit from the research capacity of the Macquarie University team both during the project and in the longer term future.
Community direction to the project will be guided by/through the *Yamandhu Marang* Reference Group.

Respect for Aboriginal traditions and cultural property
The research will always:
- Respect and protect Griffith Aboriginal community cultural rights and intellectual property
- Respect Wiradjuri cultural traditions and local cultural values of Aboriginal community members and their organisations
- Seek guidance from the *Yamandhu Marang* Reference Group on these matters where needed and respond to the guidance provided promptly and respectfully.

Ethical research, confidentiality and protection of privacy
Written plans and protocols will be prepared to ensure that participants in this project who provide information to researchers are able to provide clear, free and informed consent and to ensure protection of personal privacy and confidentiality of sensitive information.
Once agreed, these protocols will be included in an application for ethical approval for the research to proceed from the Macquarie University Human Research Ethics Committee, with written support from the *Yamandhu Marang* Reference Group to be included in that application.

Benefit to the community
The project aims to ensure benefits to the Aboriginal community of Griffith by
- Engaging community members in the development, design and conduct of a research project that reflects the aims and objectives of the community
- Providing clear, evidence-based information that can be used by the community to plan future actions and advocacy
- Providing educational opportunities to assist community members to develop basic research and other skills to enhance their personal and professional development.
- supporting self-determination of Griffith Aboriginal community
- providing guidance about access to information and how information is presented
- ensuring acknowledgement and attribution of Griffith community members in the research process and final reports and outcomes
- delivering appropriate presentation and use of information and research findings to benefit the community

Notes

1 The *Aboriginal Land Rights Act (NSW) 1983* created limited rights to claim unwanted Crown Land and former Aboriginal Reserves across the state. For detailed history of the legislation and its context and shortcomings see Wilkie (1985) and Norman (2015). Judicial recognition of common law Native Title by the Australian High Court was rendered into statute law as the *Native Title Act (Aust) 1993*, which allowed limited claims for recognition of continuing rights arising from Aboriginal custom, but these have proved difficult (although not impossible) to secure in NSW (see e.g., Foley 2007; also Teehan 2003).
2 Unauthorised occupation of land outside the so-called limits of settlement controlled by colonial authorities in NSW from 1825 to 1860 created a class of Australian society known as "squatters". Squatting not only drove unofficial frontier wars across the landscape but also provided the foundation of imperial trade in wool that formed massive private fortunes and colonial power.
3 McCaughey has an important link to Australian geography as he bequeathed £1million (current value over $AU80 million; see https://sydney.edu.au/news-opinion/news/2017/04/03/how-giving-has-created-history.html, accessed 3 April 2020) to the University of Sydney, where Janice Monk completed her undergraduate and honours study. This funding endowed nine chairs at the university, including the McCaughey Chair in Geography, which was occupied, *inter alia*, by Griffith Taylor, J. Macdonald Holmes, Trevor Langford-Smith and Maurie Daly.
4 See also: https://www.dpi.nsw.gov.au/about-us/science-and-research/centres/yanco/our-history.
5 Bremer (2021) offers a powerful account of this stewardship. Wiradjuri geographer Michael-Shawn Fletcher also advocates the need "to embrace Aboriginal people and Aboriginal knowledge ... [and the] need to educate [our children] on the way this country needs to be, the way this country can be, and about the people who created this country" (Fletcher 2020; see also Fletcher et al. 2021).
6 The Murray–Darling Basin is a one million square kilometre area in the southeast of Australia in the catchment area of the two major Basin rivers, the Murray and the Darling. Griffith is one of the major centres within the Murrumbidgee Catchment region of the Basin (https://www.mdba.gov.au/water-management/catchments/murrumbidgee).
7 *Yamandhu Marang* translates from Wiradjuri language into English as "Are you well?"(Source:http://ourlanguages.org.au/yamandhu-marang-language-does-not-belong-to-people-it-belongs-to-country/).
8 Aboriginal Medical Service.
9 The term "Stolen Generations" refers to children of Aboriginal and Torres Strait Islander descent removed from their families under state and territory "assimilation" and "protection" policies up until the early 1970s. See Read (1998).
10 Condobolin.
11 The term "clever man" generally refers to people whose cultural, spiritual and ecological knowledge gave them the highest degree of recognition as healers, doctors and people of integrity in their communities across Aboriginal Australia.
12 A NSW Government "white card" is required by anyone carrying out construction or labouring work.

References

Bamblett, Lawrence. 2013. *Our Stories Are Our Survival*. Canberra: Aboriginal Studies Press.

Behrendt, Larissa. 2005. "Law stories and life stories: Aboriginal women, the law and Australian society." *Australian Feminist Studies* 20 (47): 245–254. doi: 10.1080/08164640500090434.

Bremer, Rudi, "Awaye!" Broadcast: Sat 10 Jul 2021, 6:05pm, 2021, in *Healing Our Rivers and Country*, produced by Daniel Browning and Rudi Bremer, 1hr 47m 56s. https://www.abc.net.au/radionational/programs/awaye/saturday-10-july-2021/13439188

Cohen, Patsy, and Margaret Somerville. 1990. *Ingelba and the Five Black Matriarchs*. Sydney: Allen & Unwin.

Commonwealth of Australia. 2020. *Closing the Gap Report 2020*. Australian Government (Canberra). https://ctgreport.niaa.gov.au/sites/default/files/pdf/closing-the-gap-report-2020.pdf

Conifer, Dan. 2017. "Abbott government's Indigenous Advancement Strategy shows how not to spend $5b taxpayers' dollars" (News Report)." *ABC News*. https://www.abc.net.au/news/2017-02-04/analysis-how-not-to-spend-$5-billion-in-taxpayers-dollars/8240968

Cowper, W. Richard. 1987. *The Barren Jack Scandal and Its Effects on the M.I.A.* Bonnells Bay, NSW: Self-published.

Davidson, Robyn. 2017. *Travelling Light*. Sydney: ETT Imprint.

Dillon, Michael C., and Neil D. Westbury. 2007. *Beyond Humbug: Transforming Government Engagement with Indigenous Australia*. Adelaide: Sea View Press.

Fletcher, Michael-Shawn. 2020. "Our Country, Our Way: The 2020 Narrm Oration." In *The Narrm Oration (University of Melbourne)*, 1h 16m 52s. https://findanexpert.unimelb.edu.au/news/13836-our-country--our-way

Fletcher, Michael-Shawn, Tegan Hall, and Andreas Nicholas Alexandra. 2021. "The loss of an indigenous constructed landscape following British invasion of Australia: an insight into the deep human imprint on the Australian landscape." *Ambio* 50 (1): 138–149. doi: 10.1007/s13280-020-01339-3.

Foley, Denis. 2007. "What has native title done to the urban Koori in New South Wales who is also a traditional custodian?" In *The Social Effects of Native Title: Recognition, Translation, Coexistence*. B. R. Smith and F. Morphy, 167–183. Canberra: ANU Press.

Ford, Lisa, and Tim Rowse, eds. 2013. *Between Indigenous and Settler Governance*. London and New York: Routledge.

Fredericks, Bronwyn. 2008. "Researching with Aboriginal women as an Aboriginal woman researcher." *Australian Feminist Studies* 23 (55): 113–129. http://www.informaworld.com/10.1080/08164640701816272

Gale, Fay. 1964. *A Study of Assimilation: Part-Aborigines in South Australia*. Adelaide: Libraries Board of South Australia.

———. 1983. *We Are Bosses Ourselves: The Status and Role of Aboriginal Women Today*. Canberra: Australian Institute of Aboriginal Studies.

———. 1990. "The participation of Australian aboriginal women in a changing political environment." *Political Geography Quarterly* 9 (4): 381–395. http://www.sciencedirect.com/science/article/B6X2W-468J5YG-2G/2/41f1dfdcb60738165e1883e5c4b077e4

Griffith Visitors Information Centre. 2010. *Griffith NSW: Love the Lifestyle*. Griffith: Griffith Visitors Information Centre.

Hartwig, Lana D., Sue Jackson, Francis Markham, and Natalie Osborne. 2021. "Water colonialism and Indigenous water justice in south-eastern Australia." *International Journal of Water Resources Development*: 1-34. doi: 10.1080/07900627.2020.1868980.

Hocking, Jenny. 2018. "'A transforming sentiment in this country': the Whitlam government and Indigenous self-determination." *Australian Journal of Public Administration* 77 (S1): S5–S12. doi: 10.1111/1467-8500.12353.

Howitt, Richard. 2012. "Sustainable indigenous futures in remote Indigenous areas: relationships, processes and failed state approaches." *GeoJournal* 77 (6): 817–828. doi: 10.1007/s10708-010-9377-3.

Howitt, Richard, Claire Colyer, Janice Monk, David Crew, and Stephanie Hull. 2016. *Looking Forward – Looking Back: Changing Social and Economic Conditions of Aboriginal People in Rural NSW, 1965-2015*. Sydney: Department of Geography & Planning, Macquarie University.

Howitt, Richard, David Crew, Janice Monk, Claire Colyer, and Stephanie Hull. 2018. "Giving back after fifty years: connecting, returning, and reflecting – new research in old settings." In *Giving Back: Research and Reciprocity in Indigenous Settings*, edited by R. D. K. Herman, 128–148. Corvallis: Oregon State University Press.

Huber, Rina. 1981. "Italians in Griffith, NSW." In *Beyond the City: Case Studies in Community Structure and Development*, edited by Margaret Bowman, 45–70. Melbourne: Longman Cheshire.

Jackson, Sue, and Lesley Head. 2020. "Australia's mass fish kills as a crisis of modern water: understanding hydrosocial change in the Murray-Darling Basin." *Geoforum* 109: 44–56. http://www.sciencedirect.com/science/article/pii/S0016718519303641

Jeffcoat, Kevin. 1988. *More Precious Than Gold: An Illustrated History of Water in New South Wales*. Edited by Resources New South Wales. Dept. of Water. Parramatta, NSW: NSW Dept. of Water Resources in association with Kangaroo Press.

Locke, Michelle Lea. 2018. "Wirrawi Bubuwul – aboriginal women strong." *Australian Journal of Education* 62 (3): 299–310. doi: 10.1177/0004944118799483.

Macdonald, Gaynor. 1998. "Master narratives and the dispossession of the Wiradjuri." *Aboriginal History* 22: 162–179. http://www.jstor.org/stable/24046165.

———. 2013. "Autonomous selves in a bureaucratised world: challenges for Mardu and Wiradjuri." *Anthropological Forum* 23 (4): 399–413. doi: 10.1080/00664677.2013.842889.

McHugh, Siobhan. 1991. "Water, More Precious than Gold." *Radio Broadcasts*. Sydney: ABC Radio and NSW Department of Water Resources.

McKillop, Bob. 2016. "Pioneer work: the Murrumbidgee irrigation area towns of Leeton and Griffith." *Walter Burley Griffin Society*. Accessed 11 March. http://www.griffinsociety.org/lives_and_works/a_leeton_griffith.html

Monk, Janice. 1972. *Socio-Economic Characteristics of Six Aboriginal Communities in Australia: A Comparative Ecological Study*. PhD thesis, Department of Geography, University of Illinois at Urbana-Champaign.

Moreton-Robinson, Aileen. 2011. "The white man's burden." *Australian Feminist Studies* 26 (70): 413–431. doi: 10.1080/08164649.2011.621175.

Norman, Heidi. 2015. *"What Do We Want?": A Political History of Aboriginal Land Rights in New South Wales*. Canberra: Aboriginal Studies Press.

Poelina, Anne. 2020. "A coalition of hope! A regional governance approach to indigenous Australian cultural wellbeing." In *Located Research: Regional Places, Transitions and Challenges*, edited by Angela Campbell, Michelle Duffy and Beth Edmondson, 153–179. Singapore: Springer Singapore.

Read, Peter. 1983. " 'A rape of the soul so profound': some reflections on the dispersal policy in New South Wales." *Aboriginal History* 7 (1/2): 23–33. http://www.jstor.org/stable/24045577.

———. 1984. " 'Breaking up these camps entirely': the dispersal policy in Wiradjuri Country 1909-1929." *Aboriginal History* 8 (1/2): 45–55. http://www.jstor.org/stable/24045796

———. 1998. *The Stolen Generations: The Removal of Aboriginal Children in New South Wales 1883 to 1969*. Sydney: NSW Department of Aboriginal Affairs.
Rose, Deborah Bird. 1999. "Indigenous ecologies and an ethic of connection." In *Global Ethics and Environment*, edited by N. Low, 175–187. London: Routledge.
Rowley, Charles D. 1971. *Outcasts in White Australia. Canberra: Aboriginal Policy and Practice Volume II*. Canberra: ANU Press.
———. 1986. *Recovery: The Politics of Aboriginal Reform*: Ringwood: Penguin Books Ltd.
Rowse, Tim. 2006. "Towards a history of Indigenous statistics in Australia." In *Assessing the Evidence on Indigenous Socioeconomic Outcomes: A Focus on the 2002 NATSISS*, edited by Boyd Hunter, 1–10. Canberra: Centre for Aboriginal Economic Policy Development.
———. 2010. "The reforming state, the concerned public and indigenous political actors." *Australian Journal of Politics & History* 56 (1): 66–81. doi: 10.1111/j.1467-8497.2010.01542.x.
Taylor, Katherine Selena, Bradley J. Moggridge, and Anne Poelina. 2016. "Australian indigenous water policy and the impacts of the ever-changing political cycle." *Australasian Journal of Water Resources* 20 (2): 132–147. doi:10.1080/13241583.2017.1348887.
Teehan, Maureen. 2003. "A hope disillusioned, an opportunity lost? Reflections on common law native title and ten years of the Native Title Act." *Melbourne University Law Review* 27(2): 523–71.
Tynan, Lauren, and Michelle Bishop. 2019. "Disembodied experts, accountability and refusal: an autoethnography of two (ab)original women." *Australian Journal of Human Rights* 25 (2): 217–231. doi: 10.1080/1323238X.2019.1574202.
Walker, Brett. 2019. *Murray-Darling Basin Royal Commission Report*. Adelaide: Government of South Australia.
Wilkie, Meredith. 1985. *Aboriginal Land Rights in NSW*. Sydney: Alternative Publishing Cooperative.

18 Gender and the Food History of the Caribbean

The Case of Cassava in Barbados

Janet Momsen

Jan Monk and I first met at an Annual Meeting of the American Association of Geographers in 1978 in New Orleans. There we both gave papers on gender and the rural Caribbean and so I felt it was important to offer a paper here to highlight our joint interest in the region. In this chapter I take a historical approach to the rural economy and the role of gender, migration and tourism in the development of one of the Caribbean islands.

Cassava (manihot esculenta) has recently been identified by Caribbean governments as a priority crop with great potential to contribute to the food and agriculture sector of the region (FAO October 2014). It is the third most important crop of the tropics after rice and maize. Food and Agriculture Organization (FAO) suggested that with appropriate policies and quality standards, cassava could easily be transformed from a 'poor man's food' into a commercial commodity for sustainable food security, poverty alleviation and income generation (Ibid). Most Caribbean countries are net food importers and so the development of a viable cassava industry is a key component of the regional strategy for addressing the high food import bill, food insecurity, rural development and climate change (Ibid). Cassava flour can partially replace imported wheat flour in bread; cassava chips can replace imported animal feed and the juice can be used instead of imported high fructose corn syrup in beer. It is also seen, especially in Barbados, as beneficial against diet-related non-communicable diseases such as diabetes and colon cancer and as a vegan alternative to meat. Cassava can be grown in dry environmental conditions and in poor soils. Its roots can be left in the ground unharvested for long periods as a food reserve, so it is also being promoted as a climate change crop for the region (Ford and Dorodnykh 2016).

Such a new appreciation of cassava ignores the long history of the crop in Barbados and the role of gender in cassava production and utilization. In this chapter the production and dietary importance of this staple is traced through historical documents, several field surveys of Barbadian small farms since 1963 and local cookbooks published since 1911. This multi-sectoral approach reveals a distinctive gendered view of the role of cassava in Barbadian life and the changing role of migration in the island's diet.

DOI: 10.4324/9781032275611-22

History of Settlement in Barbados

Barbados was settled by the English in 1627 and remained a British colony until independence in 1966. The island was uninhabited when the English landed; although, there is evidence of earlier Amerindian settlement. The first migrants were largely hunters and fishers; but the Saladoid, arriving about 600 AD from South America, had pottery, agriculture and a complex social and political organization. Higman (2011, 27) argues that these second-wave migrants appear to have intended to settle with familiar food resources and brought in cassava along with the technologies appropriate for its cultivation, processing and cooking.'

> As the most important plant introduced to the islands prior to 1492, cassava represented a new attitude to life in the islands.... Equally important, it represented a new attitude to manipulation of the landscape, a willingness to transform natural land and water resources to extract a living.
> (Higman 2011, 27)

In 1627, the island was densely forested and the colonists knew little about the tropical environment. They had few tools for clearing the forest, so obtained most of their food through gathering fruits and nuts from within the forest while awaiting the arrival of seeds from England (Watts 1966, 38). Captain Powell, who was in charge of the colonizing ships, visited Guyana two weeks after his arrival in Barbados with the intention of inducing a small number of Amerindians to travel to Barbados to introduce local methods of cultivation to the settlers (Ibid). Some 32 people were brought to Barbados, carrying with them 'rootes, plants, foules, tobacco seeds, suggar canes... which said rootes, plants and other materials were the first that were ever planted there' (Powell 1656 quoted in Watts 1966, 38). The seasonal rainforest was hard to clear and as late as 1647 sweet potatoes, maize, beans and peas were planted between the cut boughs of trees still lying on the ground (Ligon 1657).

Seventeenth century migrants from various countries played a distinctive role in the development of Barbadian agriculture. As Monk with Alexander (1993, 167) point out,

> The literature on migration has begun to pay attention to gender differences in the composition of migration streams from the Caribbean, but few studies attempt to analyze these differences in any detail or to link them to other changes underway in the region.

Through an understanding of gender roles in agriculture it is possible to arrive at an assessment of the gender composition of these migration streams. Although the historical accounts do not identify the gender of these early migrants to Barbados, it is reasonable to assume that the people brought from Guyana were mostly women since they were the agriculturists and specifically had knowledge of the cultivation and the all-important processing of cassava.

Ligon (1657, 29–30) recorded the following description of cassava in Barbados:

> Bread, which is accounted the staff, or main supporter of mans (sic) life, has not here thate full taste it has in England; but yet they account it nourishing and strengthening. It is made of the root of a small tree or shrub, which they call *Cassavie*.
>
> This root only, which we are now to consider, (because our bread is made of it) is large and round. This root, before it come to be eaten, suffers a strange conversion; for being an absolute poyson when 'tis gathered, by good ordering comes to be wholsome and nourishing.'

This transformation is achieved by grating the root and squeezing out the juice. The grated root is then dried in the sun. The resulting flour can be used to make a type of bread with the introduction of cassava came sedentary agriculture.

Ligon does not say whether men or women prepare the cassava, but it is the women who do it today in Amazonas and the Garifuna women in Belize still do it. The Garifuna, then known as Caribs, were transported to Belize from the island of St Vincent, just south of Barbados, by the English in 1748 because they were preventing colonization of the island. Ligon (1657) goes on to describe how, in Barbados, the Indians made thick or thin cassava bread but did not add salt. He suggests that the best way to eat it is in milk. He also indicates how he learned from an Indian woman how to make cassava piecrust (Ligon 1657, 30). Making cassava bread in the seventeenth century has some similarities with the making of maize tortillas today and was probably also done by women. Monk (1993) noted a similar form of agriculture in Margarita Island with both women and men combining farming and selling cassava to local processors.

The migrants from Guyana also introduced sugar cane as a valued plant for chewing. After a few years, the small number of Amerindians was reduced by disease (Watts 1966, 47) and sugar cane disappeared from the island. It was re-introduced in 1637 but did not become the predominant crop until 1647 when Portuguese-Jewish refugees from Brazil introduced new techniques of refining sugar and the colonists turned to African slaves for its cultivation. Women slaves dominated in the field and as domestics in the homes of the white planters. The slaves brought with them knowledge of cassava and its processing and so the cultivation of this crop was continued in the slave gardens.

Dietary Traditions in Barbados

The Barbadian diet reflects the mixing of three dietary traditions – British, Amerindian and African. The mingling of these three strands has influenced today's cultural heritage. While most temperate agricultural produce had to be imported, the tropical climate enabled slaves to cultivate familiar crops such as cassava, okra, yams, bananas, coconuts and later breadfruit carried to the West Indies from the Pacific by Captain Bligh in a first phase of the globalization of foodstuffs. Among Caribbean islands, Barbados was unusual in that Britain was the only colonial power, whereas many other islands experienced settlement by several European countries. Thus, although naturally Barbados adopted some dishes from neighboring islands, the main influences on the island's diet are clear.

The staple foods have varied in their relative importance over time and include the early settlers' use of cassava and maize to add to wheat flour and the long-term popularity of root crops and plantains which made up the main sources of carbohydrate. Later guinea corn (sorghum) came on slave ships from West Africa and dominated slave rations. More recently, imported rice mainly from Guyana after the 1880s and of wheat bread in recent decades became important. Watts (1965) noted that the drier parts of the island continued to grow tobacco and cotton into the eighteenth century. Fieldwork in 1963 revealed that pigeon peas and cassava were often planted around the edges of the cane fields while crops such as eddoes and yams were planted around individual canes in cane-holes (Momsen 1969). A random sample survey of 213 small farms revealed that 56 (26 per cent) grew cassava (Ibid).

It is difficult to trace the changing importance of cassava in local diets as seen in cropping patterns on Barbadian farms because cassava has usually been a crop grown on small farms. Also, the measurement unit varies from acres/hectares, to weight, to number of farms. Cassava was grown on sugar plantations during World War II as a basic source of food/nutrition when the island was vulnerable to trade blockades by German submarines. Under wartime legislation plantations had to grow 12 per cent of their land in food crops for local consumption. In 1944–1945, 12 tons of cassava flour were produced every day. In 1950, 750 acres of cassava were grown, but by 1964 the acreage had fallen to 142 acres (Agricultural Statistics 1965) and a gender analysis of a survey of small farms in 1963 revealed it was grown mostly by elderly women who used it to starch clothes (Henshall 1966). Henshall's (1981) factor analysis of this data, however, revealed that women-operated farms were associated with root crops, especially cassava, unlike findings of similar surveys in neighboring islands and were distinctive from other categories of small farms (Henshall 1981).

Clearly, cassava was a more popular staple on the dry coralline island of Barbados than in the volcanic and more humid islands nearby, despite the shallow soils in Barbados. In a similar survey in 1987, cassava was hardly mentioned, but in a later survey in 2003 it was the most common root vegetable grown (Momsen 2005). In 2008, 400 hectares of cassava were grown in Barbados. In the period between 2008 and 2009, production of cassava on the island increased 48 per cent (Ministry of Agriculture 2010) but production then fell from 690,530 kg in 2009 to 184,850 kg in 2012, the lowest level this century (Ministry of Agriculture 2013). Since then, there has been a steady increase in cassava production and consumption with the introduction of new higher yielding varieties and improved cultivation methods plus growing appreciation of the import substitution and health benefits. In a 2017 video, the Barbados Government Information Service described the use of 40 per cent of cassava flour in bread. As sugar had become a less competitive crop, it was planned to increase the acreage in cassava.

Preparation and Consumption of Cassava

Since the seventeenth century introduction of cassava to Barbados, women have been key to its preparation. Ligon (1657) described how the Amerindians:

> have a piece of Iron, which I guess is cast round, the diameter of which, is about twenty inches, a little hollowed in the middle ... with three feet like a pot, about six inches high, that fire may be underneath. To such a temper they heat this Pone, (as they call it) as to bake, but not burn. When 'tis made thus hot, the *Indians*, whom we trust to make it, because they are best acquainted with it, cast the meal upon the Pone, the whole breadth of it, and put it down with their hands, and it will presently stick together.... . so turn and return it so often ... which is presently done.

He went on to say how he learned from an Amerindian woman how to make cassava piecrust (Ligon 1657, 30) and how they can make thick or thin cassava bread but do not add salt. A traditional dish in Barbados is called cassava pone, the name conflating the food and the utensil. It is made from cassava flour with grated coconut and spices and mixed with coconut water and shortening and then baked (Grey 1965). The boiled juice squeezed out of the cassava is called cassareep and is used to preserve meat in long-lasting stews such as pepper pot. A 1911 cookbook mentions cassava cakes, or flat breads, as described by Ligon, being steeped in milk and brandy for a pudding and also has recipes for cassava cakes, conkies and soup as well as for pone (Yearwood 1911).

A cookbook aimed at reducing food imports to Barbados during the World War II (Hodson 1942) suggested its use in savory dishes and had recipes for cassava pudding, cakes, biscuits, pone and even cassava donuts. Recipe books produced in the 1960s (Child Care Committee 1964; Grey 1965) also have recipes for cassava pone. Frazer (1981) has at least three recipes for cassava in a book aimed at promoting local foods and published by the Ministry of Agriculture. Sworder and Hamilton (1983) include suggestions of ways to cook sweet cassava in chunks and cassava pone. This was admittedly a heritage cookbook in that they were promoting a Caribbean culinary renaissance. Cookbooks from the wider Caribbean list cassava biscuits as being from Barbados (Wolfe, 1985). Slater (1965) offers recipes for cassava pastry and for pepperpot with cassareep.

Rita Springer (2007, 10–11) describes how food in the island has changed since the 1930s when poverty was widespread and people depended on homegrown foods and had few kitchen facilities. As electricity and gas replaced

Gender and the Food History of the Caribbean 209

charcoal for cooking and external influences grew following increased migration and tourism, with remittances raising living standards and encouraging the use of modern cooking equipment, new ideas about food grew. The early cookbooks were aimed at cooks working for local middle-class families, but more recently they have been directed to encouraging people to eat healthily using local fresh foods (Miller 2010). Recently, Marion Hart of the Food Promotion Unit of the Barbados Agricultural Development & Marketing Corporation has been producing leaflets giving recipes for new dishes using cassava such as in milk shakes and cassava salad.

Given the colonization of Barbados by white settlers from England who then brought in African slaves, it is necessary to consider the moral economy of the island's diets (Jackson et al. 2009). The popularity of cassava in the Barbadian diet has fluctuated over the last four centuries. As one of the first root crops grown on the island, it has remained a basic element in the diet supplemented by yams, eddoes, sweet potatoes and maize. However, recent changes in dietary preferences among both residents and tourists have given cassava a new status.

Working in Puerto Rico and Margarita Island, Monk with Alexander (1993) found migration and development led to women abandoning their home gardens and food production. However, in Barbados women had long been the main local food producers on small farms making up 53 per cent in 1963 falling to 26 per cent in 1987 (Momsen 1993) still among the highest proportion in the region. More women farmers than men farmers depended on remittances, but on the whole women were better educated and some combined professional jobs with part-time farming. Analysis of the 1963 data showed that the characteristics of farms with female decision-makers became more clearly identified as small-scale agriculture developed. Such farms gradually became more commercialized and adjusted to available resources (Henshall 1981). Many women started to work in the tourism industry and so learned new types of cuisine. Some women farmers began to grow food specifically for the tourism industry and there was increasing interest in introducing tourists to local foods and dishes. Tourism has achieved backward linkages to agriculture as a side effect of the globalization of food regimes. At the same time, women are developing small-scale agri-businesses such as the manufacture of jams, pickles, spices, fruit juices and cakes (Momsen 1997).

Conclusion

Cassava has remained an important element in the Barbadian diet since it was first introduced to the island in 1627 and distinguishes Barbadian diets from those of other Caribbean islands. Its cultivation, processing and preparation have always been associated with women, and some recipes can be traced back almost 500 years. Many can be found in local cookbooks published over the last century. Since the early 1990s, Barbadian interest in healthy and traditional foods has grown alongside the demands of tourism and interest from return migrants. Harris (1991) has called this the period of the Caribbean Renaissance. The epidemic of diabetes on the island has made people aware of the effect of diet on health as seen in the impact of changes in eating habits away from traditional foods to fast foods have had on the growth of diabetes (Steyne et al. 2002).

Migration has been key to maintaining cassava production and consumption and has been implicated in the development process in Barbados and in the transition from an agricultural economy to one based largely on tourism, as Monk with Alexander (1993) note elsewhere in the region. Return migrants were given land by the Barbadian government on which they were encouraged to produce for the local market and for the hotels. They have often introduced new crops and an appreciation of organic produce (Momsen 2005) and the link between health and food. In this way, the dietary renaissance has come full circle to include one of the most traditional of Barbadian foods, cassava. Women's role in the introduction of cassava, the preparation and its consumption has remained of great importance over the centuries, although rarely recognized. Today it is women who work in the island's factory making cassava flour and produce leaflets offering new recipes for the use of cassava (Agrobeat 2017). It is the basis of the concept of food sovereignty in Barbados grounded in protecting agricultural production and local foods with a view to achieving sustainable rural development (Caro 2012).

References

Agricultural Statistics. 1965. *Current Estimates of Agriculture*, October 1964. Barbados: Regional council of Ministers.
Agrobeat. 2017. Barbados Government Information Service.
Caro, Pamela. 2012. "Food sovereignty and women's rights in Latin America." *Insights: IDS* 82: 8.
Child Care Committee (compiler). 1964. *Bajan Cook Book*. Barbados.
Food and Agriculture Organization of the United Nations (FAO). 2014. "Contributing to the development of a cassava industry." *Issue Brief #11*. Subregional office for the Caribbean, Barbados.
Ford, J. R. Deep, and Ekatarina Dorodnykh. 2016. "Addressing food and nutrition security threats in the Caribbean: lessons from the cassava value chain in Barbados." *Farm and Business* 8 (1): 2–30.
Frazer, C. 1981. "Come eat with us the Bajan way: let's eat what we grow and grow what we eat." Ministry of Agriculture and Consumer Affairs and FAO, Barbados.
Grey, Winifred. 1965. *Caribbean Cookery*. London: Collins.
Harris, Jessica. 1991. *Sky Juice and Flying Fish Fireside*. New York: Simon and Schuster.
Henshall, Janet D. 1966. "The demographic factor in the structure of agriculture in Barbados." *Transactions of the Institute of British Geographers* 38: 183–195.
Henshall, Janet D. 1981. "Women and small scale farming in the Caribbean." In *Papers in Latin American Geography in Honor of Lucia Harrison*, Conference of Latin American Geographers edited by O. Horst, 44–55. Muncie, Indiana.
Higman, B. W. 2011. *A Concise History of the Caribbean*. Cambridge: Cambridge University Press.
Hodson, Mrs St John. 1942. *Wartime Recipes for Use in the West Indies*. Published for the Ministry of Food, Barbados.

Jackson, Peter, Neil Ward, and Polly Russell. 2009. "Moral economies of food and geographies of responsibility." *Transactions of the Institute of British Geographers* 34 (1): 12–24.
Ligon, R. 1657. *A True and Exact History of the Island of Barbados.* London.
Miller, Sally. 2010. *Bajan Cooking in a Nutshell.* Barbados: Miller Publishing Company Ltd.
Ministry of Agriculture. 2010. *Agricultural Statistics.* Barbados.
Ministry of Agriculture. 2013. *Agricultural Statistics.* Barbados.
Momsen, Janet D. 1969. *The Geography of Land and Population in the Caribbean* (with special reference to Barbados and the Windward Islands. Unpublished doctoral dissertation, University of London.
Momsen, Janet H. 1993. "Development and gender divisions of labour in the eastern Caribbean." In *Women and Change in the Caribbean*, edited by Janet H. Momsen, 232–246. London: James Currey Ltd and Kingston, Jamaica: Ian Randle Publishers and Bloomington: Indiana University Press.
Momsen, Janet H. 1997. "Linkages between tourism and agriculture in the Caribbean." In *Land, Sea and Human Effort in the Caribbean* edited by Beate M. W. Ratter and Wolf-Dietrich Sahr, 55–62. Hamburg: Institut für Geographie der Universität.
Momsen, Janet H. 2005. "Caribbean Peasantry revisited: Barbadian farmers over four decades." *Southeastern Geographer* 45 (2): 42–57.
Monk, Janice, with Charles S. Alexander. 1993. "Migration, development and the gender division of labour: Puerto Rico and Margarita Island, Venezuela." In *Women and Change in the Caribbean*, edited by Janet H. Momsen, 167–177. London: James Currey Ltd and Kingston, Jamaica: Ian Randle Publishers and Bloomington: Indiana University.
Powell, H. 1656. Statement to the Masters of Chancery. Reprinted (1891) in *Papers Relating to the Early History of* Barbados, Georgetown, British Guiana.
Slater, Mary. 1965. *Cooking the Caribbean Way.* London: Paul Hamlyn.
Springer, Rita G. 2007. *Caribbean Cookbook. A Lifetime of Recipes.* Barbados: Miller Publishing Co. Ltd..
Steyne, N. P., J. Mann, P. H. Bennett, N. Temple, P. Zimmer, J. Tuomilehto, J. Lindstrom, and A. Louheranta. 2002. "Diet, nutrition and the prevention of Type 2 diabetes." *Public Health Nutrition* 7 (1A): 147–165.
Sworder, Peggy and Jill Hamilton (Compilers). 1983. *The Barbados Cookbook.* Barbados: Cox Caribbean Graphics.
Watts, David. 1965. *Population Changes in Barbados in the Pre-emancipation Period.* Paper presented at *the Meeting of the Institute of British Geographers*, January. Mimeographed.
Watts, David. 1966. *Man's influence on the vegetation of Barbados, 1627-1800.* University of Hull Occasional Papers in Geography, 4. Hull: University of Hull.
Wolfe, Linda. 1985. *Recipes: The Cooking of the Caribbean Islands.* London: Macmillan Publishers.
Yearwood, Mrs A. Graham (compiler). 1911. *West Indian and Other Recipes.* Bridgetown, Barbados: The Agricultural Reporter.

19 COVID-19 and Tourism in the Island Pacific

Gender Tribulations and Transformations in Different Seas

John Connell

Despite growing up on the shores of the Pacific, Janice Monk rarely focused on oceans and their islands in her research. Only twice did she turn to islands, and once to islands and tourism, in a paper that tends to sit outside her pioneering work in feminist geography and on continental arid landscapes. It too, however, was innovative; hence, this chapter seeks to highlight her research on island economies and gender and points to its contemporary relevance in the era of COVID-19.

The gendered implications of COVID-19 in the Pacific Islands, considered here for Fiji, Vanuatu and Samoa, have been considerable. Despite COVID-19 not reaching any of these islands until mid-2021, it has had major repercussions through the loss of the dominant tourism industry and related businesses and employment. It has had both negative socio-economic impacts (the rise of domestic violence) and positive effects (the ability of women to restructure livelihoods) and has implications for a better understanding of women's experiences of (economic) shocks and women's capabilities and resilience in disaster recovery. In some parts these impacts and experiences parallel those that emerged from Janice Monk's analysis of the tourist economy of one Venezuelan island.

Margarita, Venezuela

Janice Monk, much like her distinguished colleague and friend Janet Momsen, worked in the Caribbean on agricultural change in Puerto Rico before working on tourism in the Venezuelan island of Margarita (Monk and Alexander 1986). That paper focused on structural changes in migration and employment that marked the recent emergence of a tourism economy and the accompanying transformation of livelihoods. Tourist studies were still in their infancy – derided as soft and irrelevant to hard core economic development, but the long boom meant that tourism became crucial to many small islands like Margarita. Employment and income-earning opportunities for poor agriculturalists and fisher folk seemed promising, and broader development issues in this emerging industry were largely ignored.

Janice Monk made an early and valuable analytical contribution to the structure of economic change in small island tourist economies. Tourist

DOI: 10.4324/9781032275611-23

development in Margarita proved to be quickly marked by outsiders taking over some key economic activities, with local ownership confined to small stores and guesthouses. Men gained positions as drivers and in construction while women found menial service jobs but lost vital productive roles as local agriculture collapsed. Many younger women migrated to the mainland for work. Households were split and new gender divides created. Female employment and economic activity proved disappointing amidst an economic growth that marginalised women in both new and old arenas. In what might have seemed to offer promise, tourism failed to provide decent employment and livelihoods, divided households and prompted out-migration.

This was virtually the first time that serious academic analysis pointed to the ways in which tourist 'development' could be illusory, that gender divides typified the industry and that it was crucial to consider gender relations from both perspectives of economic development and cultural change. The study offered an early analysis of how tourism employment is overtly gender biased, reflecting local and transnational norms of 'women's work' even as an economy grew. It played a key part in opening up a new way of thinking about gender in tourism (Kinnaird and Hall 1994) that could subsequently scarcely be ignored.

Pacific Island States

Unlike the Caribbean, the Pacific includes some of the most recent islands to have embraced tourism because of costs and conservatism, distance from markets and intervening opportunities: a combination of well-known structural and scalar disadvantages (Connell and Taulealo 2021). Like tourism itself, more sophisticated analysis of gender dynamics in Pacific tourism also came rather late. Broadly similar issues emerged, as they had on Margarita (and elsewhere in the Caribbean), as economies evolved – in a loosely upwards economic trajectory that stifled questions over employment and gender relations as agriculture faded away, and urbanisation added to a coastal environmental squeeze. What Janice Monk and Charles Alexander (1986) concluded of Margarita was still true of the Pacific a quarter of a century later: 'Island women have lost traditional productive roles but have not been incorporated into employment in the modern sector as fully as men' (1986, 411). 'Fully' effectively meant 'equitably'. Fortunately, traditional productive roles in the Pacific had not been entirely 'lost' and forgotten.

Few jobs in tourism are well paid and come with limited promotion prospects. Women occupy many of these jobs where alternative wage labour may be scarce, and resort development increased labour-intensive elements (Shakeela et al. 2011). Much employment is in the informal sector, including marketing and handicraft production, as tourism is characterised by both ease of entry and intense competition. Tourism work is precarious (Connell and Rugendyke 2008; Robinson et al. 2019), but formal employment opportunities for women have enabled some empowerment, resistance and resilience even, where, as in Fiji, employment is routine and menial. Kanemasu (2005) conducted a rare study in the region that drew on feminist theories to show how individuals challenge power relationships through embodied practices. Despite scarce prospects, tourism has offered women new opportunities for social mobility and greater control over household incomes and, in some contexts, a break from patriarchal society.

Social costs have sometimes ensued with uneven development and conflicts over land, incomes, and gendered inequality, but alongside recognition that intrinsic values, centred on kinship relations, were usually resilient while tourism enabled superior lifestyles and positive means of self-representation. In this century, new cruise ship tourism failed to generate the full-time employment of land-based tourism, but offered short-term economic opportunities for the local provision of goods, particularly café food and handicrafts, and services especially transport and tours. By the end of the 2010s, the cruise ship industry was increasingly being viewed negatively as both environmentally more hazardous and economically less beneficial to destinations than previously assumed.

The growing focus on tourism since the global economic boom of the 1970s, but particularly in this century, reflects a wider transition in many Small Island Developing States (SIDS) from the productive to the service sector. As agriculture and other economic activities declined, steady growth had insulated the industry from criticism. In most Pacific Island states roughly three quarters of all employment in the tourism industry is of women (Connell 2021). It seemed impolitic to suggest that few women were in the upper echelons of the industry.

Tourism and the COVID crash in the Pacific Islands

Early in 2020, a period of steady tourism growth in many Pacific Island states ended suddenly with the global spread of COVID-19. By the end of March, all ports (and borders) had closed and cruise ship tourism collapsed. Land-based tourism ended almost as quickly and by April many hotels and resorts were closing down alongside related activities such as restaurants, dive shops, local travel agents and car hire companies. That process of decline and closure continued through the year. COVID thus raised urgent questions about the role of tourism in this economy and in small island states more generally and provided an unparalleled pause to reconsider.

Closures were dramatic, but not catastrophic. In Samoa, for example, within a month of the border being closed in March, some 70 hotels, resorts and other businesses closed, at least half the industry, leaving 1,000 people without employment where there was little job security and no social security safety net. The Return to Paradise, one of the few Samoan-owned resort hotels, put 100 of its 130 staff on extended leave, retaining only a skeleton staff of 30 with reduced roles and hours (Connell and Taulealo 2021). Other hotels did much the same. The country made efforts to stimulate local tourism by reducing costs and introducing special offers. Vanuatu sought to stimulate demand by highlighting that tourism was not just for international visitors, adopting a *Sapotem lokol turisim* ('Support local tourism' in the Bislama lingua franca) campaign. With a very small potential local market and widespread recession that only delayed the inevitable. By the end of the year, most large resorts had closed.

Skeleton crews usually remained, which meant the retention of maintenance staff (such as gardeners and handypersons) and the loss of housekeeping staff and most wait staff, almost all of whom were women. Most hotels also sought to retain skilled chefs and office workers, some of whom were international migrants. Some of the key people retained were alternated and rotated during subsequent weeks to enable a broader access to employment.

Much the same collapse was experienced in Fiji and Vanuatu but accentuated there by the immediate and complete disappearance of cruise ship tourism (so involving bars, restaurants, stores and markets patronised by cruise ship tourists) which provided income-earning opportunities for people in the informal sector and in disadvantaged socio-economic groups. These include taxi and bus drivers, souvenir sellers, hair braiders and participants in 'cultural villages' on the fringes of Port Vila who displayed dance, explained traditional food and medicinal practices and sold artefacts.

The absence of tourists had direct multiplier effects. Resorts, such as The Havannah in Vanuatu, effectively ended most community-engagement activities, including sourcing supplies from local markets, handcraft producers, tour operators, taxi services and local village 'businesses' who provided security, conservation, handyman, gardening and cleaning services (Naupa et al. 2021). All hotels and restaurants needed less food; hence, they patronised local markets less and regularly turned down unsolicited offers of food and fish from local producers. Such restructuring had parallels elsewhere, with complex impacts on national and international supply chains. Local stores, partly dependent on sales to tourists at nearby resorts, shut down. That pattern was replicated elsewhere. Urban markets were particularly affected by what became an over-supply of local products, especially of handicraft goods.

Tourists were no longer visiting the islands and domestic travel declined rapidly, especially where public health criteria discouraged travel between islands. The national airlines, often subsidised by the states, declined quickly. Here too the 'skilled' workers, the pilots and engineers, were retained and the flight attendants were the first to go. Fiji Airways, the largest airline based in the Pacific, had laid off all its cabin crew by March.

In every country, an employment crisis existed, and tourism and its supply chain collapsed. The crisis was most serious in and around urban areas, where much of the tourism sector was concentrated and where there was greater dependence on cash incomes, more utility bills (notably water and electricity) and less ability to achieve some subsistence support. Poverty increased especially amongst those in the already disadvantaged informal sector, and the burden initially fell on women, as the bulk of the workforce.

Women's burdens

The COVID pandemic highlighted the marginalisation of women in the tourism industry and in the related informal sector. Women were usually the first to be displaced from the formal sector (the cleaners and waitresses, but rarely the chefs and accountants) and lost their roles in the more informal markets, handicraft production and cultural performances. Conscious of the disadvantages that women faced through the simultaneous loss of jobs in tourism, small business and the informal sector, some resorts sought to retrench people as equitably as was feasible and retain women (Naupa et al. 2021). Others simply wanted to reduce costs.

Many displaced workers had to – and could – return to agricultural livelihoods. However, since agriculture could not immediately be productive and output marketable, the transition – led by women – was difficult. Local food production could not immediately compensate for the lost incomes that enabled food purchases. In several Pacific states governments introduced programmes to train local youth in agricultural techniques and distributed seeds and planting material. In Samoa, the role and significance of the Ministry of Women, Community and Social Development increased with village women's committees playing an expanded role in encouraging food security through undertaking more home gardening. Such changes increased self-reliance but added to the domestic labour burden of women. Not all displaced workers from urban and/or tourist employment could reclaim and revitalise rural lives, thus put a burden on local ecologies and environments and on women who were the primary producers there. Tensions could easily occur over land and sea tenure, as people sought to claim land they had rarely seen for years. Theft of kava plants, sandalwood trees and root crops was reported mainly in peri-urban areas. Re-establishing agricultural livelihoods proved challenging.

Social costs became evident. In urban areas especially, and in Fiji amongst Indo-Fijians (with no real claim to land), loss of employment was marked by a rise in domestic violence (Connell 2021). Both men and women lost employment and marketing opportunities and women took on more caring and home-schooling responsibilities. Many were now 'stuck' at home, in overcrowded houses with few facilities in urban settlements. Women faced a greater economic and emotional load and an old employment 'double burden' was also re-established. When schools reopened, in Fiji at least, girls were less likely to return as households were less able to afford the school fees and girls were more expendable (and could engage in 'domestic duties'). Overall, the economic collapse that stemmed primarily from the end of tourism, in countries with limited social welfare systems, caused a rise in poverty with the burden being borne by the poorest households and by women within these households.

Revivals of livelihoods

Many women in tourism had worked in service, hospitality and housekeeping positions that did not require specific qualifications, and implied poor working conditions, incomes and job security. Partly in consequence women retained stronger social and economic ties with home. After COVID-19, practices such as returning home for significant social events, a disadvantage to formal employers, became key social and economic advantages as women retained social networks, and indigenous knowledge, so ensuring that a safety net was still in place. Formal sector marginality suddenly became valuable.

While women (and men) experienced major setbacks, they spearheaded key developments, alongside fishing and agriculture that enabled more effective coping with the loss of tourism. Women, however, had retained 'traditional' skills associated with garden production, inshore fishing and gleaning of reefs. As cash became less evident, bartering grew in significance in several island states (Boodoosingh 2020). Organised by women, garden foods were exchanged for fish, pigs for roofing iron or tutoring and various household goods for immediate needs. In an electronic age (that meant some degree of urban bias) older exchange systems were being revitalised in new form. In Solomon Islands it was referred to as *'trade bilong iumi'* (our trade). Food that could no longer be sold to hotels was distributed through Facebook. Bartering was paralleled in the revival of the 'silent markets' that had existed even in pre-contact times as coastal and small island people exchanged marine produce for the root crops of inland people. Most such goods were produced by women, as small-scale, localised activities prospered where money was less visible and less useful.

Backyard agriculture boomed in urban areas, and public spaces were claimed for production as 'pop-up gardens'. At a different scale from bartering, sharing goods and food between households within local social networks expanded. Small roadside stalls proliferated in urban areas and throughout the main islands, with households anxious to make some income from agricultural produce, and also fish, or from selling homemade doughnuts, but handicraft stalls closed. Some women traded and exchanged from their homes, selling plants and home-cooked food but had to adjust to living on reduced incomes. Fewer households bought such produce and prices were low. Households had lower incomes, selling the same goods and undercutting each other. The overall negative impact was greatest on the urban informal sector in and around the urban centres: urban residents, with minimal access to land and social support, were more likely to experience poverty. The livelihoods of those in the poorest socio-economic groups had almost entirely disappeared. Despite the re-establishment of agriculture and fishing, and rebuilding social networks, food prices increased as supply chains struggled, and although diets became more composed of local foods, food security worsened. Malnutrition would have been more widespread without the maintenance of rural production. Sharing and reciprocity could not always succeed when there was less food available.

In a sense the island states were returning to an older order of more localised lives where mobility was constrained, a moral economy was in place and strangers were problematic. That was even more evident as several states imposed bans on travelling between islands. In difficult and unprecedented times reversals to past practices could never be wholly convincing, where alternatives had so recently existed, but they stemmed a damaging tide, enabled survival, emphasised and revisited the vital role of women. Retention of diverse skills, knowledge and experiences and the willingness to share and exchange within local social networks were part of a diversity of small-scale cultural strategies, with legacies from the past. In the midst of a pandemic with severe economic consequences, they could never have been entirely successful, female-coping mechanisms ensured survival.

As in the face of other disasters, resourceful women, often unacknowledged, proved invaluable in response and reconstruction through mobilising capital, working collectively and being innovative small-scale entrepreneurs. In past Pacific environmental and political crises, from cyclones to civil wars, women revived social economies despite being burdened by a gendered and inequitable system (Clissold et al. 2020; Donahue et al. 2016; McNamara et al. 2020; Saovana-Spriggs 2003). Despite the additional burdens, including higher workloads, placed on women in crises – and especially during COVID-19, as the tourism industry collapsed – women's greater familiarity with 'traditional' values, and a willingness to work cooperatively, enabled households to cope even in extreme adversity.

Islands in the stream

The once vibrant if flawed tourism industries of Margarita and the island Pacific are in acute decline. As Venezuela's economy crashed so did the tourist industry of Margarita, badly affected by organised and violent crime and an international hub for the illegal drug trade. The spectacular crash of tourism in the Pacific was even more disruptive. In better times, in both contexts, women numerically dominated the tourist industry. Indeed, the Pacific of the 2010s was remarkably similar to the tourist industry of Margarita that Janice Monk described in the 1980s. Marginalisation and precarity endured.

Ironically, following the COVID collapse, and despite the persistent double burden experienced by many Pacific islander women, women had the cultural flexibility to lead the necessary revitalisation of social and economic lives. As the COVID-19 crisis demonstrated, women were, as in environmental and political crises, both 'victims and caretakers' (Resurreccion 2013). In such difficult circumstances that could never be universally successful, efforts are still needed to improve and support women's wellbeing, agency, livelihoods and prospects.

The devastating impact of COVID-19, ironically still largely absent in Pacific Island tourist destinations, provides the ultimate example of the costs of absolute dependence on international tourism. No economic sector is more sensitive to external shocks, and no shock more devastating than COVID-19 because of the abrupt and absolute demise of tourism, where 'conventional' shocks (such as coups, bombs or cyclones) are of immediate rather than indeterminate duration. Its demise raises questions about its future. Conceivably, revival outside the tourist industry might lead to a post-COVID future that offers not so much a 'new normal' as a more inclusive tourism where women and local linkages take a more prominent place.

Revitalisation of economies raises continually tested and contested issues of power, ownership, participation and representation. It was the nascence of these processes in Margarita that Janice Monk recognised.

In the Pacific, gender discourses and practices were only occasionally and belatedly challenged. Yet that hesitancy meant women retaining ties with home, enabling them to better withstand and cope with the exigencies of COVID-19 and the collapse of tourism, despite their being most affected. Retaining social networks proved invaluable, pointing to the virtues of a more localised and culturally hybrid economy. Pacific women were incidentally engaged in securing the regenerative and resilient economies later to be suggested as post-COVID ideals (e.g. Leach et al. 2021). The uneven involvement in the industry that led Janice Monk to reflect on its damaging impacts in small islands and its repercussions for women's lives had unusual and unexpected outcomes. Janice Monk showed how to go beyond the superficial and be more critical of an industry and to examine the capacities for change and development which in the contemporary Pacific took unexpected turns. Women may remain vulnerable, and there can be no great expectation that the post-COVID tourism industry will exemplify a 'new normal', but women's roles and contributions are at least better understood.

In a different sea, far from Margarita, a female-led revival pointed to a different future that has the potential to strengthen the role and prospects of women in and beyond the tourist industry. Janice would appreciate that and be pleased that a small and perhaps largely forgotten part of a great career had been influential. My conversations in Sydney suggest that she rather missed the opportunity to have worked in the Pacific, and 'compare and contrast'. She did however stimulate ways of thinking in and about the Pacific, and would have recognised the exigencies of Margarita in the contemporary livelihoods of Pacific women in the tourist industry, and appreciated their struggles beyond it.

References

Boodoosingh, Ramona. 2020. "Bartering in Samoa during COVID-19." *DevPolicy Blog* (blog). Development Policy Centre. June 30. https://devpolicy.org/bartering-in-samoa-during-covid-19-2020630-1/

Clissold, Rachel, Ross Westoby, and Karen E. McNamara. 2020. "Women as recovery enablers in the face of disasters in Vanuatu." *Geoforum* 113: 101–110.

Connell, John. 2021. "COVID-19 and tourism in Pacific SIDS: lessons from Fiji, Vanuatu and Samo." *The Round Table* 110(1): 149–158.

Connell, John, and Barbara Anne Rugendyke. 2008. "Tourism and local people in the Asia-Pacific region." In *Tourism at the Grassroots*, edited by John Connell and Barbara Anne Rugendyke, 1–40. London: Routledge.

Connell, J., and Tautalaaso Taulealo. 2021. "Island tourism and COVID-19 in Vanuatu and Samoa: an unfolding crisis." *Small States and Territories* 4(1): 105–124.

Donahue, Jaclyn, Kate Eccles, and May Miller-Dawkins. 2016. "Responding to shocks: women's experiences of economic shocks in the Solomon Islands and

Vanuatu." In *Household Vulnerability and Resilience to Economic Shocks*, edited by Simon Feeny, 43–66. London: Routledge.

Kanemasu, Yoko. 2005. "Weapons of the workers: employees in the Fiji hotel scene." In *Tourism at the Grassroots*, edited by John Connell and Barbara Anne Rugendyke, 114–130. London: Routledge.

Kinnaird, Vivian, and Derek Hall. 1994. "Tourism: gender perspectives." In *Tourism: A Gender Analysis*, edited by Vivian Kinnaird and Derek Hall, 1–34. Chichester: Wiley.

Leach, Melissa, Hayley MacGregor, Ian Scoones, and Annie Wilkinson. 2021. "Post-pandemic transformations: how and why COVID-19 requires us to rethink development." *World Development* 138: 105233.

McNamara, Karen E., Rachel Clissold, and Ross Westoby. 2020. "Women's capabilities in disaster recovery and resilience must be acknowledged, utilized and supported." *Journal of Gender Studies* 30 (1): 119–125.

Monk, Janice, and Charles Alexander. 1986. "Free port fallout. Gender, employment and migration on Margarita Island." *Annals of Tourism Research* 13: 393–413.

Naupa, Anna, Sarah Mecartney, Liz Pechan, and Nick Howlett. 2021. "An industry in crisis: how Vanuatu's tourism sector is building for economic recovery." In *COVID in the Islands: A Comparative Perspective on the Caribbean and the Pacific*, edited by Yonique Campbell and John Connell, 231–252 Singapore: Palgrave Macmillan.

Resurreccion, Bernadette. 2013. "Persistent women and environmental linkages in climate change and sustainable development goals." *Women's Studies International Forum* 40: 33–43.

Robinson, Richard, Antje Martins, David Solnet, and Tom Baum. 2019. "Sustaining precarity: critically examining tourism and employment." *Journal of Sustainable Tourism* 27 (7): 1008–125.

Saovana-Spriggs, R. 2003. "Bougainville women's role in conflict resolution in the Bougainville peace process." In *A Kind of Mending: Restorative Justice in the Pacific Islands*, edited by Sinclair Dinnen, Anita Jowitt, and Tess Newton, 195–213. Canberra: Pandanus.

Shakeela, Aishath, Lisa Ruhanen, and Noreen Breakey. 2011. "The role of employment in the sustainable development paradigm: the local tourism market in small island developing states." *Journal of Human Resources in Hospitality and Tourism* 10 (4): 331–353.

20 Women and Waste Recycling in the State of São Paulo, Brazil

Margarida Queirós

Women, waste, infrastructure and place

In this chapter, nature–society relations are analyzed through the study of women, who used to collect recyclable materials from waste dumps or the streets and have now organized themselves into formal collectives, known today as cooperatives. At such sites, recyclable materials, the equipment and associated infrastructure are a fundamental part of the reconstitution of the world of these women (Whatmore 2002; Lorimer 2012).

This discussion addresses the interaction between the self and the world, not as separate but as a continuum (Labanyi 2010) and examines the social conditions of the women waste pickers (Howitt et al. 2016). From this standpoint "waste has agency to act upon society" (Van Bemmel and Parizeau 2020, 208). Also, as Janice Monk and Susan Hanson wrote in 'On not excluding half of the Human in Human Geography' (1982), I did not want to exclude from my own geographical research people whose livelihood depends on something that society rejects. With a focus on women, the chapter also contributes to deepening knowledge on gender geographies in the Global South.

Waste management is commonly associated with environmental problems and is usually carried out by poor and colored people (Gregson and Crang 2010). The buildings, objects, and environment where they perform their work are generally classified as "dangerous/hazardous" because of the nature of the materials and the potential for contamination (Thomas-Hope 1998). Yet they contain a liberating potential for the women who work at these sites. Such women become responsible for these places and objects, and at the same time feel they can challenge their role in society through formal recognition of their profession, achievement of social rights, growing income, and the strengthening of class solidarity and self-esteem. These feelings are the result of unique and situated contexts that have been altered and reformulated (Valentine 1997). Waste thus becomes a resource, but the most important aspect discussed in this chapter is not "what waste is" but "what waste does".

This study reflects on the implications of hybrid relationships between human and non-human objects/materials (Demeritt 2002; Braun 2005; Hinchliffe and Whatmore 2006). The notion of 'atmosphere' as a feeling that

DOI: 10.4324/9781032275611-24

emanates from the dynamics between humans and the non-human (Labanyi 2010; Vannini and Vannini 2020; Tan 2021) is central to this study.

Methodology

This chapter is drawn from a study of Cooperlix (Presidente Prudente Recyclable Products Workers Cooperative), a cooperative of about 90 people who collect recyclable waste (metals, paper, plastic, glass) from Presidente Prudente municipality in São Paulo state (for details on this cooperative, see Queirós, Leal and Fuzzi 2020). Women waste pickers (collectors of recyclable materials) survived for years without any social protection, until they made the decision to formally organize themselves. Today, they are able to obtain equipment and infrastructure to recover the value of the materials collected and improve their working conditions at specific sites. Qualitative methodologies were used to capture the experiences of these women waste pickers in the west of the state of São Paulo (SP), Brazil, in 2018 and 2019.

Initially, a meeting was held to get to know the workers, their working conditions and the waste management practices. Later other meetings took place to understand the role of women in the cooperative, factors that influenced their personal and working trajectories, the interpersonal relations within the treatment facility and the connections with the site and the materials with which they work in order to capture the process of transforming waste into resources and examine its potential to disrupt and transform human actions. Women volunteers aged between 18 and 35 shared their daily lives through semi-formal interviews and a focus group discussion was conducted. Observation notebooks, descriptions of field experiences, photos, audio, and records at the site were used to capture details of the socio-spatial configuration of living spaces and the relationship between humans and non-human agents.

In small-scale studies such as this, walking with the participants enables close relationships to develop and thus has the potential to adjust our representations of the space where social practices are performed, materiality is embodied, and rules of space are lived (Streule 2020). Walks through the waste treatment terrain allowed some of the interviews to be done on the move, while others were conducted using standard techniques in specific working places. This method, alongside with the field observation, was particularly relevant as it allowed us to become engaged with the working environment revealing the atmosphere in which the relationships between humans and the objects (recyclable waste, technical equipment and place) are forged. Reflexive participant observation revealed a place filled with human and non-human presence, full of energy, vibrancy, and life.

The interviews included questions about sociodemographic information (age, sex, skin color, marital status, children, education, place of birth and living, prior working activity, etc.) and personal life trajectories/narratives. The photos and talks were recorded with informed consent. The focus group activity was held in the workplace canteen, allowing for the exchange of opinions, ideas, effects, and emotions between the participants concerning the objects they work with and the waste treatment facilities where they work.

Colleagues from the São Paulo State University (UNESP) at the Presidente Prudente campus were facilitators in introducing the cooperative members. The information colleagues shared encouraged the cooperation between us (researchers from the "North" and the "South"), and the exploration of common grounds to deepen the research (Monk, Manning and Denman 2003). As the research progressed, I became more aware of women's roles, their knowledge, and practices. In their reflexive commitment to the processes and methodologies used to create and apply knowledge, Monk, Manning, and Denman (2003, 26) called for attention to "women's lives constructed within the dominant relations of production and reproduction."

In Cooperlix women revealed that they seek and remain in the cooperative for several reasons: the domestic work is unpaid, thus not socially recognized as this one; the lack of better jobs with a social security plan; the unemployment of the partner; the need for financial support for their children; and the fact that they feel "independent" from the moment they obtain their own money through working with recyclables.

The context: from waste pickers to recyclable materials collectors

Brazil is marked by unemployment and exclusion from the formal labor market. According to IBGE 2020, the unemployed constitute about 14 million and unemployment affects 1/3 of the lowest income families. Consequently, it is common for many jobless persons to find refuge in informal economic activities, often combined with precarious working conditions, as is the case of the recyclable material collectors (Thomas-Hope 1998). In most cases, the activities they perform are informal and start in the cities' streets or at garbage dumps – as "waste pickers" or "scavengers" (in Portuguese, "catadores"). About 10% of the nearly 500,000 collectors of recyclable materials in Brazil are formally organized into collective working groups. These associations and/or cooperatives encompass around 1,000 collective organizations of waste pickers (Paiva 2016; Queirós, Leal and Fuzzi 2020).

In examining the changing impacts of development on women and men, Momsen (2020) exposes serious problems with garbage in poor countries, particularly in densely populated urban areas, but at the same time notes this can be an opportunity for poor people to earn from the discards of the wealthier. The activity of collecting recyclable materials (disposable paper, glass, metal, and plastic stuff) is particularly relevant in society because, among other factors, it deals with waste as a non-human object with emergent properties that enable networks of agency (Gregson and Crang 2010; Moore 2012; Gutberlet 2015; Millington and Lawhon 2018; Momsen 2020; Van Bemmel and Parizeau 2020). This perspective defines the properties of waste as an actant, meaning that they act upon individuals and society – rather than only the reverse (Moore 2012). This relationality is an important aspect of waste studies. While human actions and technologies may transform waste into recyclable materials, the value of these materials and the activities related to its preparation for sale can therefore influence the life and behavior of actors who encounter them, including the formation of cooperatives.

In 2010, in Brazil, waste pickers were recognized officially as service providers (Momsen 2020). Today the Brazilian Employment Ministry identifies the activities of recyclable material collectors and selection workers as collecting and selecting recyclable and reusable stuff, selling the collected material, and preparing it for shipment. In Brazil, this activity has been formally acknowledged since 2010 through the National Solid Waste Policy (PNRS, Law n°12, 305) which identifies the need for social inclusion of waste pickers and represents a normative advance for social and environmental issues. This solid waste policy is also significant as it offers legal and technical bases for solid waste management to contain the problems caused by the generation of waste. The PNRS corresponds not only to a national regulatory framework for sustainable practices related to waste and to urban solid waste management but also reveals a concern about social protection through the inclusion of recyclable material collectors and the recognition of the value of their work (Gonçalves et al. 2016).

Another significant initiative to improve the working conditions of collectors was also launched in 2010, known as the "Pro-Catador" Program (Decree n°7, 405/2010). Thus, according to this act, policies aimed at collectors would be established through the so-called Inter-ministerial Committee for Social and Economic Inclusion of Reusable and Recyclable Material Collectors (CIISC). This program articulates the actions of the federal government to support the productive organization of recyclable material collectors, improve their working conditions, expand opportunities for social and economic inclusion, and develop, in partnership with collectors, the selective collection of solid waste, reuse and recycling.

With the National Solid Waste Policy, the carrying out of waste picker activities in dumps was prohibited – but they were not eliminated. The law established that, by 2012, Brazilian municipalities needed to have an integrated solid waste management plan and implement selective collecting systems, and by 2014, to eradicate dumps. These legal deadlines were not met by all municipalities, revealing their financial and technical weaknesses in planning and management of solid waste. Therefore, many of the waste pickers are still in open-air dumps; others carry out the activity in landfills complying with legal and engineering requirements (IPEA 2013).

As Thomas-Hope (1998, 2) observed in tackling waste in developing counties, "there is a general lack of a culture of cooperation". In fact, throughout Brazil, in the early stages of the process, it was challenging to organize waste workers into collectives. Yet today it can be noted that the changes and collectivization that took place generated confidence, self-esteem, reciprocity, and group identity. In addition, the formal recognition of the profession, designation of a place, infrastructure, equipment, and technologies to work with, strengthens identities, empowers waste pickers, gives meaning to their interactions and entrepreneurship, and expands their life opportunities.

The Cooperlix treatment facility: origins and stabilization

In the early 2000s, the waste pickers of Presidente Prudente collected, separated, and sold recyclable waste randomly deposited in the urban perimeter, or directly in the municipal dump. Most of them faced class and race discrimination. They lived and worked in precarious conditions and supplied to recycling companies that paid low prices for materials (Leal 2002, 2004; Gonçalves et al. 2016; Carvalho and Rondini 2017). Fortunately, this scenario changed with the Recyclable Products Workers Cooperative (Cooperlix) being formed in 2002. The cooperative's headquarters were provided by the municipal government and the equipment was acquired through projects developed in partnership with the Bank of Brazil Foundation, FAPESP (Research Support Foundation of the State of São Paulo) and UNESP (Presidente Prudente University), among other sources of support, including organized community groups (trade unions, churches, etc.) (Leal 2002, 2004).

Today Cooperlix is a non-profit entity, where the income is divided among its members, used to meet losses, and for technical, educational, and social assistance. At first, many collectors did not want to join the cooperative due to the overall lack of trust in society, greater earnings from solo work or working in small groups. The buyers of recyclable materials had no interest in the formal organization of waste collectors and at that time, only 37 collectors (21 men and 16 women) agreed to participate in the formal creation of Cooperlix (Queirós, Leal and Fuzzi 2020).

Between 2004 and 2015, the size of the cooperative fluctuated due to financial difficulties. The low turnover was one of the reasons for the drop out of collectors, mostly men. As the formal labor market employment opportunities available to women in the city-region are not sufficient, they continue in activities with lower remuneration and social prestige to support their families. In the small group that remained, women took over the leadership of the cooperative, fighting for the continuity of the project, which they feel is an environmental service extremely relevant to society. Thus, there was a change in the composition of the board, with an increase in the number of women and in 2006 a woman assumed the presidency of Cooperlix until 2019 (Leal 2002, 2004).

The financial stability of the cooperative was achieved in 2015, when it was hired by the municipality for collection of waste materials, allowing a fixed monthly income, complemented by sales of collected recyclable waste. In 2016, the activity of waste scavengers was banned in the municipal dump, so they were voluntarily incorporated into Cooperlix. Thus, the impossibility of continuing to work in the dump, as well as the growing empowerment and gains of collective work, enlarged the number of its members: in December 2018, the collective had 88 workers, of which 41 were women and 47 men (Queirós, Leal and Fuzzi 2020).

Currently, the work has evolved and become more specialized and gendered among the 90 members. As Momsen (2020) noticed, men tend to deal with the heavier and more hazardous materials. At Cooperlix this also occurs, while additionally men usually drive the collection trucks. The internal organization of the facility is almost an empty space, yet it also reveals gender and spatial divisions of labor. Women concentrate and work on the sorting belt while selective collection, transport, and pressing are carried out mainly by men. Some craftwork with metals is men's responsibility as well. But, as women become more powerful in the cooperative, these divisions of labor become less rigid (Queirós, Leal and Fuzzi 2020).

226 *Margarida Queirós*

The Cooperlix treatment facility: a more-than-human atmosphere

Anderson (2014) explains that it is necessary to understand how a diverse grouping of people come together to speculate on how an atmosphere forms and unfolds. The concept of atmosphere is described as a feeling that emanates from the dynamics between humans and the non-human (Labanyi 2010; Vannini and Vannini 2020; Tan 2021). It occurs in specific spaces and an affective materiality can be felt through human bodies in motion. Atmospheres are "melded between and within the affective and emotional, the individual and collective" (Tan 2021, 3). So, affect and emotion are dynamic, simultaneous experiences that people encounter as they are entangled by an atmosphere. Since the foundation of Cooperlix there has been a huge process of transformation and empowerment.

It must be remembered that the women in this collective do not have much education, consider themselves "negras" and "pardas" (colored), have never travelled outside the state of São Paulo, and in the past did not have the capacity to support themselves financially (Katz and Monk 1993). The transformation starts as soon as those women leave their informal activity and move into a formalized setting with the help of UNESP researchers (Figure 20.1). In general, the history of cooperatives shows how the materialities associated with the workplace play an important role in social transitions, as

Figure 20.1 Mural with the beginnings of Cooperlix (with the help of an action-research project from UNESP, Dept. Geography – the colleague in the mural is Cezar Leal, the collectors say that "God is in heaven and Cezar is in earth to help us").

well as offering the beneficial effects of social inclusion. The waste pickers are affected by mandatory regulations related to their activity, which firstly makes them suspicious, but then encourages them to organize in collectives. Recyclable materials collectors are empowered by the objects they select from consumption, and these again become raw materials to the production cycle.

In the sheds/infrastructure we find material components – equipment, as well as the recyclable objects – through which the women separate the different materials according to their composition and market value, where the process of empowerment takes place (Figure 20.2). They take over the entire space to perform the activity and the happiness and rhythm that we feel there contributes to the formation of an atmosphere that does not constrain individuals.

Among the interviewees, there was a common idea that the infrastructure and equipment reduced physical effort, making their work easier and more efficient. They all shared the opinion that the shed protects them from the heat, the conveyor belt helps the separation of materials in a safer way, and the truck allows a greater amount to be collected, thus creating a better income (Figures 20.3 and 20.4). While performing this activity, they experience positive feelings/emotions, especially if they remember the previous working conditions.

The increase in infrastructure quality, adequate equipment, and better technologies enhance working conditions, increase the quantities of selected and packaged materials for sale, enable workers to perform specialized

Figure 20.2 At Cooperlix site: plastic objects separated by composition and market value, ready to be transported to destination.

228 *Margarida Queirós*

Figure 20.3 A shelter for working women: the shed from inside, the conveyor belts and the separation process.

Figure 20.4 The Cooperlix shed from outside (the truck unloading paper and cardboard).

activities, provide closer dynamics between them, improving efficiency and resulting in overall gains. The condition of the place thus allows for an equal and close relationship to develop and a sense of motivation. The workplace gives a feeling of refuge to these women. They showed me the facilities with great pride and joy, claiming "see and photograph without any problem, we are happy here and we want our visitors to feel happy" (Elsa, interview June 2019) (Figure 20.5).

Many of these women also shared painful aspects of their past. They revealed that their fathers exchanged them for money, furniture, or other possessions to their future husband. Most of them experienced motherhood when they were adolescents and afterwards were abandoned by their partners. Obviously in most cases, they became economically dependent, invisible, and subservient as a mother and/or attending to the male partner's needs. Today, through the cooperative, women share feelings of freedom, self-esteem, and confidence.

Despite their struggles, these women persist in improving their work and living conditions. The precarious conditions of their lives forced them to collect garbage in the streets and taking the step to form and join a collective was at the time the best and most liberating solution they found. Today they show pride in their achievements and refer to garbage with knowledge of its physical properties and with affection, recognizing that it has brought them autonomy, dignity, hope, and joy in living. The treatment equipment is felt by

Figure 20.5 The Cooperlix: a detail of a showcase of collected and reused materials for room decoration.

everyone as a collective acquisition, earned through individual and joint work, only possible due to the warm and protective environment they found at Cooperlix. An individual and collective energy is noticeable in the execution of the hard work, in times to eat and rest, and in the hours of meetings to discuss issues and take decisions.

The impact of the place of the cooperative is the product of a complex mixture between the technological "apparatus" for separating and compiling recyclable materials, and the local environment, such as fauna, flora, light, and temperature that make these people surprisingly hopeful, connected, protected and emotional – quoting Elsa (interview, June 2018), "we are constantly striving to have all this equipment and this place to do our work; (…) I'm here with friends, I share my problems with them and together we find solutions" (Queirós, Leal and Fuzzi 2020).

Women at Cooperlix have gained leadership positions and are aware of their achievements despite being born and living in unfavorable male-dominated environments. Today, they consider themselves recyclable material collectors, a position where they "work for the benefit of the environment and public health" (Silvia, interview June 2018). Thus, from the awareness of their role and actions, the unexpected emerges: a pleasure in what they do, leadership capacity and the sense of "sororidade", an affection of sisterhood, as the united "family" that they did not have in their past existence.

Recyclable waste thus does not represent the end; it is a beginning for the reframing of these women's lives (Queirós, Leal and Fuzzi 2020). The line between staying in a collective or returning to the dump is thin and fluid. Women who remain in the collective believe in the strength of the group and the emergence of a sense of "home" and protection.

As a researcher, the initial discomfort I felt when hearing about the tragic stories of women waste pickers was transformed into admiration in the course of my research. 'Overcoming' is a great word to describe the experiences of these women and sharing these proved therapeutic. Janice Monk's lifelong research inspires feminist researchers to establish bridges between studies from the margins to the mainstream of the privileged. Inspired by her telling the stories of women who live by collecting and separating waste and the consequent socio-materiality of these materials is part of my mission. According to Katz and Monk (1993, 26), research such as this opens paths towards change that begins in all of the many 'locations' in which women find themselves and which go 'full circle' to address the webs of sociocultural and political-economic relations in their lives. I pay tribute to Janice Monk, through making known the value of these women, interpreting parts of their stories and, above all, establishing bonds between researchers and recyclable waste collectors.

Acknowledgements

Part of this research was presented in a previous published article – Queirós, Leal and Fuzzi (2020). My thanks go to all the people who made this research possible: field work was funded by UNESP and facilitated by colleagues, especially Antonio Cezar Leal, who invited me several times to go to Brazil to collaborate in the post graduate courses and do research in underprivileged communities; and to the women who shared their feelings and emotions. Finally, I am grateful to Mário Vale, for always being there for me, sharing his views, photos, and insights.

References

Anderson, Ben. 2014. *Encountering Affect: Capacities, Apparatuses, Conditions.* Farnham: Ashgate.

Braun, Bruce. 2005. "Environmental issues: Writing a more-than-human urban geography." *Progress in Human Geography* 29 (5): 635–650.

Carvalho, Ana M. R. and Carina A. Rondini. 2017. "Perfil Socioprofissional de catadoras e catadores em associações e cooperativas do Oeste Paulista" [Socio-professional profile of female waste pickers in associations and cooperatives in the west of São Paulo). In *A Economia Solidária e os Desafios Globais do Trabalho, 1^{a}ed*, edited by A. R. Souza and M. Zanin, 251–261. São Carlos – SP: Ed.UFScar.

Demeritt, David. 2002. "What is the 'social construction of nature'? A typology and sympathetic critique." *Progress in Human Geography* 26 (6): 767–790.

Gonçalves, Marcelino, Margarida Queirós do Vale and Alexandre H. Gonçalves. 2016. "Um estudo comparado entre a realidade brasileira e portuguesa sobre a gestão dos resíduos sólidos urbanos [A comparative study between the Brazilian and Portuguese reality on the management of urban solid waste]." *Sociedade & Natureza* 28 (1): 9–20.

Gregson, Nicky and Mike Crang. 2010. "Materiality and Waste: Inorganic vitality in a networked world." *Environment and Planning A: Economy and Space* 42 (5): 1026–1032.

Gutberlet, Jutta. 2015. "Cooperative urban mining in Brazil: Collective practices in selective household waste collection and recycling." *Waste Management* 45: 22–31.

Hinchliffe, Steve and Sarah Whatmore. 2006. "Living cities: Towards a politics of conviviality." *Science as Culture* 15 (2): 123–138.

Howitt, Richard, Clare Colyer, Janice Monk, David Crew and Stephanie Hull. 2016. *Looking Forward – Looking Back. Changing Social and Economic Conditions of Aboriginal People in Rural NSW, 1965-2015*. Macquire University, Department of Geography and Planning.

IPEA. 2013. *Situação Social das Catadoras e dos Catadores de Material Reciclável e Reutilizável – Brasil* [*Social Situation of Collectors and Collectors of Recyclable and Reusable Material – Brazil*]. Brasília: Instituto de Pesquisa Econômica Aplicada.

Katz, Cindi and Janice Monk. 1993. "When in the world are women?" In *Full Circles. Geographies of Women over the Life Course*, edited by Cindi Katz and Janice Monk, 1–26. London: Routledge.

Labanyi, Jo. 2010. "Doing things: Emotion, affect, and materiality." *Journal of Spanish Cultural Studies* 11 (3-4): 223–233.

Leal, António C. (coord.). 2002/ 2004. Educação Ambiental e o gerenciamento integrado de resíduos sólidos em Presidente Prudente – SP: desenvolvimento de metodologias para a coleta seletiva, beneficiamento do lixo e organização do trabalho. [Environmental education and integrated solid waste management in Presidente Prudente – SP: development of methodologies for selective collection, waste processing and work organization. Report]. Relatório Científico, Fase I (2002) e Fase II (2004). Presidente Prudente: UNESP/FAPESP.

Lorimer, Jamie. 2012. "Multinatural geographies for the Anthropocene." *Progress in Human Geography* 36 (5): 593–612.

Millington, Nate and Mary Lawhon. 2018. "Geographies of waste: Conceptual vectors from the Global South." *Progress in Human Geography* 43 (6): 1044–1063.

Momsen, Janet. 2020. *Gender and Development*, 3rd ed. London and New York: Routledge.

Monk, Janice and Susan Hanson. 1982. "On not excluding half of the human in Human Geography." *The Professional Geographer* 34 (1): 11–23.

Monk, Janice, Patricia Manning, Catalina Denman. 2003. "Working together: Feminist perspectives on collaborative research and action." *ACME* 2 (1): 91–106.

Moore, Sarah A. 2012. "Garbage matters: Concepts in new geographies of waste." *Progress in Human Geography* 36 (6): 780–799.

Paiva, Camila C. 2016. "Mulheres catadoras: articulação política e ressignificação social através do trabalho [Waste pickers: political articulation and social resignification through work]." *Idéias* 7 (2): 151–174.

Queirós, Margarida, Cezar Leal and Fernanda Fuzzi. 2020. "Trabalho e empoderamento: mulheres catadoras de materiais recicláveis no estado de São Paulo, Brasil" [Work and empowerment: women collectors of recyclable materials in the state of São Paulo]. In *Terra e Trabalho: territorialidades e desigualdades*, Vol. II, Rosa Ester Rossini, Maria Rita Machado and Sampaio (orgs.), 204–242. São Paulo: FFLCH/USP. doi: 10.11606/9786587621333.

Streule, M. 2020. "Doing mobile ethnography: Grounded, situated and comparative." *Urban Studies* 57 (2): 421–438.

Tan, Xin W. A. 2021. "Atmospheres of street performance in Taipei: Affect and emotion as dynamic, simultaneous, more-than-representational experiences." *Emotion, Space and Society* 38: 100766.

Thomas-Hope, Elisabeth. ed. 1998. *Solid Waste Management: Critical Issues for Developing Countries*. Kingston, Jamaica: Canoe Press, University of the West Indies.

Valentine, Gill. 1997. "Tell me about using interviews as a research methodology." In *Methods in Human Geography. A Guide for Students Doing a Research Project*, edited by Robin Flowerdew and David Martin, 110–253. London: Longman.

Van Bemmel, Alexis and Kate Parizeau. 2020. "Is it food or is it waste? The materiality and relational agency of food waste across the value chain." *Journal of Cultural Economy* 13 (2): 207–220.

Vannini, Philip and April Vannini. 2020. "Attuning to wild atmospheres: Reflections on wildeness as feeling." *Emotion, Space and Society* 36: 100711.

Whatmore, Sarah. 2002. *Hybrid Geographies: Natures Cultures Spaces*. London: Sage.

21 Women's Stories of Loss and Recovery from Climatic Events in the Pacific Islands

Rachel Clissold and Karen E. McNamara

Introduction

This chapter is inspired by Janice Monk's work in highlighting the invisibility of women in human geography and her dedication to inclusivity (Monk and Hanson 1982). Across her career, Monk examined women's roles in modifying the landscape and environment, their 'spaces of action' but also the changing lives of women (Rengert and Monk 1982; Monk 2007). In this chapter, we explore the shifting roles and everyday lives of a group of Pacific Island women, their 'spaces of action' and contributions to modifying their environment and landscapes in the face of unprecedented global climate change. Pacific Islander women are often considered to be at the forefront of experiencing and responding to climate change impacts. We focus on women from the Cook Islands and Vanuatu and outline their accounts of loss from climatic events as well as their critical contributions to disaster preparedness, response and recovery.

These insights are important as women's voices and needs related to disasters and climate change are largely ignored within communities (Alam and Habibur Rahman 2014) and in formal decision-making processes (Fulu 2007; Bradshaw and Fordham 2013; Nadiruzzaman and Wrathall 2015). In the Pacific Islands region, women's diverse skills, experiences and knowledge remain largely undocumented (see exceptions Anderson 2005; Charan et al. 2016; Clissold et al. 2020), as well as underutilised in preparedness, response and recovery strategies (Raj et al. 2019). Recognising women's diverse needs and vulnerabilities, together with utilising and building on women's capacities are critical for equitable recovery and resilience-building prospects (Scanlon 1998; Soares and Mullings 2009; Gender and Disaster Network 2009; Yonder et al. 2009) – that is, "not excluding half the human" (Monk and Hanson 1982, 11). This is not to say that gender-responsive programming is not already being rolled out in the region (see Lane and McNaught 2009; Charan et al. 2016; Raj et al. 2019), but improvements are needed, and detailed case studies can be critical for this.

DOI: 10.4324/9781032275611-25

Dominant narratives of women in disasters

Speaking to Resurrección's (2013: 34) statement of "women as the environment's victims and caretakers", women and girls globally are depicted as being disproportionately affected by disasters and climatic events, while also being "responsible caregivers", working at the frontlines of risk reduction and recovery processes (MacGregor 2009; Arora-Jonsson 2011; Tschakert and Machado 2012). Women have been portrayed as systematically disadvantaged and, therefore, more likely to be hurt or killed (Neumayer and Plümper 2007), have compromised privacy, health and safety (Fulu 2007; Bradshaw and Fordham 2013), face post-disaster psychological problems (Başoğlu et al. 2004; Galea et al. 2008) or violence (Fulu 2007; Whittenbury 2013) and have low coping capacities due to restricted mobility and access to relief (Scanlon 1998; Sultana 2010; Ayeb-Karlsson et al. 2019).

The vulnerabilisation of women in the literature has been recognised as concealing women's agency, situated knowledge and resilience (Arora-Jonsson 2011). There has been growing documentation of women's critical capacities to mobilise their own responses, adapt to changing conditions and acquire the skillset needed to manage a crisis and support family, community and country (Enarson and Morrow 1998; Viñas 1998; Soares and Mullings 2009; Gaillard et al. 2015). There are many specific avenues – across 'private' and 'public' spaces (Monk 2007) – through which women have made critical contributions to crisis management and rehabilitation, political lobbying and local activism (Branco 2009; Yonder et al. 2009; Enarson 2012); using traditional knowledge to maintain food and water security for households (Charan et al. 2016); taking leading roles in mitigating shocks to household incomes through establishing businesses and diversifying economic resources (Branco 2009; Soares and Mullings 2009; Islam et al. 2014); and supporting communities through communal kitchens and re-establishing educational facilities (Fulu 2007). Women's social capital including formal and informal networks and collectives have proved critical for distributing critical resources (Drolet et al. 2015), providing psychological support (Branco 2009; Soares and Mullings 2009; Ganapati 2012), mitigating the impacts of gender-based violence (Enarson 1999; Fisher 2009), promoting inclusive recovery for those that are marginalised (Yonder et al. 2009; Enarson 2012), and creating a platform from which women can assert their needs in formal disaster relief processes (Fisher 2009; Enarson 2012; Drolet et al. 2015).

Despite these critical roles and contributions, women's voices and needs continue to be marginalised in disaster-related decision-making across scales – from formal decision-making bodies to within households and families (Scanlon 1998; Fulu 2007; Bradshaw and Fordham 2013; Alam and Habibur Rahman 2014; Nadiruzzaman and Wrathall 2015). In many contexts, the organisational structures of disaster recovery can be shaped by male culture and workforce (Fulu 2007; Neumayer and Plümper 2007). The needs and voices of all genders must, however, be centred in disaster management and risk reduction (Mulyasari and Shaw 2013; Drolet et al. 2015; Whittaker et al. 2016) if we are to avoid 'entrenchment' (i.e. disempowerment and reinforcing existing inequalities; Sovacool et al. 2018) and take advantage of the opportunity that disasters provide to challenge social inequalities and renegotiate gender norms and roles (Fulu 2007; Drolet et al. 2015; Elmhirst 2015; Rao et al. 2019).

It is also important to note that, in some contexts, women's critical roles in risk management, response, relief and recovery can emanate from gendered power configurations which impose a range of pressures, obligations and burdens (Ariyabandu 2003; Enarson et al. 2007). Expected roles as 'caregivers' means disasters can magnify women's responsibilities, burdening them with the urgent need to secure resources and assistance for survival (Wiest et al. 1994; Viñas 1998; Drolet et al. 2015). Women and girls (among other marginalised individuals) often sacrifice their adaptive preferences because of structural forces that shape trade-offs in freedom and wellbeing (Béné et al. 2014).

Study site, methods and limitations

Arising from two research projects in Vanuatu and the Cook Islands that explored women's perspectives, experiences and responses to climatic events, this chapter draws from a series of in-depth interviews ($n = 7$) and focus groups ($n = 10$) with 60 women. Both nations are in the South Pacific and are highly exposed to temperature rises, changing rainfall patterns (including flooding and drought), intense tropical cyclones, storm surges and sea level rise, among other impacts (NACCC 2007; Cook Islands Meteorological Service et al. 2011). In Vanuatu, 10 focus groups were conducted in December 2018 with 53 women ranging between 26 and 76 years of age, each having between one to seven children. All participants had marketplace-based livelihoods, such as selling crops or handicrafts in marketplaces on Efate and Santo Island ($n = 46$; see Figure 21.1) or as executive members of associations that oversee the operation of marketplaces ($n = 7$). Marketplaces are an appropriate space to explore women's everyday lives as, due to gendered norms and expectations, most marketplace vendors in the Pacific and Vanuatu are women (Brookfield et al. 1969; Barnett-Naghshineh 2019; DFAT 2019).

The chapter also draws on structured interviews with seven women from the Cook Islands, most of whom were living in the capital of Avarua on Rarotonga ($n = 4$) while the remaining were living in outer islands (Penrhyn [$n = 1$], Aitutaki [$n = 1$] and Mauke [$n = 1$]) (see Figure 21.2). Staff at the Cook Islands National Council for Women selected participants based on their networks. Data was collected in October and November 2020. As it was not always possible to conduct in-person interviews, structured interview schedules were sent out to participants in most cases. Participants from the Cook Islands ranged between 45 and 61 years of age and had at least two children each. Most participants (except two) had semi-subsistence livelihoods, dependent to some extent on home gardens and marine resources. For income, participants owned small businesses, worked for a non-government organisation, sold flowers or engaged in contract work.

236 *Rachel Clissold and Karen E. McNamara*

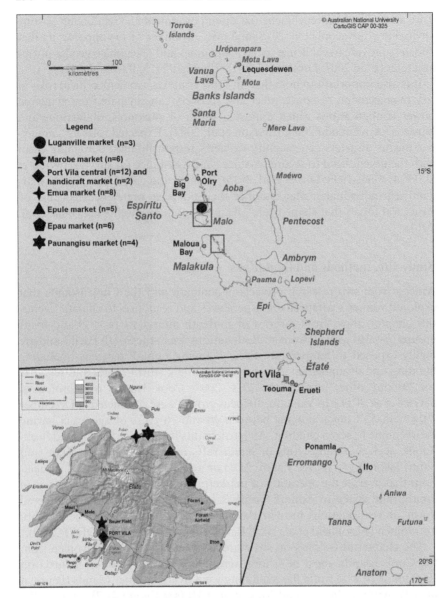

Figure 21.1 Map of Vanuatu and the approximate locations of the marketplaces that participants' livelihoods are tied to (including number of participants tied to the specific marketplace in brackets).

Source: Adapted from ANU (2018a, 2018b)

All in-person focus groups and interviews were recorded and transcribed. These transcripts, including the completed structured interview schedules, were exported into NVivo. Content analysis was conducted to identify key patterns and overarching 'themes' within the data (Graneheim and Lundman 2004;

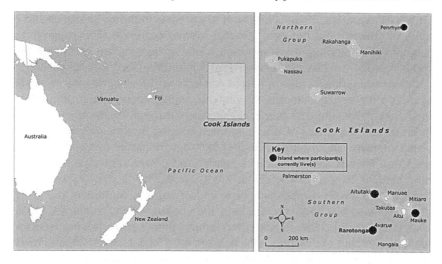

Figure 21.2 Location of the Cook Islands in relation to Australia and New Zealand (left) and the country's islands with indication of where participants live (right).

Source: Adapted from Blacka et al. (2013)

Bengtsson 2016). Ethics approval was granted through the University of Queensland (approval numbers 2018001985 and 2020000640) and for the research in Vanuatu, a research permit was granted from the Vanuatu Cultural Centre. All participants gave informed consent to participate in these studies.

Key findings

Although our findings provide critical insights, the experiences presented here are not representative of all women across time and space. There is always internal heterogeneity among women (Katz and Monk 1993; Islam et al. 2014) and gender is continuously being re-constructed (Resurrección 2011).

Loss, damage and changes to everyday lives

Drought and cyclones were the most prominent climatic events discussed by women in Vanuatu and the Cook Islands. Key impacts from drought included water and food insecurity, difficulty in looking after livestock and loss of income and livelihoods. The devastating impacts of cyclones were also expressed; destruction of homes and infrastructure, coastal areas being washed away, loss of water and power for weeks, food insecurity from destruction of gardens and crops, loss of livelihoods and loss of lives. Resource loss and decreased ability of women to meet household needs resulted in many participants feeling "very down" (Focus Group #3, Vanuatu, 2018), "worried and helpless" (Participant #7, Cook Islands, 2020) as well as "unhappy and tired" (Participant #4, Cook Islands, 2020): "she cried because… [she had] no crops. It's the only income [that] they get…" (Focus

Group #8, Vanuatu, 2018). This is not to say that emotional resilience and a sense of stoicism did not exist. Several women expressed their capacity to "accept the situation and just move on... one learns to adapt because at the end of the day you can still survive" (Participant #3, Cook Islands, 2020).

Losses and damages also impacted women's workloads and their capacity to carry out everyday activities. In Vanuatu, women spend a large amount of their time gardening and preparing products through cleaning, cutting or husking, and the effects of drier conditions on soil quality and crop growth posed intensive labour burdens as they had to work harder to secure food. In the Cook Islands, lack of access to water and power after cyclones added time burdens to women's workloads as they undertook daily tasks stating they "had to travel... some distance to collect water in containers and bring [them] back to our home for drinking and cooking" (Participant #3, Cook Islands, 2020) and "Have to go to [our] family's [homes] on low lying areas for bathing, washing the clothes" (Participant #4, Cook Islands, 2020). Power shortages also added to workloads by forcing one woman to cook an entire freezer worth of food quickly over a couple of days which, without the cyclone, "would have lasted us up to a month" (Participant #3, Cook Islands, 2020).

Women as resourceful enablers of recovery and resilience

The women were active actors with diverse strategies to prepare, respond and recover in the face of climatic events. 'Spaces of action' were once understood as separated into the binary of 'private' and 'public' but are now being understood as more complex and fluid (Rengert and Monk 1982; Monk 2007). In the face of environmental change and disasters which can destabilise and challenge gender norms and roles (Resurrección 2011; Elmhirst 2015; Rao et al. 2019), the fluidity and complex nature of 'spaces of action' are clear with women migrating between and within these multi-dimensional and multi-scalar spaces in complex ways. We touch on some of the contributions of women to shaping and building resilience within different spaces.

First, the women had critical roles in shaping their 'home' or 'private' space for themselves and their families (compared to men in the 'public' space) in the immediate aftermath of cyclone impact: "... I was at home trying to tidy our grounds etc with our children while my husband was out on the road with the rest of the men in the village cutting and clearing trees" (Participant #3, Cook Islands, 2020). The women also shared their critical role in preparing their households for cyclone impact by stocking up on "batteries for the radio", "water, batteries, torches, lantern... a generator", "essential foodstuffs", and "bottled and dried foodstuffs and a heap of coconuts" (Participants #7, #3, #7, #1, Cook Islands, 2020). Women would also harvest crops to preserve and freeze in preparation for food shortages. As a longer-lasting insidious event, drought is more difficult to prepare for, but participants indicated that they would often ration water use within households to enable survival throughout the long-haul drought conditions.

Related to preparedness, women in Vanuatu and the Cook Islands demonstrated their capacities as innovators though adaptive farming behaviours in their home gardens. The extensive experimentation and innovation related to gardens is reflective of the women's responsibilities but also priorities: "it's the only form of income and only form of way to get food ... the first thought after every cyclone is the garden" (Focus Group #2, Vanuatu, 2018). Adaptations undertaken in the gardens were based on local knowledge, and included planting crops in different soils and areas to maximise the likelihood of survival (e.g. planting sensitive crops closer to home so they can be attended to quickly if a cyclone hits), planting crops depending on rainfall and cyclone season (e.g. taro and manioc in drier seasons and only taro in cyclone season as they are less vulnerable to damage), and trimming crops such as yam sticks to reduce damage when cyclones hit. One woman in the Cook Islands also emphasised the shift towards local crops: "we figured out that there was no point in trying to grow some common NZ [New Zealand] crops, [it's] better to stick with those adapted to our conditions" (Participant #1, Cook Islands, 2020). Some ni-Vanuatu women had also created a system of redundancy in their garden plots that acted as insurance in the face of cyclones: "They're planting little gardens everywhere within their own land... so if water comes down the hill one time and destroys one, they will [have a] reserve garden left..." (Focus Group #1, Vanuatu, 2018). Here, we find critical insights into the role women play in shaping and modifying the environment, and the creativity of women as they respond to and build resilience in the face of climatic events (Rengert and Monk 1982).

The diversity in 'spaces of action' of the women, however, was also clear, illuminating the intersections of work, households and community (Monk 2007). Not only are women making critical contributions to, and shaping, their home and interior spaces and landscapes, they also act simultaneously, in complex ways, in 'public' spaces that are traditionally associated with men (Rengert and Monk 1982). For example, ni-Vanuatu women articulated their critical roles as collectivising and leading forces, lobbying for their needs in 'public' spaces during cyclone response and recovery. In several instances where post-disaster relief and assistance from governments and NGOs were inadequate, the women would collectivise and determine their own solutions or assert their rights: "If we are having difficulties [in securing formal help]... we take initiative first to find somebody who can work with us" (Focus Group #10, Vanuatu, 2018). In one instance, a group of ni-Vanuatu women lobbied against the organisations that they perceived as excluding them during post-cyclone recovery efforts:

> ... most organisations, they just take maybe young people and men... I just went there to force that they take some ladies... We know where we can use our women... Not just stand there and let other people do it. We can do it.
>
> (Focus Group #10, Vanuatu, 2018)

Similarly, after Cyclone Pam, women handicraft market vendors lobbied against undesirable government strategies (i.e., the relocation of women to a new area with little prospective customers) which they perceived as conflicting with their priorities and livelihoods. The women successfully negotiated with local government agencies for a more appropriate solution to secure their post-disaster incomes and support recovery. Despite not being a perfect solution, this was a critical outcome as many people, including the women and their families, were reliant on this income stream: "that would be a social problem if we were not served" (Focus Group #4, Vanuatu, 2018). It became clear that engagement in these activities in the 'public' space prompted some consciousness-raising so that the women began to function differently, becoming more vocal and confident in asserting their needs and rights (Monk 2007): "That's when I find out that we empower women so they will never face another disaster" (Focus Group #10, Vanuatu, 2018).

Participants also highlighted their roles as mobilisers of social capital, drawing upon extensive informal social network systems within and between islands to reduce risk, respond and recover. The women would often support each other in rebuilding homes or through sharing and trading critical resources (e.g. crops, seeds, food and garden tools):

> you have the opportunity to ask another mother to help.
> (Focus Group #7, Vanuatu, 2018)

> ... in times like this it brings a community together – we were borrowing or lending things like wheel barrows, chain saws, bush knives, sharing food etc.
> (Participant #3, Cook Islands, 2020)

In Vanuatu, participants also spoke of using networks to generate grassroots insurance schemes and financial risk-sharing which supported speedier recovery and reconstruction processes: "they [women] get together and do a little saving kind of scheme with each other" (Focus Group #3, Vanuatu, 2018). The networks among the ni-Vanuatu women vendors also promoted inclusive financial recovery processes as women who were less abled or more burdened by disasters were able to maintain their income flow through the support of other women (i.e., those more abled would sell products for those less abled). The above roles demonstrate the critical contributions that women make in shaping socio-political landscapes in the face of disasters and their gains in resilience from collective action (across both 'public' and 'private' spaces) (Rengert and Monk 1982).

These networks can also become critical pathways of knowledge and skill transfers, leading to the diversification of livelihoods as women learn from each other: "having other information from other women, how they're actually earning money, she's doing [it] now [too]... she's doing other things to gain money" (Focus Group #1, Vanuatu, 2018). In Vanuatu, the women were building resilience and diversifying livelihoods through selling a wider range of products or using savings to springboard into other activities such as guesthouses, canteens, jam-making, sewing and weaving. Some were also taking advantage of the arrival of international aid workers after Cyclone Pam and selling them locally made handicrafts.

Related to increased rates of diversification, participants emphasised their growing roles as entrepreneurs and their increased self-esteem from this 'business-woman' identity. These changes also related to some changes in household roles and responsibilities. Some women gained more control over financial decision-making, and, for others, husbands were becoming increasingly involved in household work: "The husbands give the support. They help... they look after the homes. To me, there are changes... Before maybe the fathers take the money... [but now] we work together as a team at home" (Focus Group #8, Vanuatu, 2018). Despite not being ubiquitous or automatic, this shift in gendered relations reminds us that women's lives are changing and that women's roles and activities in the face of disasters can play a part in destabilising the reproduction of gendered roles and expectations (Resurrección 2011; Elmhirst 2015; Rao et al. 2019). Thus, engagement in business activities prompted a re-shaping of identities, where some women began to function differently within 'private' spaces and became more involved and confident in decision-making (Monk 2007). This demonstrates the complex, multi-dimensional and multi-scalar nature of the once assumed 'public-private' binary (Monk 2007).

Despite these critical roles and some sense of empowerment, it was clear that participants also faced gender-related challenges and uneven gains. This was exemplified through the tendency of some women to have significantly high workloads: "Mothers have a lot of work to do" (Focus Group #3, Vanuatu, 2018). The women in Vanuatu also asserted that in past disasters, their needs and desires were often overlooked by government agencies: "[they] forget all about us" (Focus Group #8, Vanuatu, 2018). Further, some women found that their voices are filtered through a male manager before reaching higher levels of government. Despite women noticing changes in gendered household relations, restrictions in financial decision-making persisted and some still had to "show the Papa the money" that they earned to determine spending (Focus Group #7, Vanuatu, 2018). These issues remind us that empowerment is not necessarily a linear process and may involve ambiguities and contradictions (Monk 2007). Despite a heightened consciousness and capacity for public and collective action to mitigate disaster risk and impact, women continue to operate in an inequitable and gendered system that marginalises them across different spaces (Ariyabandu 2003; Enarson et al. 2007). It is, therefore, important to avoid perpetuating the narrative of women as empowered, resourceful enablers of resilience and recovery without also recognising the hidden costs and persisting need for transformations in underlying power structures (Arora-Jonsson, 2011; Tschakert and Machado, 2012).

Conclusion

This chapter has showcased some accounts of loss from climatic events, as well as women's critical roles as resourceful enablers of resilience and disaster preparedness, response and recovery. Building on Monk's work, these accounts illustrate the complex and fluid nature of 'public' and 'private' spaces in women's activism and adaptive capacity, as well as the changing lives of women (Monk 2007). Overlooking these experiences, roles and contributions risks underutilising women's capacities and neglecting their specific needs and vulnerabilities, thereby undermining prospects for improved and equitable resilience-building and recovery efforts (Scanlon 1998; Soares and Mullings 2009; Ganapati 2012; Charan et al. 2016). Women should no longer be at the margins but, alongside men, be central to disaster response and recovery conversations, policy and practice (Soares and Mullings 2009; Ganapati 2012; Charan et al. 2016). Disaster policy and practice should recognise women's social networks, traditional agricultural knowledge and innovation, and leading role in financial resilience and loss mitigation.

We also find that collective and individual women-initiated movements and creative strategies for survival and recovery can transcend or transform restrictions to traditional roles. Empowerment, however, is not necessarily linear and gains can still be partial, contested and uneven (Monk 2007). Women still operate in a system of inequality, and it is important to recognise these challenges to avoid exacerbating gendered inequalities. Therefore, although it is important to centralise women in disaster and climate change efforts, we cannot do this without simultaneous efforts to address the underlying causes of inequality and improve women's overall wellbeing, agency, livelihoods and prospects (Arora-Jonsson 2011; Tschakert and Machado 2012).

References

Alam, Khurshed, and Md. Habibur Rahman. 2014. "Women in Natural Disasters: A Case Study from Southern Coastal Region of Bangladesh." *International Journal of Disaster Risk Reduction* 8: 68–82. doi: 10.1016/j.ijdrr.2014.01.003.

Anderson, Cheryl L. 2005. "Decolonizing Disaster: A Gender Perspective of Disaster Risk Management in the United States-Affiliated Pacific Islands." PhD Thesis, Hawai'i: University of Hawai'i. https://www.proquest.com/openview/3a13e49e2837c432cbf2df35decdd398/1?pq-origsite=gscholar&cbl=18750&diss=y

Ariyabandu, Madhavi. 2003. "Women: The Risk Managers in Natural Disasters." *Voice Women* 6 (1): 1–8.

Arora-Jonsson, Seema. 2011. "Virtue and Vulnerability: Discourses on Women, Gender and Climate Change." *Global Environmental Change* 21 (2): 744–751. doi: 10.1016/j.gloenvcha.2011.01.005.

Australian National University (ANU). 2018a. "Vanuatu." http://asiapacific.anu.edu.au/mapsonline/base-maps/vanuatu-0.

———. 2018b. "Efate, Vanuatu." https://asiapacific.anu.edu.au/mapsonline/base-maps/efate-vanuatu-0.

Ayeb-Karlsson, Sonja, Dominic Kniveton, Terry Cannon, Kees Van Der Geest, Istiakh Ahmed, Erin M. Derrington, Ebinezer Florano, and Denis Opiyo Opondo. 2019. "I Will Not Go, I Cannot Go: Cultural and Social Limitations of Disaster Preparedness in Asia, Africa, and Oceania." *Disasters* 43 (4): 752–770. doi: 10.1111/disa.12404.

Barnett-Naghshineh, Olivia. 2019. "Shame and Care: Masculinities in the Goroka Marketplace." *Oceania* 89 (2): 220–236. doi: 10.1002/ocea.5219.

Başoğlu, Metin, Cengiz Kiliç, Ebru Şalcioğlu, and Maria Livanou. 2004. "Prevalence of Posttraumatic Stress Disorder and Comorbid Depression in Earthquake Survivors in Turkey: An Epidemiological Study." *Journal of Traumatic Stress* 17 (2): 133–141. doi: 10.1023/B:JOTS.0000022619.31615.e8.

Béné, Christophe, Andrew Newsham, Mark Davies, Martina Ulrichs, and Rachel Godfrey-Wood. 2014. "Review Article: Resilience, Poverty and Development." *Journal of International Development* 26 (5): 598–623. doi: 10.1002/jid.2992.

Bengtsson, Mariette. 2016. "How to Plan and Perform a Qualitative Study Using Content Analysis." *NursingPlus Open* 2: 8–14. doi: 10.1016/j.npls.2016.01.001.

Blacka, Matt, Francois Flocard, and Ben Parakoti. 2013. "Coastal Adaptation Needs for Extreme Events and Climate Change, Avarua, Rarotonga, Cook Islands. Project Stage 1: Scoping and Collation of Existing Data." *WRL Technical Report 2013/11*. Manly Vale, Australia: Water Research Laboratory, University of NSW.

Bradshaw, Sarah, and Maureene Fordham. 2013. *Hazards, Risks and, Disasters in Society*. Elsevier Inc. doi: 10.1016/B978-0-12-396451-9.00014-7.

Branco, Adélia de Melo. 2009. "Women Responding to Drought in Brazil." In *Women, Gender and Disaster: Global Issues and Initiatives*, edited by E. Enarson and P.G.D. Chakrabarti, 261–272. New Delhi, Thousand Oaks, London and Singapore: SAGE Publications.

Brookfield, Harold C., Paula B. Glick, and Doreen Hart. 1969. "Melanesian Mélange: The Market at Vila, New Hebrides." In *Pacific Market-Places*, edited by H. C. Brookfield. Canberra, Australia: Australian National University Press.

Charan, Dhrishna, Manpreet Kaur, and Priyatma Singh. 2016. "Indigenous Fijian Women's Role in Disaster Risk Management and Climate Change Adaptation." *Pacific Asia Inquiry* 7 (1): 106–122.

Clissold, Rachel, Ross Westoby, and Karen E. McNamara. 2020. "Women as Recovery Enablers in the Face of Disasters in Vanuatu." *Geoforum* 113: 101–110. doi: 10.1016/j.geoforum.2020.05.003.

Cook Islands Meteorological Service, Australian Bureau of Meteorology, and Commonwealth Scientific and Industrial Research Organisation (CSIRO). 2011. "Current and Future Climate of the Cook Islands." *Pacific Climate Change Science Program Partners*. https://www.pacificclimatechangescience.org/wp-content/uploads/2013/06/9_PCCSP_Cook_Islands_8pp.pdf

DFAT (Department of Foreign Affairs and Trade). 2019. "Pacific Women Shaping Pacific Development: Vanuatu Country Plan Summary." DFAT, Australian Government. https://pacificwomen.org/wp-content/uploads/2019/01/Vanuatu-Pacific-Women-country-plan-summary-Jan-2019.pdf

Drolet, Julie, Lena Dominelli, Margaret Alston, Robin Ersing, Golam Mathbor, and Haorui Wu. 2015. "Women Rebuilding Lives Post-Disaster: Innovative Community Practices for Building Resilience and Promoting Sustainable Development." *Gender & Development* 23 (3): 433–448. doi: 10.1080/13552074.2015.1096040.

Elmhirst, Rebecca. 2015. *The Routledge Handbook of Political Ecology*. London: Taylor and Francis Inc.

Enarson, Elaine. 1999. "Women and Housing Issues in Two U.S. Disasters: Case Studies from Hurricane Andrew and the Red River Valley Flood." *International Journal of Mass Emergencies and Disasters* 17 (1): 39–63.

———. 2012. *Women Confronting Natural Disaster: From Vulnerability to Resilience*. Boulder, CO, US: Lynne Rienner Publishers.

Enarson, Elaine, and Betty Hearn Morrow. 1998. "Women Will Rebuild Miami: A Case Study of Feminist Response to Disaster." In *The Gendered Terrain of Disaster: Through Women's Eyes*, edited by Elaine Enarson and Betty H. Morrow, 185–99. Miami, FL: Laboratory for Social and Behavioral Research, Florida International University.

Enarson, Elaine, Alice Fothergill, and Lori Peek. 2007. "Gender and Disaster: Foundations and Directions." In *Handbook of Disaster Research*, edited by Havidán Rodríguez, Enrico L. Quarantelli, and Russell R. Dynes, 130–146. New York: Springer.

Fisher, Sarah. 2009. "Sri Lankan Women's Organisations Responding to Post-Tsunami Violence." In *Women, Gender and Disaster: Global Issues and Initiatives*, edited by Elaine Enarson and P. G. Dhar Chakrabarti, 233–249. New Delhi, India: SAGE Publications. doi: 10.4135/9788132108078.n18.

Fulu, Emma. 2007. "Gender, Vulnerability, and the Experts: Responding to the Maldives Tsunami." *Development and Change* 38 (5): 843–864. doi: 10.1111/j.1467-7660.2007.00436.x.

Gaillard, J. C., Maureen Fordham, and Kristinne Sanz. 2015. "Culture, Gender and Disaster: From Vulnerability to Capacities." In *Cultures and Disasters: Understanding Cultural Framings in Disaster Risk Reduction*, edited by Fred Krüger, Greg Bankoff, Terry Cannon, Benedikt Orlowski, and E. Lisa F. Schipper, 222–234. Oxon and New York: Routledge.

Galea, Sandro, Melissa Tracy, Fran Norris, and Scott F. Coffey. 2008. "Financial and Social Circumstances and the Incidence and Course of PTSD in Mississippi during the First Two Years after Hurricane Katrina." *Journal of Traumatic Stress* 21 (4): 357–368. doi: 10.1002/jts.20355.

Ganapati, N. Emel. 2012. "In Good Company: Why Social Capital Matters for Women during Disaster Recovery." *Public Administration Review* 72 (3): 419–427. doi: 10.1111/j.1540-6210.2011.02526.x.

Gender and Disaster Network. 2009. "Gender Equality in Disasters: Six Principles for Engendered Relief and Reconstruction." https://www.gdnonline.org/resources/GDN_GENDER_EQUALITY_IN_DISASTERS.pdf.

Graneheim, Ulla H., and Berit Lundman. 2004. "Qualitative Content Analysis in Nursing Research: Concepts, Procedures and Measures to Achieve Trustworthiness." *Nurse Education Today* 24 (2): 105–112. doi: 10.1016/j.nedt.2003.10.001.

Islam, Mir Rabiul, Valerie Ingham, John Hicks, and Ian Manock. 2014. "The Changing Role of Women in Resilience, Recovery and Economic Development at the Intersection of Recurrent Disaster: A Case Study from Sirajgang, Bangladesh." *Journal of Asian and African Studies* 52 (1): 50–67. doi: 10.1177/0021909614560244.

Katz, Cindi, and Janice Monk. 1993. *Full Circles: Geographies of Women over the Life Course*. Oxon and New York: Routledge.

Lane, Ruth, and Rebecca McNaught. 2009. "Building Gendered Approaches to Adaptation in the Pacific." *Gender and Development* 17 (1): 67–80. doi: 10.1080/13552070802696920.

MacGregor, Sherilyn. 2009. "A Stranger Silence Still: The Need for Feminist Social Research on Climate Change." *The Sociological Review* 57 (2_suppl): 124–140. doi: 10.1111/j.1467-954X.2010.01889.x.

Monk, Janice. 2007. "Engendering Change." In *Companion Encyclopedia of Geography: From the Local to the Global*, 2nd ed., Vol. 2, edited by I. Douglas, R. Huggett, and C. Perkins, 993–1003 Oxon and New York: Routledge.

Monk, Janice, and Susan Hanson. 1982. "On Not Excluding Half of the Human in Human Geography." *The Professional Geographer* 34 (1): 11–23. doi: 10.1111/j.0033-0124.1982.00011.x.

Mulyasari, Farah, and Rajib Shaw. 2013. "Role of Women as Risk Communicators to Enhance Disaster Resilience of Bandung, Indonesia." *Natural Hazards* 69 (3): 2137–2160. doi: 10.1007/s11069-013-0798-4.

Nadiruzzaman, M. D., and David Wrathall. 2015. "Participatory Exclusion – Cyclone Sidr and Its Aftermath." *Geoforum* 64 (August): 196–204. doi: 10.1016/j.geoforum.2015.06.026.

National Advisory Committee on Climate Change (NACCC). 2007. "National Adaptation Programme for Action (NAPA)." unfccc.int/resource/docs/napa/vut01.pdf.

Neumayer, Eric, and Thomas Plümper. 2007. "The Gendered Nature of Natural Disasters: The Impact of Catastrophic Events on the Gender Gap in Life Expectancy, 1981-2002." *Annals of the Association of American Geographers* 97 (3): 551–566. doi: 10.1111/j.1467-8306.2007.00563.x.

Raj, Subhashni, Brigitte Laboukly, and Shantony Moli. 2019. "Disaster, Response and Relationships: A Gendered Approach to Localising Disaster Risk Reduction in the Pacific." In *Making Humanitarian Action Work for Women and Girls*, edited by Wendy Fenton, Women Deliver, and Matthew Foley, 30–32. Humanitarian Exchange Special Feature No. 75. London, UK: Overseas Development Institute.

Rao, Nitya, Arabinda Mishra, Anjal Prakash, Chandni Singh, Ayesha Qaisrani, Prathigna Poonacha, Katharine Vincent, and Claire Bedelian. 2019. "A Qualitative Comparative Analysis of Women's Agency and Adaptive Capacity in Climate Change Hotspots in Asia and Africa." *Nature Climate Change* 9 (12): 964–971. doi: 10.1038/s41558-019-0638-y.

Rengert, Arlene C., and Janice Monk, eds. 1982. *Women and Spatial Change: Learning Resources for Social Science Courses*. Dubuque, Iowa: Kendall/Hunt Publishing Company.

Resurrección, Bernadette P. 2011. "The Gender and Climate Debate: More of the Same or New Pathways of Thinking and Doing?" *Asia Security Initiative Policy Series, Working Paper No. 10*. Singapore: RSIS Centre for Non-Traditional Security Studies.

———. 2013. "Persistent Women and Environment Linkages in Climate Change and Sustainable Development Agendas." *Women's Studies International Forum* 40: 33–43. doi: 10.1016/j.wsif.2013.03.011.

Scanlon, Jennifer. 1998. "The Perspective of Gender: A Missing Element in Disaster Response." In *The Gendered Terrain of Disaster: Through Women's Eyes*, edited by Elaine Enarson and Betty H. Morrow, 45–54. Westport, CT: Greenwood.

Soares, Judith, and Audrey Y. Mullings. 2009. "'A We Run Tings': Women Rebuilding Montserrat." In *Women, Gender and Disaster: Global Issues and Initiatives*, edited by Elaine Enarson and P. G. Dhar Chakrabarti, 250–260. B-42, New Delhi, India: SAGE Publications. doi: 10.4135/9788132108078.n19.

Sovacool, Benjamin K., May Tan-Mullins, and Wokje Abrahamse. 2018. "Bloated Bodies and Broken Bricks: Power, Ecology, and Inequality in the Political Economy of Natural Disaster Recovery." *World Development* 110 (October): 243–255. doi: 10.1016/j.worlddev.2018.05.028.

Sultana, Farhana. 2010. "Living in Hazardous Waterscapes: Gendered Vulnerabilities and Experiences of Floods and Disasters." *Environmental Hazards* 9 (1): 43–53.

Tschakert, Petra, and Mario Machado. 2012. "Gender Justice and Rights in Climate Change Adaptation: Opportunities and Pitfalls." *Ethics and Social Welfare* 6 (3): 275–289. doi: 10.1080/17496535.2012.704929.

Viñas, Serrat. 1998. "Women's Disaster Vulnerability and Response to the Colima Earthquake." In *The Gendered Terrain of Disaster: Through Women's Eyes*, edited by Elaine Enarson and Betty H. Morrow, 161–172. Westport, CT: Greenwood.

Whittaker, Joshua, Christine Eriksen, and Katharine Haynes. 2016. "Gendered Responses to the 2009 Black Saturday Bushfires in Victoria, Australia." *Geographical Research* 54 (2): 203–215. doi: 10.1111/1745-5871.12162.

Whittenbury, Kerri. 2013. "Climate Change, Women's Health, Wellbeing and Experiences of Gender Based Violence in Australia." In *Research, Action and Policy: Addressing the Gendered Impacts of Climate Change*, edited by Margaret Alston and Kerri Whittenbury, 207–221. Dordrecht: Springer Netherlands. doi: 10.1007/978-94-007-5518-5_15.

Wiest, Raymond E., Jane S. P. Mocellin, and D. Thandiwe Motsisi. 1994. "The Needs of Women in Disasters and Emergencies." *Report prepared for the Disaster Management Training Programme of the United Nations Development Programme and the Office of the United Nations Disaster Relief Coordinator*. Winnipeg, Manitoba: Disaster Research Institute, University of Manitoba. https://www.gdnonline.org/resources/women-in-disaster-emergency.pdf.

Yonder, Ayse, Sengül Akçar, and Prema Gopalan. 2009. "Women's Participation in Disaster Relief and Recovery." In *Women, Gender and Disaster: Global Issues and Initiatives*, edited by Elaine Enarson and P. G. Dhar Chakrabarti, 189–211. New Delhi, India: SAGE Publications. doi: 10.4135/9788132108078.n15.

Index

2008 global economic crisis 147, 149

Aboriginal people/communities/land 98, 101, 112, 181, 182, 183–187, 189–200
abortion 38, 43
academic career 49, 56, 78, 91, 97, 101, 102, 103, 111, 115, 117
academic freedom 44, 123
academic landscapes 9–15
academic lives 75, 77
acculturation 184
Africa 21, 23, 29, 30, 31, 32, 33, 34, 49, 53, 66
African: feminism 29, 33; slaves 206, 209
agency 20, 25, 32,75, 164, 218, 221, 223, 234, 242
aggression 66, 91, 122, 126, 138
agriculture 10, 32, 50, 182, 187, 205–206, 212, 213, 214, 216, 216, 217; backyard 217; change 212
agri-food industry 159, 162
Albania 37
American Association of Geographers (AAG) 48, 49, 56, 79, 101, 111, 198, 204; annual meeting 118
American education system 124
American Indian 2
androcentricity 1, 2
Anglophone: Africa 49; journals 13; work 9, 11, 145, 154
anti-imperialist 64, 66
Antipodean 76, 97, 101
anti-war 66
Antwerp 50
Aotearoa New Zealand 73, 74, 76, 77, 78, 80, 103
Arab 169, 170, 171, 173, 175
ARACIS (Romanian Agency for Quality Assurance in Higher Education) 38, 41

Argentina 13, 48, 50, 51, 54, 69
Arizona University 1, 4, 9, 11, 12, 14, 15, 77, 79, 101
artefacts 68, 215
ashram 25
aspirations 50, 73, 80, 115, 151, 153
Aspiring Academics: A Resource Book for Graduate Students and Early Career Faculty 111, 116, 117, 118
assemblage 181, 183
Australasia 77, 78
Australia 1, 2, 4, 10, 11, 52, 73, 76, 77, 78, 81, 82,97, 98, 99, 100, 101, 102, 103, 104, 106, 108, 112, 181, 182, 183, 184, 186, 189, 195, 197, 198, 237
Australian/Antipodean 97, 101
Australian geography 98, 103, 200
Australian National University 100
Australian Office of Naval Research 100
Australian women geographers 105
autobiographical methods 2, 30
autoethnography 30
Autonomous University of Barcelona 10, 12, 14, 15

Baber, Zonia 63–71
backlash 25, 38, 43
bananas 207
Barbados 204, 205–209
barter 217
Bedouin 171–175
Belgium 51, 52
Belize 206
Bengal 137, 141
Bern 50, 51
Bologna 41, 42
boundaries 14, 81, 87, 114, 135, 138, 146
braided streams 14, 97, 108, 142
Brazil 2, 4, 11, 13, 48, 52, 77, 84, 85, 88, 94, 206, 222–225

248 *Index*

Brazilian geography 84–88, 89, 94
bread 204, 206, 207, 208
breadfruit 207
bride price 174
brotherhood 70
Bulgaria 43, 54

Cairo 51
Cambridge University 30
Canada 11, 48, 52, 67, 68, 69, 103, 105, 149; Canadian 69, 76, 99, 106
cancer 204
care: giving/giver 122, 150, 153, 234, 235; invisible work 136; migration 146, 150; work 136, 139, 140, 147, 149, 150; takers 145, 147, 218, 234
Caribbean 204, 205, 207, 208, 209, 210
cassava 204–210
catadores 223
Catalan 11, 12, 13, 14, 16, 113
Catalonia, Spain 12, 16, 159, 160, 161
CEE (Central and Eastern Europe) 37, 40, 43
Cerarols, Rosa 16
Champagne, Illinois 19
chefs 215, 216
Chicago Geographic Society 64
childcare 38, 140, 152, 208
children 43, 44, 49, 65, 75, 77, 84, 86, 90, 91, 93, 136, 137, 138, 140, 141, 142, 152, 162, 163, 171, 172, 190, 192, 193, 196, 222, 223, 235, 238
China 2, 21, 50
Christian spirituality 68
classism 37
climate change 204, 223, 242
clitoridectomy 21
coastal 213, 217, 237
coconut 207, 208, 238
Coffs Harbour, NSW 184, 186, 187, 198
Collective: work 223; numbers 225
colonial discourses 182
colonialism 35, 124, 195; in teaching 124
communal kitchens 234
communism 37, 38
community-based professional development 117
contamination 20
Cook Islands 233, 235, 237, 238, 239, 240
cookbook 204, 208, 209
cooperative 34, 164, 221, 222, 223, 225, 229, 230
Cooperlix (Presidente Prudente Recyclable Products Workers Cooperative): facilities 222–230

Cork 52
cotton 207
course learning objectives 127
Covid-19 77, 138, 154, 157, 212–219
Cowra, NSW 184, 186, 187
creative economic activities 164, 165
Cresswell, Tim 16
critical geography 4, 63, 73, 82, 121
cross-cultural comparison 23
cruise ships 214, 215
Cuba 51
cultural geography 9, 15, 29, 42; landscapes 181, 182, 198; performance 216
cyclone 238, 239, 240, 241
Czech Republic 37

Datta, Anindita 2, 41, 135, 137
Davidson, Robyn 181
Delhi 136, 137, 138, 141, 142
Deniliquin, NSW 184, 186, 187, 198
development: discourse 30, 33
diabetes 204, 210
diet 204, 206, 207, 209, 210, 217
dignity 140, 229
disability 41, 77
disaster recovery 212, 234
disasters 218, 233, 234, 235, 238, 240, 241
discipline of Geography 3, 19, 22, 48, 49, 73, 74, 77, 97, 111, 114, 121, 122
dive shops 214
diversification 240, 241
diversity and inclusion in academia 126
Documents d'Anàlisi Geogràfica 15
domestic violence 21, 190, 212, 216
domestic work/service/help 86, 136, 137, 138, 141, 145, 223
domesticity 139
Down Under 73, 74, 75, 77
dowry 20, 21, 24, 174; murder 20, 21, 24
drivers 137, 152, 213, 215
Droogleveer Fortuijn, Joos 11, 40, 52, 53
drought 235, 237, 238
drugs (illegal trade) 218
Dublin 52
Durban 29

early career academics 111
East Africa 66
Eastern Europe 27, 38, 39, 40, 41, 146, 147, 149, 154
economic crisis 147, 149, 153, 158, 162, 165
economic development 22, 213
economic woman 34

eddoes 207, 209
EDGE (Enhancing Departments and Graduate Education) 79, 112, 115, 116, 117
Egypt 51
employment: formal, informal 149, 213, 137–139, 140, 146, 150, 196, 213, 214
England/English 11, 12, 13, 32, 78, 107, 145, 150, 205, 206
entrepreneurs 32, 150, 157, 159, 161–164, 165, 166, 172, 174, 218, 241
entrepreneurs: small scale 218, 222
entrepreneurship 39, 157, 158, 161, 163, 165, 166, 170, 172, 173, 174, 175, 177, 224
environmental problems 221
Europe 4, 9, 123, 15, 30, 33, 38, 39, 40, 41, 43, 52, 54, 56, 57, 146, 147, 148, 149, 154, 157
European Union (EU) 13, 38, 145, 147
everyday lives 4, 30, 41, 136, 137, 139, 141, 162, 233, 235, 237
exoticism 20

faculty development 79, 111, 115, 116, 117
family farms 157, 158
family life 136, 142
Far East 66
feminine identities 157
feminist associations 65
feminist geographers 1, 2, 3, 4, 11, 12, 19, 20, 27, 39, 41, 49, 54, 84, 87, 94, 97, 105, 107, 108, 109, 114, 142, 145, 169
Feminist Geographies Specialty Group (FGSG) of the AAG 3, 4
feminist geography 1, 2, 3, 4, 29, 31, 39, 42, 64, 73, 74, 84, 85, 87, 88, 94, 103, 106, 111, 114, 118, 119, 135, 169, 212
feminist pedagogy 126
feminist scholarship 1, 2, 19, 37, 38, 41, 42
fertility rate 171, 173
field trips 64
Fincher, Ruth 52, 103, 106
Finding a Way 118, 119
fireside knowledge 29, 33, 34
First Nations 101, 181, 183, 184, 189, 197
flour 204, 206, 207, 208, 210
food, sovereignty 210
food: prices, security, home cooked 34, 138, 204, 216, 217
foreign-born faculty 122, 123

France 4, 11, 43, 48, 51, 52, 53, 54, 74, 78
friendship 4, 114, 165
Full Circles 75, 84, 95, 135, 145, 158, 161, 166

Galicia, Spain 159, 160, 164
Garcia Ramon, Maria Dolors 9, 10, 12, 15, 16, 53, 54, 106, 119
gardening: home 215, 216, 238
Garifuna 206
gatekeeper 41
Gatundu, Kenya 30
Gender and Development 1, 3, 5, 34, 40
Gender and Geography: IGU Commission on 39, 40, 105, 107
gender/gendered: age 166; bias 213; inequality 94, 126, 165, 175; perspective 157; response to place 19; economic work 138; right to the city 135; rurality 162; social construction of 42, 163
generation 4, 31,33, 34, 35, 74, 81, 119, 145, 146, 147, 149, 150, 153, 154, 163, 165, 171, 172, 175, 192, 204, 224
Geneva 50
geographic curricula 27, 38, 79, 118; education 14, 19, 38, 64, 79, 98, 101, 117, 118, 121, 123, 169; nineteenth and twentieth centuries 99
Geographical Society of Argentina 51
geohumaities 9, 14, 16
Germany 4, 43, 77, 146, 148, 149, 150, 151
GFDA (Geography Faculty Development Alliance) 111, 115, 116, 118
Ghana 2, 13, 49, 54
Gibson, Katherine 108
Gibson-Graham, J. K. 100, 103, 105, 107, 108
Glasgow 56
global capitalism 136, 153
global links 161, 165
global resource economy 31
Global South 22, 26, 27, 75, 138, 142, 221
GPOW (Geographic Perspectives on Women) 3
graduate education 50, 79, 100, 112, 115, 116, 118; students 102, 114, 117
Griffith 181–184
Grupo de Estudos Territoriais 84
guinea corn 207
Guyana 205, 206

250 *Index*

hair braiding 97, 107
Haiti 66
handicrafts: production 214, 235, 241, 119
Hansen, Ellen 112, 119
Havana 68
health 29, 44, 55, 140, 150, 169,185,187, 189, 198, 208,210, 215, 230, 234
heritage 68, 69, 70, 164, 206, 208
hierarchy 24, 101
higher education 19, 27, 38, 41, 44, 85, 100, 115, 116, 117, 123, 126, 151, 154, 166
Hindu 25, 26
Hispanic 2
historical studies 2
history of education 2
home-based employment 138
Hong Kong 49, 76
honours program 98
hospitality 184, 216
household work 40, 93, 241; housekeeping 215, 216
housing, illegal 137
Howitt, Ritchie 101, 112, 114, 119
human geography 1, 37, 40, 41,53, 63, 84, 97, 102, 114, 135, 169, 221, 233
human trafficking 43
Hungary 43, 48, 77, 145, 146, 147, 148, 149, 151, 152, 153, 154
husband's education 171
hybrid relationships 221

identity 44, 69, 70, 73, 82, 95, 118, 124, 61, 164, 181, 191, 194, 224, 241
IGU (International Geographical Union) 1, 2, 3, 10, 12, 29, 34, 39, 40, 50–56, 63, 71, 73, 77, 81, 83, 105, 106, 107, 109, 113
India 2, 4, 11, 13, 20, 21, 22, 23, 24, 25, 26, 41, 49, 106, 135, 136, 137, 183
Indiana Dunes National Park 65
Indigenous 1, 4, 32, 34, 51, 81, 101, 114, 187,189, 190, 192, 195, 197, 198, 217; knowledge 217; peoples 4, 51
Indonesia 50
informal economy 32, 34, 35; sector 153, 213, 215, 216, 217
insider and outsider 9, 10
intergenerational 2, 135, 140, 152, 171
international collaboration 9, 111, 119
international exchange programmes 39
interviews 32, 84, 93, 101, 104, 117, 146, 158, 159, 162, 170, 173, 174, 186, 188, 189, 190, 222, 235

Iran 49
Ireland 49, 54, 78
Iron Curtain 37, 39
Islam 170, 234, 237
Islamic feminists 170
Israel 4, 11, 13, 49, 77, 169, 170, 171, 173, 175
Italy 4, 43, 51, 52, 68, 184

Jan Monk Distinguished Lecture 107, 108
Jan Monk Service Award 4
Japan 2, 3, 11, 50, 51, 54, 68
Jerusalem 106, 174
Jewish 171, 174, 206
Johnson, Louise C. 98, 99, 103, 106
junior female faculty 115, 121, 125

Kenya 2, 4, 29, 30, 32, 33, 34, 49, 54
Kenyatta University 30
knowledge production 2, 37, 87
Kolkata 138
Krakow 2, 49
Kropotkin 34, 63, 141

labour migration 145, 146, 149, 151, 153, 157
land rights 181, 189, 190, 197
landfills 224
landscape 2, 9, 10, 14, 15, 16, 23, 26, 36, 55, 64, 70, 94, 102, 135, 164, 167, 169, 176, 182, 183, 198, 200, 205, 233; contestations 23, 26
Latin America 9, 14, 53, 84, 124, 125, 210
LGBTQ (lesbian, gay, bisexual, transgender, and queer (or questioning)) 44, 107
leadership 4, 80, 100, 105, 118, 188, 225, 230
leisure 55, 86, 138, 141
Liège, Belgium 52
life: course 4, 25, 73, 74, 75, 78, 84, 88, 93, 135, 136, 137, 142, 146, 157, 158, 161, 165; journeys 162; stage 158, 162, 166; transitions 75, 136, 143
literary materials 23
live-in 137, 146; care work 149, 150; live-out 137
livelihoods 29, 212, 213, 216, 217, 218, 219, 235, 236, 237, 240
local linkages 218
local production/specialties 161, 164
loss 24, 31, 161, 191, 212, 215, 216, 217, 225, 233, 237, 238, 241, 242

Louvain, Belgium 52
low status of women 170
Luna Garcia, Antonio 112, 119, 145
Luna, Antoni 15, 16

Macdonald Holmes, James 98
maintenance staff 215
maize 204, 205, 206, 207, 209
male aggression 66; domination 56
managerialism in higher education 123, 126, 127
Māori 73, 74, 77, 79, 80, 81, 82; geography 82
Margarita Island 206, 209, 212–213, 218, 219
marginalization 2, 55, 107
margins 11, 29, 30, 31, 32, 33, 34, 35, 230, 242
market places 33
markets 164, 193, 213, 215, 216, 217
marriage age 171
marriage migration 137
masculinity: in academia 126; studies 42
menial service jobs 213
Mentor/mentoring/mentorship 1, 2, 3, 4, 27, 39, 50, 73, 74, 78, 79, 82, 106, 111, 112, 113, 114–116, 119, 121, 122
metropolitan city 136
Mexican 2, 10, 15, 52
Mexico 9, 14, 15, 29, 52, 67, 68, 77
microaggression in academia 122, 126
Middle East 16, 169–170
migrants 137, 145, 205, 206, 209, 210, 215; women 136, 142
migration 99, 104, 145, 146, 147, 148, 149, 150, 151, 153, 154, 157, 184, 185, 195, 204, 205, 209, 210, 212
Momsen, Janet 1, 10, 11, 39, 40, 54, 73, 212
Monash University 102
Monk, Jan and Cindi Katz 145, 158, 161, 166
Morocco 51
Mozambique 50
multigenerational narratives 153
murder 20, 21, 24
Muslim world 169, 170
Musyoki, Agnes 29
mutual aid relationships 141, 142

Nairobi 30, 33
nanny 138
Nara, Japan 3
Narayan, Uma 21, 22
National Solid Waste Policy, Brazil 224

nature-society relations 221
Negev 170, 171
neighborhood 137, 141
neo-liberal 40, 136; academia 122, 125; policies 30
Netherlands 4, 11, 13, 48, 52, 54
networks 2, 4, 5, 10, 27, 39, 44, 57, 74, 88, 97, 105, 114, 122, 157, 163, 173, 185, 217, 218, 219, 223, 234, 235, 240, 242
New Orleans 3, 204
New South Wales (NSW) 98, 101, 181, 182, 183, 184, 185, 187, 189, 193
New Zealand 4, 11, 49, 51, 73, 74, 76, 77, 78, 79, 80, 103, 237, 239
Newcastle University 1
Newsletter of the IGU Gender Commission 3, 11, 111
Nigeria 2, 54
non-Western: contexts 19; cultures 20; societies 20
North Africa 170
Norwood, Vera 2, 15, 169
NSF (U.S. National Science Foundation) 115

Oberhauser, Ann 3, 113, 114, 119
Oceania 53, 54, 242
office workers 215
On not excluding half-of-the-human 1, 63, 84, 97, 102, 135, 20
organic farming 161
Orientalist 22
Other – otherness 19, 20, 22, 23, 24, 27, 99, 169
Ottoman Empire 170
out-migration 147, 169, 213

Pacific 76, 18, 207, 212, 213, 214, 215, 216, 218, 219, 233, 235
Pacific Islands 214, 233
Pākehā 76, 78, 81
Palestine 170, 182
patriarchal society 20, 214
patriarchal: violence 20; systems 25
patriarchy 19, 20, 24, 25, 41, 42, 136, 143, 163
patrilocality 175
peace monuments 67, 69, 70; symbols: spatial categories 67
peasant agriculture 32
pedagogy 22, 23, 32, 64, 126, 130; border 22, 23
Peking 49, 50
personal care 50, 86

pigeon peas 207
plantation 207
Poland 37, 43, 78, 150
political geography 55
Portugal 4, 51, 54
Portuguese 11, 206, 223
post-Socialist countries 146, 149, 153
poverty 25, 31, 152, 157,185, 196, 198, 204, 208, 215, 216, 217
practicing Geography 111, 117, 118
precarious labor 122, 137, 145, 146, 150, 151, 153, 154, 198, 213, 223, 225, 229
pregnancy 38
preparedness 233, 239, 242
private space 86, 88, 89, 238
Pro-catador Programme 224
professional activities 86, 157, 163, 164
public: domain 136, 141; health 215, 230; spaces 43, 141, 217, 234, 239
Puerto Rico 65, 66, 209, 212

Qualis System 85
qualitative methodology 158, 222
qualitative research 126
questionnaires 32, 170

race 23, 41, 42, 65, 66, 75, 88, 97, 101, 119, 123, 124, 125, 194, 225
racial prejudice 65
racism 30, 37, 124, 125, 126, 189, 194, 195, 196
Reclus 63
recovery 212, 233, 234, 235, 238–241, 242
recyclable materials: collectors 222, 223–224, 225, 227, 230
region 15, 22, 23, 24, 25, 32, 40, 43, 124, 135, 137, 141, 145, 146, 148, 171, 172, 173, 181, 182, 183–184, 204, 205, 209, 210, 213, 225, 233
regional differences 172, 173
religious pacifism 68
remittances 209
residential growth 157
resilience 212, 213, 233, 234, 238–241
resistance 32, 34, 38, 41, 42, 88, 123, 140–142, 166, 213
resort 213, 214, 215, 216, 137
restaurant 151, 165, 172, 214, 215
RGS/IBG (Royal Geographical Society/Institute of British Geographers) 3
rice 204, 207
Rio de Janeiro 84

Rockefeller Foundation 14, 49
roles-male and female 19, 154
Romania 4, 37, 38, 39, 40, 41, 42, 43, 44, 49, 54, 77
Rome 50, 51, 68, 145
Routledge 1, 3, 11, 40
rural: agrarian economy 158; areas 145, 154, 157, 161, 164–165, 166; development 204, 210; entrepreurship 158, 161; market systems 29; re-ruralization 157–158, 165, 166; tourism 162
Russia 37, 43

safe cities 43
Samoa 212, 214, 216
Sanders, Rickie 113, 119
scavengers 223, 225
scheduled caste 137
school fees 216
scientific production 84, 85, 87, 88, 92, 93
scientific trajectory 84, 92
Seattle, Washington 52
SEI (Student Evaluation of Instruction) 121, 123, 126
self-care 138
semi-peripheral rural regions 153
services 81, 157, 161, 183, 214, 215; work 111
settler 76, 78, 81, 181, 182, 183, 195
sex work 43
sex/sexism 37, 79, 102, 125; biases 135
sexuality 41, 42, 84, 88, 106
SIDS (Small Island Developing States) 214
single women 140, 152
SIROW (Southwest Institute for Research on Women) 14, 77, 101, 169
Slater, Frances 74
Slovakia 37
slum 155
small farms 182, 204, 207, 209
social: costs 214, 216; location 1, 25, 31; mobility 146, 148, 149, 151, 152, 153, 154, 214; networks 163, 173, 185, 217, 218, 219, 242; reproduction 90, 135, 136, 137; security 214, 223
Socialism 40, 147, 153
Society of Woman Geographers (SWG) 65
Sociology 37, 170
soil 68, 204, 207, 238, 239; erosion 30

solidarities 140–142
sorghum 207
South Africa 29, 51, 65
South America 68, 205
South Asia 20, 23, 24, 25, 26, 140
southeastern USA 2
souvenirs: sellers 215
Spain 4, 11, 12–14, 14–16, 31, 48, 49, 51, 54, 106, 157, 158, 159, 162, 165
spatial mobility 139–140, 147, 154
spread of basic services 161
Sri Lanka 11, 25
St Vincent 206
Stokes, Evelyn 74–78, 81, 82
subaltern women 33, 34
subsidies 162
sugar cane 206
Surabaya 50
Surinam 50
survival 140–142, 150, 218, 235, 238, 239, 242; strategies 4
Sweden 4, 52, 69, 149, 152
sweet potatoes 205, 209
Switzerland 4, 11, 13, 49, 52
Sydney, Australia 1, 10, 82, 98, 99, 102, 103, 104, 193, 219
Szeged University 40
São Paulo, Brazil 222, 223, 225

Taiwan 2, 11, 49, 54, 77, 78
teaching evaluations 122, 123
tenure: land and sea 216
tenured and tenure-track faculty 121, 123
Timosoara, Romania 38, 40
tobacco 205, 207
Tolstoy 63
totalitarian 39
tourism 55, 157, 159, 161, 162, 164, 165, 183, 204, 209, 210, 212, 213, 214–215, 216, 217, 218; tourist studies 212
trade 30, 31, 32, 198, 207, 217, 218, 225, 235
Transcarpathia, Ukraine 145, 146, 147, 149, 151, 153, 154, 156
transport 34, 64, 102, 139, 150, 157, 214, 225
Tuan, Yi Fu 15

Union of Socialist Geographers 99
United Kingdom (UK) 30, 50, 51, 76
United Nations 31, 70
University of Arizona 4, 9, 11, 12, 14, 15, 77, 101, 107

University of Auckland 76, 81
University of Canterbury 74
University of Illinois 1, 76, 77, 81, 100, 101, 104
University of Melbourne 98, 99, 104
University of Sydney 1, 98, 102, 103
University of Waikato 74, 76, 103
unmarried women 174, 175
urban life 136, 157
urban space 139
urbanization 30, 135
USA (United States of America) 1, 2, 4, 39, 40, 42, 98, 99, 100, 102, 106, 151
US-Fulbright exchange program 39
utu feminism 29, 33, 34

Vanuatu 212, 214, 215, 233, 235, 236, 237, 238, 239, 240, 241
Venezuela 212–213
victims 20, 21, 125, 218, 234
violence 20, 21, 22, 24, 43, 174, 190, 212, 216, 234; backlash 25, 38, 43; gender 234
volcanic 207

waged work 137–139, 140
Washington, D. C. 11, 50, 51, 64, 104, 105
waste: dumps 20, 223, 224; management 221, 222, 224; pickers 221, 222, 223, 224, 227, 230
Water (film) 20, 25, 26
well-being 175, 185
West Indies 207
West University Timisoara (WUT) 38, 39, 40, 41, 42, 43, 44
Western 19, 20, 21, 24, 26, 31, 32, 33, 39, 49, 102, 121, 126
white: whiteness 22, 76, 78, 81, 84, 98, 122, 123, 125, 126, 138, 150, 184, 192, 193, 194, 206, 209; male/masculinity 122, 126; planters 206; settler 76, 78, 81, 209; supremacy 125; women 84, 123
widow 25, 26, 27
WILPF (Women's International League for Peace and Freedom) 66, 67, 69
Wiradjuri 181, 182, 183, 191, 192, 194
Wiradjuri geographies 181, 183
women/women's: business leaders 157; education 171, 172, 173; entrepreneurship 157, 165, 172, 173; faculty 113; gender 19, 26, 169; in geography 11, 29, 48, 49, 53–56; inheritance rights

171, 175; labor migration 145; lives 2, 19, 20, 75, 135, 142, 146, 219, 223, 230, 241; rights 51, 65, 169, 171; under representation of 48, 50; work 2, 4
Women's Studies in Australia 102, 103

work 221, 222, 223
work-life balance 118; relations 165

yams 207, 209
young adult entrepreneurs 157–158, 161
young professionals 161

Printed and bound by CPI Group (UK) Ltd, Croydon, CR0 4YY

19/11/2024

01791328-0017